College Accounting

Seventeenth Edition

D0896470

James A. Heintz
University of Kansas

Robert W. Parry, Jr.
Indiana University

SOUTH-WESTERN
TM
THOMSON LEARNING

Australia · Canada · Mexico · Singapore · Spain · United Kingdom · United States

CONTENTS

STUDY GUIDE

WORKING PAPERS

CHAPTER 1
INTRODUCTION TO ACCOUNTING

LEARNING OBJECTIVES

Chapter 1 is designed to introduce you to accounting—its purpose, process, and career opportunities. Businesses that keep good accounting records benefit in many ways. Users of accounting information are able to make sound decisions, which will affect the business's future. Accounting offers many career opportunities, some of which are entry-level and task-oriented and others that involve decision making and planning.

Objective 1. Describe the purpose of accounting.

Accounting is the process by which businesses keep track of daily transactions and determine how the business is doing. Accounting provides needed information for its many users, from owners to government agencies and others.

Objective 2. Describe the accounting process.

The accounting process contains six major steps:

Step 1 Analyzing: Looking at information available and figuring out what to do with it. This first step in the accounting process usually occurs when the business receives some type of information, such as a bill, that needs to be properly entered into the business's records. This first step also involves deciding if the piece of information should result in an accounting entry or not.

Step 2 Recording: Entering the information, manually or via a computer, into the accounting system.

Step 3 Classifying: Grouping like things together.

Step 4 Summarizing: Bringing together all information items to determine a result, such as profit or loss.

Step 5 Reporting: Communicating the results, such as profit or loss, commonly using tables to tell the financial status of the business.

Step 6 Interpreting: Examining the financial statements to evaluate the financial health of the business.

Objective 3. Define three types of business ownership structures.

Businesses can be classified according to the number of owners. A sole proprietorship is owned by one person who assumes all risks for the business and makes all business decisions. A partnership is owned by two or more persons who share the risks and decision making. Corporations have many owners (shareholders) whose risk is limited to their investment and who have little influence in business decisions.

Objective 4. Classify different types of businesses by activities.

Businesses also can be classified by the type of service or product they provide. A service business provides a service, a merchandising business purchases a product from another business to sell, and a manufacturing business makes a product to sell.

Objective 5. Identify career opportunities in accounting.

Accounting has varied and diverse opportunities, depending on the education and experience of the worker, the type of business, and the accounting processes used within the business.

Accounting clerks record, sort, and file accounting information. Bookkeepers supervise clerks, help with daily accounting work, and summarize information.

Public accountants offer services such as auditing, tax advice, and management consulting. Managerial accountants offer services to private businesses, such as designing accounting information systems, general accounting, cost accounting, budgeting, tax accounting, and internal auditing. Government and not-for-profit organizations also employ accountants.

Accounting is a professional field, which includes organizations and certifications for those who pass examinations and have relevant work experience.

REVIEW QUESTIONS

Instructions: Analyze each of the following items carefully before writing your answer in the column at the right.

Question	Answer

1. The purpose of accounting is to provide current information to users. For each user below, briefly describe what type of information is needed.

 a. Owners (present and future)

 b. Managers who make decisions for the business

 c. Creditors (present and future)

 d. Government agencies (state, local, and national)

2. A travel agency is an example of this type of business................. _____

3. The ownership structure where owners share risks and decision making is called a(n) _____. ... _____

4. A(n) _____ business makes a product to sell......................... _____

5. A business that purchases a product from another business to sell to customers is called a(n) _____ business............................. _____

6. Under the _____ ownership structure, the owner's personal assets can be taken to pay creditors.. _____

7. The Financial Accounting Standards Board develops procedures and guidelines called _____ to be followed in the accounting process. _____

8. The owners' risk is usually limited to their initial investment in this type of ownership structure... _____

9. By meeting education and experience requirements, and passing an examination, a public accountant can achieve recognition as a(n)

 _____. ... _____

10. The six major steps of the accounting process are listed in the box at the right. In front of each term, write the letter that identifies the correct description provided in the column on the left.

 a. The process of entering financial information about events affecting the business

 b. The process of bringing together various items of information to determine a result

 c. The process of sorting or grouping like things together, rather than merely keeping a simple, diary-like narrative record of numerous and varied transactions

 d. The process of determining the effect of various events on the business

 e. The process of deciding the importance of the information in various reports

 f. The process of communicating the results of operations

_____	Analyzing
_____	Recording
_____	Classifying
_____	Summarizing
_____	Reporting
_____	Interpreting

CHAPTER 2
ANALYZING TRANSACTIONS:
THE ACCOUNTING EQUATION

LEARNING OBJECTIVES

Chapter 2 continues the introductory discussion of accounting—its elements, equation, and transactions. The accounting equation provides a structure for analyzing transactions. After all transactions have been analyzed, the financial statements—income statement, statement of owner's equity, and balance sheet—are prepared. Let's look at each of these learning objectives in detail.

Objective 1. Define the accounting elements.

Accounting elements are the parts that make up the accounting equation: assets, liabilities, and owner's equity. **Assets** are items *owned* by the business that will provide future benefits. **Liabilities** are debts *owed* by the business and will require a future outflow of assets. **Owner's equity** (also called net worth or capital) is the difference between assets and liabilities. **Revenues** represent the amount a business charges customers for products sold or services provided. Revenues create an inflow of assets. **Expenses** represent an outflow of assets (or increase in liabilities) as a result of the efforts made to generate revenues.

Objective 2. Construct the accounting equation.

The accounting equation shows the relationship among assets, liabilities, and owner's equity (the accounting elements):

$$\textbf{Assets} = \textbf{Liabilities} + \textbf{Owner's Equity}$$

When given two of the numbers for the equation above, you can calculate the missing number by adding or subtracting.

The accounting equation may be expanded to include revenues, expenses, and drawing. Although drawing is not considered a major element in the accounting equation, it is a very special type of owner's equity account. It represents the withdrawals of assets from the business by the owner.

Assets Items Owned		=	Liabilities Amounts Owed	+	Owner's Equity Owner's Investment + Earnings				
Cash	+ Delivery Equipment	=	Accounts Payable	+	Jessica Jane, Capital	–	Jessica Jane, Drawing	+ Revenues	– Expenses

Objective 3. Analyze business transactions.

Analyzing is the first step in the accounting process. Three questions must be answered: (1) What happened? (2) Which accounts are affected, and what kind of accounts are they (asset, liability, owner's equity)? (3) How is the accounting equation affected? (Accounts will increase or decrease, but the equation always remains in balance.)

Objective 4. Show the effects of business transactions on the accounting equation.

Each transaction will affect asset, liability, owner's equity, revenue, or expense accounts. For example, when an owner invests cash in the business, the asset account called *Cash* increases, and the owner's equity account *Capital* also increases.

For each transaction, you must decide what accounts are affected and whether the accounts increase or decrease. After each transaction, the equation must still be in balance.

Objective 5. Prepare an income statement, statement of owner's equity, and balance sheet.

After the transactions are completed, the financial statements are prepared to show the results of those transactions. All financial statements have a heading that indicates the name of the firm, title of the statement, and time period or date covered by the statement. The income statement reports revenues, expenses, and the net income for the period. The statement of owner's equity shows the beginning balance of the owner's capital account, plus investments and net income, less withdrawals to compute the ending capital balance. The balance sheet reports all assets, liabilities, and the owner's capital on a certain date.

Objective 6. Define the three basic phases of the accounting process.

The three basic phases of the accounting process are input, processing, and output. The inputs to the accounting process are the business transactions. These transactions are processed to recognize their effects on the assets, liabilities, owner's equity, revenues, and expenses of the business. The results of these events are then reported as outputs of the accounting process in the financial statements.

REVIEW QUESTIONS

Instructions: Analyze each of the following items carefully before writing your answer in the column at the right.

Question	Answer
1. The entire accounting process is based on one simple equation called the _____.	_____
2. An individual, association, or organization that engages in business activities is called a(n) _____.	_____
3. An item owned by a business that will provide future benefits is a(n) _____.	_____
4. Something owed to another business entity is a(n) _____.	_____
5. A(n) _____ is an unwritten promise to pay a supplier for assets purchased or a service rendered.	_____
6. The amount by which assets exceed the liabilities of a business.	_____
7. According to the _____ concept, nonbusiness assets and liabilities are not included in the business entity's records.	_____
8. Assets – liabilities = _____.	_____
9. Assets – owner's equity = _____.	_____
10. Assets = liabilities + _____.	_____

11. The outflow of assets (or increase in liabilities) as the result of efforts to produce revenue is called a(n) _____. _____

12. When total revenues exceed total expenses, the difference is called.. _____

13. When expenses are greater than revenues, the difference is called.... _____

14. Any accounting period of twelve months' duration is called a(n)...... _____

15. Withdrawals, or _____, represent a reduction in owner's equity because the owner takes cash or other assets for personal use. _____

16. The financial statement that reports the profitability of the business for a period of time is the _____. _____

17. The financial statement that shows investments and withdrawals by the owner, as well as profit or loss generated by the business, is the _____

18. The financial statement that reports the assets, liabilities, and owner's equity on a specific date is the _____. _____

19. On the balance sheet, assets are listed in order of _____, or the ease with which they can be converted to cash. _____

EXERCISES AND PROBLEMS

Exercise 1 (LO 2) THE ACCOUNTING EQUATION

Using the accounting equation provided below, compute the missing amounts.

	ASSETS	=	LIABILITIES	+	OWNER'S EQUITY
(a)	24,000	=	$ 4,000	+	$20,000
(b)	$25,000	=	$8,000	+	17,000
(c)	$50,000	=	40,000	+	$10,000

Exercise 2 (LO 2) THE ACCOUNTING EQUATION

Using the accounting equation provided below, compute the missing amounts.

	ASSETS	=	LIABILITIES	+	CAPITAL	–	DRAWING	+	REVENUE	–	EXPENSES
(a)	38,000	=	$60,000	+	$20,000	–	$10,000	+	$80,000	–	$60,000
(b)	$80,000	=	35,000	+	$35,000	–	$ 5,000	+	$70,000	–	$55,000
(c)	$90,000	=	$25,000	+	60,000	–	$ 2,000	+	$57,000	–	$50,000
(d)	$60,000	=	$20,000	+	$30,000	–	$ 5,000	+	45,000	–	$40,000
(e)	$40,000	=	$25,000	+	$40,000	–	$ 5,000	+	$30,000	–	50,000
(f)	$75,000	=	$20,000	+	$50,000	–	10,000	+	$40,000	–	$25,000

Exercise 3 (LO 5) STATEMENT OF OWNER'S EQUITY

If owner's equity was $38,000 at the beginning of the period and $45,000 at the end of the period, compute the net income or loss for the period. (There were no investments or withdrawals during the period.)

_____ Net income of $7,000. _____

Exercise 4 (LO 2) ACCOUNTING EQUATION

If Irma Elkton, a dentist, owns office equipment amounting to $3,500, laboratory equipment amounting to $10,000, and other property that is used in the business amounting to $4,620, and owes business suppliers a total of $5,000, the owner's equity in the business is:

$$18,120 = 5,000 + 13,120$$
$$22,000 = 6,000$$

Exercise 5 (LO 2) ACCOUNTING EQUATION

One year later, the amount of Dr. Elkton's business assets has increased to a total of $22,000, and the amount of business liabilities has increased to a total of $6,000. Assuming that Dr. Elkton has not made any additional investments or withdrawals, compute:

(a) Owner's equity at year end $ __16,000__

(b) Net income or loss for the year $ __14,680 Net income__

Exercise 6 (LO 3/4) EFFECTS OF TRANSACTIONS (BALANCE SHEET ACCOUNTS)

Rich Brite has started his own business. During the first month, the following transactions occurred:

(a) He invested $15,000 cash in the business, and the money was used to open a bank account.
(b) Purchased office equipment for cash, $4,000.
(c) Purchased a computer on account for $9,000.
(d) Paid $2,000 on account for the office equipment.

Using the lines provided below, show the effect of each transaction on the basic elements of the accounting equation: assets, liabilities, and owner's equity. Compute the new amounts for each element after each transaction to satisfy yourself that the accounting equation has remained in balance.

	ASSETS	=	LIABILITIES	+	OWNER'S EQUITY
(a)	15,000		∅		15,000
Bal.	15,000		∅		15,000
(b)	-4,000 +4000				
Bal.	15,000		∅		15,000
(c)	15,000 + 9,000		9,000		15,000
Bal.	24,000				24,000
(d)	-2,000		-2,000		15,000
Bal.	22,000		22,000		

Problem 5 (LO 5) BALANCE SHEET

Based on the transactions in Problem 2, prepare a balance sheet as of October 31, 20—, in the form provided below.

SusanCole Consulting Firm
Balance Sheet
Oct. 31, 2002

Assets		Liabilities	
Cash	7 850 00	Accts. Payable	4 500 00
Office Equipment	8 300 00		
Prepaid Insurance	200 00	Owner's Equity	
		SusanCole, capital	12 000 00
Total Assets	16 350 00	Susan Cole, drawing	(1 000 00)
		Revenues	7 000 0
		Expenses	(7 500 00)
		Liabilities and	
		Owner's Equity Totals	16 350 00

Problem 6 (LO 3/4/5) ANALYZE THE EFFECTS OF BUSINESS TRANSACTIONS ON THE ACCOUNTING EQUATION AND PREPARE FINANCIAL STATEMENTS

Stuart Cassady is opening a typing service. During the first month (April, 20—), the following transactions occurred.

(a) Stuart invested $10,000 in the business.

(b) Purchased office supplies for $200 cash.

(c) Purchased office supplies for $800, $400 on account and $400 in cash.

(d) Received typing fees of $300 cash.

(e) Paid the rent, $600.

(f) Withdrew $100 for personal use.

(g) Earned typing fees of $600, $200 in cash and $400 on account.

(h) Made partial payment for office supplies in (c) of $200.

(i) Received $200 cash for typing fees earned on account in (g).

Required:

1. Record the effect of each transaction on the accounting equation below. Compute new amounts in accounts after each transaction.

	ASSETS			= LIABILITIES +		OWNER'S EQUITY			
	Cash +	Accounts Receivable +	Office Supplies =	Accounts Payable	S. Cassady, +Capital −	S. Cassady, Drawing +	Revenues −	Expenses	Description
(a)	_____	_____	_____	_____	_____	_____	_____	_____	_____
Bal.	_____	_____	_____	_____	_____	_____	_____	_____	_____
(b)	_____	_____	_____	_____	_____	_____	_____	_____	_____
Bal.	_____	_____	_____	_____	_____	_____	_____	_____	_____
(c)	_____	_____	_____	_____	_____	_____	_____	_____	_____
Bal.	_____	_____	_____	_____	_____	_____	_____	_____	_____
(d)	_____	_____	_____	_____	_____	_____	_____	_____	_____
Bal.	_____	_____	_____	_____	_____	_____	_____	_____	_____
(e)	_____	_____	_____	_____	_____	_____	_____	_____	_____
Bal.	_____	_____	_____	_____	_____	_____	_____	_____	_____
(f)	_____	_____	_____	_____	_____	_____	_____	_____	_____
Bal.	_____	_____	_____	_____	_____	_____	_____	_____	_____
(g)	_____	_____	_____	_____	_____	_____	_____	_____	_____
Bal.	_____	_____	_____	_____	_____	_____	_____	_____	_____
(h)	_____	_____	_____	_____	_____	_____	_____	_____	_____
Bal.	_____	_____	_____	_____	_____	_____	_____	_____	_____
(i)	_____	_____	_____	_____	_____	_____	_____	_____	_____
Bal.	======	======	======	======	======	======	======	======	======

Problem 6 (Concluded)

2. Based on the transactions in part 1 of Problem 6, prepare an income statement, statement of owner's equity, and balance sheet for Stuart Cassady.

CHAPTER 3
THE DOUBLE-ENTRY FRAMEWORK

LEARNING OBJECTIVES

Objective 1. Define the parts of a T account.

The **T account** gets its name from the fact that it resembles the letter *T*. There are three major parts of an account. The title of the account is on top. The left side of the T account is the debit side, and the right side is the credit side.

Objective 2. Foot and balance a T account.

To determine the balance of a T account, simply total the dollar amounts of the debit and credit sides. These totals are known as **footings.** The difference between the footings is called the *balance* of the account. The balance is written on the side with the larger footing.

Objective 3. Describe the effects of debits and credits on specific types of accounts.

Assets are on the left side of the accounting equation. Thus, increases are entered on the left, or debit, side; and decreases are entered on the right, or credit, side. The normal balance of an asset account is a debit.

Liabilities and owner's equity are on the right side of the equation. Thus, increases are entered on the right, or credit, side; and decreases are entered on the left, or debit, side. The normal balance of a liability and owner's equity account is a credit.

Revenues increase owner's equity. Thus, increases in revenue are recorded as credits. The normal balance of a revenue account is a credit.

Expenses decrease owner's equity. Thus, increases in expenses are recorded as debits. The normal balance of an expense account is a debit.

Withdrawals of cash and other assets by the owner for personal reasons decrease owner's equity. Thus, an increase in drawing is recorded as a debit. The normal balance of a drawing account is a debit.

The following figure should be helpful in developing your understanding of debits and credits and the accounting equation.

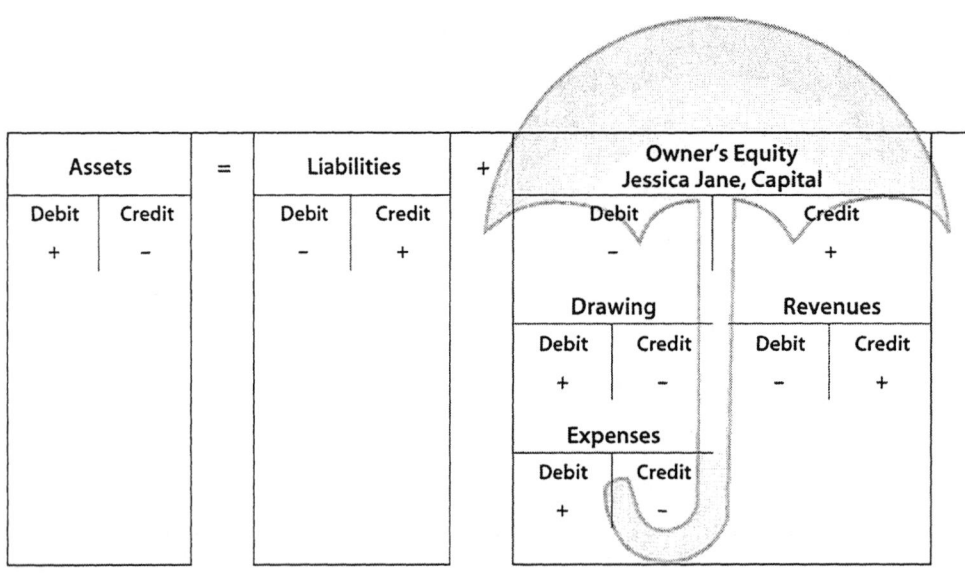

Objective 4. Use T accounts to analyze transactions.

There are three basic questions that must be answered when analyzing a transaction: (1) What happened? (2) Which accounts are affected? and (3) How is the accounting equation affected? After analyzing the transaction, in every instance, debits will equal credits.

Objective 5. Prepare a trial balance.

There are two very important rules in double-entry accounting: (1) The sum of the debits must equal the sum of the credits. This means that at least two accounts are affected by each transaction. (2) The accounting equation must remain in balance.

A **trial balance** is a list of all accounts showing the title and balance of each account. The total debits and credits must be equal.

REVIEW QUESTIONS

Instructions: Analyze each of the following items carefully before writing your answer in the column at the right.

Question	Answer

1. The fact that each transaction has a dual effect on the accounting elements provides the basis for what is called _____. _____

2. A form or record used to keep track of the increases and decreases in each type of asset, liability, owner's equity, revenue, and expense is known as a(n) _____. .. _____

3. The left side of a T account is called the _____ side. _____

4. The right side of a T account is called the _____ side. _____

5. The process of entering totals in small pencil figures in the debit and credit side of a T account is referred to as _____. _____

6. The amount of the difference between the debits and credits recorded in a T account is called the _____. _____

7. An increase in the asset cash is recorded by a(n) _____. _____

8. An increase in the liability accounts payable is recorded by a(n)....... _____

9. A list of all of the accounts showing the title and balance of each account is called the _____. .. _____

10. The normal balance of a revenue account is on the _____ side. ... _____

11. A decrease in the liability accounts payable is recorded by a(n)........ _____

12. The normal balance of a liability account is on the _____ side. ... _____

EXERCISES AND PROBLEMS

Exercise 1 (LO 3) EFFECTS OF DEBITS AND CREDITS

Indicate whether each of the following types of accounts would normally have a debit or credit balance by circling either debit or credit in the column at the right:

Type of Account	Normal Balance (Circle one)	
(a) Assets..	Debit	Credit
(b) Liabilities...	Debit	Credit
(c) Owner's Equity..	Debit	Credit
(d) Revenues..	Debit	Credit
(e) Expenses..	Debit	Credit

Exercise 2 (LO 1) DEFINING THE PARTS OF THE T ACCOUNT

Provided below are T accounts for the five types of accounts discussed to this point. Identify the debit and credit side of each type of account by writing debit on the debit side and credit on the credit side.

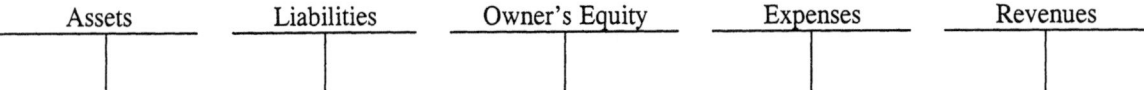

Assets	Liabilities	Owner's Equity	Expenses	Revenues

Exercise 3 (LO 3) INCREASING AND DECREASING ACCOUNTS WITH DEBITS AND CREDITS

Provided below are T accounts representing the five types of accounts discussed. Indicate how each account would be increased and decreased by placing a (+) or (−) on the debit and credit side of each account.

Assets	Liabilities	Owner's Equity	Expenses	Revenues

Exercise 4 (LO 4) USING T ACCOUNTS TO ANALYZE TRANSACTIONS

The following transactions were completed by Jacque Hamon, an educational consultant. Analyze each transaction and enter the amounts in the proper debit and credit positions in the T accounts at the right.

(a) Hamon invested $3,000 cash in the business.

 Cash Jacque Hamon, Capital

(b) Received $1,000 in cash for consulting services rendered.

 Cash Professional Fees

(c) Bought office equipment from Gusse Supply Co. on account, $500.

 Office Equipment Accounts Payable

(d) Paid electric bill, $75.

 Cash Utilities Expense

(e) Paid Gusse Supply $200 on account.

Cash | Accounts Payable

(f) Received $300 in cash for consulting services
rendered.

Cash | Professional Fees

(g) Borrowed $1,000 from bank by signing a note.

Cash | Notes Payable

(h) Paid the telephone bill, $50.

Cash | Telephone Expense

Exercise 5 (LO 4) USING T ACCOUNTS TO ANALYZE TRANSACTIONS (BALANCE SHEET ACCOUNTS)

Connie Sung has started her own typing business. During the first month, the following transactions occurred.

(a) Connie invested $12,000 cash in the business, and the money was deposited in a bank account.
(b) A new computer and printer were purchased on account from Stahl Electronics for $8,000.
(c) Paid the premium on a one year insurance policy on computer equipment, $75 cash.
(d) A bank loan was secured by signing a note for $5,000.
(e) A $3,000 payment was made to Stahl Electronics on account.

Required:

Record the above transactions in the T accounts provided below.

Assets	=	Liabilities	+	Owner's Equity
Debit + / Credit −		Debit − / Credit +		Debit − / Credit +

Cash

Office Equipment

Prepaid Insurance

Accounts Payable

Notes Payable

C. Sung, Capital

Exercise 6 (LO 4) USING T ACCOUNTS TO ANALYZE TRANSACTIONS (ALL ACCOUNTS)

In late April, Frazier Baar opened a psychiatry practice by investing $9,000 cash and purchasing a couch, chair, and leather covered note pad on account for $2,500. These events were properly entered in the accounting records. In May, Dr. Baar began seeing patients and entered into the following transactions.

(a) Received $500 for counseling services rendered.
(b) Paid $100 for *Psychology Today* and other magazines for patients to read in the waiting room.
(c) Paid $1,200 office rent for the month.

Required:

1. Enter the balances as of May 1 in the following accounts: Cash, Office Furnishings, Accounts Payable, and F. Baar, Capital.

2. Record the May transactions in the accounts listed below.

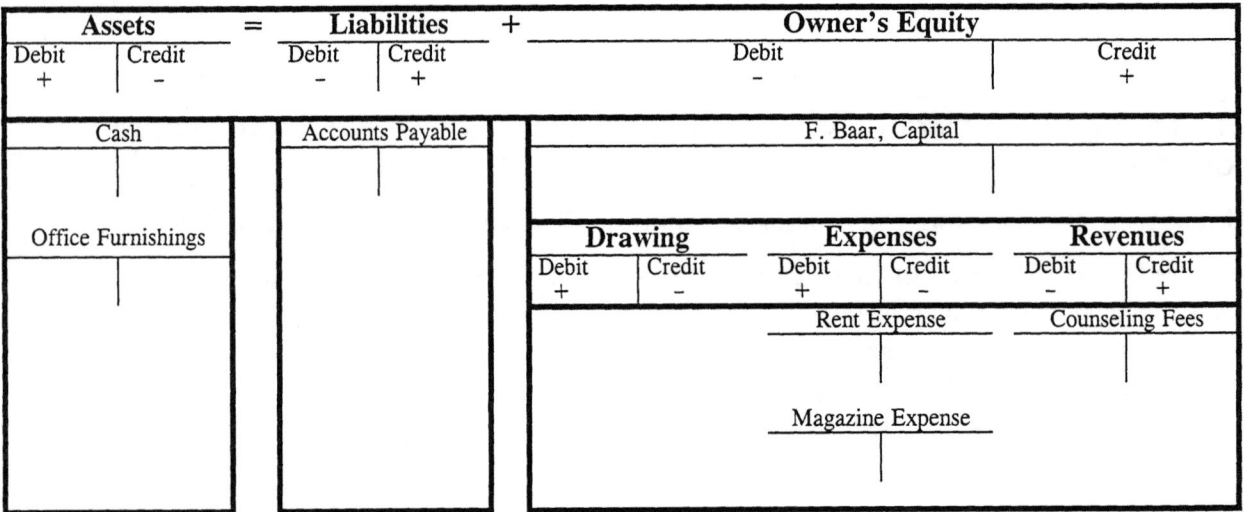

Exercise 7 (LO 2/4) USING T ACCOUNTS TO ANALYZE TRANSACTIONS, FOOTING AND BALANCING T ACCOUNTS.

In January, 20—, Blanca Estavez, CPA, started her own accounting practice. The following is a list of transactions for the first month.

(a) Invested $20,000 cash in the business.
(b) Purchased office supplies, $500 cash.
(c) Purchased office furniture, $6,000 cash.
(d) Purchased a computer and printer for $9,000: $5,000 cash and $4,000 on account.
(e) Paid $800 for accounting software programs.
(f) Performed accounting services and earned fees totaling $1,800: $1,200 in cash and $600 on account.
(g) Paid $700 rent for the month.
(h) Withdrew $200 for personal use.
(i) Paid $2,000 on account for the computer.

Exercise 7 (Continued)

Required:

1. Record the transactions in the T accounts that follow.
2. After all transactions have been entered, foot and balance the T accounts.

Assets		Liabilities		+	Owner's Equity	
Debit +	Credit –	Debit –	Credit +		Debit –	Credit +

Cash		Accounts Payable		B. Estavez, Capital	

Accounts Receivable

				Drawing		Expenses		Revenues	
				Debit +	Credit –	Debit +	Credit –	Debit –	Credit +
				B. Estavez, Drawing		Rent Expense		Accounting Fees	

Office Supplies

Office Furniture

Computer Equipment

Computer Software

Exercise 8 (LO 5) PREPARE A TRIAL BALANCE

Based on the transactions recorded in Exercise 7, prepare a trial balance at the end of the first month of operations using the form provided below.

ACCOUNT	DEBIT BALANCE	CREDIT BALANCE

Problem 1 (LO 2/4/5) ANALYZING TRANSACTIONS WITH T ACCOUNTS, FOOTING AND BALANCING ACCOUNTS, AND PREPARING A TRIAL BALANCE

Jali Abdul has decided to offer his services as a promoter for local rock-n-roll bands. Following is a narrative of selected transactions completed during January, the first month of J.A. Productions' operations.

(a) Abdul invested $10,000 in the business and opened a checking account.

(b) Office furniture was purchased on account at a cost of $5,000.

(c) Computer equipment was purchased for $4,500. Abdul paid $1,500 cash and promised to pay the balance over the next three months.

(d) Office supplies were purchased for cash, $350.

(e) Letters were sent to numerous performing groups throughout the region explaining the services available through J.A. Productions. Postage of $200 was paid in cash.

(f) After securing contracts with several groups, Abdul began arranging performances throughout the region. The telephone bill came to $300 and was paid in cash.

(g) Abdul earned promotion revenue of $2,500: $2,000 in cash and $500 on account.

(h) Paid part-time receptionist $600.

(i) Withdrew $1,000 for personal use.

(j) Abdul paid $2,500 on account for the office furniture.

(k) Collected $250 for promotional fees earned on account.

Required:

1. Record the transactions in the T accounts provided.

2. Foot and balance the accounts.

3. Prepare a trial balance of the accounts as of January 31, 20—, using the form provided.

Problem 1 (Continued)

Assets	=	Liabilities	+	Owner's Equity	

Debit +	Credit −	Debit −	Credit +	Debit −	Credit +

Cash

Accounts Payable

J. Abdul, Capital

Accounts Receivable

Drawing		Expenses		Revenues	
Debit +	Credit −	Debit +	Credit −	Debit −	Credit +

Office Supplies

J. Abdul, Drawing **Wages Expense** **Promotion Fees**

Office Furniture

Telephone Expense

Computer Equipment

Postage Expense

Problem 1 (Concluded)

ACCOUNT	DEBIT BALANCE	CREDIT BALANCE

Problem 2 REVIEW: ACCOUNTING EQUATION AND FINANCIAL STATEMENTS

Based on the transactions recorded in Problem 1, select the information needed to fill in the blank space in the following statements.

(a) Total revenue for the month $ _____

(b) Total expenses for the month $ _____

(c) Net income for the month $ _____

(d) Abdul's original investment in the business $ _____

 + the net income for the month $ _____

 – owner's drawing _____

 increase in capital _____

 = owner's equity at the end of the month $ _____

(e) End-of-month accounting equation:

ASSETS	=	LIABILITIES	+	OWNER'S EQUITY
$ _____		$ _____		$ _____

Problem 3 REVIEW: PREPARATION OF FINANCIAL STATEMENTS

Refer to the trial balance in Problem 1 and to the analysis of the change in owner's equity in Problem 2.

(a) Prepare an income statement for J.A. Productions for the month ended January 31, 20—.

(b) Prepare a statement of owner's equity for J.A. Productions for the month ended January 31, 20—.

(c) Prepare a balance sheet for J.A. Productions as of January 31, 20—.

Problem 3 (Concluded)

CHAPTER 4
JOURNALIZING AND POSTING TRANSACTIONS

LEARNING OBJECTIVES

Chapter 3 introduced the double-entry framework and illustrated the impact of debits and credits on the accounting equation and T accounts. In Chapter 4, business transactions are entered into the general journal and posted to general ledger accounts.

Objective 1. Describe the flow of data from source documents through the trial balance.

The flow of financial data from the source documents through the accounting information systems follows the steps listed below.

1. Analyze what happened by using information from source documents and the firm's chart of accounts.
2. Enter business transactions in the general journal.
3. Post entries to accounts in the general ledger.
4. Prepare a trial balance.

INPUT PROCESSING

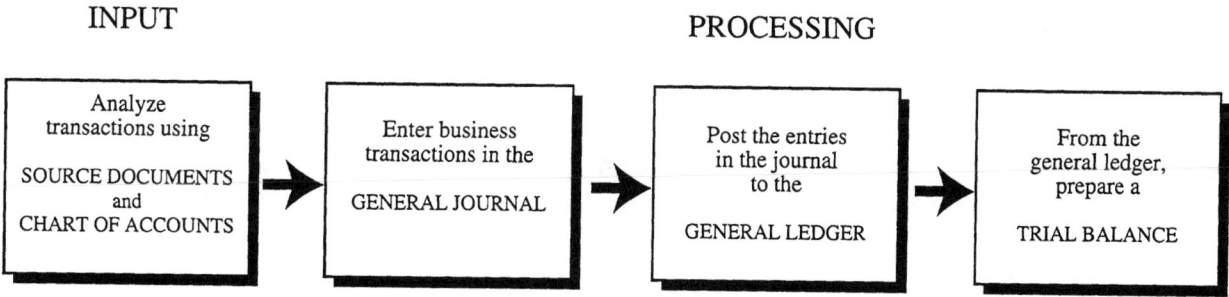

Objective 2. Describe the chart of accounts as a means of classifying financial information.

The **chart of accounts** lists in numerical order all of the accounts being used by a business. Assets are listed first (begin with "1"); liabilities are second (begin with "2"); owner's equity accounts are third (begin with "3"); revenues are fourth (begin with "4"); and expenses are last (begin with "5"). In a three-digit account numbering system, for example, Cash may be account number 101 and Accounts Receivable may be account number 122. Spacing numbers this way permits easy addition of new accounts as the business grows.

Objective 3. Describe and explain the purpose of source documents.

A **source document** provides objective information needed to record a transaction. Examples include check stubs, receipts, cash register tapes, sales invoices, and memos. Source documents are analyzed to determine which accounts should be increased or decreased.

Objective 4. Journalize transactions.

Journalizing is the process of entering information into the journal, or book of original entry. This simply means the journal is the first place a transaction is recorded. The general journal has space to enter the date of

the transaction, the name of the accounts being debited and credited, the account numbers, and the amounts of the debits and credits. A brief description follows each journal entry stating the reason for the entry.

Objective 5. Post to the general ledger.

Once the transactions are entered into the general journal, they must be **posted** to (copied to) the individual accounts, which are located in the general ledger. The accounts are in the general ledger in the chart of accounts order. That is, the assets are first, followed by liabilities, owner's equity, revenue, and expense accounts.

In this chapter, the general ledger accounts are in the form of four-column accounts. This is better than the T account because a running balance is maintained.

The **trial balance** is a listing of account balances at the end of the month—after all the transactions have been posted from the general journal to the general ledger accounts. The total of the debit balances must equal the total of the credit balances.

Objective 6. Explain how to find and correct errors.

Finding errors can be a long and frustrating process. But there are some methods to reduce the time and effort needed. The first thing to do is double-check your calculations and the accuracy of the posting activities. Common errors include sliding ($230 could become $23 or $2300), and transposing numbers (326 could become 236). Taking the difference between the debits and credits and dividing by 9 or by 2 may help locate the error.

There are two methods of correcting errors. The **ruling method** may be used before the transaction has been posted. Under this method, you draw a line through the incorrect title or amount and write in the correct information above the ruling. The **correcting entry method** is used after an entry has been posted to the general ledger. The correcting entry increases and decreases accounts in a manner that corrects the errors made in previous transactions.

REVIEW QUESTIONS

Instructions: Analyze each of the following items carefully before writing your answer in the column at the right.

Question	Answer
1. A list of all the accounts used by a business enterprise is called a(n)…	_____
2. Accounts that begin with the number "3" are _____. ………………	_____
3. Expenses are accounts that begin with which number? ………………	_____
4. A document that provides information about a business transaction is called a(n) _____. ……………………………………………………	_____
5. A document that provides a day-by-day listing of transactions of a business is called a(n) _____. ……………………………………	_____
6. A journal is commonly referred to as a(n) _____ because it is here that the first formal accounting record is made. …………………	_____
7. Transactions affecting more than two accounts are called _____. ….	_____
8. The act of entering transactions into a journal is called _____. ……	_____

9. In a journal, debits are entered first; then credits are entered and indented _____ (how much space)..................................... _____

10. A complete set of all accounts used by a business is known as the....... _____

11. A(n) _____ account allows the accountant to keep a running balance. _____

12. The process of copying debits and credits from the journal to the ledger accounts is called _____. _____

13. Posting from the journal to the ledger is done _____ or at frequent intervals. ... _____

14. The information in the Posting Reference columns of the journal and the ledger accounts provides a link known as a(n) _____. _____

15. A(n) _____ is taken after transactions are posted to the general ledger accounts to be sure that debit and credit balances in the ledger are equal. ... _____

16. A(n) _____ error occurs when you move a number a decimal place to the right or left. ... _____

17. A(n) _____ error occurs when you use the right numbers but in the wrong order. ... _____

18. Drawing a line through the incorrect amount or account title and writing correct information above it is an example of the _____ method. ... _____

19. When an incorrect entry has been journalized and posted, a(n) _____ entry is required. .. _____

EXERCISES AND PROBLEMS

Exercise 1 REVIEW: TRANSACTION ANALYSIS

Before a transaction is recorded in the journal, it should be analyzed to determine:

(a) What accounts are affected by the transaction.
(b) Whether each affected account is to be increased or decreased.
(c) Whether the increase or decrease is to be accomplished by a debit or credit.

In the following list of transactions for Abbott Service Co., indicate the names of the accounts to be debited and credited. Place a check mark in either the plus (+) or minus (−) column to indicate whether the account has been increased or decreased. The first transaction is entered as an illustration.

Transaction		Account	(+)	(−)
1. J.A. Abbott invested cash in a business enterprise.	Debit:	Cash	✓	
	Credit:	J.A. Abbott, Capital	✓	_____
2. Received cash for services provided.	Debit:			
	Credit:			

Transaction	Account	(+)	(−)
3. Paid cash for rent on the office.	Debit:		
	Credit: _____ _____ _____		
	_____ _____ _____		
4. Purchased office equipment on account.	Debit:		
	Credit: _____ _____ _____		
	_____ _____ _____		
5. Paid cash to a creditor for a debt previously owed.	Debit:		
	Credit: _____ _____ _____		
	_____ _____ _____		
6. Paid the telephone bill for the month.	Debit:		
	Credit: _____ _____ _____		
	_____ _____ _____		
7. Paid supplier for office equipment purchased in transaction 4 above.	Debit:		
	_____ _____ _____		
	Credit: _____ _____ _____		
8. Paid cash for a car for the owner's personal use.	Debit:		
	Credit: _____ _____ _____		
	_____ _____ _____		
9. Paid temporary secretary's wages.	Debit:		
	_____ _____ _____		
	Credit: _____ _____ _____		
10. Performed services that will be paid for later.	Debit:		
	_____ _____ _____		
	Credit: _____ _____ _____		

Exercise 2 (LO 4) JOURNALIZING TRANSACTIONS

Susan Poe started a business, Poe's Connections. She provides resource referral services whereby she helps businesses locate vendors of specialty products and vice versa. She charges a referral fee to her clients who may be businesses or vendors. She has a part-time clerk who enters information into a database to match requests with potential users or suppliers. Her chart of accounts is as follows:

Assets
101 Cash
122 Accounts Receivable
182 Office Furniture

Liabilities
202 Accounts Payable

Owner's Equity
311 Susan Poe, Capital
312 Susan Poe, Drawing

Revenues
401 Referral Fees

Expenses
511 Wages Expense
521 Rent Expense

Exercise 2 (Continued)

Required: Enter the following transactions in the two-column journal provided below.

2000

May	1	Susan invested $5,000 cash to start the business.
	5	Purchased office furniture on account, $3,000.
	9	Paid office rent for the month, $450.
	10	Received fees for referral services, $500.
	15	Made payment on account (for office furniture), $100.
	20	Earned referral fees: $125 cash and $175 on account.
	25	Paid wages to clerk for part-time work, $400.
	28	Withdrew cash for personal use, $100.
	29	Received cash for referral services previously rendered, $150.

GENERAL JOURNAL PAGE

	DATE	DESCRIPTION	POST. REF.	DEBIT	CREDIT	
1						1
2						2
3						3
4						4
5						5
6						6
7						7
8						8
9						9
10						10
11						11
12						12
13						13
14						14
15						15
16						16
17						17
18						18
19						19
20						20
21						21
22						22

Exercise 2 (Concluded)

GENERAL JOURNAL

PAGE _____

	DATE	DESCRIPTION	POST. REF.	DEBIT	CREDIT	
1						1
2						2
3						3
4						4
5						5
6						6
7						7
8						8
9						9
10						10
11						11
12						12
13						13
14						14
15						15

Exercise 3 (LO 5) POST TO THE GENERAL LEDGER

Post the transactions from Exercise 2 to the general ledger accounts provided on pages 34–36. Be sure to enter the appropriate cross-reference information in the Posting Reference columns of the general ledger accounts and the general journal.

GENERAL LEDGER

ACCOUNT Cash ACCOUNT NO. 101

DATE	ITEM	POST. REF.	DEBIT	CREDIT	BALANCE	
					DEBIT	CREDIT

Exercise 3 (Continued) **GENERAL LEDGER**

ACCOUNT Accounts Receivable ACCOUNT NO. 122

DATE	ITEM	POST. REF.	DEBIT	CREDIT	BALANCE		
					DEBIT	•	CREDIT

ACCOUNT Office Furniture ACCOUNT NO. 182

DATE	ITEM	POST. REF.	DEBIT	CREDIT	BALANCE		
					DEBIT	•	CREDIT

ACCOUNT Accounts Payable ACCOUNT NO. 202

DATE	ITEM	POST. REF.	DEBIT	CREDIT	BALANCE		
					DEBIT	•	CREDIT

ACCOUNT Susan Poe, Capital ACCOUNT NO. 311

DATE	ITEM	POST. REF.	DEBIT	CREDIT	BALANCE		
					DEBIT	•	CREDIT

ACCOUNT Susan Poe, Drawing ACCOUNT NO. 311

DATE	ITEM	POST. REF.	DEBIT	CREDIT	BALANCE		
					DEBIT	•	CREDIT

ACCOUNT Referral Fees ACCOUNT NO. 401

DATE	ITEM	POST. REF.	DEBIT	CREDIT	BALANCE		
					DEBIT	•	CREDIT

Exercise 3 (Concluded) **GENERAL LEDGER**

ACCOUNT Wages Expense ACCOUNT NO. 511

DATE	ITEM	POST. REF.	DEBIT	CREDIT	BALANCE		
					DEBIT	•	CREDIT

ACCOUNT Rent Expense ACCOUNT NO. 521

DATE	ITEM	POST. REF.	DEBIT	CREDIT	BALANCE		
					DEBIT	•	CREDIT

Exercise 4 REVIEW: PREPARE A TRIAL BALANCE

After the transactions are posted in Exercise 3, prepare the trial balance.

ACCOUNT	ACCT. NO.	DEBIT BALANCE	CREDIT BALANCE

Problem 1 (LO 4/5) JOURNALIZING AND POSTING TRANSACTIONS FOLLOWED BY PREPARATION OF A TRIAL BALANCE

Della Jordan started her own business, D.J. Parties. For about $50 per hour, Della and a group of part-time associates serve as disc jockeys for parties held at the client's home. As part of the service, Della provides a lighting system, stereo equipment, compact discs, and two disc jockeys working as a team for each party. A wide range of music is offered, and the client may provide additional tapes or discs to be played. A chart of accounts is provided below.

<div align="center">

D. J. Parties

Chart of Accounts

</div>

Assets			Owner's Equity		
101	Cash		311	Della Jordan, Capital	
122	Accounts Receivable		312	Della Jordan, Drawing	
181	Stereo Equipment		Revenue		
182	Office Furniture		401	Disc Jockey Fees	
183	Discs and Tapes				
184	Lighting Equipment		Expenses		
185	Van		511	Wages Expense	
			521	Rent Expense	
Liabilities			525	Telephone Expense	
202	Accounts Payable		538	Gas Expense	

The following transactions occurred during May, the first month of operation.

May	1	Jordan invested $30,000 cash in the business. The funds were deposited in a business checking account.
	3	Purchased stereo equipment and speaker systems from Big Al's Discount Stereo for $7,000: $3,000 cash and $4,000 on account.
	4	Purchased compact discs and tapes for $2,500.
	4	Purchased lighting equipment for $2,000.
	5	Purchased office furniture on account, $500.
	7	Purchased a van to be used to haul the equipment to the clients' homes, $9,500.
	18	Earned fees for services rendered, $3,800: $800 cash and $3,000 on account.
	20	Paid part-time associates for work performed, $600.
	21	Made payment on account for stereo equipment bought on May 3, $1,500.
	25	Paid for gas for the van, $40.
	27	Paid telephone bill, $80.
	28	Received cash for services previously rendered, $1,500.
	29	Paid part-time associates $1,100.
	30	Paid the rent, $500.
	30	Made payment on account for stereo equipment bought on May 3, $1,200.
	30	Jordan made withdrawal for personal use, $1,000.

Required:

1. Enter the transactions in the two-column journal provided on pages 38–39. Use Journal page 1 for transactions through May 20. Enter the remainder on page 2.

2. Post the transactions from the journal to the four-column ledger accounts on pages 40–43.

3. Prepare a trial balance.

Problem 1 (Continued)

[Instructor: Account numbers in Post Ref. column are entered when completing requirement 2.]

GENERAL JOURNAL

PAGE 1

	DATE		DESCRIPTION	POST. REF.	DEBIT	CREDIT	
1							1
2							2
3							3
4							4
5							5
6							6
7							7
8							8
9							9
10							10
11							11
12							12
13							13
14							14
15							15
16							16
17							17
18							18
19							19
20							20
21							21
22							22
23							23
24							24
25							25
26							26
27							27
28							28
29							29
30							30
31							31
32							32
33							33

Problem 1 (Continued)

GENERAL JOURNAL

PAGE 2

	DATE	DESCRIPTION	POST. REF.	DEBIT	CREDIT	
1						1
2						2
3						3
4						4
5						5
6						6
7						7
8						8
9						9
10						10
11						11
12						12
13						13
14						14
15						15
16						16
17						17
18						18
19						19
20						20
21						21
22						22
23						23
24						24
25						25
26						26
27						27
28						28
29						29
30						30
31						31
32						32
33						33
34						34

Problem 1 (Continued)

GENERAL LEDGER

ACCOUNT Cash ACCOUNT NO. 101

DATE	ITEM	POST. REF.	DEBIT	CREDIT	BALANCE		
					DEBIT	•	CREDIT

ACCOUNT Accounts Receivable ACCOUNT NO. 122

DATE	ITEM	POST. REF.	DEBIT	CREDIT	BALANCE		
					DEBIT	•	CREDIT

ACCOUNT Stereo Equipment ACCOUNT NO. 181

DATE	ITEM	POST. REF.	DEBIT	CREDIT	BALANCE		
					DEBIT	•	CREDIT

Problem 1 (Continued)

ACCOUNT Office Furniture ACCOUNT NO. 182

DATE	ITEM	POST. REF.	DEBIT	CREDIT	BALANCE		
					DEBIT	•	CREDIT

ACCOUNT Discs and Tapes ACCOUNT NO. 183

DATE	ITEM	POST. REF.	DEBIT	CREDIT	BALANCE		
					DEBIT	•	CREDIT

ACCOUNT Lighting Equipment ACCOUNT NO. 184

DATE	ITEM	POST. REF.	DEBIT	CREDIT	BALANCE		
					DEBIT	•	CREDIT

ACCOUNT Van ACCOUNT NO. 185

DATE	ITEM	POST. REF.	DEBIT	CREDIT	BALANCE		
					DEBIT	•	CREDIT

ACCOUNT Accounts Payable ACCOUNT NO. 202

DATE	ITEM	POST. REF.	DEBIT	CREDIT	BALANCE		
					DEBIT	•	CREDIT

Problem 1 (Continued)

ACCOUNT Della Jordan, Capital ACCOUNT NO. 311

DATE	ITEM	POST. REF.	DEBIT	CREDIT	BALANCE		
					DEBIT	•	CREDIT

ACCOUNT Della Jordan, Drawing ACCOUNT NO. 312

DATE	ITEM	POST. REF.	DEBIT	CREDIT	BALANCE		
					DEBIT	•	CREDIT

ACCOUNT Disc Jockey Fees ACCOUNT NO. 401

DATE	ITEM	POST. REF.	DEBIT	CREDIT	BALANCE		
					DEBIT	•	CREDIT

ACCOUNT Wages Expense ACCOUNT NO. 511

DATE	ITEM	POST. REF.	DEBIT	CREDIT	BALANCE		
					DEBIT	•	CREDIT

ACCOUNT Rent Expense ACCOUNT NO. 521

DATE	ITEM	POST. REF.	DEBIT	CREDIT	BALANCE		
					DEBIT	•	CREDIT

Problem 1 (Concluded)

ACCOUNT Telephone Expense ACCOUNT NO. 525

DATE	ITEM	POST. REF.	DEBIT	CREDIT	BALANCE DEBIT	•	CREDIT

ACCOUNT Gas Expense ACCOUNT NO. 538

DATE	ITEM	POST. REF.	DEBIT	CREDIT	BALANCE DEBIT	•	CREDIT

ACCOUNT	ACCT. NO.	DEBIT BALANCE	CREDIT BALANCE

Problem 2 REVIEW: PREPARATION OF FINANCIAL STATEMENTS

From the information in Problem 1, prepare an income statement, a statement of owner's equity, and a balance sheet.

Problem 2 (Concluded)

Problem 3

1. The Ruling Method (LO 6) CORRECTION OF ERRORS

The following journal entries were made but not posted. On January 1, $500 cash was withdrawn by the owner for personal use (R.J. Hammond) but was charged to Wages Expense. On January 2, $230 was paid on account. Make corrections using the ruling method.

GENERAL JOURNAL PAGE

	DATE		DESCRIPTION	POST. REF.	DEBIT	CREDIT	
1	20— Jan.	1	Wages Expense		5 0 0 00		1
2			Cash			5 0 0 00	2
3			Paid R. J. Hammond				3
4							4
5		2	Accounts Payable		3 2 0 00		5
6			Cash			3 2 0 00	6
7			Payment on account				7
8							8

Problem 3 (Concluded)

2. The Correcting Entry Method

On January 10, Office Equipment was debited for $800 when the debit should have been to Office Supplies. Since the entry has been posted, show the appropriate correcting entry made in the general journal on January 15.

GENERAL JOURNAL PAGE

	DATE	DESCRIPTION	POST. REF.	DEBIT	CREDIT	
1						1
2						2
3						3
4						4
5						5
6						6
7						7
8						8

CHAPTER 5
ADJUSTING ENTRIES AND THE WORK SHEET

LEARNING OBJECTIVES

We are coming to the end of the accounting cycle, and certain things must be done at the end of the period that are not done during the regular accounting period. In Chapter 5, adjusting entries and the work sheet are presented.

Objective 1. Prepare end-of-period adjustments.

In Chapters 2 through 4, we learned how to account for business transactions—events based primarily on arms length exchanges with other parties. During the accounting period, however, other changes occur which affect the financial condition of the business. For example, supplies are being used, equipment is wearing out, insurance is expiring, and employees may have earned wages that have not yet been paid. It is important for information reported on the financial statements to accurately reflect the results of business transactions with outside parties <u>and</u> other activities taking place inside the business. Therefore, adjustments must be made at the end of the accounting period to properly report assets and liabilities on the balance sheet and to comply with the matching principle. This principle requires the matching of revenues earned with expenses incurred to produce the revenues.

Objective 2. Prepare a work sheet.

The work sheet is a tool used by accountants to help organize work done at the end of the accounting period. This document is not a formal part of the accounting system. Therefore, information recorded here has no affect on the accounts or financial statements. The main purposes of the work sheet are to prepare the adjusting entries and accumulate information that will be used in the preparation of the financial statements. There are five steps taken to prepare a work sheet.

Step 1 Prepare a trial balance to ensure that the general ledger is in balance before adjusting the accounts.

Step 2 Analyze and enter the adjusting entries in the Adjustment columns of the work sheet. Every adjustment must have an equal debit and credit; and on completion, the total debits and credits must be equal in the Adjustment columns.

Step 3 Prepare the adjusted trial balance. Every account appearing in the Trial Balance columns will be extended to the Adjusted Trial Balance columns and include any changes due to the adjusting entries. On completion, the total of the debits and credits in the Adjusted Trial Balance columns must be equal.

Step 4 Extend the balances in the adjusted trial balance to either the Income Statement or Balance Sheet columns. All revenue and expenses are extended to the Income Statement columns. All other accounts (assets, liabilities, owner's capital, owner's drawing) are extended to the Balance Sheet columns.

Step 5 Complete the work sheet. Initially, the totals of the Income Statement columns will not be equal. Similarly, the totals of the Balance Sheet columns will not be equal. If the Income Statement Credit column exceeds the Income Statement Debit column, the difference represents net income. If the Income Statement Debit column exceeds the Income Statement Credit column, the difference represents net loss. The difference in the Balance Sheet columns will be exactly the same as the difference in the Income Statement columns. The amount of net income should be added to the Income Statement Debit column and the Balance Sheet Credit column for total debits to equal total credits for all four columns. If there is a net loss, this amount should be added to the Income Statement Credit column and the Balance Sheet Debit column.

<div align="center">Partial Work Sheet</div>

	For Net Income					For Net Loss			
	Income Statement		Balance Sheet			Income Statement		Balance Sheet	
	Debit	Credit	Debit	Credit		Debit	Credit	Debit	Credit
Net Income	2,500	3,200	6,200	5,500	Net Loss	3,000	2,500	7,000	7,500
	700			700			500	500	
	3,200	3,200	6,200	6,200		3,000	3,000	7,500	7,500

<div align="center">Apart Together</div>

Objective 3. Describe methods for finding errors on the work sheet.

The following tips may help in finding errors on the work sheet:

1. Check the addition of all columns.
2. Check the addition and subtraction required when extending to the Adjusted Trial Balance columns.
3. Make sure the adjusted account balances have been extended to the appropriate columns.
4. Make sure that the net income or net loss has been added to the appropriate columns.

Objective 4. Journalize adjusting entries.

Once the adjustments have been "penciled in" on the work sheet, the next step is to journalize the adjusting entries. "Adjusting Entries" is written in the Description column in the journal, and the adjusting entries are copied from the work sheet into the journal.

Objective 5. Post adjusting entries to a general ledger.

After the adjusting entries are journalized, the next step is to post them to the general ledger. The word "Adjusting" is written in the Item column in the general ledger, and each adjustment is posted to the proper general ledger account.

REVIEW QUESTIONS

Instructions: Analyze each of the following items carefully before writing your answer in the column at the right.

Question	Answer

1. The matching principle in accounting requires the matching of _____ and _____. .. _____

2. The asset account Supplies is adjusted to the income statement account entitled _____. .. _____

3. The asset account Prepaid Insurance is adjusted to the income statement account entitled _____. .. _____

4. The adjustment to Wages Expense will also affect a liability account title called _____. .. _____

5. The period of time a plant asset is expected to help produce revenues is called its _____. .. _____

6. The purpose of _____ is to spread the cost of a plant asset over its useful life. .. _____

7. A plant asset's original cost less salvage value is called _____.

8. A _____ has a credit balance and is deducted from the related asset account on the balance sheet.

9. The depreciation adjusting entry consists of a debit to Depreciation Expense and a credit to _____.

10. The difference between the original cost of a plant asset and its accumulated depreciation is called _____.

11. A _____ is helpful in preparing end-of-period adjustments and financial statements. ..

12. The first two monetary columns of a work sheet are called the _____ columns. ..

13. To which columns of the work sheet are asset and liability accounts extended? ..

14. To which columns of the work sheet are revenue and expense accounts extended? ..

15. To which columns of the work sheet are the capital and drawing accounts extended? ..

16. If the total of the Income Statement Credit column exceeds the total of the Debit column, the business has earned _____.

EXERCISES AND PROBLEMS

Exercise 1 (LO 1) PREPARING END-OF-PERIOD ADJUSTMENTS: SUPPLIES

The beginning balance of the supplies account was $300. During the year, additional supplies costing $600 were purchased and entered as debits to the supplies account. An end-of-period inventory determined that $200 worth of supplies are still on hand.

Required:

1. Determine the balance of the supplies account just prior to making any end-of-period adjustments.

2. When preparing the balance sheet, what should be reported for Supplies at the end of the year?

3. Determine the balance of the supplies expense account just prior to making any end-of-period adjustments.

4. When preparing the income statement, what should be reported for Supplies Expense? (What was the cost of the supplies used?)

5. What adjustment must be made to the supplies and supplies expense accounts?

Exercise 2 (LO 1) PREPARING END-OF-PERIOD ADJUSTMENTS: DEPRECIATION

Office equipment with an expected life of ten years and no salvage value was purchased on January 1 for $5,000. Assume the business has no other office equipment and straight-line depreciation is used.

Required:

1. What is the balance of the office equipment account at the end of the year? _____

2. What expense amount should be reported on the income statement for the use of the office equipment? _____

3. What book value should be reported on the balance sheet for the office equipment at the end of the first year? _____

4. What adjustment must be made at the end of the year to report information about the office equipment on the income statement and balance sheet? _____

Exercise 3 (LO 1/4/5) PREPARING, JOURNALIZING, AND POSTING ADJUSTING ENTRIES: SUPPLIES

The Maddie Hays modeling agency began the current period with office supplies that cost $1,225. During the period, additional supplies costing $4,545 were purchased. At the end of the accounting period, December 31, 20—, only $800 in supplies remain.

Required:

1. Enter the appropriate adjusting entry in a two-column journal.
2. Post this entry to the ledger accounts provided.

GENERAL JOURNAL PAGE

	DATE	DESCRIPTION	POST. REF.	DEBIT	CREDIT	
1						1
2						2
3						3
4						4

GENERAL LEDGER

ACCOUNT Supplies ACCOUNT NO. 141

DATE		ITEM	POST. REF.	DEBIT	CREDIT	BALANCE DEBIT	BALANCE CREDIT
20—— Jan.	1	Balance	√			1 2 2 5 00	
	12		J2	4 5 4 5 00		5 7 7 0 00	

ACCOUNT Supplies Expense ACCOUNT NO. 524

DATE	ITEM	POST. REF.	DEBIT	CREDIT	BALANCE	
					DEBIT •	CREDIT

Exercise 4 (LO 1/4/5) PREPARING, JOURNALIZING, AND POSTING ADJUSTING ENTRIES: DEPRECIATION

The Billy Willis Detective Agency began the accounting period by purchasing three cars that cost a total of $75,000. The estimated useful lives of these cars is only two years with no salvage value.

Required:

1. Enter the appropriate adjusting entry at the end of the first year in a two-column journal. Willis uses straight-line depreciation.
2. Post this entry to the ledger accounts provided on pages 51 and 52.

GENERAL JOURNAL PAGE

	DATE	DESCRIPTION	POST. REF.	DEBIT	CREDIT	
1						1
2						2
3						3
4						4

GENERAL LEDGER

ACCOUNT Automobiles ACCOUNT NO. 185

DATE	ITEM	POST. REF.	DEBIT	CREDIT	BALANCE	
					DEBIT •	CREDIT
20— Jan. 2	Balance	J1	75,00000		7500000	

ACCOUNT Accumulated Depreciation—Automobiles ACCOUNT NO. 185.1

DATE	ITEM	POST. REF.	DEBIT	CREDIT	BALANCE	
					DEBIT •	CREDIT

Exercise 4 (Continued)

ACCOUNT Depreciation Expense—Automobiles ACCOUNT NO. 541

DATE	ITEM	POST. REF.	DEBIT	CREDIT	BALANCE DEBIT	•	CREDIT

Exercise 5 (LO 1/4/5) PREPARING, JOURNALIZING, AND POSTING ADJUSTING ENTRIES: PREPAID INSURANCE

On June 1, the Straw Basket Herb Farm purchased a one-year liability insurance policy for $600. As of June 30, an additional $120 was earned by the employees but not yet paid.

Required:

1. Enter the appropriate adjusting entries at the end of June in the following general journal.
2. Post the entries to the ledger accounts provided.

GENERAL JOURNAL PAGE

	DATE	DESCRIPTION	POST. REF.	DEBIT	CREDIT	
1						1
2						2
3						3
4						4
5						5
6						6
7						7
8						8

GENERAL LEDGER

ACCOUNT Prepaid Insurance ACCOUNT NO. 145

DATE	ITEM	POST. REF.	DEBIT	CREDIT	BALANCE DEBIT	•	CREDIT
20— June 1	Balance	J2	6 0 0 00		6 0 0 00		

Exercise 5 (Concluded)

ACCOUNT **Wages Payable** ACCOUNT NO. 219

DATE	ITEM	POST. REF.	DEBIT	CREDIT	BALANCE DEBIT	•	CREDIT

ACCOUNT **Wages Expense** ACCOUNT NO. 511

DATE	ITEM	POST. REF.	DEBIT	CREDIT	BALANCE DEBIT	•	CREDIT
20—— June 14	Balance	J5	5 0 0 00		5 0 0 00		
12		J5	5 0 0 00		1 0 0 0 00		

ACCOUNT **Insurance Expense** ACCOUNT NO. 535

DATE	ITEM	POST. REF.	DEBIT	CREDIT	BALANCE DEBIT	•	CREDIT

Problem 1 (LO1/2/) PREPARING ADJUSTMENTS AND THE WORK SHEET

Kim Ho offers employment counseling to middle managers unemployed due to corporation downsizing. On January 1 of the current year, Ho purchased office equipment with an expected life of 12 years and no salvage value. Computer equipment with an expected life of four years and no salvage value was purchased on July 1 of the current year. Ho uses straight-line depreciation. Office supplies on hand at year-end amounted to $150. Employees earned $300 in wages that have not yet been paid. Provided below are the general ledger accounts as of December 31, prior to adjustment.

Required:

1. Using the ledger accounts below, complete the Trial Balance columns of the year-end work sheet provided.

2. Prepare the necessary year-end adjustments.

3. Complete the work sheet.

Problem 1 (Continued)

GENERAL LEDGER

ACCOUNT Cash ACCOUNT NO. 101

DATE		ITEM	POST. REF.	DEBIT	CREDIT	BALANCE DEBIT	•	CREDIT
20— Dec.	1	Balance	√			2 4 0 0 00		
	21		J20	10 8 0 0 00		13 2 0 0 00		
	27		J20		4 2 0 0 00	9 0 0 0 00		

ACCOUNT Office Supplies ACCOUNT NO. 142

DATE		ITEM	POST. REF.	DEBIT	CREDIT	BALANCE DEBIT	•	CREDIT
20— Dec.	1	Balance	√			2 0 0 00		
	6		J20	3 0 0 00		5 0 0 00		

ACCOUNT Office Equipment ACCOUNT NO. 181

DATE		ITEM	POST. REF.	DEBIT	CREDIT	BALANCE DEBIT	•	CREDIT
20— Dec.	1	Balance	√			6 0 0 0 00		

ACCOUNT Accumulated Depreciation—Office Equipment ACCOUNT NO. 181.1

DATE		ITEM	POST. REF.	DEBIT	CREDIT	BALANCE DEBIT	•	CREDIT

ACCOUNT Computer Equipment ACCOUNT NO. 187

DATE		ITEM	POST. REF.	DEBIT	CREDIT	BALANCE DEBIT	•	CREDIT
20— Dec.	1	Balance	√			8 0 0 0 00		

Problem 1 (Continued) **GENERAL LEDGER**

ACCOUNT Accumulated Depreciation—Computer Equipment ACCOUNT NO. 187.1

DATE		ITEM	POST. REF.	DEBIT	CREDIT	BALANCE		
						DEBIT	•	CREDIT

ACCOUNT Accounts Payable ACCOUNT NO. 202

DATE		ITEM	POST. REF.	DEBIT	CREDIT	BALANCE		
						DEBIT	•	CREDIT
20— Dec.	1	Balance	√					3 0 0 00
	6		J20		2 0 0 00			5 0 0 00
	27		J20	1 0 0 00		9 0 0 00		4 0 0 00

ACCOUNT Wages Payable ACCOUNT NO. 219

DATE		ITEM	POST. REF.	DEBIT	CREDIT	BALANCE		
						DEBIT	•	CREDIT

ACCOUNT Kim Ho, Capital ACCOUNT NO. 311

DATE		ITEM	POST. REF.	DEBIT	CREDIT	BALANCE		
						DEBIT	•	CREDIT
20— Dec.	1	Balance	√					10 2 0 0 00

ACCOUNT Kim Ho, Drawing ACCOUNT NO. 312

DATE		ITEM	POST. REF.	DEBIT	CREDIT	BALANCE		
						DEBIT	•	CREDIT
20— Dec.	1	Balance	√			1 5 0 0 00		
	30		J20	1 0 0 0 00		2 5 0 0 00		

Problem 1 (Continued) GENERAL LEDGER

ACCOUNT Counseling Fees ACCOUNT NO. 401

DATE		ITEM	POST. REF.	DEBIT	CREDIT	BALANCE DEBIT	•	BALANCE CREDIT
20— Dec.	1	Balance	√					22 0 0 0 00
	31		J20					32 1 7 0 00

ACCOUNT Wages Expense ACCOUNT NO. 511

DATE		ITEM	POST. REF.	DEBIT	CREDIT	BALANCE DEBIT	•	BALANCE CREDIT
20— Dec.	1	Balance	√			7 0 0 0 00		
	31		J20	1 5 0 0 00		8 5 0 0 00		

ACCOUNT Rent Expense ACCOUNT NO. 521

DATE		ITEM	POST. REF.	DEBIT	CREDIT	BALANCE DEBIT	•	BALANCE CREDIT
20— Dec.	1	Balance	√			4 4 0 0 00		
	4		J20	1 2 0 0 00		5 6 0 0 00		

ACCOUNT Supplies Expense ACCOUNT NO. 524

DATE	ITEM	POST. REF.	DEBIT	CREDIT	BALANCE DEBIT	•	BALANCE CREDIT

ACCOUNT Utilities Expense ACCOUNT NO. 533

DATE		ITEM	POST. REF.	DEBIT	CREDIT	BALANCE DEBIT	•	BALANCE CREDIT
20— Dec.	1	Balance	√			1 3 0 0 00		
	31		J20	5 7 0 00		1 8 7 0 00		

Problem 1 (Continued) **GENERAL LEDGER**

ACCOUNT Depreciation Expense ACCOUNT NO. 541

DATE		ITEM	POST. REF.	DEBIT	CREDIT	BALANCE	
						DEBIT •	CREDIT

ACCOUNT Depreciation Expense—Computer Equipment ACCOUNT NO. 542

DATE		ITEM	POST. REF.	DEBIT	CREDIT	BALANCE	
						DEBIT •	CREDIT

ACCOUNT Miscellaneous Expense ACCOUNT NO. 549

DATE		ITEM	POST. REF.	DEBIT	CREDIT	BALANCE DEBIT •	CREDIT
20—							
Dec.	1	Balance	√			6 0 0 00	
	22		J20	2 0 0 00		8 0 0 00	

Problem 1 (Concluded)

KIM HO EMPLOYMENT

WORK

FOR MONTH ENDED

	ACCOUNT TITLE	TRIAL BALANCE			ADJUSTMENTS		
		DEBIT	•	CREDIT	DEBIT	•	CREDIT
1							
2							
3							
4							
5							
6							
7							
8							
9							
10							
11							
12							
13							
14							
15							
16							
17							
18							
19							
20							

COUNSELING SERVICES

SHEET

DECEMBER 31, 20--

ADJUSTED TRIAL BALANCE		INCOME STATEMENT		BALANCE SHEET	
DEBIT	CREDIT	DEBIT	CREDIT	DEBIT	CREDIT

Problem 2 (LO 1/2) PREPARING ADJUSTMENTS AND THE WORK SHEET

The trial balance for Juan's Speedy Delivery Service as of September 30, 20— is shown on the work sheet on pages 60–61.

Data to complete the adjustments are as follows:

(a) Supplies inventory as of September 30, $450.
(b) Insurance expired, $200.
(c) Depreciation on delivery equipment, $350.
(d) Wages earned by employees but not paid as of September 30, $215.

Required:

1. Enter the adjustments in the Adjustments columns on the work sheet.
2. Complete the work sheet.

Problem 2 (Continued)

	ACCOUNT TITLE	TRIAL BALANCE			ADJUSTMENTS		
		DEBIT	•	CREDIT	DEBIT	•	CREDIT
1	Cash	1 5 4 5 00					
2	Accounts Receivable	8 5 0 00					
3	Supplies	7 2 5 00					
4	Prepaid Insurance	1 5 0 0 00					
5	Delivery Equipment	6 3 0 0 00					
6	Accum. Depr.—Delivery Equip.						
7	Accounts Payable			9 8 0 00			
8	Wages Payable						
9	Juan Garcia, Capital			9 0 0 0 00			
10	Juan Garcia, Drawing	1 2 0 0 00					
11	Delivery Fees			5 2 4 0 00			
12	Wages Expense	1 4 7 5 00					
13	Advertising Expense	4 2 0 00					
14	Rent Expense	7 5 0 00					
15	Supplies Expense						
16	Telephone Expense	1 8 0 00					
17	Insurance Expense						
18	Repair Expense	1 9 0 00					
19	Oil & Gas Expense	8 5 00					
20	Depreciation Expense—Del. Equip.						
		15 2 2 0 00		15 2 2 0 00			

DELIVERY SERVICE
SHEET

SEPTEMBER 30, 20--

ADJUSTED TRIAL BALANCE		INCOME STATEMENT		BALANCE SHEET		
DEBIT	CREDIT	DEBIT	CREDIT	DEBIT	CREDIT	
						1
						2
						3
						4
						5
						6
						7
						8
						9
						10
						11
						12
						13
						14
						15
						16
						17
						18
						19
						20
						21
						22
						23

Problem 3 (LO 3) FINDING AND CORRECTING ERRORS ON A WORK SHEET

A work sheet for George Green's Landscaping Service follows. It should include these adjustments:

(a) Ending inventory of supplies as of July 31, $350.
(b) Insurance expired as of July 31, $225.
(c) Depreciation on tractor, $460.
(d) Wages earned but not paid as of July 31, $320.

Required:

Errors have been intentionally placed in the following work sheet. Review the work sheet for addition mistakes, transpositions, and other errors and make all necessary corrections.

Problem 3 (Continued)
(Note: Errors are intentional.)

GREEN'S LANDSCAPING

WORK

FOR MONTH ENDED

#	ACCOUNT TITLE	TRIAL BALANCE DEBIT	TRIAL BALANCE CREDIT	ADJUSTMENTS DEBIT	ADJUSTMENTS CREDIT
1	Cash	1 8 2 5 00			
2	Accounts Receivable	7 2 0 00			
3	Supplies	6 0 0 00			(a) 3 5 0 00
4	Prepaid Insurance	8 5 0 00			(b) 2 2 5 00
5	Tractor	6 5 5 0 00			(c) 4 6 0 00
6	Accum. Depr.—Tractor				
7	Accounts Payable		5 2 0 00		
8	Wages Payable				(d) 3 2 0 00
9	George Green, Capital		8 2 5 0 00		
10	George Green, Drawing	1 2 0 0 00			
11	Landscaping Fees		6 1 0 0 00		
12	Wages Expense	1 5 4 0 00		(d) 3 2 0 00	
13	Advertising Expense	2 5 0 00			
14	Rent Expense	7 7 5 00			
15	Supplies Expense			(a) 3 5 0 00	
16	Telephone Expense	1 4 0 00			
17	Utilities Expense	2 2 0 00			
18	Insurance Expense			(b) 2 2 5 00	
19	Depr. Expense—Tractor			(c) 4 6 0 00	
20	Miscellaneous Expense	2 0 0 00			
21	Net Income	14 8 7 0 00	14 8 7 0 00	1 3 5 5 00	1 3 5 5 00
22					
23					
24					

Problem 3 (Continued)

SERVICE

SHEET

JULY 31, 20--

	ADJUSTED TRIAL BALANCE		INCOME STATEMENT		BALANCE SHEET		
	DEBIT	CREDIT	DEBIT	CREDIT	DEBIT	CREDIT	
	1 8 2 5 00				1 8 2 5 00		1
	7 2 0 00				7 2 0 00		2
	2 5 0 00				2 5 0 00		3
	6 5 0 00				6 5 0 00		4
	6 0 9 0 00				6 0 9 0 00		5
							6
		5 2 0 00				5 2 0 00	7
		3 2 0 00		3 2 0 00			8
		8 2 5 0 00				8 2 5 0 00	9
	1 2 0 0 00		1 2 0 0 00				10
		6 1 0 0 00		6 1 0 0 00			11
	1 5 4 0 00		1 5 4 0 00			1 8 4 0 00	12
	2 5 0 00		2 5 0 00				13
	7 7 5 00		7 7 5 00				14
	3 5 0 00		3 5 0 00				15
	1 4 0 00		1 4 0 00				16
	2 2 0 00		2 2 0 00				17
	2 2 5 00		2 2 5 00				18
	4 6 0 00		4 6 0 00				19
	2 0 0 00		2 0 0 00				20
	13 3 5 5 00	15 1 9 0 00	2 4 1 7 00	6 4 2 0 00	8 3 4 7 00	8 7 7 0 00	21
			1 7 2 0 00			1 7 2 0 00	22
			4 1 3 7 00	6 4 2 0 00	8 3 4 7 00	10 4 9 0 00	23
							24

CHAPTER 5 APPENDIX
DEPRECIATION METHODS

APPENDIX LEARNING OBJECTIVES

In Chapter 5, the straight-line method of depreciation was illustrated. In the appendix to Chapter 5, three additional methods are explained. These methods are used when a different schedule of expenses provides a more appropriate matching with the revenues generated.

Objective 1. **Prepare a depreciation schedule using the straight-line method.**

Objective 2. **Prepare a depreciation schedule using the sum-of-the-years'-digits method.**

Objective 3. **Prepare a depreciation schedule using the double-declining-balance method.**

Objective 4. **Prepare a depreciation schedule for tax purposes using the Modified Accelerated Cost Recovery System.**

Exercise 1 (LO 1) STRAIGHT-LINE DEPRECIATION

Office equipment was purchased on January 1 at a cost of $48,000. It has an estimated useful life of 4 years and a salvage value of $6,000. Prepare a depreciation schedule showing the depreciation expense, accumulated depreciation, and book value for each year under the straight-line method.

STRAIGHT-LINE DEPRECIATION

Exercise 2 (LO 2) SUM-OF-THE-YEARS'-DIGITS DEPRECIATION

Using the information given in Exercise 1, prepare a depreciation schedule showing the depreciation expense, accumulated depreciation, and book value for each year under the sum-of-the-years'-digits method.

SUM-OF-THE-YEARS'-DIGITS DEPRECIATION

Exercise 3 (LO 3) DOUBLE-DECLINING-BALANCE DEPRECIATION

Using the information given in Exercise 1, prepare a depreciation schedule showing the depreciation expense, accumulated depreciation, and book value for each year under the double-declining-balance method.

DOUBLE-DECLINING-BALANCE DEPRECIATION

Exercise 4 (LO 4) DEPRECIATION UNDER THE MODIFIED ACCELERATED COST RECOVERY SYSTEM

Using the information given in Exercise 1 and the rates shown in Figure 5A-4 of the text, prepare a depreciation schedule showing the depreciation expense, accumulated depreciation, and book value for each year under the Modified Accelerated Cost Recovery System. For tax purposes, assume that the office equipment has a useful life of 5 years. (The IRS schedule will spread depreciation over six years.)

MODIFIED ACCELERATED COST RECOVERY SYSTEM

CHAPTER 6
FINANCIAL STATEMENTS AND THE CLOSING PROCESS

LEARNING OBJECTIVES

Chapter 5 introduced the work sheet and demonstrated how it is used to prepare year-end adjustments. Chapter 6 completes the discussion of the work sheet by illustrating its role in the preparation of financial statements and closing entries. The purpose of the post-closing trial balance is also explained. It is prepared after closing entries have been posted to the general ledger accounts.

Objective 1. Prepare financial statements with the aid of a work sheet.

The work sheet contains almost all information needed to prepare the income statement, the statement of owner's equity, and the balance sheet. Numbers can be taken directly from the Income Statement columns for the income statement. The owner's capital account must be reviewed before completing the statement of owner's equity. If additional investments were made, they must be added to the beginning capital balance to compute the total investment. The net income (or net loss) is added to the total investment, and withdrawals (drawing) are subtracted, giving the ending owner's equity. The balance sheet is prepared using the ending owner's equity balance reported on the statement of owner's equity and the permanent accounts listed in the Balance Sheet columns of the work sheet.

Objective 2. Journalize and post closing entries.

After the work sheet is completed, the financial statements are prepared. Then the adjusting and closing entries are journalized and posted. All temporary accounts need zero balances to begin the new accounting period. The closing process has four journal entries:

1. to close the revenue account(s) to Income Summary
2. to close the expense accounts to Income Summary
3. to close the Income Summary account to the capital account, and
4. to close the Drawing account to the Capital account.

Objective 3. Prepare a post-closing trial balance.

The **post-closing trial balance** lists all the permanent accounts that have balances to begin the new accounting period. It is prepared to prove the equality of the debit and credit balances in the general ledger accounts following the closing process. Since temporary accounts (drawing, revenues, and expenses) are closed at the end of the period, they do not appear on the post-closing trial balance.

Objective 4. List and describe the steps in the accounting cycle.

This chapter concludes the accounting cycle that began in Chapter 1. The ten steps are

1. analyze source documents
2. journalize transactions
3. post transactions to general ledger accounts
4. prepare the trial balance (work sheet)
5. determine and prepare needed adjustments (work sheet)

6. complete the work sheet
7. prepare the financial statements (income statement, statement of owner's equity, and balance sheet)
8. journalize the adjusting and closing entries
9. post the adjusting and closing entries, and
10. prepare the post-closing trial balance.

REVIEW QUESTIONS

Instructions: Analyze each of the following items carefully before writing your answer in the column at the right.

Question	Answer

1. The work sheet provides all of the needed information to prepare which three financial statements?.. _____

2. The income statement contains which two major types of accounts?.. _____

3. The statement of owner's equity adds _____ to the beginning owner's equity and subtracts _____. _____

4. Amounts owed that will be paid within a year are called _____. _____

5. Expenses are listed on the income statement in the order they appear on the chart of accounts or in descending order by _____ amount. _____

6. To find if the owner made any additional investments during the period, we must review the _____ account in the general ledger. _____

7. When net income and additional investments are greater than withdrawals, the difference is called a(n) _____ in capital for the month. .. _____

8. When the balance sheet is shown in _____ form, liabilities and owner's equity sections are placed below the assets section. _____

9. When the balance sheet is shown in _____ form, assets are on the left and liabilities and owner's equity are on the right. _____

10. A(n) _____ balance sheet groups similar items together such as current assets and current liabilities. _____

11. Cash and assets that will be converted to cash or consumed within a year or the normal operating cycle are called _____ assets. _____

12. The _____ is the period of time required to purchase supplies and services and convert them back into cash. _____

13. Accounts Payable and Wages Payable are classified as _____ liabilities. ... _____

14. Assets, liabilities, and the owner's capital account accumulate information across accounting periods; they are called _____ accounts. .. _____

15. Revenue, expense, and drawing accounts accumulate information for the specific period only, then they go back to _____ balances. _____

Question	Answer

16. Because revenue, expense, and drawing accounts are closed each accounting period, they are called _____ accounts.

17. The _____ account is used to summarize the effects of revenue and expense accounts; it is then closed to the Capital account.

18. When closing entries are posted to the general ledger, the word _____ is written in the Item column of each general ledger account affected. ...

19. The _____ trial balance only lists permanent accounts.

20. The _____ begins with analyzing source documents and ends with the post-closing trial balance.

EXERCISES AND PROBLEMS

Exercise 1 REVIEW: COMPUTE NET INCOME

From the information given below, compute net income:

Revenue:	Delivery Fees	$4,826
Expenses:	Wages Expense	2,700
	Rent Expense	350
	Supplies Expense	55
	Insurance Expense	33
	Depreciation Expense	100

Exercise 2 REVIEW: COMPUTE OWNER'S EQUITY

Using the net income from Exercise 1 and the following information, compute the (a) increase to owner's equity and (b) ending owner's equity balance. Assume no additional investments were made by the owners.

(a)_____

(b)_____

Beginning Owner's Equity:	$5,680
Withdrawals by Owner:	1,000

Exercise 3 (LO 2) THE CLOSING PROCESS

Based upon Exercises 1 and 2 above, list the accounts that must be closed at the end of the accounting cycle (in addition to the income summary account).

PROBLEMS

A completed work sheet for Collins Cycle Service as of April 30, 20— appears on pages 70–71. The general ledger is provided on pages 74–78.

Required:

From the work sheet on pages 70–71, complete the problems that follow.

Problem 1 (LO 1) PREPARE AN INCOME STATEMENT

Prepare the income statement.

Problem 1 (Continued)

COLLINS CYCLE

WORK

FOR MONTH ENDED

	DESCRIPTION	TRIAL BALANCE		ADJUSTMENTS	
		DEBIT	CREDIT	DEBIT	CREDIT
1	Cash	4 8 0 0 00			
2	Supplies	8 2 6 00			(a) 3 2 6 00
3	Prepaid Insurance	1 3 0 0 00			(b) 2 0 0 00
4	Repair Equipment	2 6 0 0 00			
5	Accum. Depr.—Repair Equip.		4 0 0 00		(c) 4 0 0 00
6	Accounts Payable		1 3 0 0 00		
7	Wages Payable				(d) 1 0 0 00
8	Jean Collins, Capital		6 0 0 0 00		
9	Jean Collins, Drawing	3 0 0 00			
10	Repair Fees		2 8 3 9 00		
11	Wages Expense	2 7 5 00		(d) 1 0 0 00	
12	Rent Expense	4 0 0 00			
13	Supplies Expense			(a) 3 2 6 00	
14	Telephone Expense	3 8 00			
15	Insurance Expense			(b) 2 0 0 00	
16	Depreciation Exp.—Repair Equip.			(c) 4 0 0 00	
17		10 5 3 9 00	10 5 3 9 00	1 0 2 6 00	1 0 2 6 00
18	Net Income				
19					

Problem 1 (Concluded)

SERVICE _____

SHEET _____

APRIL 30, 20--

	ADJUSTED TRIAL BALANCE		INCOME STATEMENT		BALANCE SHEET		
	DEBIT	CREDIT	DEBIT	CREDIT	DEBIT	CREDIT	
	4 8 0 0 00				4 8 0 0 00		1
	5 0 0 00				5 0 0 00		2
	1 1 0 0 00				1 1 0 0 00		3
	2 6 0 0 00				2 6 0 0 00		4
		8 0 0 00				8 0 0 00	5
		1 3 0 0 00				1 3 0 0 00	6
		1 0 0 00				1 0 0 00	7
		6 0 0 0 00				6 0 0 0 00	8
	3 0 0 00				3 0 0 00		9
		2 8 3 9 00		2 8 3 9 00			10
	3 7 5 00		3 7 5 00				11
	4 0 0 00		4 0 0 00				12
	3 2 6 00		3 2 6 00				13
	3 8 00		3 8 00				14
	2 0 0 00		2 0 0 00				15
	4 0 0 00		4 0 0 00				16
	11 0 3 9 00	11 0 3 9 00	1 7 3 9 00	2 8 3 9 00	9 3 0 0 00	8 2 0 0 00	17
			1 1 0 0 00			1 1 0 0 00	18
			2 8 3 9 00	2 8 3 9 00	9 3 0 0 00	9 3 0 0 00	19

Problem 2 (LO 2) PREPARE A STATEMENT OF OWNER'S EQUITY

Prepare the statement of owner's equity. Be sure to check the capital account in the general ledger.

Problem 3 (LO 1) PREPARE A BALANCE SHEET

Prepare the balance sheet in report form.

Exercise 4-6A (Concluded)

Problem 4 REVIEW: PREPARE ADJUSTING ENTRIES

Journalize the adjusting entries and post them to the general ledger accounts. (Use the General Journal provided on page 73 for Problems 4 and 5.) The balances shown in the general ledger accounts are *Trial Balance* amounts—that is, before adjusting and closing entries are entered.

Problems 4 and 5 (Continued)

ACCOUNT Accumulated Depreciation—Repair Equipment ACCOUNT NO. 188.1

DATE		ITEM	POST. REF.	DEBIT	CREDIT	BALANCE		
						DEBIT	•	CREDIT
20— Apr.	1	Balance	√					4 0 0 00

ACCOUNT Accounts Payable ACCOUNT NO. 202

DATE		ITEM	POST. REF.	DEBIT	CREDIT	BALANCE		
						DEBIT	•	CREDIT
20— Apr.	30	Balance	√					1 3 0 0 00

ACCOUNT Wages Payable ACCOUNT NO. 219

DATE	ITEM	POST. REF.	DEBIT	CREDIT	BALANCE		
					DEBIT	•	CREDIT

ACCOUNT Jean Collins, Capital ACCOUNT NO. 311

DATE		ITEM	POST. REF.	DEBIT	CREDIT	BALANCE		
						DEBIT	•	CREDIT
20— Apr.	1	Balance	√					5 0 0 0 00
	15		J1		1 0 0 0 00			6 0 0 0 00

Problems 4 and 5 (Continued)

ACCOUNT Jean Collins, Drawing ACCOUNT NO. 312

DATE		ITEM	POST. REF.	DEBIT	CREDIT	BALANCE	
						DEBIT •	CREDIT
20— Apr.	30	Balance	√			3 0 0 00	

ACCOUNT Income Summary ACCOUNT NO. 313

DATE		ITEM	POST. REF.	DEBIT	CREDIT	BALANCE	
						DEBIT •	CREDIT
20— Apr.			√				

ACCOUNT Repair Fees ACCOUNT NO. 401

DATE		ITEM	POST. REF.	DEBIT	CREDIT	BALANCE	
						DEBIT •	CREDIT
20— Apr.	30	Balance	√				2 8 3 9 00

ACCOUNT Wages Expense ACCOUNT NO. 511

DATE		ITEM	POST. REF.	DEBIT	CREDIT	BALANCE	
						DEBIT •	CREDIT
20— Apr.	30	Balance	√			2 7 5 00	

Problems 4 and 5 (Continued)

ACCOUNT Rent Expense ACCOUNT NO. 521

DATE		ITEM	POST. REF.	DEBIT					CREDIT					BALANCE								
														DEBIT			•	CREDIT				
20— Apr.	3	Balance	√											4	0	0	00					

ACCOUNT Supplies Expense ACCOUNT NO. 524

DATE		ITEM	POST. REF.	DEBIT					CREDIT					BALANCE								
														DEBIT			•	CREDIT				
20— Apr.																						

ACCOUNT Telephone Expense ACCOUNT NO. 525

DATE		ITEM	POST. REF.	DEBIT					CREDIT					BALANCE								
														DEBIT			•	CREDIT				
20— Apr.	30	Balance	√											3	8	00						

ACCOUNT Insurance Expense ACCOUNT NO. 535

DATE		ITEM	POST. REF.	DEBIT					CREDIT					BALANCE								
														DEBIT			•	CREDIT				
20— Apr.																						

Problems 4 and 5 (Concluded)

ACCOUNT Depreciation Expense—Repair Equipment ACCOUNT NO. 542

DATE	ITEM	POST. REF.	DEBIT	CREDIT	BALANCE DEBIT	BALANCE CREDIT
20— Apr.						

Problem 6 (LO 3) PREPARE A POST-CLOSING TRIAL BALANCE

Prepare the post-closing trial balance.

ACCOUNT	ACCT. NO.	DEBIT BALANCE	CREDIT BALANCE

CHAPTER 6 APPENDIX
STATEMENT OF CASH FLOWS

APPENDIX LEARNING OBJECTIVES

In Chapter 6, we reviewed in greater detail the preparation of three financial statements: the income statement, statement of owner's equity, and balance sheet. A fourth important financial statement is the statement of cash flows. The main purpose of this statement is to report the sources and uses of cash. These sources and uses are categorized into three types of business activities: operating, investing, and financing.

Objective 1. Categorize business transactions as operating, investing, or financing.

Operating activities include those cash flows that are related to the revenues and expenses reported on the income statement. Examples include cash received for services performed and the payment of cash for expenses.

Investing activities are those transactions associated with buying and selling long-term assets, lending money, and collecting the principal on the related loans.

Financing activities are those cash transactions with owners and creditors. Examples include cash received from the owner to finance the operations and cash paid to the owner as withdrawals. Financing activities also include the receipt of cash from loans and the repayment of the loans.

Objective 2. Prepare a statement of cash flows by analyzing and categorizing a series of business transactions.

The main body of the statement of cash flows consists of three sections: operating, investing, and financing activities.

Name of Business
Statement of Cash Flows
For Period Ended Date

Cash flows from operating activities:
 Cash received from customers $ x,xxx
 List cash paid for various
 expenses $ (xxx)
 Total cash paid for operations (x,xxx)
 Net cash provided by (used
 for) operating activities $ xxx

Cash flows from investing activities:
 List cash received from the
 sale of long-term assets
 and other investing
 activities $ x,xxx

List cash paid for the purchase
 of long-term assets
 and other investing
 activities (x,xxx)
 Net cash provided by (used
 for) investing activities (x,xxx)
Cash flows from financing activities:
 List cash received from
 owners and creditors $ x,xxx
 List cash paid to owners and
 creditors (xxx)
 Net cash provided by (used
 for) financing activities x,xxx
Net increase (decrease) in cash $ xxx

Exercise 1 REVIEW: ENTERING TRANSACTIONS IN T-ACCOUNTS

Sung Joon Lee opened an overseas mailing business, "Lee's Quick Sail." The following transactions occurred during August of the current year. Enter the transactions in the Cash T account provided below, identifying each with its corresponding letter.

(a) Lee invested $5,000 in the business.
(b) Paid office rent, $500.
(c) Bought supplies for the month, $200.
(d) Lee made an additional investment in the business, $1,000.
(e) Bought a new scale for $1,200, $700 cash and $500 on account.
(f) Received $600 for mailing services.
(g) Paid $200 on loan (see transaction (e)).
(h) Paid electricity bill, $64.
(i) Paid gas bill, $70.
(j) Received $900 for mailing services.
(k) Paid part-time employee, $90.
(l) Lee withdrew cash for personal use, $400.

CASH

Exercise 2 REVIEW: FOOTING AND BALANCING A T-ACCOUNT

Foot and balance the T account in Exercise 1. The cash balance at the end of August is _____ .

Problem 1 (LO 1) CLASSIFYING BUSINESS TRANSACTIONS AS OPERATING, INVESTING, OR FINANCING

Label each transaction in the Cash T account of Exercise 1 as an operating (O), investing (I), or financing (F) activity.

Problem 2 (LO 2) PREPARING A STATEMENT OF CASH FLOWS BY ANALYZING BUSINESS TRANSACTIONS.

Prepare a statement of cash flows based on the transactions and Cash T account in Exercises 1 through 2 and Problem 1.

CHAPTER 7
ACCOUNTING FOR CASH

LEARNING OBJECTIVES

Managing cash is an essential part of every business's operations. In Chapter 7, we explore the cash account—setting up a bank account, writing checks and making deposits, preparing a bank reconciliation and the journal entries needed, operating a petty cash fund, establishing a change fund and using a cash short and over account.

Objective 1. Describe how to open and use a checking account.

Most banks have standard procedures for opening and using a **checking account.** They begin with a signature card, whereby the depositor's social security number or EIN number and signature are provided. Preparing deposit tickets, endorsing properly, and writing checks, are parts of using a checking account wisely.

Objective 2. Prepare a bank reconciliation and related journal entries.

On a monthly basis, banks send **bank statements** to their checking account customers. The bank statement must be reconciled—compared to the checkbook. Adjustments are made to the ending bank balance and the checkbook balance until they are equal. Once the bank reconciliation is prepared, any changes to the book (checkbook) balance will require journal entries.

Objective 3. Describe how to establish and use a petty cash fund.

A **petty cash fund** is both convenient and cost-effective. Rather than writing checks for small amounts, costing time and money, a sum of money is set aside for petty (small) cash payments during the month. Vouchers are issued for all money paid out; the petty cash record is replenished at the end of the month (brought back up to its original amount). A journal entry is made to record all of the expenses shown in the petty cash record.

Objective 4. Establish a change fund and use the cash short and over account.

Businesses that receive cash from customers generally need to establish a change fund of currency and coins to use in handling cash sales. When many cash transactions occur, there often will be a difference between what the cash register tape says and the amount of cash actually found in the drawer. An account called Cash Short and Over is used to account for these differences. At the end of the month, if there is more cash short than over, it is an expense to the business. If there is more cash over than short, it is a revenue to the business.

REVIEW QUESTIONS

Instructions: Analyze each of the following carefully before writing your answer in the column at the right.

Question	Answer

Question **Answer**

1. To open a checking account, each person authorized to sign checks must fill out a(n) _____. .. _____

2. A(n) _____ lists items being deposited to a checking account. ... _____

3. Each check deposited is identified by its _____. _____

4. A(n) _____ consists of stamping or writing the depositor's name and other information on the back of a check. _____

5. A(n) _____ endorsement consists of a signature on the back of a check. .. _____

6. A(n) _____ endorsement consists of a signature together with words such as "For Deposit."... _____

7. Depositors using ATM machines must first key in their _____. ... _____

8. A(n) _____ is a document ordering a bank to pay cash from the depositor's account. .. _____

9. The _____ is the bank on which a check is drawn. _____

10. The _____ is the person being paid the cash. _____

11. The _____ is the depositor who orders the bank to pay the cash... _____

12. Space is contained to record all relevant information about a check on its _____. .. _____

13. A statement issued to the depositor once a month is called a _____. ... _____

14. Checks paid by the bank and returned to the depositor are called _____. ... _____

15. The process of bringing the bank and book balances into agreement is called preparing a(n).. _____

16. Checks issued during the period but not yet processed by the bank are called _____. ... _____

17. Deposits made but not yet recorded by the bank are called _____. _____

18. Bank charges for services are called _____. _____

19. Checks deposited but not paid because the depositor did not have enough money in the account are called _____ checks............. _____

20. Transactions can be completed by _____ rather than by the manual process of writing checks or using cash. _____

21. A fund called _____ is established to pay for small items with cash. .. _____

22. A receipt called a(n) _____ is prepared for every payment from
the fund. ...

23. The _____ is a special multi-column record where petty cash pay-
ments are recorded. ...

24. At the end of the month, the petty cash fund is _____, or brought
up to its original amount. ...

25. The cash short and over account is used when actual cash on hand
is different from what is on the _____ tape plus the change fund.

26. When actual cash on hand exceeds what is on the register tape plus the
change fund, this difference is a(n) _____.

27. When actual cash on hand is less than what is on the register tape plus
the change fund, this difference is a(n) _____...........................

EXERCISES AND PROBLEMS

Exercise 1 (LO1) PREPARE DEPOSIT TICKET

Using the deposit ticket shown below, enter the following information:

Date:	March 28, 20—	Checks:	33-11	$202.00
Currency:	$318.00		123-666	48.00
Coin:	33.00		2-9	211.00

DEPOSIT TICKET

PEOPLE'S BANK
Wilkes-Barre, PA 18704-1456

Date_____ 20____
CHECKS AND OTHER ITEMS ARE RECEIVED FOR DEPOSIT SUBJECT TO
THE TERMS AND CONDITIONS OF THIS FINANCIAL INSTITUTION'S
ACCOUNT AGREEMENT.

SIGN HERE ONLY IF CASH RECEIVED FROM DEPOSIT

⑈063112094⑈ 0001632475⑈'

CURRENCY		
COIN		
CHECKS		
TOTAL FROM OTHER SIDE		
SUBTOTAL		
LESS CASH RECEIVED		
TOTAL DEPOSIT		

Exercise 2 (LO1) PREPARE CHECK AND STUB

During the month of October, you made the following payments by check. Fill in the stubs and write the checks. Use the blank checks provided on page 85. Enter $825.50 as the balance brought forward on Check No. 138, and add a deposit for $85 on October 10.

Oct. 3 Issued Check No. 138 to Emerald Lawn Care, Inc. for work done on the shrubbery around the office building, $125.00. (Miscellaneous Expense)

8 Issued Check No. 139 to Maxwell Office Supply for stationery, $85.90. (Office Supplies)

10 Issued Check No. 140 to Wesley's Towing for cost of towing company car to repair shop, for $50.00. (Automobile Expense)

Exercise 2 (Continued)

No. 138

DATE _____ 20_____
TO _____
FOR _____

ACCT. _____

	DOLLARS	CENTS
BAL BRO'T FOR'D		
AMT. DEPOSITED		
TOTAL		
AMT. THIS CHECK		
BAL CAR'D FOR'D		

No. 138 60-55/313

_____ 20 _____

PAY
TO THE
ORDER OF _____ $ _____

_____ Dollars

PEOPLE'S BANK FOR CLASSROOM USE ONLY
Wilkes-Barre, PA 18704-1456

MEMO _____ _____

⑈1300555 16 3247 5⑊

No. 139

DATE _____ 20_____
TO _____
FOR _____

ACCT. _____

	DOLLARS	CENTS
BAL BRO'T FOR'D		
AMT. DEPOSITED		
TOTAL		
AMT. THIS CHECK		
BAL CAR'D FOR'D		

No. 139 60-55/313

_____ 20 _____

PAY
TO THE
ORDER OF _____ $ _____

_____ Dollars

PEOPLE'S BANK FOR CLASSROOM USE ONLY
Wilkes-Barre, PA 18704-1456

MEMO _____ BY _____

⑈1300555 16 3247 5⑊

No. 140

DATE _____ 20_____
TO _____
FOR _____

ACCT. _____

	DOLLARS	CENTS
BAL BRO'T FOR'D		
AMT. DEPOSITED		
TOTAL		
AMT. THIS CHECK		
BAL CAR'D FOR'D		

No. 140 60-55/313

_____ 20 _____

PAY
TO THE
ORDER OF _____ $ _____

_____ Dollars

PEOPLE'S BANK FOR CLASSROOM USE ONLY
Wilkes-Barre, PA 18704-1456

MEMO _____ BY _____

⑈1300555 16 3247 5⑊

Exercise 3 (LO2) BANK RECONCILIATION PROCEDURES

The bank reconciliation is a process of matching the checkbook balance with the bank statement balance—adding and subtracting items until the two are equal. In the exercise below, indicate which action is taken:

 a. Add to checkbook balance.

 b. Subtract from checkbook balance.

 c. Add to bank statement balance.

 d. Subtract from bank statement balance.

_____ 1. Deposits in transit

_____ 2. Error in checkbook whereby a check for $128 was entered into the checkbook as $182

_____ 3. NSF check

_____ 4. Checks outstanding (not yet processed by the bank)

_____ 5. Bank service fees

_____ 6. Credit memo, telling depositor that a note was collected

_____ 7. Error in checkbook whereby a check for $181 was entered into the checkbook as $118

Exercise 4 (LO 2) PREPARE JOURNAL ENTRIES FOR BANK RECONCILIATION

Based on the following bank reconciliation, prepare the necessary journal entries as of January 28, 20—:

Bank statement balance, January 28		$1,896.00
Add: Deposits in transit:		
1/26	$118.00	
1/28	92.00	210.00
		$2,106.00
Deduct: Outstanding checks:		
No. 683	$ 23.00	
No. 685	6.50	
No. 687	102.50	
No. 688	13.00	
No. 689	208.00	353.00
Adjusted bank balance		$1,753.00
Book balance, January 28		$1,994.00
Add: Error on check*	$ 28.00	
Note collected**	142.00	170.00
		$2,164.00
Deduct: Unrecorded ATM withdrawal***	$ 30.00	
Service charge	11.00	
NSF check	370.00	411.00
Adjusted book balance		$1,753.00

* Accounts Payable was debited.
** Credit Notes Receivable.
*** Debit Gail Bennett, Drawing

Exercise 4 (Concluded)

GENERAL JOURNAL

PAGE _____

	DATE		DESCRIPTION	POST. REF.	DEBIT	CREDIT	
1							1
2							2
3							3
4							4
5							5
6							6
7							7
8							8
9							9
10							10
11							11
12							12
13							13
14							14
15							15
16							16
17							17
18							18
19							19
20							20
21							21
22							22

Exercise 5 (LO3) PETTY CASH JOURNAL ENTRIES

Based on the following petty cash information, prepare journal entries to establish the petty cash fund and to replenish the fund.

1. On March 1, a check is written for $100 to establish a petty cash fund.

2. During the month, the following petty cash payments are made:

Telephone Expense	$ 3.50
Automobile Expense	11.00
Postage Expense	4.50
B. Crenshaw, Drawing	35.00
Charitable Contributions Expense	25.00
Miscellaneous Expense	3.00

Exercise 5 (Concluded)

GENERAL JOURNAL

PAGE 1

	DATE	DESCRIPTION	POST. REF.	DEBIT	CREDIT	
1						1
2						2
3						3
4						4
5						5
6						6
7						7
8						8
9						9
10						10
11						11
12						12
13						13
14						14
15						15
16						16
17						17
18						18
19						19
20						20
21						21
22						22
23						23
24						

Exercise 6 (LO4) CASH SHORT AND OVER JOURNAL ENTRIES

Based on the following information, prepare weekly entries for cash receipts from service fees and cash short and over. A change fund of $100 is maintained.

August		Cash in drawer:		Cash register amount:	
	5	Cash in drawer:	$318.00	Cash register amount:	$ 218.00
	12		402.00		300.00
	19		388.00		292.00
	26		411.50		309.50

Exercise 6 (Concluded)

JOURNAL

	DATE		DESCRIPTION	POST. REF.	DEBIT	CREDIT	
1							1
2							2
3							3
4							4
5							5
6							6
7							7
8							8
9							9
10							10
11							11
12							12
13							13
14							14
15							15
16							16
17							17
18							18
19							19
20							20
21							21
22							22
23							23
24							24
25							25
26							26
27							27
28							28

Problem 1 (LO2) BANK RECONCILIATION AND RELATED JOURNAL ENTRIES

The following information relates to the bank account of the Mini Donut House:

Balance, March 31, per check stub		$2,923.00
Balance, March 31, per bank statement		3,199.00
March deposits not shown on bank statement	$302.00	
	206.00	508.00
Bank service charge shown on bank statement		14.00
Unrecorded ATM withdrawal*		60.00
NSF check shown on bank statement		153.00

Error on Check 144, where stub shows $132.00, but the check was made in the amount of $123.00. Accounts Payable was originally debited.

Checks outstanding, March 31:

No. 148	$201.00
No. 151	300.00
No. 155	501.00

*Funds were withdrawn by the owner, Paolo Goes, for personal use.

Required:

1. Prepare the bank reconciliation.

2. Prepare the needed journal entries.

Problem 1 (Continued)

1.

Problem 1 (Concluded)

2.

			JOURNAL			PAGE 1

JOURNAL PAGE 1

	DATE	DESCRIPTION	POST. REF.	DEBIT	CREDIT	
1						1
2						2
3						3
4						4
5						5
6						6
7						7
8						8
9						9
10						10
11						11
12						12
13						13
14						14
15						15
16						16

Problem 2 (LO3) PETTY CASH PAYMENTS RECORD AND JOURNAL ENTRIES

On April 1, the Fitzgibbons Furniture Repair Shop established a petty cash fund of $200.00. The following cash payments were made from the petty cash fund during the first two weeks of April. The fund was replenished to the $200.00 level on April 16.

April 1 Paid $5.28 for postage due on a package received. Petty Cash Voucher No. 10.

 5 Made a $25.00 contribution to the Washington Township Baseball League. Petty Cash Voucher No. 11.

 6 Reimbursed $6.25 to an employee for phone calls made from a pay telephone. Petty Cash Voucher No. 12.

 8 Paid $22.00 for office supplies. Petty Cash Voucher No. 13.

 10 Paid $32.00 for a newspaper advertisement. Petty Cash Voucher No. 14.

 12 Paid $33.00 for gas and an oil change for the company truck. Petty Cash Voucher No. 15.

 14 Paid $20.00 for postage stamps. Petty Cash Voucher No. 16.

 15 Made a $25.00 contribution to the Girl Scouts, Petty Cash Voucher No. 17.

Required:

 1. Prepare the journal entry to establish the petty cash fund.

 2. Enter the above payments in the petty cash payments record provided on page 94

 3. Prove the petty cash payments record.

 4. Prepare the journal entry to replenish the fund on April 16.

PETTY CASH PAYMENTS FOR MONTH OF _____ 20-- PAGE 1

DAY	DESCRIPTION	VOU. NO.	TOTAL AMOUNT	TRUCK EXPENSE	POSTAGE EXPENSE	CHARIT. CONTRIB. EXPENSE	TEL. EXPENSE	OFFICE SUPPLIES	ADVER. EXPENSE	DISTRIBUTION OF PAYMENTS ACCOUNT	AMOUNT	
1												1
2												2
3												3
4												4
5												5
6												6
7												7
8												8
9												9
10												10
11												11
12												12
13												13
14												14
15												15
16												16
17												17
18												18
19												19
20												20
21												21
22												22

Problem 2 (Concluded)

<div align="center">

JOURNAL

</div>

PAGE 1

	DATE		DESCRIPTION	POST REF.	DEBIT	CREDIT	
1							1
2							2
3							3
4							4
5							5
6							6
7							7
8							8
9							9
10							10
11							11
12							12
13							13
14							14
15							15
16							16
17							17
18							18
19							19
20							20
21							21

Problem 3 (LO4) CASH SHORT AND OVER JOURNAL ENTRIES

Mackie's Salon deposits cash weekly. A record of cash register receipts for the month of April is shown below. A change fund of $100 is maintained.

April	2	Cash in drawer:	$298.00	Cash register tape:	$196.50
	9		286.50		192.00
	16		293.50		193.50
	23		306.00		204.50
	30		301.50		203.00

Required:

Prepare weekly journal entries for cash receipts from service fees, showing cash short and over when needed.

Problem 3 (Concluded)

			JOURNAL			PAGE 1

	DATE		DESCRIPTION	POST REF.	DEBIT	CREDIT	
1							1
2							2
3							3
4							4
5							5
6							6
7							7
8							8
9							9
10							10
11							11
12							12
13							13
14							14
15							15
16							16
17							17
18							18
19							19
20							20
21							21
22							22
23							23
24							24
25							25
26							26
27							27
28							28
29							29
30							30
31							31
32							32

CHAPTER 8
PAYROLL ACCOUNTING:
EMPLOYEE EARNINGS AND DEDUCTIONS

LEARNING OBJECTIVES

Payroll accounting is an important part of any business, partly because it is such a significant expense and partly because so many laws govern its record keeping. In Chapter 8, we examine the payroll records that employers are required to keep and also those records that are maintained for administrative efficiency.

Objective 1. Distinguish between employees and independent contractors.

An **employee** is one who works under the control and direction of an employer. The employer controls how and when the job is to be done, determines working hours, and in general is responsible for all aspects of the employee's work. An **independent contractor**, on the other hand, performs a service for a fee and does not work under the control and direction of the company paying for his or her service. This is an important distinction because employers are required to maintain payroll records and file many reports for their employees but must file only one form for independent contractors.

Objective 2. Calculate employee earnings and deductions.

Three steps are required to determine how much to pay an employee for a pay period. Calculate the employee's total earnings for the pay period, determine the amounts of deductions for the same pay period, and subtract deductions from total earnings. The deductions may be required by law—for example, Social Security and Medicare taxes and federal and state income taxes—or by agreement with the employer—for example, insurance deductions and savings bond deductions.

Objective 3. Prepare payroll records.

Three types of payroll records are used to accumulate required information for federal and state tax purposes. The payroll register, the payroll check with earnings statement attached, and the employee earnings record.

The **payroll register** is a multi-column form that accumulates the necessary data to prepare the journal entry. Detailed information on earnings, taxable earnings, deductions, and net pay is provided for each employee and for the employees in total.

The **payroll check** is prepared from information in the payroll register. The detachable earnings statement attached to the employee's check shows the gross earnings, total deductions, and net pay.

A separate record of each employee's earnings is called an **employee earnings record.** This information is also obtained from the payroll register. The earnings record is designed so that quarterly and annual totals can be accumulated in order for the employer to prepare several reports.

Objective 4. Account for employee earnings and deductions.

The payroll register provides all the information needed to prepare the journal entry for any pay period. The total gross earnings is debited to a wages and salaries expense account, and each deduction is credited to a current liability account. The difference between gross earnings and total deductions is called **net pay** and is credited to cash.

Objective 5. Describe various payroll record-keeping methods.

In addition to a manual system of preparing all the necessary payroll records, payroll processing centers and electronic systems can be used to prepare the same records.

A **payroll processing center** is a business that sells payroll record-keeping services. An **electronic system** is a computer system based on a software package that performs all payroll record keeping and prepares payroll checks.

REVIEW QUESTIONS

Instructions: Analyze each of the following carefully before writing your answer in the column at the right.

Question	Answer

1. A(n) _____ is one who works under the control and direction of an employer. ... _____

2. A(n) _____ performs a service for a fee and does not work under the control and direction of the company paying for the service. _____

3. What three steps are required to determine how much to pay an employee for a pay period? .. _____

4. Compensation for managerial or administrative services, normally expressed in biweekly, monthly, or annual terms, is called _____. _____

5. Compensation for skilled or unskilled labor, normally expressed in terms of hours, weeks, or units produced, is called _____. _____

6. When compensation is based on time, _____ are helpful for keeping a record of the time worked by each employee. _____

7. An employee's total earnings is also called _____. _____

8. An employee's total earnings less all the deductions is called _____. _____

9. What are the three major categories of deductions from an employee's paycheck?.. _____

10. David Astin is married with two children, holds only one job, and has a spouse who is not employed. What number of withholding allowances is Astin entitled to claim, assuming that he does not anticipate large itemized deductions?....................................... _____

11. Upon employment, each employee is required to furnish the employer a Form _____ that details, among other things, the number of withholding allowances and marital status................................. _____

12. Name the four factors that determine the amount to be withheld from an employee's gross pay each pay period. _____

13. A form used to assemble the data required at the end of each payroll period is called a(n) _____... .. _____

14. A method of payment in which the employee's net pay is placed directly in the employee's bank account is called a(n) _____.... .. _____

15. A separate, detailed record of each employee's earnings is called a(n) _____ ... _____

16. Name two approaches in addition to a manual system used to accumulate and record payroll information. _____

EXERCISES AND PROBLEMS

Exercise 1 (LO 2) COMPUTING OVERTIME PAY RATE

Lu-yin Cheng receives a regular salary of $2,500 a month and is entitled to overtime pay at the rate of one and one-half times the regular hourly rate for any time worked in excess of 40 hours per week. Compute Cheng's overtime hourly rate.

Exercise 2 (LO 2) COMPUTING GROSS PAY

Roger Watkins earns a regular hourly rate of $12.50 and receives time and a half for any time worked over 8 hours per weekday. Roger earns double time for hours worked on Saturday or Sunday. During the past week, Roger worked 8 hours each day Monday through Wednesday, 5 hours on Thursday, 12 hours on Friday, and 6 hours on Saturday. Compute Watkins's gross pay.

Exercise 3 (LO 2) COMPUTING NET PAY

Bill Burry is married, has 3 children, and claims 5 withholding allowances for federal income tax purposes. Burry's gross pay for the week was $683.00. Using the federal income tax withholding table provided in Figure 8–4 of the text and the information provided below, compute Burry's net pay for the week.

(a) Social Security tax rate is 6.2% (Burry's prior earnings equaled $23,455.00).
(b) Medicare tax rate is 1.45%.
(c) State income tax is 2% of gross earnings.
(d) City income tax is 1% of gross earnings.
(e) Contribution to pension plan is $25.00.
(f) Health insurance deduction is $8.50.

Exercise 4 (LO 4) JOURNALIZING PAYROLL TRANSACTIONS

Using the information provided in Exercise 3, enter the payment of Bill Burry's wages in a general journal. Assume a pay period ending on July 31, 20—.

JOURNAL PAGE 1

	DATE		DESCRIPTION	POST. REF.	DEBIT	CREDIT	
1							1
2							2
3							3
4							4
5							5
6							6
7							7
8							8
9							9
10							10
11							11
12							12
13							13
14							14
15							15
16							16
17							17
18							18
19							19
20							20
21							21
22							22
23							23
24							24
25							25
26							26
27							27
28							28

Problem 1 (LO 2, 3, 4) PAYROLL REGISTER AND PAYROLL JOURNAL ENTRIES

Earl Wilson operates a business known as Wilson Enterprises. Listed below are the name, number of allowances claimed, marital status, total hours worked, and hourly rate of each employee. All hours worked in excess of 40 a week are paid for at the rate of time and a half.

The employer uses a weekly federal income tax withholding table. A portion of this weekly table is provided in Chapter 8 of your textbook. Social Security tax is withheld at the rate of 6.2%, Medicare tax is withheld at the rate of 1.45%, state income tax is withheld at the rate of 3.5%, and city earnings tax is withheld at the rate of 1%. O'Connor, Perez, Scalia, and Stephens each have $15.00 withheld this payday for group life insurance. Each employee, except Marshall, has $5.00 withheld for health insurance. All of the employees use payroll deduction to the credit union for varying amounts as listed below. Bertucci, Perez, and White each have $18.25 withheld this payday under a savings bond purchase plan.

Wilson Enterprises follows the practice of drawing a single check for the net amount of the payroll and depositing the check in a special payroll account at the bank. Individual paychecks are then drawn for the amount due each employee. The checks issued this payday were numbered consecutively beginning with No. 531.

<div align="center">

Wilson Enterprises

Payroll Information for the Week Ended January 15, 20—

</div>

Name	Allow-ances	Marital Status	Total Hours Worked	Regular Hourly Rate	Credit Union Deposit	Cumul. Earnings thru 1/8
Bertucci, Harry	3	M	45	$12.00	$114.00	$525.00
Brennan, Joyce	4	M	50	10.00	110.00	480.00
Marshall, Teddy	5	M	43	11.00	97.90	500.00
O'Connor, Sandra	2	S	48	11.00	114.40	625.00
Perez, Lucy	3	M	43	13.00	115.70	730.00
Rehnquist, Willie	5	M	40	17.00	136.00	850.00
Scalia, Tonya	2	S	38	9.00	68.40	425.00
Stephens, J.P.	6	M	47	11.00	111.10	635.00
White, Byran	1	S	60	10.00	140.00	615.00

Required:

1. Prepare a payroll register for Wilson Enterprises for the pay period ended January 15, 20—. Use the form provided on pages 104–105. (In the Taxable Earnings/Unemployment Compensation column, enter the same amounts as in the Social Security column.)

2. Assuming that the wages for the week ended January 15 were paid on January 17, enter the payment in the general journal provided on page 103.

Problem 1 (Continued)

GENERAL JOURNAL

PAGE 1

	DATE		DESCRIPTION	POST. REF.	DEBIT	CREDIT	
1							1
2							2
3							3
4							4
5							5
6							6
7							7
8							8
9							9
10							10
11							11
12							12
13							13
14							14
15							15
16							16

Problem 2 (LO 3) EMPLOYEE EARNINGS RECORD

The current employee earnings record for Joyce Brennan is provided on pages 104–105. Using the information provided in Problem 1, update Brennan's earnings record to reflect the January 15 payroll. Although this information should have been entered earlier, complete the required information at the bottom of the earnings record. The necessary information is provided below.

Name:	Joyce W. Brennan
Address:	422 Long Plain Rd.
	Leverett, MA 01054
Employee No.:	2
Gender:	Female
Department:	Sanitation
Occupation:	Janitor
S.S. No.:	336-56-7534
Marital Status:	Married
Allowances:	4
Pay Rate:	$10.00 per hour
Birth Date:	7/6/69
Date Employed:	6/22/--

Problem 1 (Continued)

PAYROLL REGISTER

	NAME	EMP. NO.	NO. ALLOW.	MARIT. STATUS	REGULAR		OVERTIME		TOTAL		CUMULATIVE TOTAL		UNEMPLOY. COMP.		SOCIAL SECURITY	
						EARNINGS								**TAXABLE EARNINGS**		
1																
2																
3																
4																
5																
6																
7																
8																
9																
10																
11																
12																
13																
14																
15																
16																

Problem 2 (Continued)

EMPLOYEES EARNINGS RECORD

	20 -- PERIOD ENDED	REGULAR		OVERTIME		TOTAL		CUMULATIVE TOTAL		UNEMPLOY. COMP.		SOCIAL SECURITY		FEDERAL INCOME TAX		SOCIAL SECURITY TAX	
			EARNINGS						**TAXABLE EARNINGS**				**DEDUCTIONS**				
1	1/1	200	00			200	00	200	00	200	00	200	00	------0	00	12	40
2	1/8	280	00			280	00	480	00	280	00	280	00	------0	00	17	36
3																	
4																	
5																	

GENDER		DEPARTMENT	OCCUPATION	SOCIAL SECURITY NO.	MARITAL STATUS	ALLOW- ANCES
M	F					

Problem 1 (Continued)

FOR PERIOD ENDED 20--

| FEDERAL INC. TAX | | SOC. SEC. TAX | | MEDICARE TAX | | STATE INC. TAX | | CITY EARN. TAX | | LIFE INS. | | HEALTH INS. | | CREDIT UNION | | OTHER | | TOTAL | | NET PAY | | CK. NO. | |
|---|
| 1 |
| 2 |
| 3 |
| 4 |
| 5 |
| 6 |
| 7 |
| 8 |
| 9 |
| 10 |
| 11 |
| 12 |
| 13 |
| 14 |
| 15 |
| 16 |

Problem 2 (Concluded)

FOR PERIOD ENDED 20--

								DEDUCTIONS											
MEDICARE TAX		STATE INCOME TAX		CITY EARNINGS TAX		LIFE INSUR		HEALTH INSUR.		CREDIT UNION		OTHER		TOTAL		NET PAY		CK. NO.	
2	90	7	00	2	00			5	00	40	00			69	30	130	70	321	1
4	06	9	80	2	80			5	00					95	02	184	98	422	2
																			3
																			4
																			5
																			6
																			7

PAY RATE	DATE OF BIRTH	DATE HIRED	NAME/ADDRESS	EMP. NO.

CHAPTER 9
PAYROLL ACCOUNTING:
EMPLOYER TAXES AND REPORTS

LEARNING OBJECTIVES

Chapter 8 discussed taxes levied on the employee and withheld by the employer. None of these taxes was an expense of the employer. In Chapter 9, we examine several taxes that represent an additional payroll expense imposed directly on the employer.

Objective 1. Describe and calculate employer payroll taxes.

Most employers are subject to a matching portion of the Social Security and Medicare taxes and to federal and state unemployment taxes. The employer's **Social Security and Medicare taxes** are levied on employers at the same rates and on the same bases as the employee Social Security and Medicare taxes. The **FUTA** tax is levied only on employers. The purpose of this tax is to raise funds to administer the federal/state unemployment compensation program. The **SUTA** tax is also levied only on employers. The purpose of this tax is to raise funds to pay unemployment benefits.

The Social Security, FUTA, and SUTA taxes are calculated from the accumulated amounts found in the Taxable Earnings columns in the payroll register. The medicare tax is calculated from the Total Earnings column.

Objective 2. Account for employer payroll taxes expense.

To journalize employer payroll taxes, debit the total of the employer Social Security, Medicare, FUTA, and SUTA taxes to a single account entitled Payroll Taxes Expense. The liabilities for the Social Security, Medicare, FUTA, and SUTA taxes payable normally are credited to separate accounts. The general format of this entry appears below:

Payroll Taxes Expense	xx	
Social Security Tax Payable		xx
Medicare Tax Payable		xx
FUTA Tax Payable		xx
SUTA Tax Payable		xx

Objective 3. Describe employer reporting and payment responsibilities.

Employer payroll reporting and payment responsibilities fall in five areas:

1. Federal income tax withholding and Social Security and Medicare taxes
2. FUTA taxes
3. SUTA taxes
4. Employee Wage and Tax Statement (W-2)
5. Summary of employee wages and taxes

The due date for federal income tax withholding and Social Security and Medicare taxes varies, depending on the amount of these taxes. Deposits are made using EFTPS or Form 8109. In addition, a Form 941 must be completed each quarter and filed with the IRS.

The federal unemployment taxes must be computed on a quarterly basis. In addition, Form 940 must be filed with the IRS at the end of the year.

Deposit rules and forms for state unemployment taxes vary among the states. Deposits usually are required on a quarterly basis.

Employers must furnish each employee with a Wage and Tax Statement (W-2) by January 31 of each year. Information needed to complete this form is contained in the employee earnings records. The employer also must file Form W-3 with the Social Security Administration by the last day of February. This form summarizes the employee earnings and tax information from Forms W-2.

Objective 4. Describe and account for workers' compensation insurance.

Workers' compensation insurance provides insurance for employees who suffer a job-related illness or injury. The cost of the insurance depends on the number of employees, the riskiness of the job, and the company's accident history. The employer usually pays the premium at the beginning of the year, based on the estimated annual payroll, and makes an adjustment at the end of the year when the actual annual payroll is known.

REVIEW QUESTIONS

Instructions: Analyze each of the following carefully before writing your answer in the column at the right.

Question	Answer

1. Name the four payroll taxes paid by the employer.

2. The textbook uses a Social Security tax rate of 6.2% applied to maximum employee earnings of _____...................................

3. The _____ is a key source of information for computing employer payroll taxes. ...

4. Individuals who own and run their own business are considered ____ .

5. The law requires persons earning self-employment income of $400 or more to pay a(n) _____..

6. The textbook uses a FUTA tax rate of 0.8% applied to maximum employee earnings of _____...

7. When journalizing the employer's payroll taxes, debit the total of the employer Social Security, Medicare, FUTA, and SUTA taxes to a single account entitled _____..

8. Name the three taxes that are associated with Form 941.

9. In addition to making quarterly deposits, employers are required to file an annual report of federal unemployment tax on Form _____. _____

10. By January 31 of each year, employers must furnish each employee with a(n) _____ ... _____

11. _____ provides insurance for employees who suffer a job-related illness or injury. .. _____

EXERCISES AND PROBLEMS

Exercise 1 (LO 1) EMPLOYER PAYROLL TAXES

The Sylvania Bookstore pays a SUTA tax of 5.4% and a FUTA tax of 0.8%. The total taxable wages for unemployment compensation on a certain payday amount to $16,800. Compute the unemployment taxes payable to the state and federal government.

Exercise 2 (LO 2) PAYROLL TAXES JOURNAL ENTRIES

The totals line from Wong Drug Store's payroll register for the week ended December 31, 20— is shown on pages 110 and 111.

Payroll taxes are imposed as follows:

Social Security tax: 6.2%
Medicare tax: 1.45%
FUTA tax: 0.8%
SUTA tax: 5.4%

Required:

1. Prepare the journal entry for payment of this payroll on December 31, 20—.

2. Prepare the journal entry for the employer's payroll taxes for the period ended December 31, 20—.

Exercise 2 (Continued)

PAYROLL REGISTER

	NAME	EMPL. NO.	NO. ALLOW.	MARIT. STATUS	EARNINGS				TAXABLE EARNINGS	
					REGULAR	OVERTIME	TOTAL	CUMULATIVE TOTAL	UNEMPLOY. COMP.	SOCIAL SECURITY
1	Totals				4,200 00	500 00	4,700 00	203,700 00	300 00	3,600 00
2										
3										
4										
5										
6										
7										
8										
9										
10										

GENERAL JOURNAL PAGE 1

	DATE	DESCRIPTION	POST. REF.	DEBIT	CREDIT	
1						1
2						2
3						3
4						4
5						5
6						6
7						7
8						8
9						9
10						10
11						11
12						12
13						13
14						14
15						15
16						16

FOR PERIOD ENDED 20--

FEDERAL INC. TAX		SOC. SEC. TAX		MEDICARE TAX		HEALTH INS.		CREDIT UNION		OTHER			TOTAL		NET PAY		CK. NO.	
420	00	223	20	68	15	80	00	200	00				991	35	3,708	65		1
																		2
																		3
																		4
																		5
																		6
																		7
																		8
																		9
																		10

Exercise 3 (LO1/2) TOTAL COST OF AN EMPLOYEE

Compute the total annual cost to an employer of employing a person whose gross salary is $45,000. (Assume a 5.4% state unemployment tax rate and a FUTA tax rate of 0.8%, both on the first $7,000 of earnings, an employer's Social Security tax rate of 6.2% on the first $76,200 of earnings and a Medicare tax rate of 1.45% on gross earnings.)

Exercise 4 (LO 4) WORKERS' COMPENSATION INSURANCE AND ADJUSTMENT

Curtis Company paid a premium of $360 for workers' compensation insurance based on the estimated payroll as of the beginning of the year. Based on actual payroll as of the end of the year, the actual premium is $397. Prepare the adjusting entry to reflect the underpayment of the insurance premium.

GENERAL JOURNAL PAGE 1

	DATE	DESCRIPTION	POST. REF.	DEBIT	CREDIT	
1						1
2						2
3						3
4						4
5						5
6						6
7						7
8						8
9						9
10						10
11						11
12						12
13						13

Problem 1 (LO 1/2) CALCULATING PAYROLL TAXES EXPENSE AND PREPARING JOURNAL ENTRY

A partial payroll register for the pay period ended August 31, 20— is provided below for the Astroscope Company.

Required:

1. Compute the total earnings subject to federal and state unemployment taxes and the Social Security tax by completing the Taxable Earnings columns of the payroll register.

2. Assume the company is in a state with an unemployment tax rate of 5.4% and a FUTA tax rate of 0.8%, both on the first $7,000 of earnings. The Social Security tax rate is 6.2% on the first $76,200 of earnings, and Medicare tax rate is 1.45% on gross earnings. Compute the state and federal unemployment taxes and the Social Security and Medicare taxes on the lines provided on page 113.

3. Prepare the entry for the employer's payroll taxes in the general journal provided on the page 114.

Problem 1 (Continued)

PAYROLL REGISTER

| | NAME | NO. ALLOW. | MARIT. STATUS | EARNINGS | | | | | | | | TAXABLE EARNINGS | | | |
				REGULAR		OVERTIME		TOTAL		CUMULATIVE TOTAL		UNEMPLOY. COMP.		SOCIAL SECURITY	
1	Coolie, Betty							350	00	7,150	00				
2	Covar, Mike							200	00	6,800	00				
3	Hagen, Frank							375	00	6,200	00				
4	Gutierrez, Bob							1,540	00	47,300	00				
5	Moten, Alice							1,500	00	50,500	00				
6	Rice, Darlene							2,300	00	78,100	00				
7															

Problem 1 (Concluded)

GENERAL JOURNAL PAGE 1

	DATE		DESCRIPTION	POST. REF.	DEBIT	CREDIT	
1							1
2							2
3							3
4							4
5							5
6							6
7							7
8							8
9							9
10							10
11							11
12							12
13							13
14							14
15							15
16							16
17							17

Problem 2 (LO 2) JOURNALIZING AND POSTING PAYROLL ENTRIES

The Rock Creek Company has five employees. All are paid on a monthly basis. The fiscal year of the business is July 1 to June 30. Payroll taxes are imposed as follows:

Social Security tax to be withheld from employees' wages and imposed on the employer, 6.2% each on the first $76,200 of earnings.

Medicare tax to be withheld from employees' wages and imposed on the employer, 1.45% each on gross earnings.

SUTA tax imposed on the employer, 5.4% on the first $7,000 of earnings.

FUTA tax imposed on the employer, 0.8% on the first $7,000 of earnings.

Problem 2 (Continued)

The accounts kept by the Rock Creek Company include the following:

Account Number	Title	Balance on July 1
101	Cash	$45,800.00
211	Employee Income Tax Payable	1,125.00
212	Social Security Tax Payable	1,580.00
213	Medicare Tax Payable	370.00
218	Savings Bond Deductions Payable	400.00
221	FUTA Tax Payable	175.00
222	SUTA Tax Payable	890.00
511	Wages and Salaries Expense	-0-
530	Payroll Taxes Expense	-0-

Following is a narrative of selected transactions relating to payrolls and payroll taxes that occurred during the months of July and August.

July	15	Paid $3,075.00 covering the following June taxes:		
		Employee income tax withheld		$1,125.00
		Social Security tax		1,580.00
		Medicare tax		370.00
		Total		$3,075.00

	31	July payroll:		
		Total wages and salaries expense		$13,000.00
		Less amounts withheld:		
		Employee income tax	$ 1,230.00	
		Social Security tax	806.00	
		Medicare tax	188.50	
		Savings bonds deductions payable	400.00	2,624.50
		Net amount paid		$10,375.50

	31	Purchased savings bonds for employees, $800.00		
	31	Data for completing employer's payroll taxes expense for July:		
		Social Security taxable wages	$13,000.00	
		Unemployment taxable wages	4,000.00	
Aug.	15	Paid $3,219.00 covering the following July taxes:		
		Employee income tax payable	$ 1,230.00	
		Social Security tax	1,612.00	
		Medicare tax	377.00	
	15	Paid SUTA tax for the quarter, $1,106.00		
	15	Paid FUTA tax, $207.00		

Problem 2 (Continued)

Required:

1. Using a general journal, journalize the preceding transactions.
2. Open T accounts for the payroll expense and liabilities. Enter the beginning balances and post the transactions recorded in the journal.

Cash	101

Employ. Inc. Tax Pay.	211

Social Security Tax Payable	212

Medicare Tax Payable	213

Savings Bond Deductions Payable	218

FUTA Tax Payable	221

Problem 2 (Continued)

SUTA Tax Payable 222 Wages and Salaries Expense 511

Payroll Taxes Expense 530

Problem 2 (Concluded)

GENERAL JOURNAL PAGE

	DATE		DESCRIPTION	POST. REF.	DEBIT	CREDIT	
1							1
2							2
3							3
4							4
5							5
6							6
7							7
8							8
9							9
10							10
11							11
12							12
13							13
14							14
15							15
16							16
17							17
18							18
19							19
20							20
21							21
22							22
23							23
24							24
25							25
26							26
27							27
28							28
29							29
30							30
31							31
32							32
32							33

Problem 3 (LO 4) WORKERS' COMPENSATION INSURANCE AND ADJUSTMENT

Jackson Manufacturing estimated its total payroll for the coming year to be $630,000. The workers' compensation insurance premium rate is 0.35%.

Required:

1. Calculate the estimated workers' compensation insurance premium and prepare the journal entry for the payment as of January 2, 20—.

2. Assume Jackson Manufacturing's actual payroll for the year is $658,000. Calculate the total insurance premium owed. Prepare a journal entry as of December 31, 20—, to record the adjustment for the underpayment. The actual payment of the additional insurance premium will take place in January of the next year.

3. Assume, instead, that Jackson Manufacturing's actual payroll for the year is $607,000. Prepare a journal entry as of December 31, 20—, for the total amount that should be refunded. The refund will not be received until the next year.

GENERAL JOURNAL PAGE 1

	DATE	DESCRIPTION	POST. REF.	DEBIT	CREDIT	
1						1
2						2
3						3
4						4
5						5
6						6
7						7
8						8
9						9
10						10
11						11
12						12
13						13
14						14
15						15
16						16
17						17

CHAPTER 10
ACCOUNTING FOR A PROFESSIONAL SERVICE BUSINESS: THE COMBINATION JOURNAL

LEARNING OBJECTIVES

The cash basis and modified cash basis are explained in Chapter 10 and then applied in the use of the combination journal. The combination journal is used for journalizing all transactions for a professional service business. Posting from a combination journal to the general ledger also is illustrated. Previously introduced, the work sheet and financial statements are also prepared following the transactions.

Objective 1. Explain the cash, modified cash, and accrual basis of accounting.

The **accrual basis** of accounting recognizes revenues when earned, regardless of when cash is received. Likewise, expenses are recognized when incurred, regardless of when they are actually paid. The **cash basis** is used by some small businesses and by individuals for income tax purposes. With the cash basis, no revenue or expenses are recognized until cash is actually received or paid.

The **modified cash basis** is a combination of the accrual and cash methods. Revenues and most expenses are recorded only when cash is received or paid (like the cash basis). However, when cash is paid for assets with useful lives greater than one accounting period, exceptions are made. Cash payments like these are recorded as assets, and adjustments are made each period as under the accrual basis. Figure 10-2 in the text compares these methods in different types of transactions.

Objective 2. Describe special records for a professional service business using the modified cash basis.

The modified cash basis is often used by small professional service businesses such as accounting, law, dentistry, medicine, and engineering. Since, under the modified cash basis, no adjusting entries are made for accrued wages expense and revenues from services performed on account are not recorded until cash is received, other records must be maintained. Two records commonly used are an appointment record and a client or patient ledger record.

Objective 3. Use the combination journal to record transactions of a professional service business.

The combination journal saves time, space, and energy in recording transactions (in comparison to the general journal). It also reduces the possibility of error since totals, rather than numerous individual entries, are posted. This is done by providing special columns for accounts frequently used. For example, the debits and credits to the cash account are posted only once—at the end of the month. Infrequently used accounts are entered in the General Debit column or the General Credit column. The Description column of a combination journal is used to enter account titles for the General Debit and General Credit columns, to identify specific creditors, to identify adjusting and closing entries, and to identify amounts forwarded from the previous page.

At the end of the accounting period, the sum of the debit columns should be compared with the sum of the credit columns to verify that they are equal. This is called proving the combination journal.

Objective 4. Post from the combination journal to the general ledger.

Accounts that have been debited or credited in the general columns are posted individually from the combination journal. "CJ" and the page number are entered into the Posting Reference column of the general

ledger account. Because individual items are posted, the totals of these columns are not posted, and check marks in parentheses are placed under the column totals.

Special columns are totaled and posted at the end of the accounting period. The account number is written in parentheses under the special column to show that the total has been posted.

The **cash balance** can be computed at any time during the month. The beginning balance (of the cash account) is added to the Cash debits (to date); the Cash credits (to date) are subtracted.

Objective 5. Prepare a work sheet, financial statements, and adjusting and closing entries for a professional service business.

When the combination journal has been posted to the general ledger, the end-of-period work sheet and financial statements are prepared in the same way as described in Chapters 5 and 6. By using the Description and General Debit and Credit columns, adjusting and closing entries are made in the combination journal in the same manner demonstrated for the general journal in Chapter 6.

REVIEW QUESTIONS

Instructions: Analyze each of the following items carefully before writing your answer in the column at the right.

Question	Answer
1. In the _____ basis of accounting, revenues are recorded when earned and expenses are recorded when incurred, regardless of when cash is received or paid. ...	_____
2. In the _____ basis of accounting, revenues are recorded only when cash is received and expenses are recorded only when cash is paid. ..	_____
3. The _____ basis of accounting uses the cash basis for some revenues and most expenses. ...	_____
4. Many small professional _____ businesses use the modified cash basis of accounting. ...	_____
5. Time and space are saved when a journal contains _____ columns for cash debits and cash credits, rather than posting each transaction separately. ..	_____
6. When accounts are used infrequently, the _____ column and the _____ column are used for individual postings.	_____
7. A journal with special columns and general columns is called a(n) _____ journal. ..	_____

8. The _____ column is used to enter account titles, specific creditors and customers; and to identify adjusting and closing entries or amounts forwarded from the previous page. .. _____

9. At the end of the month, all columns of the combination journal are _____, and the sums of the Debit columns are compared with the sums of the Credit columns. .. _____

10. Totaling and ruling the columns and comparing totals is the process of _____ the combination journal. .. _____

11. When posting from the combination journal, the letters " _____ " are used. .. _____

12. The cash balance at any time during the month is found by adding _____ to the beginning balance and subtracting _____ to date. _____

EXERCISES AND PROBLEMS

Exercise 1 (LO 1) CASH BASIS OF ACCOUNTING

In the space provided, indicate which account is debited and which account is credited, using the **cash basis** of accounting. If no entry is made, write "NO ENTRY."

1. Paid rent, $500.

2. Purchased typewriter (office equipment) for $300.

3. Revenue for week: $300 cash, $200 on account.

4. Purchased FAX machine (office equipment) for $400, on account.

5. Made payment on FAX machine, $100.

Exercise 2 (LO 1) MODIFIED CASH BASIS OF ACCOUNTING

In the space provided, indicate which account is debited and which account is credited, using the **modified cash basis** of accounting. If no entry is made, write "NO ENTRY."

1. Paid electricity bill, $50.

2. Purchased office equipment for $500, on account.

3. Revenue for week: $500 cash, $200 on account.

4. Wages earned but not paid, $500.

5. Made payment on office equipment previously purchased, $25.

Exercise 3 (LO 1) ACCRUAL BASIS OF ACCOUNTING

In the space provided, indicate which account is debited and which account is credited, using the **accrual basis** of accounting. If no entry is made, write "NO ENTRY."

1. Purchased supplies (prepaid asset), $500, on account.

2. Revenue for week: $400 cash, $250 on account.

3. Wages earned but not paid, $250.

Exercise 3 (Concluded)

4. Made payment on account, $50, for supplies previously purchased.

5. Depreciation on long-term assets, $300.

Exercise 4 (LO 3) SPECIAL COLUMNS FOR A COMBINATION JOURNAL

Ray Elkton is opening a delivery service. He owns a used van and will use it for deliveries. He has a part-time worker who is paid once a week. He receives delivery fees every three or four days and runs ads in the newspaper daily. Recommend to him which accounts should have **special columns** in a combination journal and give him three reasons why he should use a combination journal instead of a general journal.

Special Columns: _____

Reasons:

1. _____

2. _____

3. _____

Problem 1 (LO 1) CASH, MODIFIED CASH, AND ACCRUAL BASES

Mark Mosley has his own consulting business. Listed below are selected transactions from the month of April:

April 1 Paid office rent, $500.
 2 Purchased office supplies, $250.
 3 Purchased office equipment on account, $1,000.
 4 Earned consulting fees: $400 cash, $150 on account.
 5 Paid telephone bill, $48.
 6 Purchased one-year insurance policy, $200.
 7 Paid $100 on account (for office equipment previously purchased).
 8 Received $150 on account from a customer (previously owed).
 9 Depreciation on office equipment for month, $50.

Required:

Record the transactions in the space provided, using:

1. the cash basis

2. the modified cash basis

3. the accrual basis

Problem 1 (Continued)

1. Cash Basis

GENERAL JOURNAL PAGE _____

	DATE	DESCRIPTION	POST. REF.	DEBIT	CREDIT	
1						1
2						2
3						3
4						4
5						5
6						6
7						7
8						8
9						9
10						10
11						11
12						12
13						13
14						14
15						15
16						16
17						17
18						18
19						19
20						20
21						21
22						22
23						23
24						24
25						25
26						26
27						27
28						28
29						29
30						30

Problem 1 (Continued)

2. Modified Cash Basis

GENERAL JOURNAL PAGE

	DATE	DESCRIPTION	POST. REF.	DEBIT	CREDIT	
1						1
2						2
3						3
4						4
5						5
6						6
7						7
8						8
9						9
10						10
11						11
12						12
13						13
14						14
15						15
16						16
17						17
18						18
19						19
20						20
21						21
22						22
23						23
24						24
25						25
26						26
27						27
28						28
29						29
30						30

Problem 1 (Concluded)

3. Accrual Basis

GENERAL JOURNAL

PAGE _____

	DATE	DESCRIPTION	POST. REF.	DEBIT	CREDIT	
1						1
2						2
3						3
4						4
5						5
6						6
7						7
8						8
9						9
10						10
11						11
12						12
13						13
14						14
15						15
16						16
17						17
18						18
19						19
20						20
21						21
22						22
23						23
24						24
25						25
26						26
27						27
28						28
29						29
30						30

Problem 2 (LO 3) JOURNAL ENTRIES USING A COMBINATION JOURNAL

Marilyn Davis is the owner of Davis Interior Designing that offers advice to clients wishing to decorate their homes. Listed below are representative transactions for the month of February:

Feb. 1 Issued a check for $500 to Pedro Rodriguez for the February office rent.
 3 Received $300 for services rendered to Linda Johnson.
 5 Issued a check for $800 to Maxwell's Office Supply to purchase office equipment.
 10 Invested $5,000 additional cash in the business.
 28 Issued a check for $400 to Homer Utilities in payment of electric and water bill.
 28 Issued a check for $200 to Buck's Furniture for payment on office furniture previously purchased.

Required:

1. Davis uses the **modified cash basis** of accounting. Enter the above transactions in the combination journal shown on pages 130–131.

2. Total and prove the combination journal.

Problem 2 (Continued)

COMBINATION

	DATE		CASH		DESCRIPTION	POST. REF.	
			DEBIT	CREDIT			
1							1
2							2
3							3
4							4
5							5
6							6
7							7
8							8
9							9
10							10
11							11
12							12
13							13
14							14

Proving the Combination Journal:

Problem 2 (Concluded)

JOURNAL

PAGE

	GENERAL		CLIENT FEES CREDIT	RENT EXPENSE DEBIT	UTILITIES EXPENSE DEBIT	
1						1
2						2
3						3
4						4
5						5
6						6
7						7
8						8
9						9
10						10
11						11
12						12
13						13
14						14

Problem 3 (LO3/4/5) JOURNALIZING AND POSTING TRANSACTIONS AND PREPARING A TRIAL BALANCE

Jolene Knight operates a cartographer's map service, Knight Maps. During the month of May, she entered the following transactions:

May	1	Issued a check for $400 to purchase new surveying equipment.
	3	Received a check for $900 from Diane Branam for surveying her property. Earned $1,500 on account from Troy Laakman.
	4	Issued a check for $600 to CFC Rental to pay May office rent.
	6	Purchased office supplies from Bynum Office Supply on account, $250.
	10	Received a check for $3,500 from B. Sims, a real estate developer, for surveying a new subdivision.
	12	Issued a check for $300 to Oscar Miller, a part-time secretary.
	15	Issued a check for $85 to Winona's Service Station for gas and oil for the business truck.
	16	Issued a check for $200 to Bynum Office Supply in payment on account.
	18	Issued a check for $150 to George Wilson, a part-time employee.
	20	Issued a check for $200 to Winona's Service Station for work done on a company truck.
	22	Issued a check for $100 to the American Cancer Society.
	25	Received a check for $1,500 from Troy Laakman for surveying work previously performed.
	30	Issued a check for $500 as a personal withdrawal from the business.
	31	Issued a check for $300 to Oscar Miller, a part-time secretary.

Required:

1. Using the **modified cash basis** of accounting, enter the above transactions in the combination journal provided on pages 132–133.
2. Prove the combination journal.
3. Post the entries from the combination journal to the ledger accounts provided on pages 133–136.
4. Prepare a trial balance for Knight Maps as of May 31, 20—, to confirm accuracy of the debits and credits.

Problem 3 (Continued)

COMBINATION

	DATE		CASH		DESCRIPTION	POST. REF.	
			DEBIT	CREDIT			
1							1
2							2
3							3
4							4
5							5
6							6
7							7
8							8
9							9
10							10
11							11
12							12
13							13
14							14
15							15
16							16
17							17
18							18
19							19
20							20

Proving the Combination Journal:

Problem 3 (Continued)

JOURNAL

PAGE

		GENERAL		CLIENT FEES	WAGES	TRUCK	
		DEBIT	CREDIT	CREDIT	EXPENSE DEBIT	EXPENSE DEBIT	
1							1
2							2
3							3
4							4
5							5
6							6
7							7
8							8
9							9
10							10
11							11
12							12
13							13
14							14
15							15
16							16
17							17
18							18
19							19
20							20

GENERAL LEDGER

ACCOUNT Cash ACCOUNT NO. 101

DATE		ITEM	POST. REF.	DEBIT	CREDIT	BALANCE		
						DEBIT	•	CREDIT
20— May	1	Balance				1 2 0 0		

Problem 3 (Continued)

ACCOUNT Office Supplies ACCOUNT NO. 142

DATE		ITEM	POST. REF.	DEBIT				CREDIT				BALANCE							
												DEBIT				•	CREDIT		
20— May	1	Balance										1	0	0	00				

ACCOUNT Surveying Equipment ACCOUNT NO. 181

DATE		ITEM	POST. REF.	DEBIT				CREDIT				BALANCE							
												DEBIT				•	CREDIT		
20— May	1	Balance										13	0	0	0	00			

ACCOUNT Accumulated Depreciation—Surveying Equipment ACCOUNT NO. 181.1

DATE		ITEM	POST. REF.	DEBIT				CREDIT				BALANCE							
												DEBIT				•	CREDIT		

ACCOUNT Truck ACCOUNT NO. 185

DATE		ITEM	POST. REF.	DEBIT				CREDIT				BALANCE							
												DEBIT				•	CREDIT		
20— May	1	Balance										12	0	0	0	00			

ACCOUNT Accumulated Depreciation—Truck ACCOUNT NO. 185.1

DATE		ITEM	POST. REF.	DEBIT				CREDIT				BALANCE							
												DEBIT				•	CREDIT		

ACCOUNT Notes Payable ACCOUNT NO. 201

DATE		ITEM	POST. REF.	DEBIT				CREDIT				BALANCE										
												DEBIT				•	CREDIT					
20— May	1	Balance																10	0	0	0	00

Problem 3 (Continued)

ACCOUNT Accounts Payable ACCOUNT NO. 202

DATE		ITEM	POST. REF.	DEBIT	CREDIT	BALANCE			
							DEBIT	•	CREDIT
20— May	1	Balance						2 0 0 00	

ACCOUNT Jolene Knight, Capital ACCOUNT NO. 311

DATE		ITEM	POST. REF.	DEBIT	CREDIT	BALANCE			
							DEBIT	•	CREDIT
20— May	1	Balance						12 7 0 0 00	

ACCOUNT Jolene Knight, Drawing ACCOUNT NO. 312

DATE		ITEM	POST. REF.	DEBIT	CREDIT	BALANCE			
							DEBIT	•	CREDIT
20— May	1	Balance					1 0 0 0 00		

ACCOUNT Client Fees ACCOUNT NO. 401

DATE		ITEM	POST. REF.	DEBIT	CREDIT	BALANCE			
							DEBIT	•	CREDIT
20— May	1	Balance						12 0 0 0 00	

ACCOUNT Wages Expense ACCOUNT NO. 511

DATE		ITEM	POST. REF.	DEBIT	CREDIT	BALANCE			
							DEBIT	•	CREDIT
20— May	3	Balance					4 0 0 0 00		

Problem 3 (Continued)

ACCOUNT Rent Expense ACCOUNT NO. 521

DATE		ITEM	POST. REF.	DEBIT	CREDIT	BALANCE DEBIT	•	CREDIT
20— May	3	Balance				2 4 0 0 00		

ACCOUNT Truck Expense ACCOUNT NO. 526

DATE		ITEM	POST. REF.	DEBIT	CREDIT	BALANCE DEBIT	•	CREDIT
20— May	1	Balance				8 0 0 00		

ACCOUNT Charitable Contributions Expense ACCOUNT NO. 534

DATE		ITEM	POST. REF.	DEBIT	CREDIT	BALANCE DEBIT	•	CREDIT
20— May	1	Balance				4 0 0 00		

ACCOUNT Depreciation Expense—Surveying Equipment ACCOUNT NO. 541

DATE		ITEM	POST. REF.	DEBIT	CREDIT	BALANCE DEBIT	•	CREDIT

ACCOUNT Depreciation Expense—Truck ACCOUNT NO. 542

DATE		ITEM	POST. REF.	DEBIT	CREDIT	BALANCE DEBIT	•	CREDIT

Problem 3 (Concluded)

ACCOUNT	ACCT. NO.	DEBIT BALANCE	CREDIT BALANCE

Problem 4 (LO 5) PREPARING A WORK SHEET, FINANCIAL STATEMENTS, ADJUSTING AND CLOSING ENTRIES

The work sheet for Charlotte Cruz, a financial planner, is shown on pages 138–139. The Trial Balance columns have been completed. There were no additional investments by the owner.
Adjustments are as follows:

(a) Prepaid insurance expired, $200.
(b) Unused office supplies on hand, $228.
(c) Depreciation expense—office equipment, $125.

Required:

1. Finish the work sheet.

2. Prepare the income statement, statement of owner's equity, and balance sheet.

3. Record the adjusting entries and closing entries in the combination journal on pages 142–143.

Problem 4 (Continued)

CRUZ FINANCIAL

WORK

FOR MONTH ENDED

	DESCRIPTION	TRIAL BALANCE		ADJUSTMENTS	
		DEBIT	CREDIT	DEBIT	CREDIT
1	Cash	3 0 8 2 00			
2	Office Supplies	6 2 8 00			
3	Prepaid Insurance	3 5 0 00			
4	Office Equipment	1 8 0 0 00			
5	Accum. Depr.—Office Equip.		2 5 0 00		
6	Accounts Payable		9 0 0 00		
7	Charlotte Cruz, Capital		3 0 0 0 00		
8	Charlotte Cruz, Drawing	1 0 0 00			
9	Planning Fees		3 0 2 6 00		
10	Wages Expense	8 0 0 00			
11	Rent Expense	3 0 0 00			
12	Office Supplies Expense				
13	Telephone Expense	5 2 00			
14	Electricity Expense	3 8 00			
15	Insurance Expense				
16	Depreciation Exp.—Office Equip.				
17	Miscellaneous Expense	2 6 00			
18					
19	Net Income	1 7 6 00	1 7 6 00		
20					

Problem 4 (Continued)

PLANNING

SHEET

DECEMBER 31, 20--

	ADJUSTED TRIAL BALANCE		INCOME STATEMENT		BALANCE SHEET		
	DEBIT	CREDIT	DEBIT	CREDIT	DEBIT	CREDIT	
1							1
2							2
3							3
4							4
5							5
6							6
7							7
8							8
9							9
10							10
11							11
12							12
13							13
14							14
15							15
16							16
17							17
18							18
19							19
20							20

Problem 4 (Continued)

Problem 4 (Continued)

Problem 4 (Continued)

COMBINATION

	DATE		CASH				DESCRIPTION	POST. REF.	
			DEBIT		CREDIT				
1									1
2									2
3									3
4									4
5									5
6									6
7									7
8									8
9									9
10									10
11									11
12									12
13									13
14									14
15									15
16									16
17									17
18									18
19									19
20									20
21									21
22									22
23									23
24									24
25									25
26									26
27									27
28									28

Problem 4 (Concluded)

JOURNAL

PAGE _____

	GENERAL		PLANNING FEES CREDIT	WAGES EXPENSE DEBIT	MISC. EXPENSE DEBIT	
	DEBIT	CREDIT				
1						1
2						2
3						3
4						4
5						5
6						6
7						7
8						8
9						9
10						10
11						11
12						12
13						13
14						14
15						15
16						16
17						17
18						18
19						19
20						20
21						21
22						22
23						23
24						24
25						25
26						26
27						27
28						28

CHAPTER 11
ACCOUNTING FOR SALES AND CASH RECEIPTS

LEARNING OBJECTIVES

Chapter 11 introduces the merchandising business: sales transactions and the related new accounts, a new ledger, and a new schedule. Merchandise sales transactions are shown in general journal format.

Objective 1. Describe merchandise sales transactions.

Retail businesses make sales on account, as well as cash sales and credit card sales. Sales tickets and cash register receipts are produced for customers and accounting purposes.

Wholesale businesses also make sales on account, but the process is more complicated and includes purchase orders and sales invoices. Credit approval often is required for business customers.

Both types of businesses have sales returns (merchandise returned for a refund) and allowances (reductions in price because of defects, damage, or other problems with the merchandise).

Objective 2. Describe and use merchandise sales accounts.

Accounting for sales transactions requires four general ledger accounts: Sales, Sales Tax Payable, Sales Returns and Allowances, and Sales Discounts. Sales is a revenue account; Sales Tax Payable is a liability account; and Sales Returns and Allowances and Sales Discounts are contra-revenue accounts.

When a sale is made and sales tax is added to the sale, the liability account (Sales Tax Payable) is credited for the amount of tax that will be remitted to the government. Therefore, when merchandise is returned for a credit (Sales Returns and Allowances), the customer is also refunded the amount of the sales tax. (Sales Tax Payable is debited.)

Cash discounts are given to business customers who pay within a discount period such as ten days. This encourages prompt payment of bills. When a discount is taken, the sales discount account is debited for the amount of the discount.

Net sales is determined by deducting the contra-revenue accounts (Sales Returns and Allowances and Sales Discounts) from gross sales.

Objective 3. Describe and use the accounts receivable ledger.

The accounts receivable account in the general ledger provides a record of the total amount owed to a business by its customers. To help run the business, a record also is needed of the amount owed by individual customers. The accounts receivable subsidiary ledger provides this information.

When an accounts receivable subsidiary ledger is used, the accounts receivable account in the general ledger is a "controlling account." The accounts receivable ledger is "subsidiary" to this account. Transactions are posted daily from the general journal to both the general ledger and the accounts receivable ledger.

Objective 4. Prepare a schedule of accounts receivable.

Once all daily postings are completed to individual accounts, the balance in the accounts receivable general ledger account must agree with the sum of the customer balances in the accounts receivable ledger. The schedule of accounts receivable is prepared at the end of the month to verify that the total of customer balances equals the balance in the controlling account, Accounts Receivable.

REVIEW QUESTIONS

Instructions: Analyze each of the following statements carefully before writing your answer in the column at the right.

Question	Answer

Question **Answer**

1. A(n) _____ business purchases merchandise such as clothing, furniture, or computers to sell to its customers. _____

2. A(n) _____ is a transfer of merchandise from one individual or business to another in exchange for cash or a promise to pay cash. _____

3. A(n) _____ is a document created as evidence of a sale for a retail business. .. _____

4. A written order to buy merchandise, called a(n) _____ , is received from a customer. ... _____

5. A(n) _____ is prepared when merchandise ordered is shipped to a customer. .. _____

6. Merchandise returned by a customer for a refund is called a(n) _____ _____

7. Reductions in price of merchandise granted because of defect or damage are called _____ _____

8. When credit is given for merchandise returned or for an allowance, a(n) _____ is issued. .. _____

9. The sales account is a _____ account. _____

10. When a sale on account is made, _____ is debited. _____

11. When a sale is made with sales tax, a liability account, called _____ , is credited for the amount of the sales tax. _____

12. Sales Returns and Allowances is a contra- _____ account. _____

13. A(n) _____ is granted for prompt payment by customers who buy merchandise on account. ... _____

14. Sales Discounts is a contra- _____ account. _____

15. A record of each customer's account balance is contained in the _____ _____ ledger. .. _____

16. To indicate that the accounts receivable ledger has been posted, a slash and a _____ _____ are entered in the posting reference column of the general journal. .. _____

17. Sales returns and allowances are posted to both the general ledger and the _____ _____ ledger. .. _____

18. When a collection is received on account, _____ is credited. _____

19. The _____ is a listing of the balances of all customers who owe money at the end of the month. ... _____

20. The schedule of accounts receivable is used to verify that the sum of the accounts receivable ledger balances equals the _____ balance. _____

EXERCISES AND PROBLEMS

Exercise 1 (LO 1) SALES DOCUMENTS

The following is a copy of a purchase order received from Custom Builders, Inc. by Rogers Building Supplies, Inc. Assuming you are employed by Rogers Building Supplies, Inc., prepare a sales invoice (No. 491) dated July 18 billing Custom Builders, Inc. for the items specified in their order No. A208. The unit prices are as follows: #6 insulated steel doors, $290.00 each and #28 pine, six-panel doors, $125 each. Indicate terms of 30 days.

		Purchase Order		Order No. **A208**
Date	July 15, 20--	**CUSTOM BUILDERS, INC.**		
Terms	30 days	**2001 HILLSIDE DR.** **BLOOMINGTON, IN 47401-2287**		

To

Rogers Building Supplies, Inc.
So. Adams
Bloomington, IN 47401-3663

Quantity	Description	Price
10	#6 Insulated steel doors	290.00
15	#28 Pine, six-panel doors	125.00

Deliver no goods without a written order on this form. *By* _E. Taylor_

Exercise 1 (Continued)

Invoice Invoice No. Date Your Order No. Terms	ROGERS BUILDING SUPPLIES, INC. So. Adams, Bloomington, IN 47401-3663 Sold to		
Quantity	Description	Unit Price	Amount

Exercise 2 (LO 1) SALES DOCUMENTS

On July 28, Custom Builders, Inc. returned one #6 insulated steel door to Rogers Building Supplies, Inc. for credit. Using the blank form on page 148, prepare a credit memorandum (No. 17) covering the cost of the door sold on July 18.

Exercise 2 (Concluded)

Quantity	Description	Unit Price	Amount

Credit Memorandum

No.

ROGERS BUILDING SUPPLIES, INC.
So. Adams,
Bloomington, IN 47401-3663

Date To

We credit your account as follows:

Exercise 3 (LO 2/3) SALES AND SALES RETURNS AND ALLOWANCES TRANSACTIONS

Record the following transactions in a general journal, assuming a 5% sales tax.

(a) Sold $230.00 of merchandise, plus sales tax, on account. (R.B. Jones, Sale No. 28)
(b) R.B. Jones returns $30 worth of merchandise for a credit.
(c) R.B. Jones pays the balance of the account in cash.
(d) Sold $300.00 of merchandise, plus sales tax, for cash.
(e) Merchandise returned for cash refund, $15.

Exercise 3 (Concluded)

GENERAL JOURNAL

PAGE _____

	DATE	DESCRIPTION	POST. REF.	DEBIT	CREDIT	
1						1
2						2
3						3
4						4
5						5
6						6
7						7
8						8
9						9
10						10
11						11
12						12
13						13
14						14
15						15
16						16
17						17
18						18
19						19
20						20
21						21
22						22
23						23
24						24
25						25
26						26
27						27
28						28
29						29
30						30
31						31

Exercise 4 (LO3) SALES TRANSACTIONS

Diana Brewer operates the Floor and Window Treatment Center and completed the following transactions related to sales of merchandise on account during the month of February. Sales tax of 5% was included in the amount of each sale.

Feb. 2 Sold wallpaper supplies to Dresson Homes, $98.95; terms, n/30. Sale No. 255.
 12 Sold paint to Ray Acuff, $105.00; terms, n/30. Sale No 256.
 23 Sold miniblinds to Clydette Rupert, $114.83; terms, n/30. Sale No. 257.
 24 Sold decorator items to Marty Staple, $35.55; terms, n/30. Sale No. 258.
 25 Sold paint to Angel Burtin, $25.57; terms, n/30. Sale No. 259.

Required:

Enter the above transactions in a general journal.

GENERAL JOURNAL PAGE

	DATE	DESCRIPTION	POST. REF.	DEBIT	CREDIT	
1						1
2						2
3						3
4						4
5						5
6						6
7						7
8						8
9						9
10						10
11						11
12						12
13						13
14						14
15						15
16						16
17						17
18						18
19						19
20						20
21						21
22						22

Exercise 5 (LO 3) CASH RECEIPTS TRANSACTIONS

Diana Brewer of the Floor and Window Treatment Center received cash during the month of March as described below.

Mar. 2 Received cash from Dresson Homes on account, $98.95.
12 Received cash from Ray Acuff on account, $105.00.
15 Cash sale to Jean Granite, $404.76, plus 5% sales tax.
18 Cash sale to Bill Green, $2,380.95, plus 5% sales tax.
23 Received cash from Clydette Rupert on account, $114.83.
24 Received cash from Marty Staple on account, $35.55.
25 Received cash from Angel Burtin on account, $25.57.
31 Cash sales for the month were $22,000.00, including 5% sales tax. (From cash register tape.)
31 Credit card sales for the month were $28,000.00, including 5% sales tax. Bank credit card expense is $560.

Required:

Enter the above transactions in the general journal below and on page 152.

GENERAL JOURNAL

PAGE

	DATE	DESCRIPTION	POST. REF.	DEBIT	CREDIT	
1						1
2						2
3						3
4						4
5						5
6						6
7						7
8						8
9						9
10						10
11						11
12						12
13						13
14						14
15						15
16						16
17						17
18						18
19						19

Exercise 5 (Concluded)

GENERAL JOURNAL

PAGE

	DATE		DESCRIPTION	POST. REF.	DEBIT	CREDIT	
1							1
2							2
3							3
4							4
5							5
6							6
7							7
8							8
9							9
10							10
11							11
12							12
13							13
14							14
15							15
16							16
17							17
18							18
19							19
20							20
21							21
22							22
23							23
24							24
25							25
26							26
27							27
28							28
29							29
30							30
31							31

Problem 1 (LO 2/3) SALES, SALES RETURNS AND ALLOWANCES, AND CASH RECEIPTS TRANSACTIONS

The following information represents transactions for Kwan Chu's Fish Market for the month of July, 20—. Sales tax is 6 percent.

July 1 Sold merchandise on account to B.A. Smith, $137.50, plus sales tax. Sale No. 33.

3 Merchandise return by B.A. Smith, $15.00, plus sales tax, for a credit. Credit Memorandum 11.

5 Sold merchandise on account to L.L. Unis, $218.00, plus sales tax. Sale No. 34.

7 Cash sales for the week, $325.44, plus sales tax.

10 Sold merchandise on account to W.P. Clark, $208.00, plus sales tax. Sale No. 35.

11 Received $129.85 from B.A. Smith, on account.

13 Merchandise return by W.P. Clark, $22.00, plus sales tax, for a credit. Credit Memorandum 12.

14 Cash sales for the week, $411.20, plus sales tax.

16 Sold merchandise on account to B.A. Smith, $282.50, plus sales tax. Sale No. 36.

17 Received $231.08 from L.L. Unis, on account.

21 Cash sales for the week, $292.50, plus sales tax.

24 Sold merchandise on account to L.L. Unis, $224.50, plus sales tax. Sale No. 37.

28 Cash sales for the week, $300.50, plus sales tax.

31 Received $197.16 from W.P. Clark, on account.

Required:

Using the information provided, record the transactions in the general journal below and on page 154.

GENERAL JOURNAL

PAGE _____

	DATE	DESCRIPTION	POST. REF.	DEBIT	CREDIT	
1						1
2						2
3						3
4						4
5						5
6						6
7						7
8						8
9						9
10						10
11						11
12						12
13						13
14						14
15						15
16						16

Problem 1 (Concluded)

GENERAL JOURNAL PAGE _____

	DATE		DESCRIPTION	POST. REF.	DEBIT	CREDIT	
1							1
2							2
3							3
4							4
5							5
6							6
7							7
8							8
9							9
10							10
11							11
12							12
13							13
14							14
15							15
16							16
17							17
18							18
19							19
20							20
21							21
22							22
23							23
24							24
25							25
26							26
27							27
28							28
29							29
30							30

Problem 2 (LO 3/4) SALES, LEDGERS, AND SCHEDULE OF ACCOUNTS RECEIVABLE

H.K. Smythe operates Leather All, a leather shop that sells luggage, handbags, business cases, and other leather goods. During the month of May, the following sales on account were made.

May 3 Sold merchandise on account to T.A. Pigdon, $247.50, plus sales tax of $14.85. Sale No. 51.
 4 Sold merchandise on account to J.R. Feyton, $55.00, plus sales tax of $3.30. Sale No. 52.
 6 Sold merchandise on account to P.C. McMurdy, $99.00, plus sales tax of $5.94. Sale No. 53.
 10 Sold merchandise on account to J.T. Messer, $175.00, plus sales tax of $10.50. Sale No. 54.
 12 Sold merchandise on account to A.F. Schlitz, $355.00, plus sales tax of $21.30. Sale No. 55.
 13 Sold merchandise on account to J.R. Feyton, $215.00, plus sales tax of $12.90. Sale No. 56.
 20 Sold merchandise on account to P.C. McMurdy, $400.00, plus sales tax of $24.00. Sale No. 57.
 28 Sold merchandise on account to J.T. Messer, $255.00, plus sales tax of $15.30. Sale No. 58.

Required:

1. Enter the above transactions in the general journal provided below and on page 156 (start with page 7).
2. Post the entries to the general ledger and accounts receivable ledger on pages 156–158.
3. Prepare a schedule of accounts receivable as of May 31.

GENERAL JOURNAL

PAGE

	DATE	DESCRIPTION	POST. REF.	DEBIT	CREDIT	
1						1
2						2
3						3
4						4
5						5
6						6
7						7
8						8
9						9
10						10
11						11
12						12
13						13
14						14
15						15
16						16
17						17
18						18

Problem 2 (Continued)

GENERAL JOURNAL

PAGE

	DATE		DESCRIPTION	POST. REF.	DEBIT	CREDIT	
1							1
2							2
3							3
4							4
5							5
6							6
7							7
8							8
9							9
10							10
11							11
12							12
13							13
14							14
15							15
16							16
17							17
18							18

GENERAL LEDGER

ACCOUNT Accounts Receivable ACCOUNT NO. 122

DATE		ITEM	POST. REF.	DEBIT	CREDIT	BALANCE DEBIT	BALANCE CREDIT
20— May	1	Balance	√			8 3 4 00	

156

Problem 2 (Continued)

ACCOUNT Sales Tax Payable ACCOUNT NO. 231

DATE		ITEM	POST. REF.	DEBIT	CREDIT	BALANCE	
						DEBIT	CREDIT

ACCOUNT Sales ACCOUNT NO. 401

DATE		ITEM	POST. REF.	DEBIT	CREDIT	BALANCE	
						DEBIT	CREDIT

ACCOUNTS RECEIVABLE LEDGER

NAME J. R. Feyton

ADDRESS 6022 Columbia, St. Louis, MO 63139-1906

DATE		ITEM	POST. REF.	DEBIT	CREDIT	BALANCE

Problem 2 (Continued)

NAME P.C. McMurdy

ADDRESS 1214 N. 2ND St., E. St. Louis, IL 62201-2679

DATE		ITEM	POST. REF.	DEBIT	CREDIT	BALANCE
20— May	1	Balance	√			1 2 5 00

NAME J. T. Messer

ADDRESS P.O. Box 249, Chesterfield, MO 63017-3901

DATE		ITEM	POST. REF.	DEBIT	CREDIT	BALANCE
20— May	1	Balance	√			1 7 7 00

NAME T. A. Pigdon

ADDRESS 1070 Purcell, University City, MO 63130-1546

DATE		ITEM	POST. REF.	DEBIT	CREDIT	BALANCE
20— May	1	Balance	√			2 8 0 00

NAME A. F. Schlitz

ADDRESS 800 Lindbergh Blvd., St. Louis, MO 63166-1546

DATE		ITEM	POST. REF.	DEBIT	CREDIT	BALANCE
20— May	1	Balance	√			2 5 2 00

Problem 2 (Concluded)

Problem 3 (LO 2/3) SALES, SALES RETURNS AND ALLOWANCES, CASH RECEIPTS, AND LEDGERS

Paula Angelillis operates the Hard-to-Find Auto Parts Store. Much of her business is by mail. The following transactions related to sales and cash receipts occurred during June:

June 1 Received $300 from A.K. Wells, including $14.29 of sales tax, for field cash sale. (Field cash sales are not included in cash register tapes.)

 5 Received $125.60 from L. Strous on account.

 10 Received $263.25 from D. Manning on account.

 12 Q. Striker returned merchandise for credit. The sales price was $215.00, plus sales tax of $10.75.

 18 Received $58.25 from D. Warding on account.

 20 Received $1,000 from B.L. Stryker, including $47.62 tax (field cash sale).

 21 Received $29.99 from L. Clese on account.

 24 R. Popielarz returned merchandise for credit. Sales price was $116.25, plus sales tax of $5.81.

 27 Received $426.00 from L. LeCount on account.

 30 Cash and bank credit card sales for the month were $8,200, plus sales tax of $410.00. Bank credit card expense is $80.

Required:

1. Enter each transaction in the general journal provided on pages 160–161 (start with page 8).
2. Post the entries to the general and accounts receivable ledgers (pages 161–164).

Problem 3 (Continued)

GENERAL JOURNAL

PAGE _____

	DATE	DESCRIPTION	POST. REF.	DEBIT	CREDIT	
1						1
2						2
3						3
4						4
5						5
6						6
7						7
8						8
9						9
10						10
11						11
12						12
13						13
14						14
15						15
16						16
17						17
18						18
19						19
20						20
21						21
22						22
23						23
24						24
25						25
26						26
27						27
28						28
29						29
30						30
31						31
32						32
33						33
34						34
35						35
36						36

Problem 3 (Continued)

GENERAL JOURNAL

PAGE

	DATE	DESCRIPTION	POST. REF.	DEBIT	CREDIT	
1						1
2						2
3						3
4						4
5						5
6						6
7						7
8						8
9						9
10						10

GENERAL LEDGER

ACCOUNT Cash ACCOUNT NO. 101

DATE		ITEM	POST. REF.	DEBIT	CREDIT	BALANCE	
						DEBIT	CREDIT
20— June	1	Balance	√			13 2 0 0 25	

ACCOUNT Accounts Receivable ACCOUNT NO. 122

DATE		ITEM	POST. REF.	DEBIT	CREDIT	BALANCE	
						DEBIT	CREDIT
20— June	1	Balance	√			1 2 5 0 90	

Problem 3 (Continued)　　　　　**GENERAL LEDGER**

ACCOUNT　　Sales Tax Payable　　　　　　　　　　　　ACCOUNT NO. 231

DATE		ITEM	POST. REF.	DEBIT	CREDIT	BALANCE		
						DEBIT	•	CREDIT
20— June	1	Balance	√					1 2 5 00

ACCOUNT　　Sales　　　　　　　　　　　　　　　　ACCOUNT NO. 401

DATE	ITEM	POST. REF.	DEBIT	CREDIT	BALANCE		
					DEBIT	•	CREDIT

ACCOUNT　　Sales Returns and Allowances　　　　　　ACCOUNT NO. 401.1

DATE	ITEM	POST. REF.	DEBIT	CREDIT	BALANCE		
					DEBIT	•	CREDIT

ACCOUNT　　Bank Credit Card Expense　　　　　　　ACCOUNT NO. 513

DATE	ITEM	POST. REF.	DEBIT	CREDIT	BALANCE		
					DEBIT	•	CREDIT

Problem 3 (Continued)

ACCOUNTS RECEIVABLE LEDGER

NAME L. Clese

ADDRESS 875 Glenway Drive, Glendale, MO 63122-4112

DATE		ITEM	POST. REF.	DEBIT	CREDIT	BALANCE
20—						
June	1	Balance	√			2 9 99

NAME L. LeCount

ADDRESS 1439 East Broad Street, Columbus, OH 43205-9892

DATE		ITEM	POST. REF.	DEBIT	CREDIT	BALANCE
20—						
June	1	Balance	√			4 2 6 00

NAME D. Manning

ADDRESS 2101 Cumberland Road, Noblesville, IN 47870-2435

DATE		ITEM	POST. REF.	DEBIT	CREDIT	BALANCE
20—						
June	1	Balance	√			2 6 3 25

NAME R. Popielarz

ADDRESS 3001 Hillcrest Drive, Dallas, PA 18612-6854

DATE		ITEM	POST. REF.	DEBIT	CREDIT	BALANCE
20—						
June	1	Balance	√			1 2 2 06

Problem 3 (Concluded) **ACCOUNTS RECEIVABLE LEDGER**

NAME Q. Striker

ADDRESS 4113 Main Street, Beech Grove, IN 46107-9643

DATE		ITEM	POST. REF.	DEBIT	CREDIT	BALANCE
20— June	1	Balance	√			2 2 5 75

NAME L. Strous

ADDRESS 2215 N. State Road 135, Greenwood, IN 46142-6432

DATE		ITEM	POST. REF.	DEBIT	CREDIT	BALANCE
20— June	1	Balance	√			1 2 5 60

NAME D. Warding

ADDRESS 1100 W. Main Street, Carmel, IN 46032-2364

DATE		ITEM	POST. REF.	DEBIT	CREDIT	BALANCE
20— June	1	Balance	√			5 8 25

CHAPTER 12
ACCOUNTING FOR PURCHASES AND CASH PAYMENTS

LEARNING OBJECTIVES

Chapter 12 continues the study of merchandise transactions. In this chapter, purchases and cash payments are emphasized, and another new ledger and new schedule are introduced. As was done in Chapter 11, merchandise purchase transactions are shown in general journal format.

Objective 1. Define merchandise purchases transactions.

For a merchandising business, **purchases** refers to merchandise acquired for resale. There are several important documents used in the purchasing process of a merchandising business. A **purchase requisition** is a form used to request the purchasing department to purchase merchandise or other property. A **purchase order** is a written order to buy goods from a specific vendor (supplier). A **receiving report** is prepared upon receipt of merchandise and indicates what merchandise has been received. An **invoice** is a document prepared by the seller as a bill for the merchandise shipped. To the seller, this is a sales invoice. To the buyer, it is called a **purchase invoice**.

The accounting department compares the purchase invoice with the purchase requisition, purchase order, and receiving report. If the invoice is for the goods ordered at the correct price, the invoice is paid by the due date.

When credit terms such as 2/10, n/30 are offered by the seller, a **cash discount** is available to the buyer if the bill is paid within the discount period. Another type of discount, called a **trade discount**, is often offered by manufacturers and wholesalers. This discount is a reduction from the list or catalog price. By simply adjusting the trade discount percentages, companies can avoid the cost of reprinting catalogs every time there is a change in price.

Objective 2. Describe and use merchandise purchases accounts.

To account for merchandise purchases transactions, four new accounts are used. These are **Purchases, Purchases Returns and Allowances, Purchases Discounts,** and **Freight-In.**

Purchases is an account to which the cost of merchandise (i.e., inventory acquired for resale) is debited.

Purchases Returns and Allowances is a contra-purchases account to which returns of merchandise and price reductions are credited. This account is subtracted from Purchases on the income statement.

Purchases Discounts is a contra-purchases account to which any cash discounts allowed on purchases are credited. This account is subtracted from Purchases on the income statement.

Freight-In is an adjunct-purchases account to which transportation charges on merchandise purchases are debited. This account is added to Purchases on the income statement.

FOB shipping point means that transportation charges are paid by the buyer. **FOB destination** means that transportation charges are paid by the seller.

Gross profit is computed using the following format:

Sales			$xxxx	
Less sales returns				
and allowances			xxxx	
Net sales				$xxxx
Cost of goods sold				
Merchandise inventory,				
beginning of period			$xxxx	
Purchases		$xxxx		
Less: Purchases returns				
and allowances	$xxxx			
Purchases discounts	xxxx	xxxx		
Net purchases		$xxxx		
Add freight-in		xxxx		
Cost of goods purchased			xxxx	
Goods available for sale			$xxxx	
Less merchandise inventory,				
end of period			xxxx	
Cost of goods sold				xxxx
Gross profit				$xxxx

Objective 3. Describe and use the accounts payable ledger.

The accounts payable account in the general ledger provides a record of the total amount owed by a business to its suppliers. To help run the business, a record also is needed of the amount owed to each supplier. The accounts payable subsidiary ledger provides this information.

When an accounts payable subsidiary ledger is used, the accounts payable account in the general ledger is a "controlling account." The accounts payable ledger is "subsidiary" to this account. Transactions are posted daily from the general journal to both the general ledger and the accounts payable ledger.

Objective 4. Prepare a schedule of accounts payable.

The accounts payable balance in the general ledger should equal the sum of the supplier balances in the accounts payable ledger. A listing of supplier accounts and balances is called a **schedule of accounts payable**. This schedule is usually prepared at the end of the month to verify that the sum of the accounts payable ledger balances equals the accounts payable balance.

REVIEW QUESTIONS

Instructions: Analyze each of the following statements carefully before writing your answer in the column at the right.

	Question	Answer
	Question	**Answer**

1. For a merchandising business, _____ refers to merchandise acquired for resale. ... _____

2. A(n) _____ is a form used to request the purchasing department to purchase merchandise or other property. _____

3. A(n) _____ is a written order to buy goods from a specific vendor (supplier). .. _____

4. When the merchandise is received, a(n) _____ indicating what has been received is prepared. .. _____

5. To the buyer, a document prepared by the seller as a bill for the merchandise shipped is called a(n) _____. _____

6. In the credit terms 2/10, n/30, the 2 represents....................... _____

7. A(n) _____ is a type of discount offered by manufacturers and wholesalers as a reduction from the list or catalog price offered to different classes of customers. .. _____

8. List the four accounts used with merchandise purchases transactions.

9. FOB shipping point means that transportation charges are paid by the _____. ... _____

10. FOB destination means that transportation charges are paid by the _____. ... _____

11. Cost of merchandise available for sale less the end-of-period merchandise inventory is called _____. _____

12. Net sales minus cost of merchandise sold is called _____. _____

13. A separate ledger containing an individual account payable for each supplier is called a(n) _____. .. _____

14. To indicate that the accounts payable ledger has been posted, a slash and a _____ _____ are entered in the posting reference column of the general journal. .. _____

15. If a buyer returns merchandise or is given an allowance for damaged merchandise, the account _____ is credited for the dollar amount. _____

16. Purchases returns and allowances are posted to both the general ledger and the _____ _____ ledger. .. _____

17. When a payment is made on account, _____ _____ is debited. ... _____

18. To verify that the sum of the accounts payable ledger balances equals the accounts payable balance, a(n) _____ is prepared. _____

EXERCISES AND PROBLEMS

Exercise 1 (LO 1) PURCHASE REQUISITION

You are employed by Eberle Hardware, a retail hardware business, as manager of the Lawn and Garden Department. On October 1, 20—, after completing an inventory, you decide that the following merchandise should be ordered:

15	All steel rubber-tire wheelbarrows	24	Spade shovels
25	Garden hose, 1/2", 50 ft.	6	Long-handle spade shovels
3	Power mower, 21" cut	12	Spade forks
5	Heavy duty rototillers		

You would like delivery within 10 days and should be notified upon receipt of the merchandise. Using the form provided below, prepare the purchase requisition.

```
                                              ———————————————    Purchase Requisition
         ┌──────────────┐
         │    Eberle    │    110 E. Kirkwood Ave.
         │   Hardware   │    Indianapolis, IN 46011-3274
         └──────────────┘

                                                       Requisition No. 502 _____

   Required for Department _____    Date Issued _____

   Advise _____ On Delivery    Date Required _____

   ┌──────────────────┬──────────────────────────────────────────────┐
   │    Quantity      │                 Description                   │
   ├──────────────────┼──────────────────────────────────────────────┤
   │                  │                                               │
   │                  │                                               │
   │                  │                                               │
   │                  │                                               │
   │                  │                                               │
   │                  │                                               │
   │                  │                                               │
   └──────────────────┴──────────────────────────────────────────────┘

   Approved By _____    Requisition Placed By _____

   DEPARTMENT MANAGER'S MEMORANDUM
                                       Issued To _____

   Purchase Order No. _____            _____

   Date _____             _____
```

NOTE: *The department manager's memorandum at the bottom of the form should not be completed until after the purchase order is placed in Exercise 2.*

Exercise 2 (LO 1) PURCHASE ORDER

Assume you are acting as purchasing agent for Eberle Hardware. On October 2, 20—, order the merchandise specified on Requisition No. 502 in Exercise 1 from Wesner's Supply, 1476 South Spurr Drive, Miami, Florida, 33161-1516. Use the purchase order form provided below specifying shipment by AAA freight FOB destination; prices as follows:

All steel rubber-tire wheelbarrows	$ 20.35 ea.
Garden hose, 1/2", 50 ft.	4.65 ea.
Power mower, 21" cut	180.75 ea.
Heavy duty rototillers	291.50 ea.
Spade shovels	7.45 ea.
Long-handle spade shovels	9.30 ea.
Spade forks	7.70 ea.

After preparing the purchase order, fill in the department manager's memorandum at the bottom of Purchase Requisition No. 502 prepared in Exercise 1. Assume the requisition was approved by Scott Roturt.

Eberle Hardware
110 E. Kirkwood Ave.
Indianapolis, IN 46011-3274

Purchase Order

Order No. 361 _____

Date _____

To _____

Deliver By _____

Ship via _____

FOB _____

Quantity	Description	Unit Price	Total

By _____

Exercise 3 (LO 1) PURCHASE INVOICES

The purchase invoice below received from Wesner's Supply has been referred to you for verification. Compare it with Purchase Order No. 361 in Exercise 2 and verify (a) the quantities ordered, (b) the quantities shipped, (c) the unit prices, (d) the extensions, and (e) the total amount of the invoice. For each item that has been verified, report any discrepancies detected.

INVOICE NO	SOLD TO		SHIP TO	
	Eberle Hardware 110 E. Kirkwood Ave. Indianapolis, IN 46011-3274		same	

W S Wesner's Supply

1476 South Spurr Drive, Miami, FL 33161-1516

INVOICE DATE	YOUR ORDER NO & DATE	DATE SHIPPED
Oct. 7, 20--	361 Oct. 2, 20--	Oct. 7, 20--

REQUISITION NO	OUR ORDER NO

TERMS	FOB	CAR INITIALS & NO	HOW SHIPPED & ROUTE	SHIPPED FROM
2/10, n/30	Destination		Freight AAA	Miami

QUANTITY SHIPPED	DESCRIPTION	UNIT PRICE	EXTENSION
15	All steel rubber-tire wheelbarrows	20.35	305.25
25	Garden hose, 1/2", 50 ft.	4.65	116.25
4	Power mower, 21" cut	291.50	1,166.00
5	Heavy duty rototillers	180.75	903.75
24	Spade shovels	7.95	178.80
6	Long-handle spade shovels	9.30	57.00
12	Spade forks	7.70	92.40
			2,819.45

Exercise 4 (LO 1) TRADE DISCOUNT

Skirvin Enterprises purchased merchandise with a list price of $800 subject to a trade discount of 10%. Compute the amount to be paid.

Exercise 5 (LO1) CASH DISCOUNT

Geisel's Boating Supplies purchased life preservers and other boating equipment for resale costing $1,200 subject to terms of 3/10, n/60.

1. If Geisel makes payment within the discount period, how much will be paid?

2. If the invoice terms were 2/10, n/30, compute the cash discount available to Geisel if payment is made within the discount period.

Exercise 6 (LO2) GROSS PROFIT

The following information was taken from the records of Hi-Fi Specialists for the month of August, 20—:

Sales	$ 257,400
Sales returns and allowances	1,900
Merchandise inventory, August 1	38,000
Merchandise inventory, August 31	32,000
Purchases	200,000
Purchases returns and allowances	10,200
Purchases discounts	4,000
Freight-in	2,000

Required:

Using the form on page 172, show the computation of gross profit on the income statement for the month of August.

Exercise 6 (Continued)

Exercise 7 (LO) JOURNALIZING PURCHASES AND CASH PAYMENTS

O'Henesy Office Equipment and Supply purchased the following merchandise:

20	Electronic printing calculators	$ 63.95	each
10	Electric self-correcting typewriters	900.00	each
5	Microcomputers	1,995.00	each

The amount of the purchase is subject to a trade discount of 15% and credit terms of 2/10, n/30. The following transactions occurred during the month of November:

Nov. 5 Purchased the above merchandise on account.
 15 Issued a check for the amount due.

Required:

1. Journalize the above transactions in the general journal below.
2. Give the appropriate general journal entry if the payment is not made until December 5.

GENERAL JOURNAL PAGE

	DATE	DESCRIPTION	POST. REF.	DEBIT	CREDIT	
1						1
2						2
3						3
4						4
5						5
6						6
7						7
8						8
9						9
10						10
11						11

Supporting calculations:

Problem 1 (LO2) JOURNALIZING AND POSTING PURCHASES TRANSACTIONS

J.R. Lang, owner of Lang's Galleria, made the following purchases of merchandise on account during the month of November 20—.

Nov. 2 Purchase Invoice No. 611, $4,145, from Ford Distributors.

 5 Purchase Invoice No. 216, $2,165, from Mueller Wholesaler.

 15 Purchase Invoice No. 399, $2,895, from Grant White & Co.

 19 Purchase Invoice No. 106, $1,845, from Bailey & Hinds, Inc.

 22 Purchase Invoice No. 914, $3,225, from Ford Distributors.

 28 Purchase Invoice No. 661, $2,175, from Jackson Company.

 30 Purchase Invoice No. 716, $3,500, from Mueller Wholesaler.

Required:

1. Record the transactions in a general journal (page 9) on page 175.
2. Post from the journal to the general ledger accounts and the accounts payable ledger accounts (pages 176–178).

Problem 1 (Continued)

GENERAL JOURNAL

	DATE	DESCRIPTION	POST. REF.	DEBIT	CREDIT	
1						1
2						2
3						3
4						4
5						5
6						6
7						7
8						8
9						9
10						10
11						11
12						12
13						13
14						14
15						15
16						16
17						17
18						18
19						19
20						20
21						21
22						22
23						23
24						24
25						25
26						26
27						27
28						28
29						29
30						30

Problem 1 (Continued)

GENERAL LEDGER

ACCOUNT Accounts Payable ACCOUNT NO. 202

DATE	ITEM	POST. REF.	DEBIT	CREDIT	BALANCE		
					DEBIT	•	CREDIT

ACCOUNT Purchases ACCOUNT NO. 231

DATE	ITEM	POST. REF.	DEBIT	CREDIT	BALANCE		
					DEBIT	•	CREDIT

ACCOUNTS PAYABLE LEDGER

NAME Bailey & Hinds, Inc.

ADDRESS

DATE	ITEM	POST. REF.	DEBIT	CREDIT	BALANCE

Problem 1 (Concluded)

ACCOUNTS PAYABLE LEDGER

NAME Ford Distributors

ADDRESS

DATE		ITEM	POST. REF.	DEBIT	CREDIT	BALANCE

NAME Grant White & Co.

ADDRESS

DATE		ITEM	POST. REF.	DEBIT	CREDIT	BALANCE

NAME Jackson Company

ADDRESS

DATE		ITEM	POST. REF.	DEBIT	CREDIT	BALANCE

NAME Mueller Wholesaler

ADDRESS

DATE		ITEM	POST. REF.	DEBIT	CREDIT	BALANCE

Problem 2 (LO 3/4) PURCHASES TRANSACTIONS AND SCHEDULE OF ACCOUNTS PAYABLE

Tom Bowers operates a business under the name of Tom's Sporting Goods. The books of original entry include a general journal and an accounts payable ledger. Following are the transactions related to purchases for the month of February:

Feb. 3 Purchased merchandise from Ringer's on account, $498.64. Invoice No. 611; terms 2/10, net/30.
 4 Purchased merchandise on account from Klein Brothers, $780.11. Invoice No. 112; terms 30 days.
 11 Purchased merchandise from Corleon's on account, $2,300.00. Invoice No. 432; terms 30 days.
 15 Received a credit memorandum from Ringer's for $30.00 for merchandise returned that had been purchased on account.

Required:
1. Enter the above transactions in the general journal provided below (page 5).
2. Post from the journal to the general ledger and accounts payable ledger accounts on pages 179–180.
3. Prepare a schedule of accounts payable as of February 28.

GENERAL JOURNAL PAGE

	DATE	DESCRIPTION	POST. REF.	DEBIT	CREDIT	
1						1
2						2
3						3
4						4
5						5
6						6
7						7
8						8
9						9
10						10
11						11
12						12
13						13
14						14
15						15

Problem 2 (Continued)

GENERAL LEDGER

ACCOUNT Accounts Payable ACCOUNT NO. 202

DATE		ITEM	POST. REF.	DEBIT	CREDIT	BALANCE	
						DEBIT	• CREDIT
20— Feb.	1	Balance	√				3 1 2 5 50

ACCOUNT Purchases ACCOUNT NO. 501

DATE		ITEM	POST. REF.	DEBIT	CREDIT	BALANCE	
						DEBIT	• CREDIT
20— Feb.	1	Balance	√			2 5 0 0 00	

ACCOUNT Purchases Returns and Allowances ACCOUNT NO. 501.1

DATE		ITEM	POST. REF.	DEBIT	CREDIT	BALANCE	
						DEBIT	• CREDIT
20— Feb.	1	Balance	√				2 0 0 00

Problem 2 (Concluded)

ACCOUNTS PAYABLE LEDGER

NAME Corleon's

ADDRESS 1894 Winthrop Ave., White Plains, NY 10606-6915

DATE		ITEM	POST. REF.	DEBIT	CREDIT	BALANCE
20— Feb.	1	Balance	√			1 6 2 5 50

NAME Klein Brothers

ADDRESS 1728 Camino Real, San Antonio, TX 78238-4420

DATE		ITEM	POST. REF.	DEBIT	CREDIT	BALANCE
20— Feb.	1	Balance	√			6 2 5 00

NAME Ringer's

ADDRESS 1500 North Street, Bakersfield, CA 93301-4747

DATE		ITEM	POST. REF.	DEBIT	CREDIT	BALANCE
20— Feb.	1	Balance	√			8 7 5 00

Problem 3 (LO 3/4) CASH PAYMENTS TRANSACTIONS AND SCHEDULE OF ACCOUNTS PAYABLE

Chris Bultman operates a retail shoe store. The books of original entry include a general journal and an accounts payable ledger. Following are transactions related to cash payments for the month of August:

Aug.	1	Issued Check No. 47 for $900.00 in payment of rent (Rent Expense) for August.
	3	Issued Check No. 48 to Blue Suede Shoes Company in payment on account, $640.00 less 2% discount.
	9	Issued Check No. 49 to Style-Rite in payment on account, $800.00 less 3% discount.
	14	Issued Check No. 50 for $125.28 in payment of utility bill (Utilities Expense).
	20	Issued Check No. 51 to Baldo Company in payment for cash purchase, $525.00.
	22	Issued Check No. 52 to West Coast Shoes in payment on account, $625.00. A discount of 2% was lost because Bultman neglected to pay the invoice within the discount period.
	27	Issued Check No. 53 for $2,000.00 to Bultman for a cash withdrawal for personal use.

Required:

1. Enter the above transactions in a general journal (page 4) on page 182.
2. Post from the journal to the general ledger and accounts payable ledger accounts provided on pages 183–185.
3. Prepare a schedule of accounts payable for Bultman Shoes on August 31, 20— using the form on page 185.

Problem 3 (Continued)

GENERAL JOURNAL

PAGE _____

	DATE		DESCRIPTION	POST. REF.	DEBIT	CREDIT	
1							1
2							2
3							3
4							4
5							5
6							6
7							7
8							8
9							9
10							10
11							11
12							12
13							13
14							14
15							15
16							16
17							17
18							18
19							19
20							20
21							21
22							22
23							23
24							24
25							25
26							26
27							27
28							28
29							29
30							30

Problem 3 (Continued)

GENERAL LEDGER

ACCOUNT Cash ACCOUNT NO. 101

DATE		ITEM	POST. REF.	DEBIT	CREDIT	BALANCE		
						DEBIT	•	CREDIT
20— Aug.	1	Balance	√					25 0 0 0 00

ACCOUNT Accounts Payable ACCOUNT NO. 202

DATE		ITEM	POST. REF.	DEBIT	CREDIT	BALANCE		
						DEBIT	•	CREDIT
20— Aug.	1	Balance	√					3 3 6 6 00

ACCOUNT Chris Bultman, Drawing ACCOUNT NO. 312

DATE		ITEM	POST. REF.	DEBIT	CREDIT	BALANCE		
						DEBIT	•	CREDIT
20— Aug.	1	Balance	√			14 0 0 0 00		

ACCOUNT Purchases ACCOUNT NO. 501

DATE		ITEM	POST. REF.	DEBIT	CREDIT	BALANCE		
						DEBIT	•	CREDIT
20— Aug.	1	Balance	√			54 2 6 5 43		

Problem 3 (Continued)

GENERAL LEDGER

ACCOUNT Purchases Discounts ACCOUNT NO. 501.2

DATE		ITEM	POST. REF.	DEBIT	CREDIT	BALANCE DEBIT	•	BALANCE CREDIT
20— Aug.	1	Balance	√					3 2 5 20

ACCOUNT Rent Expense ACCOUNT NO. 521

DATE		ITEM	POST. REF.	DEBIT	CREDIT	BALANCE DEBIT	•	BALANCE CREDIT
20— Aug.	1	Balance	√			7 2 0 0 00		

ACCOUNT Utilities Expense ACCOUNT NO. 533

DATE		ITEM	POST. REF.	DEBIT	CREDIT	BALANCE DEBIT	•	BALANCE CREDIT
20— Aug.	1	Balance	√			8 2 2 87		

ACCOUNTS PAYABLE LEDGER

NAME Blue Suede Shoes Company

ADDRESS 2805 South Meridian, Indianapolis, IN 46225-3460

DATE		ITEM	POST. REF.	DEBIT	CREDIT	BALANCE
20— Aug.	1	Balance	√			6 4 0 00

Problem 3 (Concluded)

ACCOUNTS PAYABLE LEDGER

NAME Style-Rite

ADDRESS 6500 9th Street, New Orleans, LA 70115-1122

DATE	ITEM	POST. REF.	DEBIT	CREDIT	BALANCE
20— Aug. 1	Balance	√			1 2 0 0 00

NAME West Coast Shoes

ADDRESS 705 Rialto Avenue, Fresno, CA 93705-7845

DATE	ITEM	POST. REF.	DEBIT	CREDIT	BALANCE
20— Aug. 1	Balance	√			1 5 2 6 00

Problem 4 (LO 4) CASH PAYMENTS TRANSACTIONS

The following cash payments were made by the Demis Music Company during the month of July:

July 5 Paid $600 for rent. Issued Check No. 222.

12 Purchased $3,250 in merchandise from Hamilton Music Company. Issued Check No. 223.

18 Made a payment on account to Martinez Guitar Company for $4,500, less a 2% discount for paying within the discount period. Issued Check No. 224.

25 Paid $2,000 to First National Bank to pay off a note. Issued Check No. 225.

31 Anna Demis withdrew $5,500 from the business for personal use. Issued Check No. 226.

Required:

Enter the above transactions in a general journal.

GENERAL JOURNAL PAGE _____

	DATE		DESCRIPTION	POST. REF.	DEBIT	CREDIT	
1							1
2							2
3							3
4							4
5							5
6							6
7							7
8							8
9							9
10							10
11							11
12							12
13							13
14							14
15							15
16							16
17							17
18							18
19							19
20							20

CHAPTER 12 STUDY GUIDE
APPENDIX: THE NET-PRICE METHOD OF RECORDING PURCHASES

LEARNING OBJECTIVES

Objective 1. Describe the net-price method of recording purchases.

Under the net-price method, purchases are recorded at the net amount, assuming that all cash discounts will be taken.

Objective 2. Record purchases and cash payments using the net-price method.

At the time of purchase, Purchases is debited and Accounts Payable is credited for the gross price less the cash discount. If payment is made within the discount period, Accounts Payable is debited and Cash is credited for the net price. If payment is not made until after the discount period, Accounts Payable is debited for the net price, Purchases Discounts Lost is debited for the discount lost, and Cash is credited for the gross price.

Exercise PURCHASES AND CASH PAYMENTS TRANSACTIONS

Jiang's Accessory Shop had the following transactions during April.

April 2 Purchased merchandise on account from Sag's Apparel for $2,000, terms 2/10, n/30.
 5 Purchased merchandise on account from Lee's Wholesale for $1,800, terms 1/10, n/30.
 11 Paid the amount due to Sag's Apparel for the purchase on April 2.
 25 Paid the amount due to Lee's Wholesale for the purchase on April 5.

Required:

1. Prepare general journal entries for these transactions using the gross-price method.
2. Prepare general journal entries for these transactions using the net-price method.

GENERAL JOURNAL PAGE

	DATE	DESCRIPTION	POST. REF.	DEBIT	CREDIT	
1						1
2						2
3						3
4						4
5						5
6						6
7						7
8						8
9						9
10						10

GENERAL JOURNAL

PAGE

	DATE	DESCRIPTION	POST. REF.	DEBIT	CREDIT	
1						1
2						2
3						3
4						4
5						5
6						6
7						7
8						8
9						9
10						10
11						11
12						12
13						13
14						14
15						15
16						16
17						17
18						18
19						19
20						20
21						21
22						22
23						23
24						24
25						25
26						26
27						27
28						28
29						29
30						30

CHAPTER 13
SPECIAL JOURNALS

LEARNING OBJECTIVES

Chapter 13 continues the study of sales, cash receipts, purchases, and cash payments transactions in a merchandising business. The focus is on how to account for these transactions more efficiently. Four special journals that speed up and simplify the recording process are introduced.

Objective 1. Describe special journals and explain their purpose.

A **special journal** is a journal designed for recording only certain kinds of transactions. The types of special journals used by a business should depend on the types of transactions that occur frequently for the business. Four special journals commonly used by businesses are the sales journal, cash receipts journal, purchases journal, and cash payments journal.

Objective 2. Describe and use the sales journal.

The **sales journal** saves time and energy by simplifying the recording and posting of transactions. It is a "special journal" used to record only credit sales.

Credit sales affect Accounts Receivable (debit), Sales (credit) and, if there is a sales tax, Sales Tax Payable (credit). The sales journal provides separate columns for Accounts Receivable Debit, Sales Credit, and Sales Tax Payable Credit. The column totals are posted monthly to the general ledger accounts. Individual customer accounts in the accounts receivable ledger are posted daily.

Objective 3. Describe and use the cash receipts journal.

Like the sales journal, a **cash receipts journal** saves time and energy in recording and posting transactions. Any time cash is received, the cash receipts journal is the book of original entry, and Cash is always debited. Column headings are established for Cash and other accounts that are frequently used, such as Sales (credit), Accounts Receivable (credit), Bank Credit Card Expense (debit), and Sales Tax Payable (credit). There may also be a General Credit column for accounts that do not have a special column.

As with other special journals, column totals are posted at the end of the month. Daily postings are made for items in the General Credit column, as well as to the accounts receivable ledger.

Objective 4. Describe and use the purchases journal.

A **purchases journal** is a special journal used to record only purchases of merchandise on account. This journal may have only a single column for Purchases Dr./Accounts Payable Cr. Alternatively, there may be three columns for Purchases Dr., Freight-In Dr., and Accounts Payable Cr.

Each general ledger account used in the purchases journal requires only one posting each period. Individual supplier accounts in the accounts payable ledger are posted daily.

Objective 5. Describe and use the cash payments journal.

A **cash payments journal** is a special journal used to record only cash payments transactions. The column headings of the cash payments journal will be those accounts that are most frequently affected by the company's cash payments transactions. All column totals are posted to the general ledger account indicated in

the column headings, except for the "General Dr." column. Each amount in this column must be posted individually. Column totals are posted at the end of each month. General Debit column entries are posted daily.

Postings to the accounts payable ledger must also be made. These postings are made daily.

REVIEW QUESTIONS

Instructions: Analyze each of the following statements carefully before writing your answer in the column at the right.

Question	Answer

1. A journal designed for recording only certain kinds of transactions is called a _____. .. _____

2. Transactions that occur infrequently, and adjusting and closing entries usually are recorded in the _____. _____

3. A sale is recorded in a sales journal by entering the following information: .. _____

4. A(n) _____ journal is a special journal used to record only sales on account. .. _____

5. Sales returns and allowances are generally recorded in the _____ journal. ... _____

6. Each sales journal entry is posted to the accounts receivable ledger _____ .. _____

7. Any time the cash receipts journal is used, a debit is made to _____. ... _____

8. The cash receipts journal is a special journal used to record only _____ transactions. .. _____

9. Each amount in the General Credit column of the cash receipts journal is posted _____. .. _____

10. A(n) _____ is a special journal used to record only purchases of merchandise on account. .. _____

11. Purchases returns and allowances are recorded in the _____. _____

12. The purchases journal for a company like Northern Micro, whose suppliers generally pay the freight charges, would have only a single column labeled Purchases Dr. _____. _____

13. A separate ledger containing an individual account payable for each supplier is called a(n) _____. ... _____

14. Each purchases journal entry is posted to the accounts payable ledger

 _____. ... _____

15. A(n) _____ is a special journal used to record only cash payments

 transactions. .. _____

16. Any time the cash payments journal is used, a credit is made to the

 account called _____. ... _____

17. A cash payment is recorded in the cash payments journal by entering

 the following information: .. _____

18. Each amount in the General Debit column of the cash payments

 journal is posted _____. .. _____

EXERCISES AND PROBLEMS

Exercise 1 (LO 2) SALES JOURNAL

Diana Brewer operates the Floor and Window Treatment Center and completed the following transactions related to sales of merchandise on account during the month of February. Sales tax of 5% was included in the amount of each sale.

Feb. 2 Sold wallpaper supplies to Dresson Homes, $98.95; terms, n/30. Sale No. 255.
 12 Sold paint to Ray Acuff, $105.00; terms, n/30. Sale No 256.
 23 Sold miniblinds to Clydette Rupert, $114.83; terms, n/30. Sale No. 257.
 24 Sold decorator items to Marty Staple, $35.55; terms, n/30. Sale No. 258.
 25 Sold paint to Angel Burtin, $25.57; terms, n/30. Sale No. 259.

Required:

1. Enter the above transactions in the sales journal provided on page 192.
2. Total and rule the journal.

Exercise 1 (Concluded)

SALES JOURNAL PAGE

	DATE	SALE NO.	TO WHOM SOLD	POST. REF.	ACCOUNTS RECEIVABLE DR.	SALES CR	SALES TAX PAYABLE CR.
1							
2							
3							
4							
5							
6							
7							

Exercise 2 (LO 3) CASH RECEIPTS JOURNAL

Diana Brewer of the Floor and Window Treatment Center received cash during the month of March as described below.

Mar. 2 Received cash from Dresson Homes on account, $98.95.
 12 Received cash from Ray Acuff on account, $105.00.
 15 Cash sale to Jean Granite, $404.76, plus 5% sales tax.
 18 Cash sale to Bill Green, $2,380.95, plus 5% sales tax.
 23 Received cash from Clydette Rupert on account, $114.83.
 24 Received cash from Marty Staple on account, $35.55.
 25 Received cash from Angel Burtin on account, $25.57.
 31 Cash sales for the month were $22,000.00, including 5% sales tax. (From cash register tape.)
 31 Credit card sales for the month were $28,000.00, including 5% sales tax.

Required:

1. Enter the above transactions in the cash receipts journal on page 193.
2. Total and rule the journal.

Exercise 2 (Concluded)

CASH RECEIPTS JOURNAL PAGE

	DATE	ACCOUNT CREDITED	POST. REF.	GENERAL CR.	ACCTS. RECEIV-ABLE CR.	SALES CR.	SALES TAX PAY. CR.	CASH DR.	
1									1
2									2
3									3
4									4
5									5
6									6
7									7
8									8
9									9
10									10
11									11

Exercise 3 (LO 4) PURCHASES JOURNAL

Tom Bowers operates a business under the name of Tom's Sporting Goods. The books of original entry include a purchases journal and a general journal, in which entries such as Purchase Returns and Allowances are recorded. An accounts payable ledger is used to maintain a record of the amount owed to suppliers. Following are the transactions related to purchases for the month of February:

Feb. 3 Purchased merchandise from Ringer's on account, $498.64. Invoice No. 611; terms 2/10, net/30.

 4 Purchased merchandise on account from Klein Brothers, $780.11. Invoice No. 112; terms 30 days.

 11 Purchased merchandise from Corleon's on account, $2,300.00. Invoice No. 432; terms 30 days.

 15 Received a credit memorandum from Ringer's for $30.00 for merchandise returned that had been purchased on account.

Required:

Enter the above transactions in the purchases journal and general journal.

PURCHASES JOURNAL PAGE

	DATE	INVOICE NO.	FROM WHOM PURCHASED	POST. REF.	PURCHASES DR. ACCTS. PAY. CR.	
1						1
2						2
3						3
4						4
5						5
6						6

Exercise 3 (Concluded)

GENERAL JOURNAL
PAGE

	DATE		DESCRIPTION	POST. REF.	DEBIT	CREDIT	
1							1
2							2
3							3

Exercise 4 (LO 5) Cash Payments Journal

The following cash payments were made by the Demis Music Company during the month of July:

July 5 Paid $600 for rent. Issued Check No. 222.

12 Purchased $3,250 in merchandise from Hamilton Music Company. Issued Check No. 223.

18 Made a payment on account to Martinez Guitar Company for $4,500, less a 2% discount for paying within the discount period. Issued Check No. 224.

25 Paid $2,000 to First National Bank to pay off a note. Issued Check No. 225.

31 Anna Demis withdrew $5,500 from the business for personal use. Issued Check No. 226.

Required:

1. Enter the above transactions in the cash payments journal.
2. Total, rule, and prove the journal.

CASH PAYMENTS JOURNAL
PAGE

DATE	CK. NO.	ACCOUNT DEBITED	POST. REF.	GENERAL DR.	ACCTS. PAYABLE DR.	PURCHASES DR.	PURCHASES DISCOUNTS CR.	CASH CR.

Problem 1 (LO 2/3) SALES JOURNAL AND CASH RECEIPTS JOURNAL

The following information represents transactions for Kwan Chu's Fish Market for the month of July, 20—. Sales tax is 6 percent.

July
1 Sold merchandise on account to B.A. Smith, $137.50, plus sales tax. Sale No. 33.
3 Merchandise returned by B.A. Smith, $15.00, plus sales tax, for a credit. Credit Memorandum 11.
5 Sold merchandise on account to L.L. Unis, $218.00, plus sales tax. Sale No. 34.
7 Cash sales for the week, $325.44, plus sales tax.
10 Sold merchandise on account to W.P. Clark, $208.00, plus sales tax. Sale No. 35.
11 Received $129.85 from B.A. Smith, on account.
13 Merchandise returned by W.P. Clark, $22.00, plus sales tax, for a credit. Credit Memorandum 12.
14 Cash sales for the week, $411.20, plus sales tax.
16 Sold merchandise on account to B.A. Smith, $282.50, plus sales tax. Sale No. 36.
17 Received $231.08 from L.L. Unis, on account.
21 Cash sales for the week, $292.50, plus sales tax.
24 Sold merchandise on account to L.L. Unis, $224.50, plus sales tax. Sale No. 37.
28 Cash sales for the week, $300.50, plus sales tax.
31 Received $197.16 from W.P. Clark, on account.

Required:

1. Using the information provided, record the transactions in the sales journal, the cash receipts journal, or the general journal as required.

2. Total and rule the column totals

GENERAL JOURNAL PAGE

	DATE		DESCRIPTION	POST. REF.	DEBIT	CREDIT	
1							1
2							2
3							3
4							4
5							5
6							6
7							7
8							8
9							9
10							10
11							11
12							12

Problem 1 (Concluded)

SALES JOURNAL PAGE

	DATE	SALE NO.	TO WHOM SOLD	POST. REF.	ACCOUNTS RECEIVABLE DR.	SALES CR	SALES TAX PAYABLE CR.	
1								1
2								2
3								3
4								4
5								5
6								6
7								7
8								8

CASH RECEIPTS JOURNAL PAGE

	DATE	ACCOUNT CREDITED	POST. REF.	GENERAL CR.	ACCTS. RECEIVABLE CR.	SALES CR.	SALES TAX PAY. CR.	CASH DR.	
1									1
2									2
3									3
4									4
5									5
6									6
7									7
8									8

Problem 2 (LO 2/3) SALES JOURNAL, GENERAL LEDGER AND ACCOUNTS RECEIVABLE LEDGER

H.K. Smythe operates Leather All, a leather shop that sells luggage, handbags, business cases, and other leather goods. During the month of May, the following sales on account were made.

May 3 Sold merchandise on account to T.A. Pigdon, $247.50, plus sales tax of $14.85. Sale No. 51.

 4 Sold merchandise on account to J.R. Feyton, $55.00, plus sales tax of $3.30. Sale No. 52.

 6 Sold merchandise on account to P.C. McMurdy, $99.00, plus sales tax of $5.94. Sale No. 53.

 10 Sold merchandise on account to J.T. Messer, $175.00, plus sales tax of $10.50. Sale No. 54.

 12 Sold merchandise on account to A.F. Schlitz, $355.00, plus sales tax of $21.30. Sale No. 55.

 13 Sold merchandise on account to J.R. Feyton, $215.00, plus sales tax of $12.90. Sale No. 56.

 20 Sold merchandise on account to P.C. McMurdy, $400.00, plus sales tax of $24.00. Sale No. 57.

 28 Sold merchandise on account to J.T. Messer, $255.00, plus sales tax of $15.30. Sale No. 58.

Required:

1. Enter the above transactions in the sales journal (page 1) provided below.
2. Post the entries in the sales journal to the accounts receivable ledger on pages 198–199.
3. Total and verify the column totals and rule the sales journal. Complete the summary postings to the general ledger on page 198.

SALES JOURNAL
PAGE

	DATE	SALE NO.	TO WHOM SOLD	POST. REF.	ACCOUNTS RECEIVABLE DR.	SALES CR	SALES TAX PAYABLE CR.	
1								1
2								2
3								3
4								4
5								5
6								6
7								7
8								8
9								9
10								10
11								11
12								12
13								13
14								14
15								15
16								16

Problem 2 (Continued)

GENERAL LEDGER

ACCOUNT Accounts Receivable ACCOUNT NO. 122

DATE	ITEM	POST. REF.	DEBIT	CREDIT	BALANCE DEBIT	•	BALANCE CREDIT
20— May	Balance	√			8 3 4 00		

ACCOUNT Sales Tax Payable ACCOUNT NO. 231

DATE	ITEM	POST. REF.	DEBIT	CREDIT	BALANCE DEBIT	•	BALANCE CREDIT

ACCOUNT Sales ACCOUNT NO. 401

DATE	ITEM	POST. REF.	DEBIT	CREDIT	BALANCE DEBIT	•	BALANCE CREDIT

ACCOUNTS RECEIVABLE LEDGER

NAME J. R. Feyton

ADDRESS 6022 Columbia, St. Louis, MO 63139-1906

DATE	ITEM	POST. REF.	DEBIT	CREDIT	BALANCE

NAME P.C. McMurdy

ADDRESS 1214 N. 2^{ND} St., E. St. Louis, IL 62201-2679

DATE	ITEM	POST. REF.	DEBIT	CREDIT	BALANCE
20— May 1	Balance	√			1 2 5 00

Problem 2 (Concluded)

ACCOUNTS RECEIVABLE LEDGER

NAME J. T. Messer

ADDRESS P.O. Box 249, Chesterfield, MO 63017-3901

DATE		ITEM	POST. REF.	DEBIT	CREDIT	BALANCE
20— May	1	Balance	√			1 7 7 00

NAME T. A. Pigdon

ADDRESS 1070 Purcell, University City, MO 63130-1546

DATE		ITEM	POST. REF.	DEBIT	CREDIT	BALANCE
20— May	1	Balance	√			2 8 0 00

NAME A. F. Schlitz

ADDRESS 800 Lindbergh Blvd., St. Louis, MO 63166-1546

DATE		ITEM	POST. REF.	DEBIT	CREDIT	BALANCE
20— May	1	Balance	√			2 5 2 00

Problem 3 (LO2/3) CASH RECEIPTS JOURNAL, GENERAL JOURNAL, GENERAL LEDGER, AND ACCOUNTS RECEIVABLE LEDGER

Paula Angelillis operates the Hard-to-Find Auto Parts Store. Much of her business is by mail. The books of original entry include a cash receipts journal and a general journal. The following transactions related to sales and cash receipts occurred during June:

June	1	Received $300 from A.K. Wells, including $14.29 of sales tax, for field cash sale. (Field cash sales are not included in cash register tapes.)
	5	Received $125.60 from L. Strous on account.
	10	Received $263.25 from D. Manning on account.
	12	Q. Striker returned merchandise for credit. The sales price was $215.00, plus sales tax of $10.75.
	18	Received $58.25 from D. Warding on account.
	20	Received $1,000 from B.L. Stryker, including $47.62 tax (field cash sale).
	21	Received $29.99 from L. Clese on account.
	24	R. Popielarz returned merchandise for credit. The sales price was $116.25, plus sales tax of $5.81.
	27	Received $426.00 from L. LeCount on account.
	30	Cash and bank credit card sales for the month were $8,200, plus sales tax of $410.00. Bank credit card expense is $80.

Required:

1. Enter each transaction in either the cash receipts journal (page 18) or the general journal (page 5) provided. Total, verify the totals, and rule the cash receipts journal.
2. Make the individual postings required from the cash receipts journal and the general journal to the general and accounts receivable ledgers.
3. Make the summary postings from the cash receipts journal to the general ledger.

GENERAL JOURNAL PAGE

	DATE		DESCRIPTION	POST. REF.	DEBIT	CREDIT	
1							1
2							2
3							3
4							4
5							5
6							6
7							7
8							8
9							9
10							10
11							11
12							12

Problem 3 (Continued)

CASH RECEIPTS JOURNAL

PAGE 18

DATE	ACCOUNT CREDITED	POST. REF.	GENERAL CR.	ACCTS. RECEIV- ABLE CR.	SALES CR.	SALES TAX PAY. CR.	BANK CR. CARD EXP. DR.	CASH DR
1								
2								
3								
4								
5								
6								
7								
8								
9								
10								
11								
12								
13								
14								
15								
16								
17								
18								
19								
20								
21								

Problem 3 (Continued)

GENERAL LEDGER

ACCOUNT Cash ACCOUNT NO. 101

DATE		ITEM	POST. REF.	DEBIT	CREDIT	BALANCE		
						DEBIT	•	CREDIT
20— June	1	Balance	√			13 2 0 0 25		

ACCOUNT Accounts Receivable ACCOUNT NO. 122

DATE		ITEM	POST. REF.	DEBIT	CREDIT	BALANCE		
						DEBIT	•	CREDIT
20— June	1	Balance	√			1 2 5 0 90		

ACCOUNT Sales Tax Payable ACCOUNT NO. 231

DATE		ITEM	POST. REF.	DEBIT	CREDIT	BALANCE		
						DEBIT	•	CREDIT
20— June	1	Balance	√					1 2 5 00

ACCOUNT Sales ACCOUNT NO. 401

DATE		ITEM	POST. REF.	DEBIT	CREDIT	BALANCE		
						DEBIT	•	CREDIT

ACCOUNT Sales Returns and Allowances ACCOUNT NO. 401.1

DATE		ITEM	POST. REF.	DEBIT	CREDIT	BALANCE		
						DEBIT	•	CREDIT

Problem 3 (Continued)

ACCOUNT Bank Credit Card Expense ACCOUNT NO. 513

DATE	ITEM	POST. REF.	DEBIT	CREDIT	BALANCE DEBIT	•	BALANCE CREDIT

ACCOUNTS RECEIVABLE LEDGER

NAME L. Clese

ADDRESS 875 Glenway Drive, Glendale, MO 63122-4112

DATE		ITEM	POST. REF.	DEBIT	CREDIT	BALANCE
20— June	1	Balance	√			2 9 99

NAME L. LeCount

ADDRESS 1439 East Broad Street, Columbus, OH 43205-9892

DATE		ITEM	POST. REF.	DEBIT	CREDIT	BALANCE
20— June	1	Balance	√			4 2 6 00

NAME D. Manning

ADDRESS 2101 Cumberland Road, Noblesville, IN 47870-2435

DATE		ITEM	POST. REF.	DEBIT	CREDIT	BALANCE
20— June	1	Balance	√			2 6 3 25

Problem 3 (Concluded)

NAME R. Popielarz

ADDRESS 3001 Hillcrest Drive, Dallas, PA 18612-6854

DATE		ITEM	POST. REF.	DEBIT	CREDIT	BALANCE
20— June	1	Balance	√			1 2 2 06

NAME Q. Striker

ADDRESS 4113 Main Street, Beech Grove, IN 46107-9643

DATE		ITEM	POST. REF.	DEBIT	CREDIT	BALANCE
20— June	1	Balance	√			2 2 5 75

NAME L. Strous

ADDRESS 2215 N. State Road 135, Greenwood, IN 46142-6432

DATE		ITEM	POST. REF.	DEBIT	CREDIT	BALANCE
20— June	1	Balance	√			1 2 5 60

NAME D. Warding

ADDRESS 1100 W. Main Street, Carmel, IN 46032-2364

DATE		ITEM	POST. REF.	DEBIT	CREDIT	BALANCE
20— June	1	Balance	√			5 8 25

Problem 4 (LO 4) PURCHASES JOURNAL, GENERAL LEDGER, AND ACCOUNTS PAYABLE LEDGER

J.R. Lang, owner of Lang's Galleria, made the following purchases of merchandise on account during the month of November 20—.

Nov. 2 Purchase Invoice No. 611, $4,145, from Ford Distributors.
 5 Purchase Invoice No. 216, $2,165, from Mueller Wholesaler.
 15 Purchase Invoice No. 399, $2,895, from Grant White & Co.
 19 Purchase Invoice No. 106, $1,845, from Bailey & Hinds, Inc.
 22 Purchase Invoice No. 914, $3,225, from Ford Distributors.
 28 Purchase Invoice No. 661, $2,175, from Jackson Company.
 30 Purchase Invoice No. 716, $3,500, from Mueller Wholesaler.

Required:

1. Record the transactions in the purchases journal (page 9). Total and rule the journal.
2. Post from the purchases journal to the general ledger accounts and to the accounts payable ledger accounts.

PURCHASES JOURNAL PAGE

	DATE	INVOICE NO.	FROM WHOM PURCHASED	POST. REF.	PURCHASES DR. ACCTS. PAY. CR.	
1						1
2						2
3						3
4						4
5						5
6						6
7						7
8						8
9						9
10						10

GENERAL LEDGER

ACCOUNT Accounts Payable ACCOUNT NO. 202

DATE	ITEM	POST. REF.	DEBIT	CREDIT	BALANCE DEBIT	•	CREDIT

Problem 4 (Continued) **GENERAL LEDGER**

ACCOUNT Purchases ACCOUNT NO. 501

DATE	ITEM	POST. REF.	DEBIT	CREDIT	BALANCE	
					DEBIT	CREDIT

ACCOUNTS PAYABLE LEDGER

NAME Bailey & Hinds, Inc.
ADDRESS

DATE	ITEM	POST. REF.	DEBIT	CREDIT	BALANCE

NAME Ford Distributors
ADDRESS

DATE	ITEM	POST. REF.	DEBIT	CREDIT	BALANCE

NAME Grant White & Co.
ADDRESS

DATE	ITEM	POST. REF.	DEBIT	CREDIT	BALANCE

Problem 4 (Concluded) **ACCOUNTS PAYABLE LEDGER**

NAME Jackson Company

ADDRESS

DATE	ITEM	POST. REF.	DEBIT	CREDIT	BALANCE

NAME Mueller Wholesaler

ADDRESS

DATE	ITEM	POST. REF.	DEBIT	CREDIT	BALANCE

Problem 5 (LO 5) CASH PAYMENTS JOURNAL, GENERAL LEDGER, AND ACCOUNTS PAYABLE LEDGER

Chris Bultman operates a retail shoe store. Following are transactions related to cash payments for the month of August:

Aug. 1 Issued Check No. 47 for $900.00 in payment of rent (Rent Expense) for August.
 3 Issued Check No. 48 to Blue Suede Shoes Company in payment on account, $640.00 less 2% discount.
 9 Issued Check No. 49 to Style-Rite in payment on account, $800.00 less 3% discount.
 14 Issued Check No. 50 for $125.28 in payment of utility bill (Utilities Expense).
 20 Issued Check No. 51 to Baldo Company in payment for cash purchase, $525.00.
 22 Issued Check No. 52 to West Coast Shoes in payment on account, $625.00. A discount of 2% was lost because Bultman neglected to pay the invoice within the discount period.
 27 Issued Check No. 53 for $2,000.00 to Bultman for a cash withdrawal for personal use.

Required:

1. Enter the above transactions in the cash payments journal (page 9).
2. Enter the totals, rule, and prove the journal.
3. Complete individual postings to the general ledger and accounts payable ledger and summary postings to the general ledger. The relevant accounts are provided on pages 208–211.

Problem 5 (Continued)

CASH PAYMENTS JOURNAL

PAGE

	DATE	ACCOUNT DEBITED	POST. REF.	GENERAL DR.	ACCTS. PAYABLE DR.	PURCHASES DR.	PURCH. DISC. CR.	CASH CR.	
1									1
2									2
3									3
4									4
5									5
6									6
7									7
8									8
9									9
10									10

GENERAL LEDGER

ACCOUNT Cash ACCOUNT NO. 101

DATE		ITEM	POST. REF.	DEBIT	CREDIT	BALANCE DEBIT	•	BALANCE CREDIT
20— Aug.	1	Balance	√			25 0 0 0 00		

ACCOUNT Accounts Payable ACCOUNT NO. 202

DATE		ITEM	POST. REF.	DEBIT	CREDIT	BALANCE DEBIT	•	BALANCE CREDIT
20— Aug.	1	Balance	√					3 3 6 6 00

ACCOUNT Chris Bultman, Drawing ACCOUNT NO. 312

DATE		ITEM	POST. REF.	DEBIT	CREDIT	BALANCE DEBIT	•	BALANCE CREDIT
20— Aug.	1	Balance	√			14 0 0 0 00		

Problem 5 (Continued) **GENERAL LEDGER**

ACCOUNT Purchases ACCOUNT NO. 501

DATE		ITEM	POST. REF.	DEBIT	CREDIT	BALANCE		
						DEBIT	•	CREDIT
20— Aug.	1	Balance	√			54 2 6 5 43		

ACCOUNT Purchases Discounts ACCOUNT NO. 501.2

DATE		ITEM	POST. REF.	DEBIT	CREDIT	BALANCE		
						DEBIT	•	CREDIT
20— Aug.	1	Balance	√					3 2 5 20

ACCOUNT Rent Expense ACCOUNT NO. 521

DATE		ITEM	POST. REF.	DEBIT	CREDIT	BALANCE		
						DEBIT	•	CREDIT
20— Aug.	1	Balance	√			7 2 0 0 00		

ACCOUNT Utilities Expense ACCOUNT NO. 533

DATE		ITEM	POST. REF.	DEBIT	CREDIT	BALANCE		
						DEBIT	•	CREDIT
20— Aug.	1	Balance	√			8 2 2 87		

ACCOUNTS PAYABLE LEDGER

NAME Blue Suede Shoes Company

ADDRESS

DATE		ITEM	POST. REF.	DEBIT	CREDIT	BALANCE
20— Aug.	1	Balance	√			6 4 0 00

Problem 5 (Concluded)

ACCOUNTS PAYABLE LEDGER

NAME Style-Rite

ADDRESS

DATE		ITEM	POST. REF.	DEBIT	CREDIT	BALANCE
20— Aug.	1	Balance	√			1 2 0 0 00

NAME West Coast Shoes

ADDRESS

DATE		ITEM	POST. REF.	DEBIT	CREDIT	BALANCE
20— Aug.	1	Balance	√			1 5 2 6 00

CHAPTER 14
THE VOUCHER SYSTEM

LEARNING OBJECTIVES

This chapter explains the voucher system in the expenditure process for retail businesses. A voucher register, check register, and schedule of vouchers payable are introduced to replace a purchases journal, cash payments journal, and schedule of accounts payable. The purpose of the voucher system is security—to provide a system of control over monies paid out by a business.

Objective 1. Describe how a voucher system is used to control expenditures.

A **voucher system** adds a step in the expenditure process—it requires that a new form (the voucher) be completed and approved before cash is disbursed. The process may seem burdensome and time-consuming; it does require extra effort, but it also provides control over money being spent. Three elements of internal control—segregation of duties, proper authorization, and adequate documents and records—are present. **Duties are segregated** because different employees order, receive, and record purchases. **Authorization** is required to order the goods and to prepare the voucher. The **documents and records** include purchase requisitions, purchase orders, receiving reports, and vouchers that are prenumbered and accounted for.

Objective 2. Prepare a voucher.

A **voucher** is a prenumbered document that shows that an acquisition is proper and payment is authorized. On the front are recorded the voucher date, invoice terms and due date, supplier name and address, invoice date, description of items purchased, and invoice amount. On the back is recorded the disposition or processing information for the voucher—what account is debited, payment information, and authorization signatures.

Objective 3. Describe and use a voucher register.

The **voucher register** is a special journal used to record all purchases—whether merchandise, assets, or other services. Vouchers Payable is credited for every transaction; special columns are used for accounts frequently debited such as Purchases, Supplies, and Wages Expense. For those accounts used less frequently, the General Dr. column is used (and posted individually to the general ledger). Column totals from the voucher register are posted to the general ledger at the end of the month.

The Payments column of the voucher register is used to record payment of vouchers (date and check number). Unpaid vouchers are kept in an unpaid vouchers file and filed by due date. The unpaid vouchers file usually takes the place of an accounts payable ledger.

Objective 4. Describe the payment process using a voucher system.

On the due date, an unpaid voucher is pulled from the unpaid vouchers file. The voucher is verified, and a check is prepared. (Without the supporting voucher, no check can be issued.) A voucher check is a special type of check that includes space for entering data about the voucher being paid. Paid vouchers are then filed numerically or by supplier in a paid voucher file. Vouchers, which are prenumbered, are accounted for to identify missing or duplicate vouchers.

Objective 5. Describe and use a check register and prepare a schedule of vouchers payable.

A **check register** is a special journal that accompanies a voucher system. There are only three columns—Vouchers Payable Debit, Purchases Discounts Credit, and Cash Credit. Column totals are posted at the end of the month to the general ledger. At the end of the month, a schedule of vouchers payable is prepared—either from the voucher register or from the unpaid vouchers file.

Objective 6. Account for returns, allowances, and partial payments.

Purchases returns and allowances and partial payments require additional entries in the general journal—to debit Vouchers Payable and credit either Purchases Returns and Allowances or Purchases.

REVIEW QUESTIONS

Instructions: Analyze each of the following statements carefully before writing your answer in the column at the right.

Question	Answer
1. Sets of procedures used to ensure all activities of the business are accounted for are called _____.	_____
2. Having one employee order goods and a different employee pay for them is called _____.	_____
3. _____ and related responsibilities mean that every business activity should be properly authorized.	_____
4. Accounting documents and records should be used in such a way that every purchase is supported by a document. This describes _____.	_____
5. Vouchers are _____, used in sequence, and subsequently accounted for.	_____
6. A(n) _____ is a control technique that requires every acquisition and subsequent payment be supported by an approved voucher.	_____
7. A(n) _____ is a document that shows that an acquisition is proper and that payment is authorized.	_____
8. Every recorded purchase is supported by five documents: the voucher, the _____, the receiving report, the _____, and the purchase requisition.	_____ _____
9. When a purchase invoice arrives, it is compared with the purchase requisition, the purchase order, and the _____.	_____
10. The _____ section on the back of the voucher is not completed until the voucher is paid on the due date.	_____

11. The _____ is a special journal used to record purchases of all
 types of assets and services. .. _____

12. When a voucher register is used, it generally replaces the _____
 journal. ... _____

13. The voucher and supporting documents are filed in the _____
 until it is time for payment. .. _____

14. Unpaid vouchers are filed by _____ in the unpaid vouchers file. _____

15. For most businesses that use a voucher system, the unpaid vouchers
 file serves as a(n) _____ ledger. _____

16. Both individual and column postings are made from the voucher
 register to the _____. .. _____

17. A(n) _____ is a check with space for entering data about the
 voucher being paid. ... _____

18. After a voucher has been paid, the cashier completes the _____
 section on the back of the voucher. _____

19. The _____ is a special journal used to record all checks written
 in a voucher system. .. _____

20. The check register has only three columns—Vouchers Payable Debit,
 Purchases Discounts Credit, and _____ Credit. _____

21. The Schedule of Vouchers Payable is prepared from the unpaid
 vouchers file or from the voucher register, and the total must equal
 the balance of the _____ account. _____

22. When a complete return is made of merchandise purchased, a(n)
 _____ is received from the supplier and is attached to the voucher.
 The voucher is then filed in the _____ file. _____

23. When a partial return is made of merchandise purchased, a(n)
 _____ is received from the supplier and is attached to the voucher.
 The voucher is then filed in the _____ file. _____

24. When partial payments (installments) are planned at the time a
 purchase is made, a(n) _____ is prepared for each payment. _____

EXERCISES AND PROBLEMS

Exercise 1 (LO 1) PURCHASING PROCESS USING A VOUCHER SYSTEM

Directions: Fill in the missing information.

1. When a purchase invoice is received from a supplier, the voucher section performs the following three steps:

 a. Compares

 b. Judges

 c. Verifies

2. The voucher system provides for three elements of internal control. Explain each of these:

 a. Segregation of duties

 b. Authorization

 c. Adequate documents and records

Exercise 2 (LO 2) PREPARING A VOUCHER

Prepare the voucher on page 215 (front and back) from the information provided. The supplier, B.J. Smith & Co., 444 West Iowa Street, Tucson, AZ 82648-0444 sent you their invoice #2818, dated May 1, 20--, terms 2/10, n/30 for the following merchandise: 14 cases Regal Spray Paint at $800 a case and 12 power sprayers at $125 each. Charge the amount to Purchases, Account No. 501. We will take the discount and pay the invoice with Check No. 388, dated May 9. Today is May 3. Sign your name to indicate the voucher was prepared by you. Leave other signature spaces blank.

Exercise 2 (Concluded)

(front)

| ARIZONA PAINT SUPPLY | | Voucher No. ___**821**___ |

284 Western Blvd.
Phoenix, AZ 84101-0284

Date: _____ Terms: _____ Due: _____

To:

| | Invoice | | | |
Date	No.	Description		Amount

Authorization: _____ Prepared by: _____
Supervisor Clerk

(back)

Voucher No. ___**821**___

ACCOUNT DEBITED	ACCT. NO.	Amount	Summary

PAYMENT

Date: _____ Check No. _____ Amount: _____

APPROVED: Distribution _____ Payment _____

Exercise 3 (LO1/4) PURCHASE AND PAYMENT PROCESSES USING A VOUCHER SYSTEM

Complete the following flowcharts by inserting the missing information for the voucher system.

THE PURCHASING PROCESS

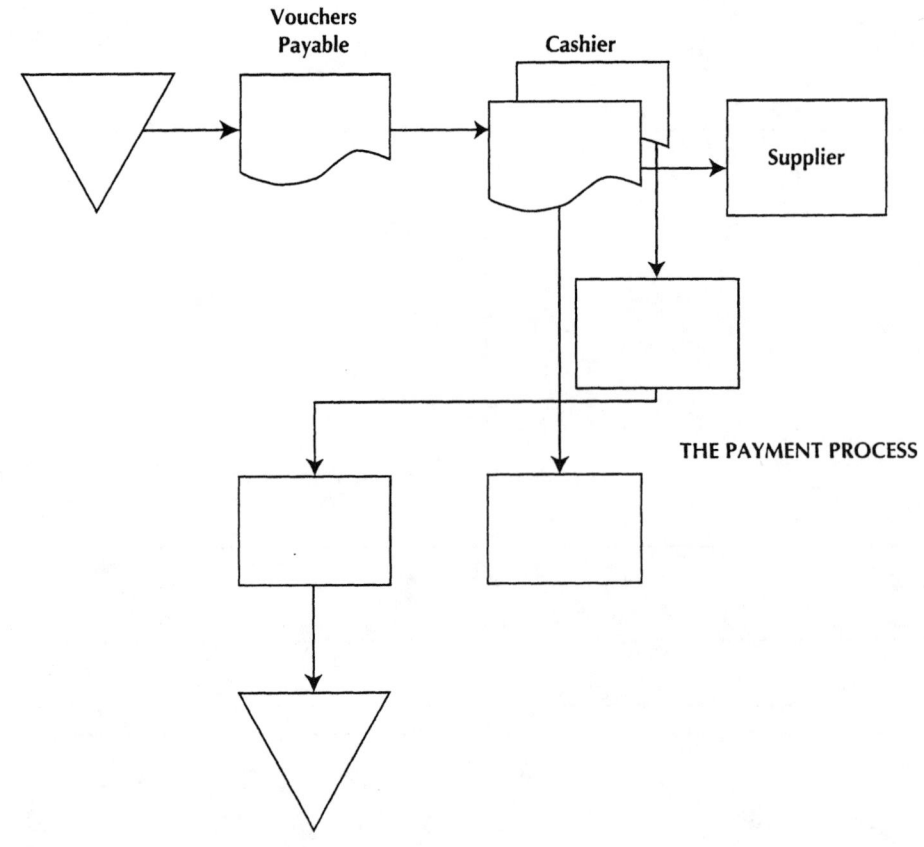

THE PAYMENT PROCESS

Problem 1 (LO 3/6) VOUCHER REGISTER, MERCHANDISE RETURNS, AND PARTIAL PAYMENTS

Based on the following information, prepare the voucher register (page 6) on pages 218–219 for Morrell's Antiques. Total, rule, and prove the register.

Date	Voucher No.	Amount	Issued To	Purpose	Payment Date	Ck. No.
1/1	101	$1,000	LaSalle Corporation	Rent	1/1	1
1/3	102	800	Messler's	Merchandise	1/11	3
1/5	103	250	JJ's Lacquers	Supplies	1/7	2
1/8	104	550	Merrick Co.	Merchandise	1/19	5
1/11	105	750	Jones & Carrothers	Merchandise	1/21	6
1/13	106	380	Messler's	Merchandise		
1/13	See below					
1/14	See below					
1/15	107	1,350	Payroll	Paychecks	1/15	4
1/18	108	900	Merrick Co.	Merchandise	1/28	7
1/22	109	660	Messler's	Merchandise		
1/25	110	840	Jones & Carrothers	Merchandise		
1/28	111	490	JJ's Lacquers	Supplies		
1/29	See below					
1/30	114	510	Wright Wholesalers	Merchandise		
1/31	115	1,350	Payroll	Paychecks	1/31	8

Record the following returns and allowances and voucher cancellation in the general journal (page 3) on page 220 and in the voucher register on pages 218–219 where appropriate.

1/13 Returned $250 in merchandise to Merrick Co.; received a credit memo and filed it in the unpaid vouchers file.

1/14 Returned $380 in merchandise to Messler's; received a credit memo and filed it in the paid vouchers file.

1/29 Canceled Voucher #110; will pay Jones & Carrothers in two installments of $420 each. (Issued two new vouchers—112 and 113)

Problem 1 (Continued)

VOUCHER

	DATE	VOUCHER NO.	ISSUED TO	PURCHASES DR.	
1					1
2					2
3					3
4					4
5					5
6					6
7					7
8					8
9					9
10					10
11					11
12					12
13					13
14					14
15					15
16					16
17					17
18					18
19					19
20					20

Problem 1 (Continued)

REGISTER

SUPPLIES DR.	WAGES AND SALARIES EXP. DR.	GENERAL DR.			VOUCHERS PAYABLE CR.	PAYMENT		
		ACCOUNT	POST. REF.	AMOUNT		DATE	CK. NO.	
								1
								2
								3
								4
								5
								6
								7
								8
								9
								10
								11
								12
								13
								14
								15
								16
								17
								18
								19
								20

Problem 1 (Concluded)

GENERAL JOURNAL PAGE

	DATE	DESCRIPTION	POST. REF.	DEBIT	CREDIT	
1						1
2						2
3						3
4						4
5						5
6						6
7						7
8						8
9						9
10						10
11						11
12						12
13						13
14						14

Problem 2 (LO 5) CHECK REGISTER

Based on information in the payment section of Problem 1 and the following, prepare a check register (page 6) for Morrell's Antiques. Assume all appropriate discounts are taken. Total, rule, and prove the register. Also, update the payment section of the voucher register in Problem 1.

Date	Ck. No.	Issued To	Voucher No.	In Payment of	Amount	Terms
1/1	1	LaSalle Corp.	101	Rent	$1,000	
1/7	2	JJ's Lacquers	103	Supplies	250	
1/11	3	Messler's	102	Merchandise	800	2/10, n/30
1/15	4	Payroll	107	Paychecks	1,350	
1/19	5	Merrick Co.	104	Merchandise	300	net 30
1/21	6	Jones & Carrothers	105	Merchandise	750	2/10, n/30
1/28	7	Merrick Co.	108	Merchandise	900	2/10, n/30
1/31	8	Payroll	115	Paychecks	1,350	

Problem 2 (Concluded)

CHECK REGISTER PAGE 6

	DATE	CHECK NO.	PAYEE	VOUCHERS PAY DR.		PURCHASES DISCOUNTS CR.	CASH CR.	
				VOU. NO.	AMOUNT			
1								1
2								2
3								3
4								4
5								5
6								6
7								7
8								8
9								9
10								10
11								11
12								12
13								13
14								14
15								15
16								16

Problem 3 (LO 3/5) VOUCHER REGISTER, CHECK REGISTER, POSTING, AND SCHEDULE OF VOUCHERS PAYABLE

Bob Adams is owner of Adams Feed & Seed. The following transactions occurred during May, 20—. Adams Feed & Seed uses a voucher register, a check register, and a general journal. Unpaid vouchers are filed and listed at the end of the month.

Enter the transactions for May in the voucher register (page 5) on pages 222–223 and the check register (page 4) on page 223. Total, rule, and prove the registers. Post the voucher register and the check register to the general ledger, and prepare a schedule of vouchers payable. Use account numbers as shown in the chapter.

Problem 3 (Continued)

VOUCHER

	DATE	VOUCHER NO.	ISSUED TO	PURCHASES DR.				
1								
2								
3								
4								
5								
6								
7								
8								
9								
10								

Vouchers issued:

Date	Voucher No.	Issued To	Amount	Purpose	Terms
5/1	522	Meadowland Corp.	$500	Rent for May	
5/6	523	Mulchers Company	300	Merchandise	2/10, n/30
5/11	524	Richard's Supply	400	Merchandise	2/10, n/30
5/14	525	Payroll	600	Bimonthly payroll	
5/18	526	Brenner's	550	Merchandise	2/10, n/30
5/23	527	McAndrews Feed	250	Merchandise	2/10, n/30
5/26	528	B&B Stationery	200	Office Supplies	
5/31	529	Payroll	600	Bimonthly payroll	

Checks issued:

Date	Check No.	Payee	Voucher No.	Amount
5/2	610	Meadowland Corp.	522	$500
5/7	611	Mulchers Company	523	300
5/11	612	Richard's Supply	524	400
5/15	613	Payroll	525	600
5/28	614	B&B Stationery	528	200
5/31	615	Payroll	529	600

Problem 3 (Continued)

REGISTER

PAGE _____

SUPPLIES DR.	WAGES AND SALARIES EXP. DR.	GENERAL DR.			VOUCHERS PAYABLE CR.	PAYMENT		
		ACCOUNT	POST. REF.	AMOUNT		DATE	CK. NO.	
								1
								2
								3
								4
								5
								6
								7
								8
								9
								10

CHECK REGISTER

PAGE _____

	DATE	CHECK NO.	PAYEE	VOUCHERS PAY DR.		PURCHASES DISCOUNTS CR.	CASH CR.	
				VOU. NO.	AMOUNT			
1								1
2								2
3								3
4								4
5								5
6								6
7								7
8								8
9								9
10								1
11								1
12								1
13								1

Problem 3 (Continued)

GENERAL LEDGER

ACCOUNT Cash ACCOUNT NO. 101

DATE		ITEM	POST. REF.	DEBIT	CREDIT	BALANCE		
						DEBIT	•	CREDIT
20— May	1	Balance	√			6 4 8 0 00		

ACCOUNT Supplies ACCOUNT NO. 141

DATE	ITEM	POST. REF.	DEBIT	CREDIT	BALANCE		
					DEBIT	•	CREDIT

ACCOUNT Vouchers Payable ACCOUNT NO. 202

DATE	ITEM	POST. REF.	DEBIT	CREDIT	BALANCE		
					DEBIT	•	CREDIT

ACCOUNT Purchases ACCOUNT NO. 501

DATE	ITEM	POST. REF.	DEBIT	CREDIT	BALANCE		
					DEBIT	•	CREDIT

ACCOUNT Purchases Discounts ACCOUNT NO. 501.2

DATE	ITEM	POST. REF.	DEBIT	CREDIT	BALANCE		
					DEBIT	•	CREDIT

ACCOUNT Wages and Salaries Expense ACCOUNT NO. 511

DATE	ITEM	POST. REF.	DEBIT	CREDIT	BALANCE		
					DEBIT	•	CREDIT

Problem 3 (Concluded)

ACCOUNT Rent Expense ACCOUNT NO. 521

DATE	ITEM	POST. REF.	DEBIT	CREDIT	BALANCE		
					DEBIT	•	CREDIT

CHAPTER 15
ADJUSTMENTS AND THE WORK SHEET
FOR A MERCHANDISING BUSINESS

LEARNING OBJECTIVES

Chapter 15 covers the end-of-period adjustments and the preparation of a work sheet for a merchandising business. Adjustments for merchandise inventory and unearned revenue are emphasized.

Objective 1. Prepare an adjustment for merchandise inventory.

During the year, the purchase and sale of merchandise is not entered in the merchandise inventory account. Thus, at the end of the year, it is necessary to adjust the merchandise inventory account to properly reflect the amount of inventory on hand. This is accomplished by removing the beginning inventory from the books (the current balance), and entering the ending inventory, based on a physical count.

The journal entry to remove the beginning inventory will always be a debit to the income summary account and a credit to Merchandise Inventory.

Income Summary	xx	
Merchandise Inventory		xx

The journal entry to enter the ending merchandise inventory, based on a physical count, will always be a debit to Merchandise Inventory and a credit to the Income Summary account.

Merchandise Inventory	xx	
Income Summary		xx

Objective 2. Prepare an adjustment for unearned revenue.

A liability account is created when cash is received before the product or service is provided. This liability is called **unearned revenue**. If all, or part, of the revenue has been earned by the end of the period, an adjustment is made in order to reduce the liability, unearned revenue, and increase the related revenue account.

Objective 3. Prepare a work sheet for a merchandising firm.

At the end of the accounting period, a work sheet is prepared to make the remaining steps of the accounting cycle easier. The work sheet is similar to the one you learned about in Chapter 5 for a service business, except for the new accounts introduced for a merchandising business and the unearned revenue account that was introduced in this chapter.

Adjusting entries are entered on the work sheet, including adjustments for supplies used, insurance expired, depreciation, and wages earned but not paid. From the adjusted trial balance columns, all amounts are extended to either the Income Statement columns or the Balance Sheet columns of the work sheet.

Of particular importance is the method of extending the amounts for Merchandise Inventory and Income Summary on the work sheet. Merchandise Inventory is extended in the usual manner. The adjusted balance is extended to the Adjusted Trial Balance columns and then to the Balance Sheet columns. However, both the debit <u>and</u> credit adjustments to Income Summary are extended to the Adjusted Trial Balance columns and then to the Income Statement columns (see page 227). The debit to Income Summary represents the beginning balance of merchandise inventory. The credit to Income Summary represents the ending balance of merchandise

inventory. Both amounts are used on the income statement. Thus, both amounts are extended to the Income Statement columns.

The other accounts identified with merchandise accounting will be extended into the Income Statement columns of the work sheet. Also, any unearned revenue that has been earned as of the balance sheet date will be adjusted into revenue (see table below).

WORK SHEET

	Trial Balance		Adjustments		Adj. Trial Balance		Income Statement		Balance Sheet	
	Dr.	Cr.	Dr.	Cr.	Dr.	Cr.	Dr.	Cr.	Dr.	Cr.
Merchandise Inv.	BI		EI	BI	EI				EI	
Unearned Rev.		xx	xx			xx				xx
Income Summary			BI	EI	BI	EI	BI	EI		
Revenue		xx		xx		xx		xx		
Sales		xx				xx		xx		
Sales Ret. & All.	xx				xx		xx			
Sales Discounts	xx				xx		xx			
Purchases	xx				xx		xx			
Purch. Ret. & All.		xx				xx		xx		
Purch. Discounts		xx				xx		xx		
Freight-In	xx				xx		xx			

All of the accounts needed to arrive at net income for a merchandising business are in the Income Statement columns of the work sheet. The difference between the debits and credits in the Income Statement columns and between the debits and credits in the Balance Sheet columns will equal either net income or net loss.

Objective 4. Journalize adjusting entries for a merchandising firm.

Just because adjusting entries were analyzed and placed on the work sheet does not mean that they have been entered into the accounts in the general ledger. Adjusting entries need to be entered in the general journal and posted to the general ledger. This information can be taken from the Adjustments columns of the work sheet.

REVIEW QUESTIONS

Instructions: Analyze each of the following items carefully before writing your answer in the column at the right.

Question	Answer

1. At the end of an accounting period, a(n) _____ is used to analyze and prepare adjustments and to determine the amount of net income or net loss for the time period. ... _____

2. The amount of inventory on hand at the end of the accounting period is determined by taking a(n) _____ of the goods on hand. _____

3. The beginning inventory is removed from the merchandise inventory account with a(n) _____ , and a debit is entered into the _____ account. ... _____

4. The ending inventory is entered by debiting Merchandise Inventory and crediting the _____ account. _____

5. Purchases less Purchases Returns and Allowances and Purchases Discounts equals _____. .. _____

6. Beginning inventory plus net purchases and freight-in equals

 _____. ... _____

7. Merchandise available for sale less ending inventory is equal to

 _____. ... _____

8. On the work sheet, both the debit and credit amounts of the income summary account are extended to the _____ and to the _____ columns of the work sheet. .. _____

9. The cash received in advance of delivering a product or performing a service is called _____. .. _____

10. Unearned revenue is reported as a(n) _____ on the balance sheet. _____

11. At the end of an accounting period, unearned revenue is adjusted into a(n) _____ account for the amount of revenue that has been earned. _____

12. Sales Returns and Allowances is deducted from _____ on the income statement. ... _____

13. Sales Returns and Allowances is classified as a(n) _____ account. _____

14. Purchases Returns and Allowances and Purchases Discounts are deducted from the _____ account on the income statement. _____

15. Purchases Returns and Allowances and Purchases Discounts are classified as _____ accounts. .. _____

16. The first step in preparing a work sheet is to prepare the............... _____

17. On the work sheet, amounts are extended from the Adjusted Trial Balance columns to the _____ and _____ columns. _____

18. If credits exceed debits on the Income Statement columns of the work sheet, this represents a net _____. _____

19. The most helpful aid in entering adjustments into the general journal is the _____. .. _____

EXERCISES AND PROBLEMS

Exercise 1 (LO 1) ADJUSTING ENTRIES FOR MERCHANDISE INVENTORY

Kendall's TV and Appliances had a merchandise inventory of $60,300 at the beginning of the year and $54,800 at the end of the year. Prepare the necessary adjusting entries in a general journal.

GENERAL JOURNAL PAGE

	DATE	DESCRIPTION	POST. REF.	DEBIT	CREDIT	
1						1
2						2
3						3
4						4
5						5
6						6
7						7
8						8
9						9

Exercise 2 (LO 1) CALCULATION OF COST OF GOODS SOLD

The following amounts are known for Casey's Card and Gift Shop:

Beginning merchandise inventory	$33,000
Ending merchandise inventory	41,000
Purchases	86,000
Purchases returns and allowances	4,500
Purchases discounts	2,500
Freight-in	1,000

Prepare the cost of goods sold section of the income statement for Casey's Card and Gift Shop.

Exercise 3 (LO 2) ADJUSTMENT FOR UNEARNED REVENUES

The following transactions took place for Hamilton Theaters. Journalize these transactions in a general journal.

Feb. 22 Sold 2,000 season tickets at $25 each, receiving cash of $50,000. Received cash before the services were provided.

Dec. 31 An end-of-period adjustment is needed to recognize that $45,000 in ticket revenue has been earned.

GENERAL JOURNAL PAGE

	DATE	DESCRIPTION	POST. REF.	DEBIT	CREDIT	
1						1
2						2
3						3
4						4
5						5
6						6
7						7
8						8
9						9
10						10

Exercise 4 (LO 4) JOURNALIZING ADJUSTING ENTRIES

The partial work sheet below is taken from the books of Long Auto Repair for the year ended December 31, 20—.

LONG AUTO REPAIR
WORK SHEET (PARTIAL)
FOR YEAR ENDED DECEMBER 31, 20--

		TRIAL BALANCE		ADJUSTMENTS		
		DEBIT	CREDIT	DEBIT	CREDIT	
1	Merchandise Inventory	60 0 0 0 00		(b) 57 0 0 0 00	(a) 60 0 0 0 00	1
2	Supplies	6 0 0 0 00			(d) 3 2 0 0 00	2
3	Building	150 0 0 0 00				3
4	Accum. Depr.—Building		45 0 0 0 00		(e) 8 0 0 0 00	4
5	Wages Payable				(f) 2 4 0 0 00	5
6	Unearned Repair Revenue		6 0 0 0 00	(c) 5 0 0 0 00		6
7	Income Summary			(a) 60 0 0 0 00	(b) 57 0 0 0 00	7
8	Repair Revenue		30 0 0 0 00		(c) 5 0 0 0 00	8
9	Wages Expense	39 0 0 0 00		(f) 2 4 0 0 00		9
10	Supplies Expense			(d) 3 2 0 0 00		10
11	Depr. Exp.--Building			(e) 8 0 0 0 00		11

Journalize the above adjustments in a general journal.

Exercise 4 (Concluded)

GENERAL JOURNAL

PAGE _____

	DATE		DESCRIPTION	POST. REF.	DEBIT	CREDIT	
1							1
2							2
3							3
4							4
5							5
6							6
7							7
8							8
9							9
10							10
11							11
12							12
13							13
14							14
15							15
16							16
17							17
18							18

Problem 1 (LO 1/2/3) PREPARE A WORK SHEET

The work sheet provided on pages 232–233 is taken from the books of Ocean Beach Sail Shop, a business owned by Nicole Smith. Adjustment information is provided below.

(a, b)	Based on a physical count, merchandise inventory on hand as of December 31, 20—, $36,000.
(c)	Supplies remaining at end of the year, $2,350.
(d)	Unexpired insurance on December 31, $1,875.
(e)	Depreciation expense on the building for 20—, $7,000.
(f)	Depreciation expense on the store equipment for 20—, $2,800.
(g)	Unearned tour revenue as of December 31, $2,700.
(h)	Wages earned but not paid as of December 31, $1,100.

Required:

1. Complete the Adjustments columns. Identify each adjustment with its corresponding letter.
2. Complete the work sheet.

Problem 1 (Continued)

OCEAN BEACH SAIL SHOP

WORK SHEET

FOR YEAR ENDED DECEMBER 31, 20--

	DESCRIPTION	TRIAL BALANCE		ADJUSTMENTS	
		DEBIT	CREDIT	DEBIT	CREDIT
1	Cash	27 0 0 0 00			
2	Accounts Receivable	9 0 0 0 00			
3	Merchandise Inventory	31 0 0 0 00			
4	Supplies	7 5 0 0 00			
5	Prepaid Insurance	4 9 0 0 00			
6	Land	40 0 0 0 00			
7	Building	60 0 0 0 00			
8	Accum. Depr.—Building		25 0 0 0 00		
9	Store Equipment	29 0 0 0 00			
10	Accum. Depr.—Store Equipment		9 0 0 0 00		
11	Accounts Payable		7 6 0 0 00		
12	Wages Payable				
13	Sales Tax Payable		6 1 0 0 00		
14	Unearned Tour Revenue		6 8 0 0 00		
15	Mortgage Payable		43 0 0 0 00		
16	Nicole Smith, Capital		124 5 9 0 00		
17	Nicole Smith, Drawing	33 0 0 0 00			
18	Income Summary				
19	Sales		122 0 0 0 00		
20	Sales Returns & Allowances	4 2 0 0 00			
21	Tour Revenue				
22	Purchases	38 0 0 0 00			
23	Purchases Returns & Allowances		2 6 0 0 00		
24	Purchases Discounts		1 4 0 0 00		
25	Freight-In	2 5 0 0 00			
26	Wages Expense	47 0 0 0 00			
27	Advertising Expense	4 8 0 0 00			
28	Supplies Expense				
29	Telephone Expense	1 8 0 0 00			
30	Utilities Expense	7 6 0 0 00			
31	Insurance Expense				
32	Depr. Expense—Building				
33	Depr. Expense—Store Equipment				
34	Miscellaneous Expense	7 9 0 00			
35		348 0 9 0 00	348 0 9 0 00		
36	Net Income				
37					
38					

Problem 1 (Continued)

OCEAN BEACH SALE SHOP

WORK SHEET (CONTINUED)

	ADJUSTED TRIAL BALANCE		INCOME STATEMENT		BALANCE SHEET		
	DEBIT	CREDIT	DEBIT	CREDIT	DEBIT	CREDIT	
1							1
2							2
3							3
4							4
5							5
6							6
7							7
8							8
9							9
10							10
11							11
12							12
13							13
14							14
15							15
16							16
17							17
18							18
19							19
20							20
21							21
22							22
23							23
24							24
25							25
26							26
27							27
28							28
29							29
30							30
31							31
32							32
33							33
34							34
35							35
36							36
37							37
38							38

Problem 2 (LO 4) JOURNALIZING ADJUSTING ENTRIES

From the work sheet prepared for Ocean Beach Sail Shop (Problem 1), record the adjusting entries in a general journal.

GENERAL JOURNAL PAGE

	DATE	DESCRIPTION	POST. REF.	DEBIT	CREDIT	
1						1
2						2
3						3
4						4
5						5
6						6
7						7
8						8
9						9
10						10
11						11
12						12
13						13
14						14
15						15
16						16
17						17
18						18
19						19
20						20
21						21
22						22
23						23
24						24
25						25
26						26
27						27
28						28
29						29
30						30

CHAPTER 15 APPENDIX
EXPENSE METHOD OF ACCOUNTING FOR PREPAID EXPENSES

LEARNING OBJECTIVES

The appendix to Chapter 15 covers the expense method of accounting for prepaid expenses.

Objective 1. Use the expense method of accounting for prepaid expenses.

Under the **expense method** of accounting for prepaid expenses, supplies and other prepaid items are entered as **expenses** when purchased. Under this method, we must adjust the accounts at the end of each accounting period to record the **unused** portions as assets.

Objective 2. Make the appropriate adjusting entries when the expense method is used for prepaid expenses.

To illustrate the appropriate entries, let's assume that the following entry was made on November 1, 20— when six months office rent was paid in advance.

```
20—
Nov. 1  Office Rent Expense          6,000
            Cash                                 6,000

        Paid 6 months office rent in advance
```

At the end of December, adjusting entries must be made to prepare year-end financial statements. The office has been used for two months. Thus, the office expense for the year should be $2,000 ($1,000 per month × 2). This leaves $4,000 that should be recorded as an asset, Prepaid Office Rent. The following adjusting entry is made for office rent:

```
20—             Adjusting Entry
Dec. 31   Prepaid Office Rent        4,000
              Office Rent Expense            4,000
```

As shown in the T accounts below, after this entry is posted, the office rent expense account has a debit balance of $2,000 ($6,000 – $4,000). This amount is reported on the income statement as an operating expense. The prepaid office rent account has a debit balance of $4,000. It is reported on the balance sheet as a current asset.

Prepaid Office Rent		Office Rent Expense	
Adj. Dec. 31 4,000		Nov. 1 6,000	Adj. Dec. 31 4,000
		Bal. Dec. 31 2,000	

EXERCISES

Exercise 1 (LO 2) EXPENSE METHOD OF ACCOUNTING FOR PREPAID EXPENSES

Dalton's Fishery paid $2,400 for a one-year insurance premium on its delivery van on October 1. The following entry was made.

20—
Oct. 1 Insurance Expense 2,400
 Cash 2,400
 Paid insurance premium

Prepare the adjusting entry on December 31.

GENERAL JOURNAL PAGE

	DATE		DESCRIPTION	POST. REF.	DEBIT	CREDIT	
1							1
2							2
3							3
4							4

Exercise 2 (LO 1/2) EXPENSE METHOD OF ACCOUNTING FOR PREPAID EXPENSES

On August 21, Georgio's Dry Goods purchased supplies costing $6,000 for cash. This amount was debited to the supplies expense account. At the end of the year, an inventory shows that supplies costing $1,000 still remain. Prepare the entries for the purchase and year-end adjustment.

GENERAL JOURNAL PAGE

	DATE		DESCRIPTION	POST. REF.	DEBIT	CREDIT	
1							1
2							2
3							3
4							4
5							5
6							6
7							7
8							8

CHAPTER 16
FINANCIAL STATEMENTS AND YEAR-END
ACCOUNTING FOR A MERCHANDISING BUSINESS

LEARNING OBJECTIVES

Chapter 16 covers the year-end accounting process as it applies to a merchandising business—the work sheet, closing and reversing entries, and the financial statements. In addition, financial ratios are introduced for the merchandising business.

Objective 1. Prepare a single-step and multiple-step income statement for a merchandising business.

The single-step form of income statement lists all revenue items and their total first, followed by all expense items and their total. The difference, which is either net income or net loss, is then calculated.

The **multiple-step income statement** contains the computation of net sales and cost of goods sold. It also reports gross profit, income from operations, and net income. The multiple-step income statement begins with gross sales less deductions to arrive at *net sales*. Then, cost of goods sold is calculated—beginning inventory plus net purchases and freight-in, less ending inventory. Net sales minus cost of goods sold results in *gross profit*. Then, operating expenses are subtracted, resulting in income from operations. Finally, other revenue and expenses not from operations (such as interest) are included to compute *net income*.

Objective 2. Prepare a statement of owner's equity.

The statement of owner's equity summarizes all changes in the owner's equity, including net income or loss and any additional investments or withdrawals by the owner.

Objective 3. Prepare a classified balance sheet.

The **classified balance sheet** distinguishes between *current* and long-term assets and liabilities. Current assets include cash and assets that will be converted to cash or consumed within the year or operating cycle (whichever is longer). Property, plant, and equipment are assets with long useful lives and much less liquidity. Current liabilities are generally due within a year and require the use of current assets. Long-term liabilities extend longer than one year.

Objective 4. Compute standard financial ratios.

Financial ratios help evaluate the current financial condition and profitability of a company. **Working capital** is current assets minus current liabilities; it tells whether a business has enough current assets to meet current operating debts.

The **current** and **quick ratios** measure a firm's ability to pay its current liabilities. The current ratio is calculated by dividing current assets by current liabilities. The desirable ratio is 2:1 ($2 of current assets for every $1 of current liabilities). **Quick assets** include cash and other very liquid assets—such as accounts receivable. The quick ratio is calculated by dividing quick assets by current liabilities. The desirable ratio is 1:1.

Return on owner's equity is calculated by dividing net income by average owner's equity (beginning equity plus ending equity, divided by 2). This rate of return can be compared with other years' rates and with other businesses' rates.

The **accounts receivable turnover** is determined by dividing net credit sales by average accounts receivable. This number is then divided into 365 days to determine the average number of days credit customers are taking to pay for their purchases.

Inventory turnover reveals how many times merchandise inventory "turns over" or was sold during the period. It is calculated by dividing cost of goods sold by the average inventory (beginning inventory plus ending inventory, divided by 2). This number is then divided into 365 days to determine the average number of days merchandise is held before it is sold.

Objective 5. Prepare closing entries for a merchandising business.

As with a professional service business, closing entries for a merchandising business are facilitated by the work sheet. All temporary accounts are closed—sales, contra-sales accounts, purchases, contra-purchases accounts, and expenses. The income summary account already contains two entries for merchandise inventory adjustments (debited to remove the old balance; credited to enter the new balance). First, all income statement accounts with credit balances are debited, crediting the income summary account. Then, all income statement accounts with debit balances are credited, debiting the income summary account. The balance in the income summary account is then transferred to the owner's equity account; a credit balance (indicating net income) is debited to close the income summary account. Finally, the drawing account is closed to the owner's capital account.

After the closing entries are posted, the post-closing trial balance is prepared. It reflects balances after the adjusting and closing entries are posted; only permanent accounts still have balances.

Objective 6. Prepare reversing entries.

Year-end adjusting entries may be reversed in the next accounting period if it helps to simplify entries made during the year. Except for the first year of operation, **reversing entries** are helpful whenever an adjusting entry has increased an asset or liability account from a zero balance. The reversing entries are made on the first day of the new accounting period.

REVIEW QUESTIONS

Instructions: Analyze each of the following items carefully before writing your answer in the column at the right.

Question	Answer
1. The primary purpose of the _____ is to serve as an aid in preparing the financial statements..	_____
2. The _____ form of income statement lists all revenue items first, followed by all expense items and their totals.	_____
3. Gross sales less sales returns and allowances is called _____	_____
4. _____ is the result of net sales less cost of goods sold.	_____
5. When operating expenses are subtracted from gross profit, the result is called _____. ...	_____

6. After other revenues are added and other expenses are subtracted, the final result is called _____. .. _____

7. The statement of owner's equity shows the net _____ or _____ in owner's equity for the period. ... _____

8. The report form of a(n) _____ balance sheet distinguishes between current and long-term assets and between current and long-term liabilities. ... _____

9. The speed with which assets can be converted to cash is called _____. ... _____

10. The difference between the cost of a long-term asset and the amount of accumulated depreciation is called _____ or book value. _____

11. _____ are obligations that are due within one year or during the normal operating cycle of the business, whichever is longer. _____

12. A(n) _____ is an example of a long-term liability based on a written agreement evidencing a debt secured by property. _____

13. The difference between current assets and current liabilities is called _____. ... _____

14. The _____ ratio is current assets divided by current liabilities. .. _____

15. _____ assets include cash and all other current assets that can be quickly converted to cash. .. _____

16. The _____ ratio is calculated by dividing net income by average owner's equity. ... _____

17. The _____ measures the number of times the accounts receivable were collected during the accounting period. _____

18. The _____ measures the number of times merchandise is sold during the accounting period. .. _____

19. All _____ owner's equity accounts are closed at the end of the accounting period. ... _____

20. The purpose of the _____ is to prove that the general ledger is in balance at the beginning of the new accounting period. _____

21. A reversing entry is the opposite of a(n) _____ entry. _____

22. Adjusting entries that increase an asset or liability account from a(n) _____ balance may be reversed. _____

EXERCISES AND PROBLEMS

Exercise 1 (LO 1) MULTIPLE-STEP INCOME STATEMENT

From the information below, prepare a multiple-step income statement for Morse Motor Company for the year ended December 31, 20—.

Merchandise Inventory, January 1, 20—	$ 28,900
Merchandise Inventory, December 31, 20—	29,600
Sales	118,300
Sales Returns and Allowances	1,280
Interest Revenue	1,900
Purchases	68,000
Purchases Returns and Allowances	2,140
Purchases Discounts	1,360
Freight-In	540
Wages Expense	21,000
Rent Expense	8,000
Supplies Expense	900
Telephone Expense	2,600
Utilities Expense	3,800
Insurance Expense	1,000
Depreciation Expense—Equipment	4,200
Miscellaneous Expense	300
Interest Expense	700

Exercise 1 (Concluded)

Exercise 2 (LO 2/3) PREPARE A STATEMENT OF OWNER'S EQUITY AND CLASSIFIED BALANCE SHEET

From the information below, prepare a statement of owner's equity and a report form of a classified balance sheet for Morse Motor Company as of December 31, 20—.

Cash	$19,200
Accounts Receivable	28,500
Merchandise Inventory	29,600
Supplies	1,800
Prepaid Insurance	1,100
Equipment (undepreciated cost)	30,000
Accum. Depr.—Equip.	2,000
Accounts Payable	18,000
Wages Payable	900
Sales Tax Payable	480
Mortgage Payable—Current Portion	1,200
Mortgage Payable	8,000
K.T. Morse, Capital, December 31, 20—	80,820
K.T. Morse, Capital, January 1, 20—	66,740
K.T. Morse, Withdrawals during year	8,000
Additional Investment by K.T. Morse, May 1, 20—	10,000

Exercise 2 (Concluded)

Exercise 3 (LO 4) FINANCIAL RATIOS

From the Morse Motor Company financial statements prepared in Exercises 1 and 2, prepare the following ratios: (Net credit sales for the year were $88,000; accounts receivable on January 1 was $24,200.)

1. Working capital

2. Current ratio

3. Quick ratio

4. Return on owner's equity

5. Accounts receivable turnover

6. Inventory turnover

Exercise 4 (LO 5/6/) CLOSING AND REVERSING ENTRIES

Based on the foregoing financial statements, prepare closing and reversing entries in the general journal on page 246. Adjusting entries included Insurance Expense, Depreciation Expense, Supplies Expense, and Accrued Wages of $280 (debit to Wages Expense and credit to Wages Payable).

Exercise 4 (Concluded)

GENERAL JOURNAL

	DATE	DESCRIPTION	POST. REF.	DEBIT	CREDIT	
1						1
2						2
3						3
4						4
5						5
6						6
7						7
8						8
9						9
10						10
11						11
12						12
13						13
14						14
15						15
16						16
17						17
18						18
19						19
20						20
21						21
22						22
23						23
24						24
25						25
26						26
27						27
28						28
29						29
30						30
31						31

Problem 1 (REVIEW) COMPLETE A WORK SHEET

Complete the work sheet for Clark's Clothing Store on pages 248–249 by using the adjustment information provided below.

(a) and (b) Merchandise Inventory, December 31, 20—, $12,400

(c) Unused supplies on December 31, 20—, $2,100

(d) Expired insurance on December 31, 20—, $500

(e) Depreciation expense on building for the year, $10,000

(f) Depreciation expense on fixtures for the year, $2,000

(g) Wages accrued (earned but not yet paid), $380

Problem 1 (Continued)

CLARK'S CLOTHING

WORK

FOR YEAR ENDED

	DESCRIPTION	TRIAL BALANCE		ADJUSTMENTS	
		DEBIT	CREDIT	DEBIT	CREDIT
1	Cash	16 4 0 0 00			
2	Accounts Receivable	7 1 0 0 00			
3	Merchandise Inventory	28 0 0 0 00			
4	Supplies	3 0 0 0 00			
5	Prepaid Insurance	2 0 0 0 00			
6	Land	10 0 0 0 00			
7	Building	100 0 0 0 00			
8	Accum. Depr.—Building		10 0 0 0 00		
9	Fixtures	33 0 0 0 00			
10	Accum. Depr.—Fixtures		6 0 0 0 00		
11	Accounts Payable		12 0 0 0 00		
12	Wages Payable				
13	Sales Tax Payable		1 2 0 0 00		
14	Mortgage Payable		58 0 0 0 00		
15	Alex Clark, Capital		73 3 0 0 00		
16	Alex Clark, Drawing	12 5 0 0 00			
17	Income Summary				
18	Sales		232 5 0 0 00		
19	Sales Returns & Allowances	2 5 0 0 00			
20	Purchases	68 5 0 0 00			
21	Purchases Returns & Allowances		1 2 0 0 00		
22	Purchases Discounts		1 3 0 0 00		
23	Freight-In	4 4 0 00			
24	Wages Expense	19 8 0 0 00			
25	Advertising Expense	7 0 0 00			
26	Rent Expense	82 6 6 0 00			
27	Supplies Expense				
28	Telephone Expense	2 1 0 0 00			
29	Utilities Expense	1 8 0 0 00			
30	Insurance Expense				
31	Depr. Expense—Building				
32	Depr. Expense—Fixtures				
33	Miscellaneous Expense	6 0 0 00			
34	Interest Expense	4 4 0 0 00			
35		395 5 0 0 00	395 5 0 0 00		
36	Net Income				
37					

Problem 1 (Concluded)

STORE

SHEET

DECEMBER 31, 20--

	ADJUSTED TRIAL BALANCE		INCOME STATEMENT		BALANCE SHEET		
	DEBIT	CREDIT	DEBIT	CREDIT	DEBIT	CREDIT	
1							1
2							2
3							3
4							4
5							5
6							6
7							7
8							8
9							9
10							10
11							11
12							12
13							13
14							14
15							15
16							16
17							17
18							18
19							19
20							20
21							21
22							22
23							23
24							24
25							25
26							26
27							27
28							28
29							29
30							30
31							31
32							32
33							33
34							34
35							35
36							36
37							37

Problem 2 (LO 5/6) ADJUSTING, CLOSING, AND REVERSING ENTRIES

From the work sheet prepared for Clark's Clothing Store (Problem 1), record the adjusting, closing, and reversing entries on the general journal page below and on page 251.

GENERAL JOURNAL PAGE

	DATE	DESCRIPTION	POST. REF.	DEBIT	CREDIT	
1						1
2						2
3						3
4						4
5						5
6						6
7						7
8						8
9						9
10						10
11						11
12						12
13						13
14						14
15						15
16						16
17						17
18						18
19						19
20						20
21						21
22						22
23						23
24						24
25						25
26						26
27						27
28						28
29						29

Problem 2 (Concluded)

GENERAL JOURNAL

PAGE

	DATE		DESCRIPTION	POST. REF.	DEBIT	CREDIT	
1							1
2							2
3							3
4							4
5							5
6							6
7							7
8							8
9							9
10							10
11							11
12							12
13							13
14							14
15							15
16							16
17							17
18							18
19							19
20							20
21							21
22							22
23							23
24							24
25							25
26							26
27							27
28							28
29							29
30							30
31							31

Problem 3 (LO 1/2/3) PREPARATION OF AN INCOME STATEMENT, STATEMENT OF OWNER'S EQUITY, AND BALANCE SHEET

Based on the work sheet for Clark's Clothing Store, prepare the following financial statements:

1. multiple-step income statement.
2. statement of owner's equity. (Alex made no additional investments during the year.)
3. classified balance sheet. (Mortgage payable—current portion is $1,000.)

Problem 3 (Concluded)

Problem 4 (LO 4) FINANCIAL RATIOS

For Clark's Clothing Store, calculate the following financial statement ratios. (Note: Net credit sales for the year were $115,000, and accounts receivable on January 1 was $8,400.)

1. Working capital

2. Current ratio

3. Quick ratio

4. Return on owner's equity

5. Accounts receivable turnover

6. Inventory turnover

WORKING
PAPERS

Name _____

Exercise 1-1A

1. _____ Owners

2. _____ Managers

3. _____ Creditors

4. _____ Governmental
agencies

a. whether the firm can pay its bills on time

b. detailed, up-to-date information to measure business
performance (and plan for future operations)

c. to determine taxes to be paid and whether other
regulations are met.

d. the firm's current financial condition

Exercise 1-2A

Order	Accounting Process	Definition
_____	Recording	_____

_____	Summarizing	_____

_____	Reporting	_____

_____	Analyzing	_____

_____	Interpreting	_____

_____	Classifying	_____

Exercise 1-1B

Users	Information
Owners (present and future):	_____

Managers:	_____

Creditors (present and future):	_____

Government agencies:	_____

Exercise 1-2B

Letter	Accounting Process
_____	Analyzing
_____	Recording
_____	Classifying
_____	Summarizing
_____	Reporting
_____	Interpreting

Definition

a. telling the results

b. looking at events that have taken place and thinking about how they affect the business

c. deciding the importance of the various reports

d. bringing together information to explain a result

e. sorting and grouping like items together

f. entering financial information into the accounting system

Exercise 2-1A

Item	Account	Classification
Money in bank	Cash	_____
Office supplies	Supplies	_____
Money owed	Accounts Payable	_____
Office chairs	Office Furniture	_____
Net worth of owner	John Smith, Capital	_____
Money withdrawn by owner	John Smith, Drawing	_____
Money owed us by customers	Accounts Receivable	_____

Exercise 2-2A

Assets	=	Liabilities	+	Owner's Equity
_____	=	$24,000	+	$10,000
$25,000	=	$18,000	+	_____
$40,000	=	_____	+	$15,000

Exercise 2-3A

	Assets	=	Liabilities	+	Owner's Equity
(a)	_____		_____		_____
Bal.	_____		_____		_____
(b)	_____		_____		_____
Bal.	_____		_____		_____
(c)	_____		_____		_____
	_____		_____		_____
Bal.	_____		_____		_____
(d)	_____		_____		_____
Bal.	_____		_____		_____

Exercise 2-4A

Assets	=	Liabilities	+	Owner's Equity							
				Capital	−	Drawing	+	Revenues	−	Expenses	Description

Bal.

(e)

Bal.

(f)

Bal.

(g)

Bal.

(h)

Bal.

(i)

Bal.

(j)

Bal.

(k)

Bal.

Exercise 2-5A

Account	Classification	Financial Statement
Cash	_____	_____
Rent Expense	_____	_____
Accounts Payable	_____	_____
Service Fees	_____	_____
Supplies	_____	_____
Wages Expense	_____	_____
Ramon Martinez, Drawing	_____	_____
Ramon Martinez, Capital	_____	_____
Prepaid Insurance	_____	_____
Accounts Receivable	_____	_____

Exercise 2-6A

Exercise 2-7A

Problem 2-1A

	Assets	=	Liabilities	+	Owner's Equity
1.	_____		_____		_____
2.	_____		_____		_____
3.	_____		_____		_____

Problem 2-2A: See page WP-7

Problem 2-3A

Problem 2-2A

	Assets					=	Liabilities	+	Owner's Equity									
	Cash	+	Accounts Receivable	+	Office Supplies	+	Prepaid Insurance	=	Accounts Payable	+	J. Pembroke, Capital	–	J. Pembroke, Drawing	+	Revenues	–	Expenses	Description
(a)																		
Bal.																		
(b)																		
Bal.																		
(c)																		
Bal.																		
(d)																		
Bal.																		
(e)																		
Bal.																		
(f)																		
Bal.																		
(g)																		
Bal.																		

Problem 2-4A

Problem 2-5A

Exercise 2-1B

Account	Classification
Cash	_____
Accounts Payable	_____
Supplies	_____
Bill Jones, Drawing	_____
Prepaid Insurance	_____
Accounts Receivable	_____
Bill Jones, Capital	_____

Exercise 2-2B

Assets	=	Liabilities	+	Owner's Equity
_____	=	$20,000	+	$5,000
$30,000	=	$15,000	+	_____
$20,000	=	_____	+	$10,000

Exercise 2-3B

	Assets	=	Liabilities	+	Owner's Equity
(a)	_____		_____		_____
Bal.	_____		_____		_____
(b)	_____		_____		_____
Bal.	_____		_____		_____
(c)	_____		_____		_____
	_____		_____		_____
Bal.	_____		_____		_____
(d)	_____		_____		_____
Bal.	_____		_____		_____

Exercise 2-4B

	Assets	=	Liabilities	+	Capital	–	Drawing	+	Revenues	–	Expenses	Description
								Owner's Equity				
Bal.												
(e)												
Bal.												
(f)												
Bal.												
(g)												
Bal.												
(h)												
Bal.												
(i)												
Bal.												
(j)												
Bal.												
(k)												
Bal.												

Exercise 2-5B

Account	Classification	Financial Statement
Cash	_____	_____
Rent Expense	_____	_____
Accounts Payable	_____	_____
Service Fees	_____	_____
Supplies	_____	_____
Wages Expense	_____	_____
Amanda Wong, Drawing	_____	_____
Amanda Wong, Capital	_____	_____
Prepaid Insurance	_____	_____
Accounts Receivable	_____	_____

Exercise 2-6B

Exercise 2-7B

Problem 2-1B

	Assets	=	Liabilities	+	Owner's Equity
1.					
2.					
3.					

Problem 2-2B: See page WP-13

Problem 2-3B

Problem 2-2B

	Assets							=	Liabilities	+	Owner's Equity							
	Cash	+	Accounts Receivable	+	Office Supplies	+	Prepaid Insurance	=	Accounts Payable	+	D. Segal, Capital	−	D. Segal, Drawing	+	Revenues	−	Expenses	Description

(a)
Bal.
(b)
Bal.
(c)
Bal.
(d)
Bal.
(e)
Bal.
(f)
Bal.
(g)
Bal.

Problem 2-4B

Problem 2-5B

Challenge Problem

Cash from customers												
Cash paid for wages												
Cash paid for rent												
Cash paid for utilities												
Cash paid for insurance												
Cash paid for supplies												
Cash paid for telephone												
Total cash paid for operating items												
Difference between cash received from customers and												
cash paid for goods and services												

Mastery Problem

1.

	Assets						=	Liabilities	+	Owner's Equity											
		Items Owned						Amts. Owed		Owner's Investment				Earnings							
Cash	+	Accts. Rec.	+	Sup-plies	+	Prepaid Ins.	+	Tools	+	Van	=	Accts. Payable	+	L. Vozniak, Capital	–	L. Vozniak, Drawing	+	Rev.	–	Exp.	Description

(a)

Bal.

(b)

Bal.

(c)

Bal.

(d)

Bal.

(e)

Bal.

(f)

Bal.

(g)

Bal.

(h)

Bal.

(i)

Bal.

(j)

Bal.

Continued on next page

Mastery Problem (Continued)

	Assets						=	Liabilities	+	Owner's Equity					
		Items Owned						Amts. Owed		Owner's Investment			Earnings		
	Cash	Accts. Rec.	Sup-plies	Prepaid Ins.	Tools	Van	=	Accts. Payable	+	L. Vozniak, Capital	L. Vozniak, Drawing	Rev.	Exp.	Description	
(k)															
Bal.															
(l)															
Bal.															
(m)															
Bal.															
(n)															
Bal.															
(o)															
Bal.															
(p)															
Bal.															

Mastery Problem (Continued)

3.

4.

Name _____

Mastery Problem (Concluded)

5.

Exercise 3-1A

Cash

Exercise 3-2A

a. The cash account is increased with a .. _____

b. The owner's capital account is increased with a.. _____

c. The delivery equipment account is increased with a _____

d. The cash account is decreased with a .. _____

e. The liability account Accounts Payable is increased with a _____

f. The revenue account Delivery Fees is increased with a.............................. _____

g. The asset account Accounts Receivable is increased with a _____

h. The rent expense account is increased with a .. _____

i. The owner's drawing account is increased with a _____

Exercise 3-3A

1. & 2.

Cash	Jim Arnold, Capital

Supplies	Utilities Expense

Exercise 3-4A

Account	Debit or Credit
1. Cash	_____
2. Wages Expense	_____
3. Accounts Payable	_____
4. Owner's Drawing	_____
5. Supplies	_____
6. Owner's Capital	_____
7. Equipment	_____

Exercise 3-5A: See page WP-23

Exercise 3-6A

Cash

Exercise 3-5A

	Assets		=		Liabilities		+		Owner's Equity	
Dr. +		Cr. –		Dr. –		Cr. +		Dr. –		Cr. +

Drawing

Dr. +	Cr. –

Expenses

Dr. +	Cr. –

Revenues

Dr. –	Cr. +

Exercise 3-7A

Assets		=	Liabilities		+	Owner's Equity								
Dr. +	Cr. −		Dr. −	Cr. +		Dr. −	Cr. +							

Drawing — Dr. + / Cr. −

Expenses — Dr. + / Cr. −

Revenues — Dr. − / Cr. +

Exercise 3-8A

ACCOUNT	DEBIT BALANCE	CREDIT BALANCE

Exercise 3-9A

ACCOUNT	DEBIT BALANCE	CREDIT BALANCE

Exercise 3-10A

Name _____

Exercise 3-11A

Exercise 3-12A

Problem 3-1A

1. & 2.

Owner's Equity

Dr.	Cr.
–	+

Revenues

Dr.	Cr.
–	+

Expenses

Dr.	Cr.
+	–

Drawing

Dr.	Cr.
+	–

=

Liabilities

Dr.	Cr.
–	+

+

Assets

Dr.	Cr.
+	–

Problem 3-1A (Concluded)

3.

ACCOUNT	DEBIT BALANCE	CREDIT BALANCE

Problem 3-2A

1.

(a) Total revenue for the month .. _____

(b) Total expenses for the month .. _____

(c) Net income for the month .. _____

2.

(a) Harold Long's original investment in the business .. _____

 + The net income for the month .. _____

 − Owner's drawing .. _____

 = Ending owner's equity ... _____

(b) End of month accounting equation:

Assets	=	Liabilities	+	Owner's Equity
_____		_____		_____

Problem 3-3A

1.

Name _____

Problem 3-3A (Concluded)

2.

3.

Exercise 3-1B

Accounts Payable

Exercise 3-2B

a. The asset account Prepaid Insurance is increased with a.................................. _____

b. The owner's drawing account is increased with a ... _____

c. The asset account Accounts Receivable is decreased with a _____

d. The liability account Accounts Payable is decreased with a.............................. _____

e. The owner's capital account is increased with a.. _____

f. The revenue account Professional Fees is increased with a............................. _____

g. The asset account Repair Expense is increased with a _____

h. The asset account Cash is decreased with a ... _____

i. The asset account Delivery Equipment is decreased with a.............................. _____

Exercise 3-3B

1. & 2.

Cash	Roberto Alvarez, Capital

Supplies	Utilities Expense

Exercise 3-4B

Account	Debit or Credit
1. Cash	_____
2. Rent Expense	_____
3. Notes Payable	_____
4. Owner's Drawing	_____
5. Accounts Receivable	_____
6. Owner's Capital	_____
7. Tools	_____

Exercise 3-5B: See page WP-34

Exercise 3-6B

Cash

Exercise 3-5B

Assets

Dr.	Cr.
+	−

=

Liabilities

Dr.	Cr.
−	+

+

Owner's Equity

Dr.	Cr.
−	+

Drawing

Dr.	Cr.
+	−

Expenses

Dr.	Cr.
+	−

Revenues

Dr.	Cr.
−	+

Name _____

Exercise 3-7B

Assets			=	Liabilities			+	Owner's Equity		
Dr. +		Cr. −		Dr. −		Cr. +		Dr. −		Cr. +

Drawing

Dr. +	Cr. −

Expenses

Dr. +	Cr. −

Revenues

Dr. −	Cr. +

Exercise 3-8B

ACCOUNT	DEBIT BALANCE	CREDIT BALANCE

Exercise 3-9B

ACCOUNT	DEBIT BALANCE	CREDIT BALANCE

Exercise 3-10B

Exercise 3-11B

Exercise 3-12B

Problem 3-1B

1. & 2.

Assets		=	Liabilities		+	Owner's Equity	
Dr. +	Cr. −		Dr. −	Cr. +		Dr. −	Cr. +

Owner's Equity subsections:

Drawing			Expenses			Revenues	
Dr. +	Cr. −		Dr. +	Cr. −		Dr. −	Cr. +

Problem 3-1B (Concluded)

3.

ACCOUNT	DEBIT BALANCE	CREDIT BALANCE	

Problem 3-2B

1.

(a) Total revenue for the month.. _____

(b) Total expenses for the month... _____

(c) Net income for the month.. _____

2.

(a) Sue Jantz's original investment in the business _____

 + The net income for the month .. _____

 – Owner's drawing .. _____

 = Ending owner's equity.. _____

(b) End of month accounting equation:

Assets	=	Liabilities	+	Owner's Equity
_____		_____		_____

Problem 3-3B

1.

Problem 3-3B (Concluded)

2.

Challenge Problem

1.

2.

Mastery Problem
1. & 2.

Name _____

Mastery Problem (Continued)

3.

ACCOUNT	DEBIT BALANCE	CREDIT BALANCE

4.

Mastery Problem (Concluded)

5.

6.

Exercise 4-1A

1. _____ Check stubs or check register

2. _____ Purchase invoice from suppliers (vendors)

3. _____ Sales tickets or invoices to customers

4. _____ Receipts or cash register tapes

a. A good or service has been sold.

b. Cash has been received by the business.

c. Cash has been paid by the business.

d. Goods or services have been purchased by the business.

Exercise 4-2A

Transaction	Debit	Credit
1. Invested cash in the business, $5,000.	_____	_____
2. Paid office rent, $500.	_____	_____
3. Purchased office supplies on account, $300.	_____	_____
4. Received cash for services rendered (fees), $400.	_____	_____
5. Paid cash on account, $50.	_____	_____
6. Rendered services on account, $300.	_____	_____
7. Received cash for an amount owed by a customer, $100.	_____	_____

Exercise 4-3A

Exercise 4-3A (Concluded)

Exercise 4-4A

<div align="center">JOURNAL</div>

PAGE 1

	DATE		DESCRIPTION	POST. REF.	DEBIT	CREDIT	
1							1
2							2
3							3
4							4
5							5
6							6
7							7
8							8
9							9
10							10
11							11
12							12
13							13
14							14
15							15
16							16
17							17
18							18
19							19
20							20
21							21
22							22
23							23
24							24

Exercise 4-5A (Continued)

ACCOUNT _____ ACCOUNT NO. _____

DATE	ITEM	POST. REF.	DEBIT	CREDIT	BALANCE	
					DEBIT	CREDIT

ACCOUNT _____ ACCOUNT NO. _____

DATE	ITEM	POST. REF.	DEBIT	CREDIT	BALANCE	
					DEBIT	CREDIT

ACCOUNT _____ ACCOUNT NO. _____

DATE	ITEM	POST. REF.	DEBIT	CREDIT	BALANCE	
					DEBIT	CREDIT

ACCOUNT _____ ACCOUNT NO. _____

DATE	ITEM	POST. REF.	DEBIT	CREDIT	BALANCE	
					DEBIT	CREDIT

Exercise 4-5A (Continued)

ACCOUNT ACCOUNT NO.

DATE	ITEM	POST. REF.	DEBIT	CREDIT	BALANCE DEBIT	CREDIT

ACCOUNT ACCOUNT NO.

DATE	ITEM	POST. REF.	DEBIT	CREDIT	BALANCE DEBIT	CREDIT

ACCOUNT ACCOUNT NO.

DATE	ITEM	POST. REF.	DEBIT	CREDIT	BALANCE DEBIT	CREDIT

ACCOUNT ACCOUNT NO.

DATE	ITEM	POST. REF.	DEBIT	CREDIT	BALANCE DEBIT	CREDIT

ACCOUNT ACCOUNT NO.

DATE	ITEM	POST. REF.	DEBIT	CREDIT	BALANCE DEBIT	CREDIT

Exercise 4-5A (Concluded)

ACCOUNT	ACCT. NO.	DEBIT BALANCE	CREDIT BALANCE

Exercise 4-6A

Exercise 4-6A (Concluded)

Name _____

Exercise 4-7A

Exercise 4-7A (Concluded)

Exercise 4-8A

<div align="center">

JOURNAL

</div>

PAGE

	DATE		DESCRIPTION	POST. REF.	DEBIT	CREDIT	
15	May	17	Office Equipment		4 0 0 00		15
16			Cash			4 0 0 00	16
17			Purchased copy paper				17
18							18
23		23	Cash	101	1 0 0 0 00		23
24			Service Fees	401		1 0 0 0 00	24
25			Received cash for services previously earned				25
26							26
27							27
28							28
29							29
30							30
31							31
32							32
33							33

Name _____

Problem 4-1A

2. (For 1. & 3., see page WP-60)

<div align="center">JOURNAL</div> PAGE 7

	DATE		DESCRIPTION	POST. REF.	DEBIT	CREDIT	
1							1
2							2
3							3
4							4
5							5
6							6
7							7
8							8
9							9
10							10
11							11
12							12
13							13
14							14
15							15
16							16
17							17
18							18
19							19
20							20
21							21
22							22
23							23
24							24
25							25
26							26
27							27
28							28
29							29
30							30
31							31
32							32
33							33
34							34

Problem 4-1A (Continued)

<div align="center">JOURNAL</div>

	DATE		DESCRIPTION	POST. REF.	DEBIT	CREDIT	
1							1
2							2
3							3
4							4
5							5
6							6
7							7
8							8
9							9
10							10
11							11
12							12
13							13
14							14
15							15
16							16
17							17
18							18
19							19
20							20
21							21
22							22
23							23
24							24
25							25
26							26
27							27
28							28
29							29
30							30
31							31
32							32
33							33
34							34
35							35
36							36

Problem 4-1A (Continued)

JOURNAL PAGE 9

	DATE		DESCRIPTION	POST. REF.	DEBIT	CREDIT	
1							1
2							2
3							3
4							4
5							5
6							6
7							7
8							8
9							9
10							10
11							11
12							12
13							13
14							14
15							15
16							16
17							17
18							18
19							19
20							20
21							21
22							22
23							23
24							24
25							25
26							26
27							27
28							28
29							29
30							30
31							31
32							32
33							33
34							34
35							35
36							36

Problem 4-1A (Continued)

1. & 3.

ACCOUNT Cash ACCOUNT NO. 101

DATE	ITEM	POST. REF.	DEBIT	CREDIT	BALANCE	
					DEBIT	CREDIT

Name _____

Problem 4-1A (Continued)

ACCOUNT Accounts Receivable ACCOUNT NO. 122

DATE	ITEM	POST. REF.	DEBIT	CREDIT	BALANCE DEBIT	BALANCE CREDIT

ACCOUNT Office Supplies ACCOUNT NO. 142

DATE	ITEM	POST. REF.	DEBIT	CREDIT	BALANCE DEBIT	BALANCE CREDIT

ACCOUNT Office Equipment ACCOUNT NO. 181

DATE	ITEM	POST. REF.	DEBIT	CREDIT	BALANCE DEBIT	BALANCE CREDIT

ACCOUNT Delivery Truck ACCOUNT NO. 185

DATE	ITEM	POST. REF.	DEBIT	CREDIT	BALANCE DEBIT	BALANCE CREDIT

Problem 4-1A (Continued)

ACCOUNT Accounts Payable ACCOUNT NO. 202

DATE	ITEM	POST. REF.	DEBIT	CREDIT	BALANCE	
					DEBIT	CREDIT

ACCOUNT Jim Andrews, Capital ACCOUNT NO. 311

DATE	ITEM	POST. REF.	DEBIT	CREDIT	BALANCE	
					DEBIT	CREDIT

ACCOUNT Jim Andrews, Drawing ACCOUNT NO. 312

DATE	ITEM	POST. REF.	DEBIT	CREDIT	BALANCE	
					DEBIT	CREDIT

ACCOUNT Delivery Fees ACCOUNT NO. 401

DATE	ITEM	POST. REF.	DEBIT	CREDIT	BALANCE	
					DEBIT	CREDIT

Problem 4-1A (Continued)

ACCOUNT Wages Expense ACCOUNT NO. 511

DATE	ITEM	POST. REF.	DEBIT	CREDIT	BALANCE DEBIT	CREDIT

ACCOUNT Advertising Expense ACCOUNT NO. 512

DATE	ITEM	POST. REF.	DEBIT	CREDIT	BALANCE DEBIT	CREDIT

ACCOUNT Rent Expense ACCOUNT NO. 521

DATE	ITEM	POST. REF.	DEBIT	CREDIT	BALANCE DEBIT	CREDIT

ACCOUNT Telephone Expense ACCOUNT NO. 525

DATE	ITEM	POST. REF.	DEBIT	CREDIT	BALANCE DEBIT	CREDIT

Problem 4-1A (Continued)

ACCOUNT Electricity Expense ACCOUNT NO. 533

DATE	ITEM	POST. REF.	DEBIT	CREDIT	BALANCE	
					DEBIT	CREDIT

ACCOUNT Charitable Contributions Expense ACCOUNT NO. 534

DATE	ITEM	POST. REF.	DEBIT	CREDIT	BALANCE	
					DEBIT	CREDIT

ACCOUNT Gas and Oil Expense ACCOUNT NO. 538

DATE	ITEM	POST. REF.	DEBIT	CREDIT	BALANCE	
					DEBIT	CREDIT

ACCOUNT Miscellaneous Expense ACCOUNT NO. 549

DATE	ITEM	POST. REF.	DEBIT	CREDIT	BALANCE	
					DEBIT	CREDIT

Problem 4-1A (Concluded)

4.

ACCOUNT	ACCT. NO.	DEBIT BALANCE	CREDIT BALANCE

Problem 4-2A
2. (For 1. & 3., see page WP-69)

JOURNAL PAGE 1

	DATE	DESCRIPTION	POST. REF.	DEBIT	CREDIT	
1						1
2						2
3						3
4						4
5						5
6						6
7						7
8						8
9						9
10						10
11						11
12						12
13						13
14						14
15						15
16						16
17						17
18						18
19						19
20						20
21						21
22						22
23						23
24						24
25						25
26						26
27						27
28						28
29						29
30						30
31						31
32						32
33						33
34						34
35						35
36						36

Problem 4-2A (Continued)

JOURNAL PAGE 2

	DATE		DESCRIPTION	POST. REF.	DEBIT	CREDIT	
1							1
2							2
3							3
4							4
5							5
6							6
7							7
8							8
9							9
10							10
11							11
12							12
13							13
14							14
15							15
16							16
17							17
18							18
19							19
20							20
21							21
22							22
23							23
24							24
25							25
26							26
27							27
28							28
29							29
30							30
31							31
32							32
33							33
34							34
35							35
36							36

Problem 4-2A (Continued)

JOURNAL PAGE 3

	DATE		DESCRIPTION	POST. REF.	DEBIT	CREDIT	
1							1
2							2
3							3
4							4
5							5
6							6
7							7
8							8
9							9
10							10
11							11
12							12
13							13
14							14
15							15
16							16
17							17
18							18
19							19
20							20
21							21
22							22
23							23
24							24
25							25
26							26
27							27
28							28
29							29
30							30
31							31
32							32
33							33
34							34
35							35
36							36

Problem 4-2A (Continued)

1. & 3.

GENERAL LEDGER

ACCOUNT Cash ACCOUNT NO. 101

DATE	ITEM	POST. REF.	DEBIT	CREDIT	BALANCE	
					DEBIT	CREDIT

ACCOUNT Office Supplies ACCOUNT NO. 142

DATE	ITEM	POST. REF.	DEBIT	CREDIT	BALANCE	
					DEBIT	CREDIT

Problem 4-2A (Continued)

ACCOUNT Office Equipment ACCOUNT NO. 181

DATE	ITEM	POST. REF.	DEBIT	CREDIT	BALANCE DEBIT	BALANCE CREDIT

ACCOUNT Accounts Payable ACCOUNT NO. 202

DATE	ITEM	POST. REF.	DEBIT	CREDIT	BALANCE DEBIT	BALANCE CREDIT

ACCOUNT Annette Creighton, Capital ACCOUNT NO. 311

DATE	ITEM	POST. REF.	DEBIT	CREDIT	BALANCE DEBIT	BALANCE CREDIT

ACCOUNT Annette Creighton, Drawing ACCOUNT NO. 312

DATE	ITEM	POST. REF.	DEBIT	CREDIT	BALANCE DEBIT	BALANCE CREDIT

Problem 4-2A (Continued)

ACCOUNT Consulting Fees ACCOUNT NO. 401

DATE	ITEM	POST. REF.	DEBIT	CREDIT	BALANCE	
					DEBIT	CREDIT

ACCOUNT Wages Expense ACCOUNT NO. 511

DATE	ITEM	POST. REF.	DEBIT	CREDIT	BALANCE	
					DEBIT	CREDIT

ACCOUNT Advertising Expense ACCOUNT NO. 512

DATE	ITEM	POST. REF.	DEBIT	CREDIT	BALANCE	
					DEBIT	CREDIT

ACCOUNT Rent Expense ACCOUNT NO. 521

DATE	ITEM	POST. REF.	DEBIT	CREDIT	BALANCE	
					DEBIT	CREDIT

Problem 4-2A (Continued)

ACCOUNT Telephone Expense ACCOUNT NO. 525

DATE	ITEM	POST. REF.	DEBIT	CREDIT	BALANCE DEBIT	BALANCE CREDIT

ACCOUNT Transportation Expense ACCOUNT NO. 526

DATE	ITEM	POST. REF.	DEBIT	CREDIT	BALANCE DEBIT	BALANCE CREDIT

ACCOUNT Utilities Expense ACCOUNT NO. 533

DATE	ITEM	POST. REF.	DEBIT	CREDIT	BALANCE DEBIT	BALANCE CREDIT

ACCOUNT Miscellaneous Expense ACCOUNT NO. 549

DATE	ITEM	POST. REF.	DEBIT	CREDIT	BALANCE DEBIT	BALANCE CREDIT

Problem 4-2A (Continued)

4.

ACCOUNT	ACCT. NO.	DEBIT BALANCE	CREDIT BALANCE

Problem 4-2A (Continued)

5.

Problem 4-2A (Concluded)

Problem 4-3A

| | | JOURNAL | | | PAGE | |

	DATE	DESCRIPTION	POST. REF.	DEBIT	CREDIT	
1						1
2						2
3						3
4						4
5						5
6						6
7						7
8						8
9						9
10						10
11						11
12						12
13						13
14						14
15						15
16						16
17						17
18						18
19						19
20						20

Exercise 4-1B

1. Cash register tape _____

2. Sales ticket (issued to customer) _____

3. Purchase invoice (received from supplier or vendor) _____

4. Check stub _____

Name _____

Exercise 4-2B

Transaction	Debit	Credit
1. Invested cash in the business, $1,000.	_____	_____
2. Performed services on account, $200.	_____	_____
3. Purchased office equipment on account, $500.	_____	_____
4. Received cash on account for services previously rendered, $200.	_____	_____
5. Made a payment on account, $100.	_____	_____

Exercise 4-3B

Total debits: _____

Total credits: _____

Exercise 4-4B

<div align="center">**JOURNAL**</div>

PAGE 1

	DATE		DESCRIPTION	POST. REF.	DEBIT	CREDIT	
1							1
2							2
3							3
4							4
5							5
6							6
7							7
8							8
9							9
10							10
11							11
12							12
13							13
14							14
15							15
16							16
17							17
18							18
19							19
20							20
21							21
22							22
23							23
24							24
25							25
26							26
27							27
28							28
29							29
30							30
31							31
32							32
33							33
34							34
35							35
36							36

Exercise 4-4B (Concluded)

JOURNAL PAGE 2

	DATE	DESCRIPTION	POST. REF.	DEBIT	CREDIT	
1						1
2						2
3						3
4						4
5						5
6						6
7						7
8						8
9						9
10						10
11						11
12						12
13						13
14						14
15						15
16						16
17						17
18						18
19						19
20						20
21						21
22						22
23						23
24						24
25						25
26						26
27						27
28						28
29						29
30						30
31						31
32						32
33						33
34						34
35						35
36						36

Exercise 4-5B

GENERAL LEDGER

ACCOUNT _____ ACCOUNT NO. _____

DATE	ITEM	POST. REF.	DEBIT	CREDIT	BALANCE	
					DEBIT	CREDIT

ACCOUNT _____ ACCOUNT NO. _____

DATE	ITEM	POST. REF.	DEBIT	CREDIT	BALANCE	
					DEBIT	CREDIT

ACCOUNT _____ ACCOUNT NO. _____

DATE	ITEM	POST. REF.	DEBIT	CREDIT	BALANCE	
					DEBIT	CREDIT

Exercise 4-5B (Continued)

ACCOUNT _____ ACCOUNT NO. _____

DATE	ITEM	POST. REF.	DEBIT	CREDIT	BALANCE	
					DEBIT	CREDIT

ACCOUNT _____ ACCOUNT NO. _____

DATE	ITEM	POST. REF.	DEBIT	CREDIT	BALANCE	
					DEBIT	CREDIT

ACCOUNT _____ ACCOUNT NO. _____

DATE	ITEM	POST. REF.	DEBIT	CREDIT	BALANCE	
					DEBIT	CREDIT

ACCOUNT _____ ACCOUNT NO. _____

DATE	ITEM	POST. REF.	DEBIT	CREDIT	BALANCE	
					DEBIT	CREDIT

Exercise 4-5B (Continued)

ACCOUNT _____ ACCOUNT NO. _____

DATE	ITEM	POST. REF.	DEBIT	CREDIT	BALANCE	
					DEBIT	CREDIT

ACCOUNT _____ ACCOUNT NO. _____

DATE	ITEM	POST. REF.	DEBIT	CREDIT	BALANCE	
					DEBIT	CREDIT

ACCOUNT _____ ACCOUNT NO. _____

DATE	ITEM	POST. REF.	DEBIT	CREDIT	BALANCE	
					DEBIT	CREDIT

ACCOUNT _____ ACCOUNT NO. _____

DATE	ITEM	POST. REF.	DEBIT	CREDIT	BALANCE	
					DEBIT	CREDIT

ACCOUNT _____ ACCOUNT NO. _____

DATE	ITEM	POST. REF.	DEBIT	CREDIT	BALANCE	
					DEBIT	CREDIT

Exercise 4-5B (Concluded)

ACCOUNT	ACCT. NO.	DEBIT BALANCE	CREDIT BALANCE

Exercise 4-6B

Exercise 4-6B (Concluded)

Exercise 4-7B

Exercise 4-7B (Concluded)

Exercise 4-8B

<div align="center">JOURNAL</div>

PAGE

	DATE		DESCRIPTION	POST. REF.	DEBIT	CREDIT	
15	Apr.	6	Office Supplies		5 3 0 00		15
16			Cash			5 3 0 00	16
17			Purchased office equipment				17
18							18
23		21	Cash	101	3 0 0 00		23
24			Service Fees	401		3 0 0 00	24
25			Revenue earned from services.				25
26							26
27							27
28							28
29							29
30							30
31							31
32							32
33							33

Problem 4-1B

2. (For 1. & 3., see page WP-90)

JOURNAL PAGE 7

	DATE		DESCRIPTION	POST. REF.	DEBIT	CREDIT	
1							1
2							2
3							3
4							4
5							5
6							6
7							7
8							8
9							9
10							10
11							11
12							12
13							13
14							14
15							15
16							16
17							17
18							18
19							19
20							20
21							21
22							22
23							23
24							24
25							25
26							26
27							27
28							28
29							29
30							30
31							31
32							32
33							33
34							34

Problem 4-1B (Continued)

	DATE		DESCRIPTION	POST. REF.	DEBIT	CREDIT	
1							1
2							2
3							3
4							4
5							5
6							6
7							7
8							8
9							9
10							10
11							11
12							12
13							13
14							14
15							15
16							16
17							17
18							18
19							19
20							20
21							21
22							22
23							23
24							24
25							25
26							26
27							27
28							28
29							29
30							30
31							31
32							32
33							33
34							34
35							35
36							36

Problem 4-1B (Continued)

<div align="center">JOURNAL</div>

PAGE 9

	DATE		DESCRIPTION	POST. REF.	DEBIT	CREDIT	
1							1
2							2
3							3
4							4
5							5
6							6
7							7
8							8
9							9
10							10
11							11
12							12
13							13
14							14
15							15
16							16
17							17
18							0
19							19
20							20
21							21
22							22
23							23
24							24
25							25
26							26
27							27
28							28
29							29
30							30
31							31
32							32
33							33
34							34
35							35
36							36

Problem 4-1B (Continued)

1. & 3.

GENERAL LEDGER

ACCOUNT Cash ACCOUNT NO. 101

DATE	ITEM	POST. REF.	DEBIT	CREDIT	BALANCE	
					DEBIT	CREDIT

ACCOUNT Accounts Receivable ACCOUNT NO. 122

DATE	ITEM	POST. REF.	DEBIT	CREDIT	BALANCE	
					DEBIT	CREDIT

Problem 4-1B (Continued)

ACCOUNT Tailoring Supplies ACCOUNT NO. 141

DATE	ITEM	POST. REF.	DEBIT	CREDIT	BALANCE DEBIT	BALANCE CREDIT

ACCOUNT Tailoring Equipment ACCOUNT NO. 183

DATE	ITEM	POST. REF.	DEBIT	CREDIT	BALANCE DEBIT	BALANCE CREDIT

ACCOUNT Accounts Payable ACCOUNT NO. 202

DATE	ITEM	POST. REF.	DEBIT	CREDIT	BALANCE DEBIT	BALANCE CREDIT

ACCOUNT Ann Tailor , Capital ACCOUNT NO. 311

DATE	ITEM	POST. REF.	DEBIT	CREDIT	BALANCE DEBIT	BALANCE CREDIT

Problem 4-1B (Continued)

ACCOUNT Ann Tailor, Drawing ACCOUNT NO. 312

DATE	ITEM	POST. REF.	DEBIT	CREDIT	BALANCE	
					DEBIT	CREDIT

ACCOUNT Tailoring Fees ACCOUNT NO. 401

DATE	ITEM	POST. REF.	DEBIT	CREDIT	BALANCE	
					DEBIT	CREDIT

ACCOUNT Wages Expense ACCOUNT NO. 511

DATE	ITEM	POST. REF.	DEBIT	CREDIT	BALANCE	
					DEBIT	CREDIT

ACCOUNT Advertising Expense ACCOUNT NO. 512

DATE	ITEM	POST. REF.	DEBIT	CREDIT	BALANCE	
					DEBIT	CREDIT

Problem 4-1B (Continued)

ACCOUNT Rent Expense ACCOUNT NO. 521

DATE	ITEM	POST. REF.	DEBIT	CREDIT	BALANCE DEBIT	BALANCE CREDIT

ACCOUNT Telephone Expense ACCOUNT NO. 525

DATE	ITEM	POST. REF.	DEBIT	CREDIT	BALANCE DEBIT	BALANCE CREDIT

ACCOUNT Electricity Expense ACCOUNT NO. 533

DATE	ITEM	POST. REF.	DEBIT	CREDIT	BALANCE DEBIT	BALANCE CREDIT

ACCOUNT Miscellaneous Expense ACCOUNT NO. 549

DATE	ITEM	POST. REF.	DEBIT	CREDIT	BALANCE DEBIT	BALANCE CREDIT

Problem 4-1B (Concluded)
4.

ACCOUNT	ACCT. NO.	DEBIT BALANCE	CREDIT BALANCE

Problem 4-2B

1.

JOURNAL PAGE 1

	DATE		DESCRIPTION	POST. REF.	DEBIT	CREDIT	
1							1
2							2
3							3
4							4
5							5
6							6
7							7
8							8
9							9
10							10
11							11
12							12
13							13
14							14
15							15
16							16
17							17
18							18
19							19
20							20
21							21
22							22
23							23
24							24
25							25
26							26
27							27
28							28
29							29
30							30
31							31
32							32
33							33
34							34
35							35
36							36

Problem 4-2B (Continued)

JOURNAL

	DATE		DESCRIPTION	POST. REF.	DEBIT	CREDIT	
1							1
2							2
3							3
4							4
5							5
6							6
7							7
8							8
9							9
10							10
11							11
12							12
13							13
14							14
15							15
16							16
17							17
18							18
19							19
20							20
21							21
22							22
23							23
24							24
25							25
26							26
27							27
28							28
29							29
30							30
31							31
32							32
33							33
34							34
35							35
36							36

Problem 4-2B (Continued)

JOURNAL

	DATE		DESCRIPTION	POST. REF.	DEBIT	CREDIT	
1							1
2							2
3							3
4							4
5							5
6							6
7							7
8							8
9							9
10							10
11							11
12							12
13							13
14							14
15							15
16							16
17							17
18							18
19							19
20							20
21							21
22							22
23							23
24							24
25							25
26							26
27							27
28							28
29							29
30							30
31							31
32							32
33							33
34							34
35							35
36							36

Problem 4-2B (Continued)

2.

GENERAL LEDGER

ACCOUNT Cash ACCOUNT NO. 101

DATE	ITEM	POST. REF.	DEBIT	CREDIT	BALANCE	
					DEBIT	CREDIT

ACCOUNT Accounts Receivable ACCOUNT NO. 122

DATE	ITEM	POST. REF.	DEBIT	CREDIT	BALANCE	
					DEBIT	CREDIT

Problem 4-2B (Continued)

ACCOUNT Office Supplies ACCOUNT NO. 142

DATE	ITEM	POST. REF.	DEBIT	CREDIT	BALANCE	
					DEBIT	CREDIT

ACCOUNT Office Equipment ACCOUNT NO. 181

DATE	ITEM	POST. REF.	DEBIT	CREDIT	BALANCE	
					DEBIT	CREDIT

ACCOUNT Accounts Payable ACCOUNT NO. 202

DATE	ITEM	POST. REF.	DEBIT	CREDIT	BALANCE	
					DEBIT	CREDIT

ACCOUNT Benito Mendez, Capital ACCOUNT NO. 311

DATE	ITEM	POST. REF.	DEBIT	CREDIT	BALANCE	
					DEBIT	CREDIT

Problem 4-2B (Continued)

ACCOUNT Benito Mendez, Drawing ACCOUNT NO. 312

DATE	ITEM	POST. REF.	DEBIT	CREDIT	BALANCE DEBIT	CREDIT

ACCOUNT Appraisal Fees ACCOUNT NO. 401

DATE	ITEM	POST. REF.	DEBIT	CREDIT	BALANCE DEBIT	CREDIT

ACCOUNT Wages Expense ACCOUNT NO. 511

DATE	ITEM	POST. REF.	DEBIT	CREDIT	BALANCE DEBIT	CREDIT

ACCOUNT Advertising Expense ACCOUNT NO. 512

DATE	ITEM	POST. REF.	DEBIT	CREDIT	BALANCE DEBIT	CREDIT

Problem 4-2B (Continued)

ACCOUNT Rent Expense ACCOUNT NO. 521

DATE	ITEM	POST. REF.	DEBIT	CREDIT	BALANCE DEBIT	CREDIT

ACCOUNT Telephone Expense ACCOUNT NO. 525

DATE	ITEM	POST. REF.	DEBIT	CREDIT	BALANCE DEBIT	CREDIT

ACCOUNT Transportation Expense ACCOUNT NO 526

DATE	ITEM	POST. REF.	DEBIT	CREDIT	BALANCE DEBIT	CREDIT

ACCOUNT Electricity Expense ACCOUNT NO. 533

DATE	ITEM	POST. REF.	DEBIT	CREDIT	BALANCE DEBIT	CREDIT

ACCOUNT Miscellaneous Expense ACCOUNT NO. 549

DATE	ITEM	POST. REF.	DEBIT	CREDIT	BALANCE DEBIT	CREDIT

Problem 4-2B (Continued)

3.

ACCOUNT	ACCT. NO.	DEBIT BALANCE	CREDIT BALANCE

Problem 4-2B (Continued)

Problem 4-2B (Concluded)

Problem 4-3B

JOURNAL

PAGE

	DATE	DESCRIPTION	POST. REF.	DEBIT	CREDIT	
1						1
2						2
3						3
4						4
5						5
6						6
7						7
8						8
9						9
10						10
11						11
12						12
13						13
14						14
15						15
16						16
17						17
18						18
19						19
20						20
21						21
22						22
23						23

Challenge Problem

Fred Phaler Consulting

Trial Balance

June 30, 20--

ACCOUNT	ACCT. NO.	DEBIT BALANCE	CREDIT BALANCE
Cash	101		
Accounts Receivable	122		
Office Supplies	142		
Accounts Payable	202		
Wages Payable	219		
Fred Phaler, Capital	311		
Fred Phaler, Drawing	312		
Professional Fees	401		
Wages Expense	511		
Rent Expense	521		
Telephone Expense	525		
Automobile Expense	526		
Utilities Expense	533		

Mastery Problem

1.

<div align="center">JOURNAL</div>

	DATE		DESCRIPTION	POST. REF.	DEBIT	CREDIT	
1							1
2							2
3							3
4							4
5							5
6							6
7							7
8							8
9							9
10							10
11							11
12							12
13							13
14							14
15							15
16							16
17							17
18							18
19							19
20							20
21							21
22							22
23							23
24							24
25							25
26							26
27							27
28							28
29							29
30							30
31							31
32							32
33							33
34							34
35							35

Mastery Problem (Continued)

<div align="center">

JOURNAL

</div>

PAGE 2

	DATE		DESCRIPTION	POST. REF.	DEBIT	CREDIT	
1							1
2							2
3							3
4							4
5							5
6							6
7							7
8							8
9							9
10							10
11							11
12							12
13							13
14							14
15							15
16							16
17							17
18							18
19							19
20							20
21							21
22							22
23							23
24							24
25							25
26							26
27							27
28							28
29							29
30							30
31							31
32							32
33							33
34							34
35							35

Mastery Problem (Continued)

JOURNAL

	DATE		DESCRIPTION	POST. REF.	DEBIT	CREDIT	
1							1
2							2
3							3
4							4
5							5
6							6
7							7
8							8
9							9
10							10
11							11
12							12
13							13
14							14
15							15
16							16
17							17
18							18
19							19
20							20
21							21
22							22
23							23
24							24
25							25
26							26
27							27
28							28
29							29
30							30
31							31
32							32
33							33
34							34
35							35

Name _____

Mastery Problem (Continued)
2.

ACCOUNT Cash ACCOUNT NO. 101

DATE	ITEM	POST. REF.	DEBIT	CREDIT	BALANCE DEBIT	BALANCE CREDIT

ACCOUNT Office Supplies ACCOUNT NO. 142

DATE	ITEM	POST. REF.	DEBIT	CREDIT	BALANCE DEBIT	BALANCE CREDIT

ACCOUNT Athletic Equipment ACCOUNT NO. 183

DATE	ITEM	POST. REF.	DEBIT	CREDIT	BALANCE DEBIT	BALANCE CREDIT

Mastery Problem (Continued)

ACCOUNT Basketball Facilities ACCOUNT NO. 184

DATE	ITEM	POST. REF.	DEBIT	CREDIT	BALANCE	
					DEBIT	CREDIT

ACCOUNT Accounts Payable ACCOUNT NO. 202

DATE	ITEM	POST. REF.	DEBIT	CREDIT	BALANCE	
					DEBIT	CREDIT

ACCOUNT Barry Bird, Capital ACCOUNT NO. 311

DATE	ITEM	POST. REF.	DEBIT	CREDIT	BALANCE	
					DEBIT	CREDIT

ACCOUNT Barry Bird, Drawing ACCOUNT NO. 312

DATE	ITEM	POST. REF.	DEBIT	CREDIT	BALANCE	
					DEBIT	CREDIT

Name _____

Mastery Problem (Concluded)

ACCOUNT	ACCT. NO.	DEBIT BALANCE	CREDIT BALANCE

Exercise 5-1A

(Balance Sheet)
Supplies

(Income Statement)
Supplies Expense

JOURNAL PAGE

	DATE	DESCRIPTION	POST. REF.	DEBIT	CREDIT	
1						1
2						2
3						3
4						4
5						5
6						6

Exercise 5-2A

(Balance Sheet)
Prepaid Insurance

(Income Statement)
Insurance Expense

JOURNAL PAGE

	DATE	DESCRIPTION	POST. REF.	DEBIT	CREDIT	
1						1
2						2
3						3
4						4
5						5
6						6

Exercise 5-3A

(Income Statement)	(Balance Sheet)
Wages Expense	Wages Payable

JOURNAL PAGE

	DATE	DESCRIPTION	POST. REF.	DEBIT	CREDIT	
1						1
2						2
3						3
4						4

Exercise 5-4A

_____ × _____ = _____

(Income Statement)	(Balance Sheet)
Depr. Expense—Delivery Equip.	Accum. Depr.—Delivery Equip.

JOURNAL PAGE

	DATE	DESCRIPTION	POST. REF.	DEBIT	CREDIT	
1						1
2						2
3						3
4						4

Exercise 5-5A

Exercise 5-6A

1.

(Balance Sheet) Supplies	(Income Statement) Supplies Expense

2.

(Balance Sheet) Supplies	(Income Statement) Supplies Expense

Exercise 5-7A

1.

(Balance Sheet) Prepaid Insurance	(Income Statement) Insurance Expense

2.

(Balance Sheet) Prepaid Insurance	(Income Statement) Insurance Expense

Exercise 5-8A

Jim Jacob's Furniture Repair

Work Sheet (Partial)

For Year Ended December 31, 20--

	DESCRIPTION	TRIAL BALANCE DEBIT	TRIAL BALANCE CREDIT	ADJUSTMENTS DEBIT	ADJUSTMENTS CREDIT	ADJUSTED TRIAL BALANCE DEBIT	ADJUSTED TRIAL BALANCE CREDIT	
1	Cash	1 0 0 0 00				1 0 0 0 00		1
2	Supplies	8 5 0 00				2 0 0 00		2
3	Prepaid Insurance	9 0 0 00				3 0 0 00		3
4	Delivery Equipment	3 6 0 0 00				3 6 0 0 00		4
5	Accum. Depr.—Delivery Equip.		6 0 0 00				8 0 0 00	5
6	Wages Payable						1 0 0 00	6
7	Jim Jacob, Capital		4 0 0 0 00				4 0 0 0 00	7
8	Repair Fees		1 6 5 0 00				1 6 5 0 00	8
9	Wages Expense	6 0 0 0 00				7 0 0 0 00		9
10	Advertising Expense	2 0 0 00				2 0 0 00		10
11	Supplies Expense					6 5 0 00		11
12	Insurance Expense					6 0 0 00		12
13	Depr. Exp.—Delivery Equip.					2 0 0 00		13
14		6 2 5 0 00	6 2 5 0 00			6 5 5 0 00	6 5 5 0 00	14
15								15
16								16
17								17
18								18
19								19
20								20
21								21
22								22
23								23
24								24
25								25

Exercise 5-9A

JOURNAL PAGE ____

	DATE		DESCRIPTION	POST. REF.	DEBIT	CREDIT	
1							1
2							2
3							3
4							4
5							5
6							6
7							7
8							8
9							9
10							10
11							11
12							12
13							13
14							14
15							15

Exercise 5-10A

	Income Statement Debit	Income Statement Credit	Balance Sheet Debit	Balance Sheet Credit
Cash				
Accounts Receivable				
Supplies				
Prepaid Insurance				
Delivery Equipment				
Accum. Depr.—Del. Equip.				
Accounts Payable				
Wages Payable				
Owner, Capital				
Owner, Drawing				
Delivery Fees				
Wages Expense				
Rent Expense				

Exercise 5-10A (Continued)

	Income Statement		Balance Sheet	
	Debit	**Credit**	**Debit**	**Credit**
Supplies Expense	_____	_____	_____	_____
Insurance Expense	_____	_____	_____	_____
Depr. Exp.—Del. Equip.	_____	_____	_____	_____

Exercise 5-11A

	Income Statement		Balance Sheet	
	Debit	**Credit**	**Debit**	**Credit**
Net Income	_____	_____	_____	_____
Net Loss	_____	_____	_____	_____

Exercise 5-12A

JOURNAL PAGE 9

	DATE		DESCRIPTION	POST. REF.	DEBIT	CREDIT	
1	20-- Dec.		Adjusting Entries				1
2		31	Supplies Expense		8 5 00		2
3			Supplies			8 5 00	3
4							4
5		31	Wages Expense		2 2 0 00		5
6			Wages Payable			2 2 0 00	6
7							7
8							8
9							9
10							10
11							11
12							12
13							13
14							14
15							15
16							16
17							17
18							18

Exercise 5-12A (Concluded)

GENERAL LEDGER

ACCOUNT Supplies ACCOUNT NO. 141

DATE		ITEM	POST. REF.	DEBIT	CREDIT	BALANCE	
						DEBIT	CREDIT
20-- Dec.	1	Balance	✓			1 5 0 00	
	15		J8	5 0 00		2 0 0 00	

ACCOUNT Wages Payable ACCOUNT NO. 219

DATE		ITEM	POST. REF.	DEBIT	CREDIT	BALANCE	
						DEBIT	CREDIT

ACCOUNT Wages Expense ACCOUNT NO. 511

DATE		ITEM	POST. REF.	DEBIT	CREDIT	BALANCE	
						DEBIT	CREDIT
20-- Dec.	1	Balance	✓			9 0 0 00	
	15		J8	3 0 0 00		1 2 0 0 00	

ACCOUNT Supplies Expense ACCOUNT NO. 523

DATE		ITEM	POST. REF.	DEBIT	CREDIT	BALANCE	
						DEBIT	CREDIT

Problem 5-1A

Mason's Delivery

Work

For Month Ended

	ACCOUNT TITLE	TRIAL BALANCE		ADJUSTMENTS	
		DEBIT	CREDIT	DEBIT	CREDIT
1	Cash	1 6 0 0 00			
2	Accounts Receivable	9 4 0 00			
3	Supplies	6 3 5 00			
4	Prepaid Insurance	1 2 0 0 00			
5	Delivery Equipment	6 4 0 0 00			
6	Accum. Depr.—Delivery Equip.				
7	Accounts Payable		1 2 2 0 00		
8	Wages Payable				
9	Jill Mason, Capital		8 0 0 0 00		
10	Jill Mason, Drawing	1 4 0 0 00			
11	Delivery Fees		6 2 0 0 00		
12	Wages Expense	1 5 0 0 00			
13	Advertising Expense	4 6 0 00			
14	Rent Expense	8 0 0 00			
15	Supplies Expense				
16	Telephone Expense	1 6 5 00			
17	Insurance Expense				
18	Repair Expense	2 3 0 00			
19	Oil & Gas Expense	9 0 00			
20	Depr. Exp.—Delivery Equip.				
21		15 4 2 0 00	15 4 2 0 00		
22					
23					
24					
25					
26					
27					
28					
29					
30					
31					
32					
33					

Problem 5-1A (Concluded)

Service _____

Sheet _____

September 30, 20-- _____

	ADJUSTED TRIAL BALANCE		INCOME STATEMENT		BALANCE SHEET		
	DEBIT	CREDIT	DEBIT	CREDIT	DEBIT	CREDIT	
							1
							2
							3
							4
							5
							6
							7
							8
							9
							10
							11
							12
							13
							14
							15
							16
							17
							18
							19
							20
							21
							22
							23
							24
							25
							26
							27
							28
							29
							30
							31
							32
							33

Problem 5-2A

	ACCOUNT TITLE	TRIAL BALANCE										ADJUSTMENTS								
		DEBIT					CREDIT						DEBIT				CREDIT			
1	Cash		9	8	0	00														
2	Accounts Receivable		5	9	0	00														
3	Supplies		5	7	5	00														
4	Prepaid Insurance	1	3	0	0	00														
5	Van	5	8	0	0	00														
6	Accumulated Depreciation—Van																			
7	Accounts Payable							9	6	0	00									
8	Wages Payable																			
9	Jason Armstrong, Capital						10	0	0	0	00									
10	Jason Armstrong, Drawing		6	0	0	00														
11	Escort Fees						2	6	0	0	00									
12	Wages Expense	1	8	0	0	00														
13	Advertising Expense		3	8	0	00														
14	Rent Expense		9	0	0	00														
15	Supplies Expense																			
16	Telephone Expense		2	2	0	00														
17	Insurance Expense																			
18	Repair Expense		3	1	5	00														
19	Oil and Gas Expense		1	0	0	00														
20	Depreciation Expense—Van																			
21		13	5	6	0	00	13	5	6	0	00									
22																				
23																				
24																				
25																				
26																				
27																				
28																				
29																				
30																				
31																				
32																				
33																				

Problem 5-2A (Concluded)

Service _____

Sheet _____

November 30, 20--

	ADJUSTED TRIAL BALANCE		INCOME STATEMENT		BALANCE SHEET		
	DEBIT	CREDIT	DEBIT	CREDIT	DEBIT	CREDIT	
							1
							2
							3
							4
							5
							6
							7
							8
							9
							10
							11
							12
							13
							14
							15
							16
							17
							18
							19
							20
							21
							22
							23
							24
							25
							26
							27
							28
							29
							30
							31
							32
							33

Problem 5-3A

<div style="text-align:center">**JOURNAL**</div>

PAGE 5

	DATE		DESCRIPTION	POST. REF.	DEBIT	CREDIT	
1							1
2							2
3							3
4							4
5							5
6							6
7							7
8							8
9							9
10							10
11							11
12							12
13							13
14							14
15							15
16							16
17							17
18							18
19							19
20							20
21							21
22							22
23							23
24							24
25							25
26							26
27							27
28							28
29							29
30							30
31							31
32							32
33							33
34							34
35							35
36							36

Problem 5-3A (Continued)

GENERAL LEDGER

ACCOUNT Supplies ACCOUNT NO. 141

DATE		ITEM	POST. REF.	DEBIT	CREDIT	BALANCE	
						DEBIT	CREDIT
20-- Nov.	1		J1	4 7 5 00		4 7 5 00	
	15		J4	1 0 0 00		5 7 5 00	

ACCOUNT Prepaid Insurance ACCOUNT NO. 145

DATE		ITEM	POST. REF.	DEBIT	CREDIT	BALANCE	
						DEBIT	CREDIT
20-- Nov.	1		J1	1 3 0 0 00		1 3 0 0 00	

ACCOUNT Accumulated Depreciation—Van ACCOUNT NO. 185.1

DATE		ITEM	POST. REF.	DEBIT	CREDIT	BALANCE	
						DEBIT	CREDIT

ACCOUNT Wages Payable ACCOUNT NO. 219

DATE		ITEM	POST. REF.	DEBIT	CREDIT	BALANCE	
						DEBIT	CREDIT

Problem 5-3A (Concluded)

GENERAL LEDGER

ACCOUNT Wages Expense ACCOUNT NO. 511

DATE		ITEM	POST. REF.	DEBIT	CREDIT	BALANCE	
						DEBIT	CREDIT
20-- Nov.	15		J3	9 0 0 00		9 0 0 00	
	26		J4	9 0 0 00		1 8 0 0 00	

ACCOUNT Supplies Expense ACCOUNT NO. 523

DATE	ITEM	POST. REF.	DEBIT	CREDIT	BALANCE	
					DEBIT	CREDIT

ACCOUNT Insurance Expense ACCOUNT NO. 535

DATE	ITEM	POST. REF.	DEBIT	CREDIT	BALANCE	
					DEBIT	CREDIT

ACCOUNT Depreciation Expense—Van ACCOUNT NO. 541

DATE	ITEM	POST. REF.	DEBIT	CREDIT	BALANCE	
					DEBIT	CREDIT

Name _____

Problem 5-4A: See pages 130 and 131

Exercise 5-1B

(Balance Sheet)
Supplies

(Income Statement)
Supplies Expense

JOURNAL PAGE

	DATE	DESCRIPTION	POST. REF.	DEBIT	CREDIT	
1						1
2						2
3						3
4						4
5						5
6						6

Exercise 5-2B

(Balance Sheet)
Prepaid Insurance

(Income Statement)
Insurance Expense

JOURNAL PAGE

	DATE	DESCRIPTION	POST. REF.	DEBIT	CREDIT	
1						1
2						2
3						3
4						4
5						5
6						6

Problem 5-4A

Joyce Lee's

Work

For Month Ended

	ACCOUNT TITLE	TRIAL BALANCE										ADJUSTMENTS										
		DEBIT					CREDIT					DEBIT					CREDIT					
1	Cash	1	7	2	5	00																
2	Accounts Receivable		9	6	0	00																
3	Supplies		5	2	5	00																
4	Prepaid Insurance		9	3	0	00																
5	Office Equipment	5	4	5	0	00																
6	Accum. Depr.—Office Equipment																					
7	Accounts Payable							4	8	0	00											
8	Wages Payable																					
9	Joyce Lee, Capital						7	5	0	0	00											
10	Joyce Lee, Drawing	1	1	2	5	00																
11	Professional Fees						5	7	0	0	00											
12	Wages Expense	1	4	2	0	00																
13	Advertising Expense		3	5	0	00																
14	Rent Expense		7	0	0	00																
15	Supplies Expense																					
16	Telephone Expense		1	3	0	00																
17	Utilities Expense		1	9	0	00																
18	Insurance Expense																					
19	Depr. Expense—Office Equipment																					
20	Miscellaneous Expense		1	7	5	00																
21		13	6	8	0	00	13	6	8	0	00											
22																						
23																						
24																						
25																						
26																						
27																						
28																						
29																						
30																						
31																						
32																						
33																						

Problem 5-4A (Concluded)

Tax Service

Sheet

March 31, 20--

ADJUSTED TRIAL BALANCE		INCOME STATEMENT		BALANCE SHEET		
DEBIT	CREDIT	DEBIT	CREDIT	DEBIT	CREDIT	
						1
						2
						3
						4
						5
						6
						7
						8
						9
						10
						11
						12
						13
						14
						15
						16
						17
						18
						19
						20
						21
						22
						23
						24
						25
						26
						27
						28
						29
						30
						31
						32
						33

Exercise 5-3B

(Income Statement) Wages Expense		(Balance Sheet) Wages Payable	

JOURNAL PAGE

	DATE	DESCRIPTION	POST. REF.	DEBIT	CREDIT	
1						1
2						2
3						3
4						4

Exercise 5-4B

_____ × _____ = _____

(Income Statement) Depr. Expense—Delivery Equipment		(Balance Sheet) Accum. Depr.—Delivery Equipment	

JOURNAL PAGE

	DATE	DESCRIPTION	POST. REF.	DEBIT	CREDIT	
1						1
2						2
3						3
4						4

Exercise 5-5B

Name _____

Exercise 5-6B

1.

(Balance Sheet) Supplies	(Income Statement) Supplies Expense

2.

(Balance Sheet) Supplies	(Income Statement) Supplies Expense

Exercise 5-7B

1.

(Balance Sheet) Prepaid Insurance	(Income Statement) Insurance Expense

2.

(Balance Sheet) Prepaid Insurance	(Income Statement) Insurance Expense

Exercise 5-8B

Jasmine Kah's Auto Detailing

Work Sheet (Partial)

For Month Ended June 30, 20--

	DESCRIPTION	TRIAL BALANCE DEBIT	TRIAL BALANCE CREDIT	ADJUSTMENTS DEBIT	ADJUSTMENTS CREDIT	ADJUSTED TRIAL BALANCE DEBIT	ADJUSTED TRIAL BALANCE CREDIT	
1	Cash	1 5 0 0 00				1 5 0 0 00		1
2	Supplies	5 2 0 0 00				9 0 0 00		2
3	Prepaid Insurance	7 5 0 0 00				2 0 0 00		3
4	Cleaning Equipment	5 4 0 0 00				5 4 0 0 00		4
5	Accum. Depr.—Cleaning Equip.		8 5 0 00				1 1 5 0 00	5
6	Wages Payable						2 5 0 00	6
7	Jasmine Kah, Capital		4 6 0 0 00				4 6 0 0 00	7
8	Detailing Fees		2 2 2 0 00				2 2 2 0 00	8
9	Wages Expense	7 0 0 0 00				9 5 0 0 00		9
10	Advertising Expense	1 5 0 00				1 5 0 00		10
11	Supplies Expense					4 3 0 0 00		11
12	Insurance Expense					5 5 0 0 00		12
13	Depr. Exp.—Cleaning Equip.					3 0 0 00		13
14		7 6 7 0 00	7 6 7 0 00			8 2 2 0 00	8 2 2 0 00	14
15								15
16								16
17								17
18								18
19								19
20								20
21								21
22								22
23								23
24								24
25								25

Exercise 5-9B

JOURNAL PAGE _____

	DATE	DESCRIPTION	POST. REF.	DEBIT	CREDIT	
1						1
2						2
3						3
4						4
5						5
6						6
7						7
8						8
9						9
10						10
11						11
12						12
13						13
14						14
15						15

Exercise 5-10B

	Income Statement		Balance Sheet	
	Debit	**Credit**	**Debit**	**Credit**
Cash				
Accounts Receivable				
Supplies				
Prepaid Insurance				
Automobile				
Accum. Depr.—Automobile				
Accounts Payable				
Wages Payable				
Owner, Capital				
Owner, Drawing				
Service Fees				
Wages Expense				
Supplies Expense				

Exercise 5-10B (Concluded)

	Income Statement		Balance Sheet	
	Debit	**Credit**	**Debit**	**Credit**
Utilities Expense				
Insurance Expense				
Depr. Exp.—Automobile				

Exercise 5-11B

	Income Statement		Balance Sheet	
	Debit	**Credit**	**Debit**	**Credit**
Net Income				
Net Loss				

Exercise 5-12B

JOURNAL PAGE 7

	DATE		DESCRIPTION	POST. REF.	DEBIT	CREDIT	
1			Adjusting Entries				1
2	20-- July	31	Insurance Expense		3 2 0 00		2
3			Prepaid Insurance			3 2 0 00	3
4							4
5		31	Depreciation Expense—Cleaning Equipment		1 4 5 00		5
6			Accumulated Depreciation—Cleaning Equipment			1 4 5 00	6
7							7
8							8
9							9
10							10
11							11
12							12
13							13
14							14
15							15
16							16

Exercise 5-12B (Concluded)

GENERAL LEDGER

ACCOUNT Prepaid Insurance ACCOUNT NO. 145

DATE		ITEM	POST. REF.	DEBIT	CREDIT	BALANCE	
						DEBIT	CREDIT
20-- July	1	Balance	✓			3 2 0 00	
	15		J6	6 4 0 00		9 6 0 00	

ACCOUNT Accumulated Depreciation—Cleaning Equip. ACCOUNT NO. 183.1

DATE		ITEM	POST. REF.	DEBIT	CREDIT	BALANCE	
						DEBIT	CREDIT
20-- July	1	Balance	✓				8 7 0 00

ACCOUNT Insurance Expense ACCOUNT NO. 535

DATE	ITEM	POST. REF.	DEBIT	CREDIT	BALANCE	
					DEBIT	CREDIT

ACCOUNT Depreciation Expense—Cleaning Equip. ACCOUNT NO. 541

DATE	ITEM	POST. REF.	DEBIT	CREDIT	BALANCE	
					DEBIT	CREDIT

Problem 5-1B

Louie's Lawn

Work

For Month Ended

	ACCOUNT TITLE	TRIAL BALANCE		ADJUSTMENTS	
		DEBIT	CREDIT	DEBIT	CREDIT
1	Cash	1 3 7 5 00			
2	Accounts Receivable	8 8 0 00			
3	Supplies	4 9 0 00			
4	Prepaid Insurance	8 0 0 00			
5	Lawn Equipment	5 7 0 0 00			
6	Accum. Depr.—Lawn Equipment				
7	Accounts Payable		7 8 0 00		
8	Wages Payable				
9	Louie Long, Capital		6 5 0 0 00		
10	Louie Long, Drawing	1 2 5 0 00			
11	Lawn Service Fees		6 1 0 0 00		
12	Wages Expense	1 1 4 5 00			
13	Advertising Expense	5 4 0 00			
14	Rent Expense	7 2 5 00			
15	Supplies Expense				
16	Telephone Expense	1 6 0 00			
17	Insurance Expense				
18	Repair Expense	2 5 0 00			
19	Depr. Expense—Lawn Equipment				
20	Miscellaneous Expense	6 5 00			
21		13 3 8 0 00	13 3 8 0 00		
22					
23					
24					
25					
26					
27					
28					
29					
30					
31					
32					
33					

Problem 5-1B (Concluded)

Service _____

Sheet _____

March 31, 20-- _____

ADJUSTED TRIAL BALANCE		INCOME STATEMENT		BALANCE SHEET		
DEBIT	CREDIT	DEBIT	CREDIT	DEBIT	CREDIT	
						1
						2
						3
						4
						5
						6
						7
						8
						9
						10
						11
						12
						13
						14
						15
						16
						17
						18
						19
						20
						21
						22
						23
						24
						25
						26
						27
						28
						29
						30
						31
						32
						33

Problem 5-2B

Nolan's Home

Work

For Month Ended

	ACCOUNT TITLE	TRIAL BALANCE			ADJUSTMENTS		
		DEBIT	CREDIT		DEBIT	CREDIT	
1	Cash	8 3 0 00					
2	Accounts Receivable	7 6 0 00					
3	Supplies	6 2 5 00					
4	Prepaid Insurance	9 5 0 00					
5	Automobile	6 5 0 0 00					
6	Accum. Depr.—Automobile						
7	Accounts Payable		1 5 0 0 00				
8	Wages Payable						
9	Val Nolan, Capital		9 9 0 0 00				
10	Val Nolan, Drawing	1 1 0 0 00					
11	Appraisal Fees		3 0 0 0 00				
12	Wages Expense	1 5 6 0 00					
13	Advertising Expense	4 2 0 00					
14	Rent Expense	1 0 5 0 00					
15	Supplies Expense						
16	Telephone Expense	2 5 5 00					
17	Insurance Expense						
18	Repair Expense	2 7 0 00					
19	Oil and Gas Expense	8 0 00					
20	Depr. Expense—Automobile						
21		14 4 0 0 00	14 4 0 0 00				
22							
23							
24							
25							
26							
27							
28							
29							
30							
31							
32							
33							

Problem 5-2B (Concluded)

Appraisals

Sheet

October 31, 20--

ADJUSTED TRIAL BALANCE		INCOME STATEMENT		BALANCE SHEET		
DEBIT	CREDIT	DEBIT	CREDIT	DEBIT	CREDIT	
						1
						2
						3
						4
						5
						6
						7
						8
						9
						10
						11
						12
						13
						14
						15
						16
						17
						18
						19
						20
						21
						22
						23
						24
						25
						26
						27
						28
						29
						30
						31
						32
						33

Problem 5-3B

JOURNAL

	DATE	DESCRIPTION	POST. REF.	DEBIT	CREDIT	
1						1
2						2
3						3
4						4
5						5
6						6
7						7
8						8
9						9
10						10
11						11
12						12
13						13
14						14
15						15
16						16
17						17
18						18
19						19
20						20
21						21
22						22
23						23
24						24
25						25
26						26
27						27
28						28
29						29
30						30
31						31
32						32
33						33
34						34
35						35
36						36

Problem 5-3B (Continued)

GENERAL LEDGER

ACCOUNT Supplies ACCOUNT NO. 141

DATE		ITEM	POST. REF.	DEBIT	CREDIT	BALANCE DEBIT	BALANCE CREDIT
20-- Oct.	2		J1	6 2 5 00		6 2 5 00	

ACCOUNT Prepaid Insurance ACCOUNT NO. 145

DATE		ITEM	POST. REF.	DEBIT	CREDIT	BALANCE DEBIT	BALANCE CREDIT
20-- Oct.	3		J1	9 5 0 00		9 5 0 00	

ACCOUNT Accumulated Depreciation—Automobile ACCOUNT NO. 185.1

DATE	ITEM	POST. REF.	DEBIT	CREDIT	BALANCE DEBIT	BALANCE CREDIT

Problem 5-3B (Continued)

ACCOUNT Wages Payable ACCOUNT NO. 219

DATE	ITEM	POST. REF.	DEBIT	CREDIT	BALANCE DEBIT	BALANCE CREDIT

ACCOUNT Wages Expense ACCOUNT NO. 511

DATE	ITEM	POST. REF.	DEBIT	CREDIT	BALANCE DEBIT	BALANCE CREDIT
20-- Oct. 15		J2	7 0 0 00		7 0 0 00	
26		J2	8 6 0 00		1 5 6 0 00	

ACCOUNT Supplies Expense ACCOUNT NO. 523

DATE	ITEM	POST. REF.	DEBIT	CREDIT	BALANCE DEBIT	BALANCE CREDIT

Problem 5-3B (Concluded)

ACCOUNT Insurance Expense

ACCOUNT NO. 535

DATE	ITEM	POST. REF.	DEBIT	CREDIT	BALANCE DEBIT	BALANCE CREDIT

ACCOUNT Depreciation Expense—Automobile

ACCOUNT NO. 541

DATE	ITEM	POST. REF.	DEBIT	CREDIT	BALANCE DEBIT	BALANCE CREDIT

Problem 5-4B

	ACCOUNT TITLE	TRIAL BALANCE											ADJUSTMENTS									
		DEBIT					CREDIT						DEBIT					CREDIT				
1	Cash	1	3	6	5	00																
2	Accounts Receivable		8	4	5	00																
3	Supplies		6	2	0	00																
4	Prepaid Insurance	1	1	5	0	00																
5	Office Equipment	6	4	0	0	00																
6	Accum. Depr.—Office Equipment																					
7	Accounts Payable							7	3	5	00											
8	Wages Payable																					
9	Dick Ady, Capital							7	8	0	0	00										
10	Dick Ady, Drawing	1	2	0	0	00																
11	Professional Fees							6	3	5	0	00										
12	Wages Expense	1	4	9	5	00																
13	Advertising Expense		3	8	0	00																
14	Rent Expense		8	5	0	00																
15	Supplies Expense																					
16	Telephone Expense		2	0	5	00																
17	Utilities Expense		2	8	5	00																
18	Insurance Expense																					
19	Depr. Expense—Office Equipment																					
20	Miscellaneous Expense			9	0	00																
21		14	8	8	5	00	14	8	8	5	00											
22																						
23																						
24																						
25																						
26																						
27																						
28																						
29																						
30																						
31																						
32																						
33																						

Problem 5-4B (Concluded)

Bookkeeping Service

Sheet

July 31, 20--

ADJUSTED TRIAL BALANCE		INCOME STATEMENT		BALANCE SHEET		
DEBIT	CREDIT	DEBIT	CREDIT	DEBIT	CREDIT	
						1
						2
						3
						4
						5
						6
						7
						8
						9
						10
						11
						12
						13
						14
						15
						16
						17
						18
						19
						20
						21
						22
						23
						24
						25
						26
						27
						28
						29
						30
						31
						32
						33

Challenge Problem

1.

Diane Kiefner's Wilderness

Work

For Summer

	ACCOUNT TITLE	TRIAL BALANCE												ADJUSTMENTS												
		DEBIT						CREDIT						DEBIT						CREDIT						
1	Cash	11	5	0	0	00																				
2																										
3																										
4																										
5	Diane Kiefner, Capital							15	0	0	0	00														
6	Tour Revenue							10	0	0	0	00														
7	Advertising Supplies Expense	1	0	0	0	00																				
8	Food Expense	2	0	0	0	00																				
9	Equipment Rental Expense	3	0	0	0	00																				
10	Travel Expense	4	0	0	0	00																				
11	Kayak Expense	3	5	0	0	00																				
12																										
13		25	0	0	0	00		25	0	0	0	00														
14																										
15																										
16																										
17																										
18																										
19																										

Challenge Problem (Concluded)

Kayaking Tours

Sheet

Ended 20--

	ADJUSTED TRIAL BALANCE		INCOME STATEMENT		BALANCE SHEET		
	DEBIT	CREDIT	DEBIT	CREDIT	DEBIT	CREDIT	
							1
							2
							3
							4
							5
							6
							7
							8
							9
							10
							11
							12
							13
							14
							15
							16
							17
							18
							19

2. _____

Mastery Problem

1.

Kristi Williams

Work

For Year Ended

	ACCOUNT TITLE	TRIAL BALANCE											ADJUSTMENTS										
		DEBIT					CREDIT						DEBIT					CREDIT					
1	Cash	8	7	3	0	00																	
2	Office Supplies		7	0	0	00																	
3	Prepaid Insurance		6	0	0	00																	
4	Office Equipment	18	0	0	0	00																	
5	Accum. Depr.—Office Equipment																						
6	Computer Equipment	6	0	0	0	00																	
7	Accum. Depr.—Computer Equipment																						
8	Notes Payable						8	0	0	0	00												
9	Accounts Payable							5	0	0	00												
10	Kristi Williams, Capital						11	4	0	0	00												
11	Kristi Williams, Drawing	3	0	0	0	00																	
12	Client Fees						35	8	0	0	00												
13	Wages Expense	9	5	0	0	00																	
14	Rent Expense	6	0	0	0	00																	
15	Office Supplies Expense																						
16	Utilities Expense	2	1	7	0	00																	
17	Insurance Expense																						
18	Depr. Expense—Office Equipment																						
19	Depr. Expense—Computer Equipment																						
20	Miscellaneous Expense	1	0	0	0	00																	
21		55	7	0	0	00	55	7	0	0	00												
22																							
23																							
24																							
25																							
26																							
27																							
28																							
29																							
30																							
31																							
32																							

Mastery Problem (Continued)

Counseling Services

Sheet

December 31, 20--

	ADJUSTED TRIAL BALANCE		INCOME STATEMENT		BALANCE SHEET		
	DEBIT	CREDIT	DEBIT	CREDIT	DEBIT	CREDIT	
							1
							2
							3
							4
							5
							6
							7
							8
							9
							10
							11
							12
							13
							14
							15
							16
							17
							18
							19
							20
							21
							22
							23
							24
							25
							26
							27
							28
							29
							30
							31
							32

Mastery Problem (Concluded)

2.

<div align="center">JOURNAL</div>

PAGE 5

	DATE		DESCRIPTION	POST. REF.	DEBIT	CREDIT	
1							1
2							2
3							3
4							4
5							5
6							6
7							7
8							8
9							9
10							10
11							11
12							12
13							13
14							14
15							15
16							16
17							17
18							18
19							19
20							20
21							21
22							22
23							23
24							24
25							25
26							26
27							27
28							28
29							29
30							30
31							31
32							32
33							33
34							34
35							35

APPENDIX EXERCISES

Exercise 5Apx-1A

Straight-Line Depreciation

Year	Depreciable Cost	x	Rate	=	Depreciation Expense	Accumulated Depreciation End of Year	Book Value End of Year
___	___		___		___	___	___
___	___		___		___	___	___
___	___		___		___	___	___
___	___		___		___	___	___

Exercise 5Apx-2A

Sum-of-the-Years'-Digits

Year	Depreciable Cost	x	Rate	=	Depreciation Expense	Accumulated Depreciation End of Year	Book Value End of Year
___	___		___		___	___	___
___	___		___		___	___	___
___	___		___		___	___	___
___	___		___		___	___	___

Exercise 5Apx-3A

Double-Declining-Balance Method

Year	Book Value Beginning of Year	x	Rate	=	Depreciation Expense	Accumulated Depreciation End of Year	Book Value End of Year
___	___		___		___	___	___
___	___		___		___	___	___
___	___		___		___	___	___
___	___		___		___	___	___

Exercise 5Apx-4A

Modified Accelerated Cost Recovery System

Year	Cost	x	Rate	=	Depreciation Expense	Accumulated Depreciation End of Year	Book Value End of Year

Exercise 5Apx-1B

Straight-Line Depreciation

Year	Depreciable Cost	x	Rate	=	Depreciation Expense	Accumulated Depreciation End of Year	Book Value End of Year

Exercise 5Apx-2B

Sum-of-the-Years'-Digits

Year	Depreciable Cost	x	Rate	=	Depreciation Expense	Accumulated Depreciation End of Year	Book Value End of Year

Exercise 5Apx-3B

Double-Declining-Balance Method

Year	Book Value Beginning of Year	x	Rate	=	Depreciation Expense	Accumulated Depreciation End of Year	Book Value End of Year

Exercise 5Apx-4B

Modified Accelerated Cost Recovery System

Year	Cost	x	Rate	=	Depreciation Expense	Accumulated Depreciation End of Year	Book Value End of Year

Exercise 6-1A

Exercise 6-2A

Exercise 6-3A

Exercise 6-4A

JOURNAL

	DATE		DESCRIPTION	POST. REF.	DEBIT	CREDIT	
1							1
2							2
3							3
4							4
5							5
6							6
7							7
8							8
9							9
10							10
11							11
12							12
13							13
14							14
15							15
16							16
17							17
18							18
19							19
20							20
21							21
22							22
23							23

Exercise 6-4A (Concluded)

Exercise 6-5A

JOURNAL

	DATE		DESCRIPTION	POST. REF.	DEBIT	CREDIT	
1							1
2							2
3							3
4							4
5							5
6							6
7							7
8							8
9							9
10							10
11							11
12							12
13							13
14							14
15							15
16							16
17							17
18							18
19							19
20							20
21							21
22							22
23							23
24							24
25							25
26							26
27							27
28							28
29							29
30							30
31							31
32							32
33							33
34							34
35							35
36							36

Exercise 6-5A (Concluded)

Accum. Depr.—Delivery Equip.	185.1
	Bal. 100

Wages Payable	219
	Bal. 200

Saburo Goto, Capital	311
	Bal. 4,000

Saburo Goto, Drawing	312
Bal. 800	

Income Summary	313

Delivery Fees	401
	Bal. 2,200

Wages Expense	511
Bal. 1,800	

Advertising Expense	512
Bal. 80	

Rent Expense	521
Bal. 500	

Supplies Expense	523
Bal. 120	

Telephone Expense	525
Bal. 58	

Electricity Expense	533
Bal. 44	

Insurance Expense	535
Bal. 30	

Gas & Oil Expense	538
Bal. 38	

Depr. Exp.—Delivery Equip.	541
Bal. 100	

Miscellaneous Expense	549
Bal. 33	

Name _____

Problem 6-1A

1.

2.

Problem 6-1A (Concluded)

3.

Problem 6-2A

Problem 6-3A
1.

JOURNAL

	DATE		DESCRIPTION	POST. REF.	DEBIT	CREDIT	
1							1
2							2
3							3
4							4
5							5
6							6
7							7
8							8
9							9
10							10
11							11
12							12
13							13
14							14
15							15
16							16
17							17
18							18

Problem 6-3A (Continued)

2.

<div align="center">

JOURNAL PAGE 11

</div>

	DATE		DESCRIPTION	POST. REF.	DEBIT	CREDIT	
1							1
2							2
3							3
4							4
5							5
6							6
7							7
8							8
9							9
10							10
11							11
12							12
13							13
14							14
15							15
16							16
17							17
18							18
19							19
20							20
21							21
22							22
23							23

<div align="center">

GENERAL LEDGER

</div>

ACCOUNT Cash ACCOUNT NO. 101

DATE		ITEM	POST. REF.	DEBIT	CREDIT	BALANCE DEBIT	BALANCE CREDIT
20-- Jan.	31	Balance	✓			3 0 8 0 00	

Name _____

Problem 6-3A (Continued)

ACCOUNT Accounts Receivable ACCOUNT NO. 122

DATE		ITEM	POST. REF.	DEBIT	CREDIT	BALANCE DEBIT	BALANCE CREDIT
20-- Jan.	31	Balance	✓			1 2 0 0 00	

ACCOUNT Supplies ACCOUNT NO. 141

DATE		ITEM	POST. REF.	DEBIT	CREDIT	BALANCE DEBIT	BALANCE CREDIT
20-- Jan.	31	Balance	✓			8 0 0 00	

ACCOUNT Prepaid Insurance ACCOUNT NO. 145

DATE		ITEM	POST. REF.	DEBIT	CREDIT	BALANCE DEBIT	BALANCE CREDIT
20-- Jan.	31	Balance	✓			9 0 0 00	

ACCOUNT Delivery Equipment ACCOUNT NO. 185

DATE		ITEM	POST. REF.	DEBIT	CREDIT	BALANCE DEBIT	BALANCE CREDIT
20-- Jan.	31	Balance	✓			3 0 0 0 00	

ACCOUNT Accumulated Depreciation—Delivery Equipment ACCOUNT NO. 185.1

DATE	ITEM	POST. REF.	DEBIT	CREDIT	BALANCE DEBIT	BALANCE CREDIT

Problem 6-3A(Continued)

ACCOUNT Accounts Payable ACCOUNT NO. 202

DATE		ITEM	POST. REF.	DEBIT	CREDIT	BALANCE DEBIT	BALANCE CREDIT
20-- Jan.	31	Balance	✓				1 1 0 0 00

ACCOUNT Wages Payable ACCOUNT NO. 219

DATE	ITEM	POST. REF.	DEBIT	CREDIT	BALANCE DEBIT	BALANCE CREDIT

ACCOUNT Monte Eli, Capital ACCOUNT NO. 311

DATE		ITEM	POST. REF.	DEBIT	CREDIT	BALANCE DEBIT	BALANCE CREDIT
20-- Jan.	31	Balance	✓				7 0 0 0 00

ACCOUNT Monte Eli, Drawing ACCOUNT NO. 312

DATE		ITEM	POST. REF.	DEBIT	CREDIT	BALANCE DEBIT	BALANCE CREDIT
20-- Jan.	31	Balance	✓			1 0 0 0 00	

ACCOUNT Income Summary ACCOUNT NO. 313

DATE	ITEM	POST. REF.	DEBIT	CREDIT	BALANCE DEBIT	BALANCE CREDIT

Problem 6-3A (Continued)

ACCOUNT Repair Fees ACCOUNT NO. 401

DATE		ITEM	POST. REF.	DEBIT	CREDIT	BALANCE	
						DEBIT	CREDIT
20-- Jan.	31	Balance	✓				4 2 3 0 00

ACCOUNT Wages Expense ACCOUNT NO. 511

DATE		ITEM	POST. REF.	DEBIT	CREDIT	BALANCE	
						DEBIT	CREDIT
20-- Jan.	31	Balance	✓			1 6 5 0 00	

ACCOUNT Advertising Expense ACCOUNT NO. 512

DATE		ITEM	POST. REF.	DEBIT	CREDIT	BALANCE	
						DEBIT	CREDIT
20-- Jan.	31	Balance	✓			1 7 0 00	

ACCOUNT Rent Expense ACCOUNT NO. 521

DATE		ITEM	POST. REF.	DEBIT	CREDIT	BALANCE	
						DEBIT	CREDIT
20-- Jan.	31	Balance	✓			4 2 0 00	

ACCOUNT Supplies Expense ACCOUNT NO. 523

DATE		ITEM	POST. REF.	DEBIT	CREDIT	BALANCE	
						DEBIT	CREDIT

Problem 6-3A (Continued)

ACCOUNT Telephone Expense ACCOUNT NO. 525

DATE		ITEM	POST. REF.	DEBIT	CREDIT	BALANCE	
						DEBIT	CREDIT
20-- Jan.	31	Balance	✓			4 9 00	

ACCOUNT Insurance Expense ACCOUNT NO. 535

DATE		ITEM	POST. REF.	DEBIT	CREDIT	BALANCE	
						DEBIT	CREDIT

ACCOUNT Gas and Oil Expense ACCOUNT NO. 538

DATE		ITEM	POST. REF.	DEBIT	CREDIT	BALANCE	
						DEBIT	CREDIT
20-- Jan.	31	Balance	✓			3 3 00	

ACCOUNT Depreciation Expense—Delivery Equipment ACCOUNT NO. 541

DATE		ITEM	POST. REF.	DEBIT	CREDIT	BALANCE	
						DEBIT	CREDIT

ACCOUNT Miscellaneous Expense ACCOUNT NO. 549

DATE		ITEM	POST. REF.	DEBIT	CREDIT	BALANCE	
						DEBIT	CREDIT
20-- Jan.	31	Balance	✓			2 8 00	

Problem 6-3A (Concluded)

3.

ACCOUNT	ACCT. NO.	DEBIT BALANCE	CREDIT BALANCE

Exercise 6-1B

Exercise 6-2B

Name _____

Exercise 6-3B

Exercise 6-4B

<div align="center">

JOURNAL

</div>

	DATE		DESCRIPTION	POST. REF.	DEBIT	CREDIT	
1							1
2							2
3							3
4							4
5							5
6							6
7							7
8							8
9							9
10							10
11							11
12							12
13							13
14							14
15							15
16							16
17							17
18							18
19							19
20							20
21							21
22							22
23							23

Exercise 6-4B (Concluded)

Exercise 6-5B

<div style="text-align: center;">**JOURNAL**</div>

PAGE

	DATE		DESCRIPTION	POST. REF.	DEBIT	CREDIT	
1							1
2							2
3							3
4							4
5							5
6							6
7							7
8							8
9							9
10							10
11							11
12							12
13							13
14							14
15							15
16							16
17							17
18							18
19							19
20							20
21							21
22							22
23							23
24							24
25							25
26							26
27							27
28							28
29							29
30							30
31							31
32							32
33							33
34							34
35							35
36							36

Problem 6-3B (Continued)

2.

JOURNAL PAGE 11

DATE	DESCRIPTION	POST. REF.	DEBIT	CREDIT	
					1
					2
					3
					4
					5
					6
					7
					8
					9
					10
					11
					12
					13
					14
					15
					16
					17
					18
					19
					20
					21
					22
					23

GENERAL LEDGER

ACCOUNT Cash ACCOUNT NO. 101

DATE	ITEM	POST. REF.	DEBIT	CREDIT	BALANCE DEBIT	BALANCE CREDIT
20-- June 30	Balance	✓			5 2 8 5 00	

Problem 6-3B (Continued)

ACCOUNT Accounts Receivable ACCOUNT NO. 122

DATE	ITEM	POST. REF.	DEBIT	CREDIT	BALANCE DEBIT	BALANCE CREDIT
20-- June 30	Balance	✓			1 0 7 5 00	

ACCOUNT Supplies ACCOUNT NO. 141

DATE	ITEM	POST. REF.	DEBIT	CREDIT	BALANCE DEBIT	BALANCE CREDIT
20-- June 30	Balance	✓			7 5 0 00	

ACCOUNT Prepaid Insurance ACCOUNT NO. 145

DATE	ITEM	POST. REF.	DEBIT	CREDIT	BALANCE DEBIT	BALANCE CREDIT
20-- June 30	Balance	✓			5 0 0 00	

ACCOUNT Office Equipment ACCOUNT NO. 181

DATE	ITEM	POST. REF.	DEBIT	CREDIT	BALANCE DEBIT	BALANCE CREDIT
20-- June 30	Balance	✓			2 2 0 0 00	

ACCOUNT Accumulated Depreciation—Office Equipment ACCOUNT NO. 181.1

DATE	ITEM	POST. REF.	DEBIT	CREDIT	BALANCE DEBIT	BALANCE CREDIT

Name _____

Problem 6-3B (Continued)

ACCOUNT Accounts Payable ACCOUNT NO. 202

DATE		ITEM	POST. REF.	DEBIT	CREDIT	BALANCE DEBIT	BALANCE CREDIT
20-- June	30	Balance	✓				1 5 0 0 00

ACCOUNT Wages Payable ACCOUNT NO. 219

DATE		ITEM	POST. REF.	DEBIT	CREDIT	BALANCE DEBIT	BALANCE CREDIT

ACCOUNT Juanita Alvarez, Capital ACCOUNT NO. 311

DATE		ITEM	POST. REF.	DEBIT	CREDIT	BALANCE DEBIT	BALANCE CREDIT
20-- June	30	Balance	✓				7 0 0 0 00

ACCOUNT Juanita Alvarez, Drawing ACCOUNT NO. 312

DATE		ITEM	POST. REF.	DEBIT	CREDIT	BALANCE DEBIT	BALANCE CREDIT
20-- June	30	Balance	✓			8 0 0 00	

ACCOUNT Income Summary ACCOUNT NO. 313

DATE		ITEM	POST. REF.	DEBIT	CREDIT	BALANCE DEBIT	BALANCE CREDIT

Problem 6-3B (Continued)

ACCOUNT Consulting Fees ACCOUNT NO. 401

DATE	ITEM	POST. REF.	DEBIT	CREDIT	BALANCE DEBIT	BALANCE CREDIT
20-- June 30	Balance	✓				4 2 0 4 00

ACCOUNT Wages Expense ACCOUNT NO. 511

DATE	ITEM	POST. REF.	DEBIT	CREDIT	BALANCE DEBIT	BALANCE CREDIT
20-- June 30	Balance	✓			1 4 0 0 00	

ACCOUNT Advertising Expense ACCOUNT NO. 512

DATE	ITEM	POST. REF.	DEBIT	CREDIT	BALANCE DEBIT	BALANCE CREDIT
20-- June 30	Balance	✓			6 0 00	

ACCOUNT Rent Expense ACCOUNT NO. 521

DATE	ITEM	POST. REF.	DEBIT	CREDIT	BALANCE DEBIT	BALANCE CREDIT
20-- June 30	Balance	✓			5 0 0 00	

ACCOUNT Supplies Expense ACCOUNT NO. 523

DATE	ITEM	POST. REF.	DEBIT	CREDIT	BALANCE DEBIT	BALANCE CREDIT

Name _____

Problem 6-3B (Continued)

ACCOUNT Telephone Expense ACCOUNT NO. 525

DATE	ITEM	POST. REF.	DEBIT	CREDIT	BALANCE DEBIT	BALANCE CREDIT
20-- June 30	Balance	✓			4 6 00	

ACCOUNT Electricity Expense ACCOUNT NO. 533

DATE	ITEM	POST. REF.	DEBIT	CREDIT	BALANCE DEBIT	BALANCE CREDIT
20-- June 30	Balance	✓			3 9 00	

ACCOUNT Insurance Expense ACCOUNT NO. 535

DATE	ITEM	POST. REF.	DEBIT	CREDIT	BALANCE DEBIT	BALANCE CREDIT

ACCOUNT Gas and Oil Expense ACCOUNT NO. 538

DATE	ITEM	POST. REF.	DEBIT	CREDIT	BALANCE DEBIT	BALANCE CREDIT
20-- June 30	Balance	✓			2 8 00	

ACCOUNT Depreciation Expense—Office Equipment ACCOUNT NO. 541

DATE	ITEM	POST. REF.	DEBIT	CREDIT	BALANCE DEBIT	BALANCE CREDIT

Problem 6-3B (Concluded)

ACCOUNT Miscellaneous Expense ACCOUNT NO. 549

DATE		ITEM	POST. REF.	DEBIT	CREDIT	BALANCE	
						DEBIT	CREDIT
20-- June	30	Balance	✓			2 1 00	

3.

ACCOUNT	ACCT. NO.	DEBIT BALANCE	CREDIT BALANCE

Name _____

Challenge Problem

Challenge Problem (Concluded)

Name _____

Mastery Problem

Mastery Problem (Continued)

Name _____

Mastery Problem (Concluded)

JOURNAL

	DATE		DESCRIPTION	POST. REF.	DEBIT	CREDIT	
1							1
2							2
3							3
4							4
5							5
6							6
7							7
8							8
9							9
10							10
11							11
12							12
13							13
14							14
15							15
16							16
17							17
18							18
19							19
20							20
21							21
22							22
23							23
24							24
25							25
26							26
27							27
28							28
29							29
30							30
31							31
32							32
33							33
34							34
35							35
36							36

Exercise 6Apx-1A

a. _____ g. _____

b. _____ h. _____

c. _____ i. _____

d. _____ j. _____

e. _____ k. _____

f.

Problem 6Apx-1A

Exercise 6Apx-1B

a. _____

b. _____

c. _____

d. _____

e. _____

f.

g. _____

h. _____

i. _____

j. _____

k. _____

Problem 6Apx-1B

Exercise 7-1A

1. _____ 5. _____
2. _____ 6. _____
3. _____ 7. _____
4. _____

Exercise 7-2A

DEPOSIT TICKET		63-1209 / 631

WIZARD BANK
3711 Buena Vista Dr.
Orlando, FL 32811-1314

Date_____ 20_____

CHECKS AND OTHER ITEMS ARE RECEIVED FOR DEPOSIT SUBJECT TO THE TERMS AND CONDITIONS OF THIS FINANCIAL INSTITUTION'S ACCOUNT AGREEMENT.

SIGN HERE ONLY IF CASH RECEIVED FROM DEPOSIT

⑆063112094⑆ 0001632475⑈

CURRENCY		
COIN		
C H E C K S		
TOTAL FROM OTHER SIDE		
SUBTOTAL		
LESS CASH RECEIVED		
TOTAL DEPOSIT		

Exercise 7-3A

No. 1	

DATE _____ 20____
TO _____
FOR _____

ACCT. _____

	DOLLARS	CENTS
BAL BRO'T FOR'D		
AMT. DEPOSITED		
TOTAL		
AMT. THIS CHECK		
BAL CAR'D FOR'D		

No. 1 63-1209 / 631

_____ 20_____

PAY
TO THE
ORDER OF _____ $_____

_____ Dollars

WIZARD BANK FOR CLASSROOM USE ONLY
3711 Buena Vista Dr.
Orlando, FL 32811-1314

MEMO_____ BY _____

⑆063112094⑆ 0001632475⑈

Exercise 7-4A

	Ending Bank Balance	Ending Check-book Balance
1.	_____	_____
2.	_____	_____
3.	_____	_____
4.	_____	_____
5.	_____	_____
6.	_____	_____
7.	_____	_____

Exercise 7-5A

JOURNAL PAGE

	DATE	DESCRIPTION	POST. REF.	DEBIT	CREDIT	
1						1
2						2
3						3
4						4
5						5
6						6
7						7
8						8
9						9
10						10
11						11
12						12
13						13
14						14
15						15
16						16
17						17
18						18
19						19
20						20
21						21

Exercise 7-6A

JOURNAL

	DATE		DESCRIPTION	POST. REF.	DEBIT	CREDIT	
1							1
2							2
3							3
4							4
5							5
6							6
7							7
8							8
9							9
10							10
11							11
12							12
13							13
14							14
15							15
16							16
17							17
18							18
19							19
20							20
21							21
22							22
23							23
24							24
25							25
26							26
27							27
28							28
29							29
30							30
31							31
32							32
33							33
34							34
35							35
36							36

Exercise 7-7A

JOURNAL PAGE

	DATE		DESCRIPTION	POST. REF.	DEBIT	CREDIT	
1							1
2							2
3							3
4							4
5							5
6							6
7							7
8							8
9							9
10							10
11							11
12							12
13							13
14							14
15							15
16							16
17							17
18							18
19							19
20							20
21							21
22							22
23							23
24							24
25							25
26							26
27							27
28							28
29							29
30							30
31							31
32							32
33							33
34							34
35							35
36							36

Problem 7-1A

1.

Problem 7-1A (Concluded)

2.

JOURNAL PAGE

	DATE	DESCRIPTION	POST. REF.	DEBIT	CREDIT	
1						1
2						2
3						3
4						4
5						5
6						6
7						7
8						8
9						9
10						10
11						11
12						12
13						13
14						14
15						15

Problem 7-2A: See page WP-217

Problem 7-3A

1. and 3.

JOURNAL PAGE

	DATE	DESCRIPTION	POST. REF.	DEBIT	CREDIT	
1						1
2						2
3						3
4						4
5						5
6						6
7						7
8						8
9						9
10						10
11						11
12						12
13						13

Problem 7-2A

1.

2.

<div align="center">

JOURNAL PAGE

</div>

	DATE	DESCRIPTION	POST. REF.	DEBIT	CREDIT	
1						1
2						2
3						3
4						4
5						5
6						6
7						7
8						8
9						9
10						10

Problem 7-3A (Concluded)
2. and 3.

Problem 7-4A

1.

<div align="center">JOURNAL</div>

PAGE 8

	DATE		DESCRIPTION	POST. REF.	DEBIT	CREDIT	
1							1
2							2
3							3
4							4
5							5
6							6
7							7
8							8
9							9
10							10
11							11
12							12
13							13
14							14
15							15
16							16
17							17
18							18
19							19

2.

ACCOUNT ACCOUNT NO.

DATE	ITEM	POST. REF.	DEBIT	CREDIT	BALANCE	
					DEBIT	CREDIT

3. The balance represents:

Exercise 7-1B

1. _____ 5. _____

2. _____ 6. _____

3. _____ 7. _____

4. _____

Exercise 7-2B

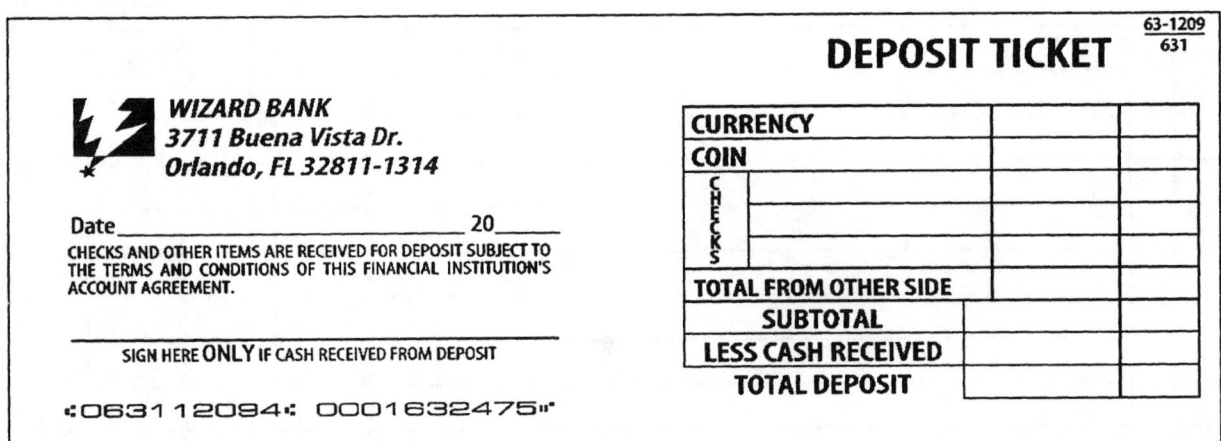

Exercise 7-3B

Exercise 7-4B

	Ending Bank Balance	Ending Check- book Balance
1.	_____	_____
2.	_____	_____
3.	_____	_____
4.	_____	_____
5.	_____	_____
6.	_____	_____
7.	_____	_____

Exercise 7-5B

JOURNAL PAGE

	DATE	DESCRIPTION	POST. REF.	DEBIT	CREDIT	
1						1
2						2
3						3
4						4
5						5
6						6
7						7
8						8
9						9
10						10
11						11
12						12
13						13
14						14
15						15
16						16
17						17
18						18
19						19
20						20
21						21

Exercise 7-6B

		JOURNAL				PAGE	
	DATE	DESCRIPTION	POST. REF.	DEBIT		CREDIT	
1							1
2							2
3							3
4							4
5							5
6							6
7							7
8							8
9							9
10							10
11							11
12							12
13							13
14							14
15							15
16							16
17							17
18							18
19							19
20							20
21							21
22							22
23							23
24							24
25							25
26							26
27							27
28							28
29							29
30							30
31							31
32							32
33							33
34							34
35							35
36							36

Exercise 7-7B

<div align="center">JOURNAL</div>

PAGE

	DATE		DESCRIPTION	POST. REF.	DEBIT	CREDIT	
1							1
2							2
3							3
4							4
5							5
6							6
7							7
8							8
9							9
10							10
11							11
12							12
13							13
14							14
15							15
16							16
17							17
18							18
19							19
20							20
21							21
22							22
23							23
24							24
25							25
26							26
27							27
28							28
29							29
30							30
31							31
32							32
33							33
34							34
35							35
36							36

Problem 7-1B

1.

Name _____

Problem 7-1B (Concluded)
2.

JOURNAL
PAGE

	DATE		DESCRIPTION	POST. REF.	DEBIT	CREDIT	
1							1
2							2
3							3
4							4
5							5
6							6
7							7
8							8
9							9
10							10
11							11
12							12
13							13
14							14
15							15

Problem 7-2B: See page WP-226.

Problem 7-3B
1. and 3.

JOURNAL
PAGE

	DATE		DESCRIPTION	POST. REF.	DEBIT	CREDIT	
1							1
2							2
3							3
4							4
5							5
6							6
7							7
8							8
9							9
10							10
11							11
12							12
13							13

Problem 7-2B

1.

2.

<div align="center">JOURNAL</div>

PAGE

	DATE	DESCRIPTION	POST. REF.	DEBIT	CREDIT	
1						1
2						2
3						3
4						4
5						5
6						6
7						7
8						8
9						9
10						10

Problem 7-3B (Concluded)
2. and 3.

Problem 7-4B

1.

<div align="center">

JOURNAL PAGE 8

</div>

	DATE		DESCRIPTION	POST. REF.	DEBIT	CREDIT	
1							1
2							2
3							3
4							4
5							5
6							6
7							7
8							8
9							9
10							10
11							11
12							12
13							13
14							14
15							15
16							16
17							17
18							18
19							19

2.

ACCOUNT ACCOUNT NO.

DATE	ITEM	POST. REF.	DEBIT	CREDIT	BALANCE	
					DEBIT	CREDIT

3. The balance represents:

Challenge Problem

1. Panera Bakery

		JOURNAL				PAGE	

	DATE	DESCRIPTION	POST. REF.	DEBIT	CREDIT	
1						1
2						2
3						3
4						4
5						5
6						6
7						7
8						8
9						9
10						10
11						11
12						12
13						13
14						14
15						15
16						16
17						17
18						18
19						19
20						20
21						21
22						22
23						23
24						24
25						25
26						26
27						27
28						28
29						29

Challenge Problem (Concluded)

2. Lawrence Bank

JOURNAL PAGE

	DATE		DESCRIPTION	POST. REF.	DEBIT	CREDIT	
1							1
2							2
3							3
4							4
5							5
6							6
7							7
8							8
9							9
10							10
11							11
12							12
13							13
14							14
15							15
16							16
17							17
18							18
19							19
20							20
21							21
22							22
23							23
24							24
25							25
26							26
27							27
28							28
29							29

Mastery Problem

1.

PETTY CASH PAYMENTS FOR MONTH OF _____ 20-- PAGE _____

DAY	DESCRIPTION	VOU. NO.	TOTAL AMOUNT	TRUCK EXPENSE	POSTAGE EXPENSE	CHARIT. CONTRIB. EXPENSE	TELEPHONE EXPENSE	ADVERT. EXPENSE	MISC. EXPENSE	ACCOUNT	AMOUNT

(Blank form — DISTRIBUTION OF PAYMENTS, rows 1–22)

Mastery Problem (Continued)
2. and 3.

JOURNAL PAGE

	DATE		DESCRIPTION	POST. REF.	DEBIT	CREDIT	
1							1
2							2
3							3
4							4
5							5
6							6
7							7
8							8
9							9
10							10
11							11
12							12
13							13
14							14
15							15
16							16
17							17
18							18
19							19
20							20
21							21
22							22
23							23
24							24
25							25
26							26
27							27
28							28
29							29
30							30
31							31
32							32
33							33
34							34
35							35

Mastery Problem (Concluded)

JOURNAL

PAGE 2

	DATE		DESCRIPTION	POST. REF.	DEBIT	CREDIT	
1							1
2							2
3							3
4							4
5							5
6							6
7							7
8							8
9							9
10							10
11							11
12							12
13							13
14							14

3.

Exercise 8-1A

a. _____ regular hours × $10.00 per hour _____

b. _____ overtime hours × $15.00 per hour _____

c. Total gross wages _____

d. Federal income tax withholding
 (from tax tables in Figure 8-4) _____

e. Social security withholding at 6.2% _____

f. Medicare withholding at 1.45% _____

g. Total withholding _____

h. Net pay _____

Exercise 8-2A

Exercise 8-3A

Exercise 8-4A

	Marital Status	Total Weekly Earnings	Number of Allowances	Amount of Withholding
a.	S	$327.90	2	_____
b.	S	410.00	1	_____
c.	M	438.16	5	_____
d.	S	518.25	0	_____
e.	M	603.98	6	_____

Exercise 8-5A

Cumulative Pay Before Current Weekly Payroll	Current Gross Pay	Year-to-Date Earnings	Social Security Max.	Amount over Max. Soc. Sec.	Amount Subject to Soc. Sec	Social Sec. Tax Withheld	Medicare Tax Withheld
$22,000	$1,200		$76,200				
54,000	4,200		76,200				
73,600	3,925		76,200				
75,600	4,600		76,200				

Exercise 8-6A

JOURNAL PAGE

	DATE	DESCRIPTION	POST. REF.	DEBIT	CREDIT	
1						1
2						2
3						3
4						4
5						5
6						6
7						7
8						8
9						9

Exercise 8-7A

JOURNAL PAGE

	DATE	DESCRIPTION	POST. REF.	DEBIT	CREDIT	
1						1
2						2
3						3
4						4
5						5
6						6
7						7
8						8
9						9

Problem 8-1A

1.

2.

JOURNAL PAGE

	DATE	DESCRIPTION	POST. REF.	DEBIT	CREDIT	
1						1
2						2
3						3
4						4
5						5
6						6
7						7
8						8
9						9
10						10
11						11
12						12
13						13
14						14
15						15

Problem 8-2A

1.

PAYROLL REGISTER

	NAME	NO. ALLOW.	MARIT. STATUS	EARNINGS							TAXABLE EARNINGS			
				REGULAR		OVERTIME		TOTAL		CUMULATIVE TOTAL		UNEMPLOY. COMP.		SOCIAL SECURITY
1														
2														
3														
4														
5														
6														
7														
8														
9														
10														
11														
12														
13														
14														

Problem 8-2A (Concluded)

FOR PERIOD ENDED _____ 20--

			DEDUCTIONS								
FEDERAL INCOME TAX	SOCIAL SECURITY TAX	MEDICARE TAX	CITY TAX	HEALTH INSUR.	OTHER			TOTAL	NET PAY	CK. NO.	
											1
											2
											3
											4
											5
											6
											7
											8
											9
											10
											11
											12
											13
											14

2.

JOURNAL

PAGE _____

	DATE	DESCRIPTION	POST. REF.	DEBIT	CREDIT	
1						1
2						2
3						3
4						4
5						5
6						6
7						7
8						8
9						9
10						10
11						11
12						12
13						13
14						14

Problem 8-3A

EMPLOYEE EARNINGS RECORD

20 -- PERIOD ENDED	EARNINGS				TAXABLE EARNINGS		DEDUCTIONS		
	REGULAR	OVERTIME	TOTAL	CUMULATIVE TOTAL	UNEMPLOY. COMP.	SOCIAL SECURITY	FEDERAL INCOME TAX	SOCIAL SECURITY TAX	
GENDER	DEPARTMENT		OCCUPATION		SOCIAL SECURITY NO.		MARITAL STATUS	ALLOW-ANCES	
M F									

Name _____

CHAPTER 8 WP-241

Problem 8-3A (Concluded)

FOR PERIOD ENDED _____ 20--

			DEDUCTIONS					
MEDICARE TAX	CITY TAX	HEALTH INSURANCE	OTHER		TOTAL	CK. NO.	AMOUNT	
								1
								2
								3
								4
								5
PAY RATE	DATE OF BIRTH	DATE HIRED	NAME/ADDRESS				EMP. NO.	6
								7

Exercise 8-1B

a. _____ regular hours × $12.00 per hour _____

b. _____ overtime hours × $18.00 per hour _____

c. Total gross wages _____

d. Federal income tax withholding
 (from tax tables in Figure 8-4) _____

e. Social security withholding at 6.2% _____

f. Medicare withholding at 1.45% _____

g. Total withholding _____

h. Net pay _____

Exercise 8-2B

Exercise 8-3B

Exercise 8-4B

	Marital Status	Total Weekly Earnings	Number of Allowances	Amount of Withholding
a.	M	$546.00	4	_____
b.	M	390.00	3	_____
c.	S	461.39	2	_____
d.	M	522.88	6	_____
e.	S	612.00	0	_____

Exercise 8-5B

Cumulative Pay Before Current Weekly Payroll	Current Gross Pay	Year-to-Date Earnings	Social Security Max.	Amount over Max. Soc. Sec.	Amount Subject to Soc. Sec	Social Sec. Tax Withheld	Medicare Tax Withheld
$31,000	$1,500		$76,200				
53,000	2,860		76,200				
73,300	3,140		76,200				
75,600	2,920		76,200				

Exercise 8-6B

JOURNAL

PAGE ____

	DATE		DESCRIPTION	POST. REF.	DEBIT	CREDIT	
1							1
2							2
3							3
4							4
5							5
6							6
7							7
8							8
9							9
10							10
11							11
12							12
13							13
14							14
15							15
16							16
17							17
18							18
19							19
20							20
21							21
22							22

Exercise 8-7B

		JOURNAL				PAGE

	DATE		DESCRIPTION	POST. REF.	DEBIT	CREDIT	
1							1
2							2
3							3
4							4
5							5
6							6
7							7
8							8
9							9
10							10
11							11
12							12
13							13

Problem 8-1B

1.

Problem 8-1B (Concluded)

2.

JOURNAL PAGE

	DATE		DESCRIPTION	POST. REF.	DEBIT	CREDIT	
1							1
2							2
3							3
4							4
5							5
6							6
7							7
8							8
9							9
10							10
11							11
12							12
13							13
14							14
15							15
16							16
17							17
18							18
19							19
20							20
21							21
22							22
23							23
24							24
25							25
26							26
27							27
28							28
29							29
30							30
31							31
32							32
33							33
34							34
35							35

Problem 8-2B

PAYROLL REGISTER

	NAME	NO. ALLOW	MARIT. STATUS	EARNINGS						TAXABLE EARNINGS			
				REGULAR		OVERTIME		TOTAL	CUMULATIVE TOTAL	UNEMPLOY. COMP.		SOCIAL SECURITY	
1													
2													
3													
4													
5													
6													
7													
8													
9													
10													
11													
12													
13													
14													

Problem 8-2B (Concluded)

FOR PERIOD ENDED 20--

				DEDUCTIONS							
FEDERAL INCOME TAX	SOCIAL SECURITY TAX	MEDICARE TAX	STATE INCOME TAX	HEALTH INSURANCE	OTHER		TOTAL	NET PAY	CHECK NO.		
											1
											2
											3
											4
											5
											6
											7
											8
											9
											10
											11
											12
											13
											14

2.

JOURNAL

PAGE

	DATE	DESCRIPTION	POST. REF.	DEBIT	CREDIT	
1						1
2						2
3						3
4						4
5						5
6						6
7						7
8						8
9						9
10						10
11						11
12						12
13						13
14						14

Problem 8-3B

EMPLOYEE EARNINGS RECORD

20 -- PERIOD ENDED	EARNINGS				TAXABLE EARNINGS		DEDUCTIONS	
	REGULAR	OVERTIME	TOTAL	CUMULATIVE TOTAL	UNEMPLOY. COMP.	SOCIAL SECURITY	FEDERAL INCOME TAX	SOCIAL SECURITY TAX

GENDER	DEPARTMENT	OCCUPATION	SOCIAL SECURITY NO.	MARITAL STATUS	ALLOW-ANCES
M F					

Problem 8-3B (Concluded)

FOR PERIOD ENDED _____ 20--

									DEDUCTIONS								
MEDICARE TAX		CITY TAX		HEALTH INSURANCE		OTHER						TOTAL		CK. NO.	AMOUNT		
																	1
																	2
																	3
																	4
																	5
PAY RATE		DATE OF BIRTH		DATE HIRED		NAME/ADDRESS									EMP NO.		6
																	7

Challenge Problem

1.

JOURNAL PAGE

	DATE		DESCRIPTION	POST. REF.	DEBIT	CREDIT	
1							1
2							2
3							3
4							4
5							5
6							6
7							7
8							8
9							9
10							10

2.

Mastery Problem

1.

	NAME	NO. ALLOW.	MARIT. STATUS	EARNINGS				TAXABLE EARNINGS	
				REGULAR	OVERTIME	TOTAL	CUMULATIVE TOTAL	UNEMPLOY. COMP.	SOCIAL SECURITY
1									
2									
3									
4									
5									
6									
7									
8									
9									
10									
11									
12									
13									
14									

3.

20 -- PERIOD ENDED	EARNINGS				TAXABLE EARNINGS		FEDERAL INCOME TAX
	REGULAR	OVERTIME	TOTAL	CUMULATIVE TOTAL	UNEMPLOY. COMP.	SOCIAL SECURITY	
11/4	330 00	33 00	363 00	6,145 50	363 00	363 00	4 00
11/11	440 00	49 50	489 50	6,635 00	489 50	489 50	22 00
11/18							
11/25							

GENDER	DEPARTMENT	OCCUPATION	SOCIAL SECURITY NO.	MARITAL STATUS
M F				

Mastery Problem (Continued)

FOR PERIOD ENDED 20--

	FEDERAL INCOME TAX		SOCIAL SECURITY TAX		MEDICARE TAX		STATE INCOME TAX		HEALTH INSURANCE		CREDIT UNION		TOTAL		NET PAY		CK. NO.	
																		1
																		2
																		3
																		4
																		5
																		6
																		7
																		8
																		9
																		10
																		11
																		12
																		13
																		14

(Header: DEDUCTIONS spans FEDERAL INCOME TAX through TOTAL)

FOR PERIOD ENDED 20--

	SOCIAL SECURITY TAX		MEDICARE TAX		STATE INCOME TAX		HEALTH INSURANCE		CREDIT UNION		TOTAL		CK. NO.	AMOUNT			
	22	51	5	26	12	71			72	60	117	08	121	245	92		1
	30	35	7	10	17	13			97	90	174	48	229	315	02		2
																	3
																	4
																	5

(Header: DEDUCTIONS spans SOCIAL SECURITY TAX through TOTAL; NET PAY spans CK. NO. and AMOUNT)

ALLOWANCES	PAY RATE	DATE OF BIRTH	DATE HIRED	NAME/ADDRESS	EMP. NO.
					6
					7

Mastery Problem (Concluded)
2.

JOURNAL PAGE

	DATE		DESCRIPTION	POST. REF.	DEBIT	CREDIT	
1							1
2							2
3							3
4							4
5							5
6							6
7							7
8							8
9							9
10							10
11							11
12							12
13							13
14							14
15							15
16							16
17							17
18							18
19							19
20							20
21							21
22							22
23							23
24							24
25							25
26							26
27							27
28							28
29							29
30							30
31							31
32							32
33							33
34							34
35							35

Name _____

Exercise 9-1A

1.

2.

JOURNAL

PAGE

	DATE		DESCRIPTION	POST. REF.	DEBIT	CREDIT	
1							1
2							2
3							3
4							4
5							5
6							6
7							7

Exercise 9-2A

JOURNAL

PAGE

	DATE		DESCRIPTION	POST. REF.	DEBIT	CREDIT	
1							1
2							2
3							3
4							4
5							5
6							6
7							7

Exercise 9-3A

Name	Total Earnings	Taxable Earnings	
		Unemploy. Comp.	Social Security
Burgos	_____	_____	_____
Ellis	_____	_____	_____
Lewis	_____	_____	_____
Mason	_____	_____	_____
Yates	_____	_____	_____
Zielke	_____	_____	_____
Total	_____	_____	_____

JOURNAL PAGE

	DATE	DESCRIPTION	POST. REF.	DEBIT	CREDIT	
1						1
2						2
3						3
4						4
5						5
6						6
7						7

Exercise 9-4A

Exercise 9-5A

JOURNAL

PAGE

	DATE		DESCRIPTION	POST. REF.	DEBIT	CREDIT	
1							1
2							2
3							3
4							4
5							5
6							6
7							7
8							8
9							9

Exercise 9-6A

1.

JOURNAL

PAGE

	DATE		DESCRIPTION	POST. REF.	DEBIT	CREDIT	
1							1
2							2
3							3
4							4
5							5

2.

JOURNAL

PAGE

	DATE		DESCRIPTION	POST. REF.	DEBIT	CREDIT	
1							1
2							2
3							3
4							4

Problem 9-1A

	Total Earnings	Taxable Earnings	
		Unemploy. Comp.	Social Security
Name	**Total Earnings**	**Unemploy. Comp.**	**Social Security**
Barnum, Alex	_____	_____	_____
Duel, Richard	_____	_____	_____
Hunt, J. B.	_____	_____	_____
Larson, Susan	_____	_____	_____
Mercado, Denise	_____	_____	_____
Swan, Judy	_____	_____	_____
Yates, Keith	_____	_____	_____
Total	_____	_____	_____

2.

JOURNAL PAGE

	DATE	DESCRIPTION	POST. REF.	DEBIT	CREDIT	
1						1
2						2
3						3
4						4
5						5
6						6
7						7
8						8
9						9
10						10

Problem 9-2A

1.

		JOURNAL				PAGE
	DATE	DESCRIPTION	POST. REF.	DEBIT	CREDIT	
1						1
2						2
3						3
4						4
5						5
6						6
7						7
8						8
9						9
10						10
11						11
12						12
13						13
14						14
15						15
16						16
17						17
18						18
19						19
20						20
21						21
22						22
23						23
24						24
25						25
26						26
27						27
28						28
29						29
30						30
31						31
32						32
33						33
34						34

Problem 9-2A (Continued)

JOURNAL PAGE

	DATE		DESCRIPTION	POST. REF.	DEBIT	CREDIT	
1							1
2							2
3							3
4							4
5							5
6							6
7							7
8							8
9							9
10							10
11							11
12							12
13							13
14							14
15							15
16							16
17							17
18							18
19							19
20							20
21							21
22							22
23							23
24							24
25							25
26							26
27							27
28							28
29							29
30							30
31							31
32							32
33							33
34							34
35							35

Name _____

Problem 9-2A (Concluded)

2.

Cash	101

Employ. Inc. Tax Pay.	211

Social Security Tax Payable	212

Medicare Tax Payable	213

Savings Bond Deductions Payable	218

FUTA Tax Payable	221

SUTA Tax Payable	222

Wages and Salaries Expense	511

Payroll Taxes Expense	530

Problem 9-3A

1.

JOURNAL PAGE

	DATE		DESCRIPTION	POST. REF.	DEBIT	CREDIT	
1							1
2							2
3							3
4							4
5							5
6							6

2.

JOURNAL PAGE

	DATE		DESCRIPTION	POST. REF.	DEBIT	CREDIT	
1							1
2							2
3							3
4							4
5							5
6							6

Problem 9-3A (Concluded)

3.

JOURNAL PAGE

	DATE		DESCRIPTION	POST. REF.	DEBIT	CREDIT	
1							1
2							2
3							3
4							4
5							5

Exercise 9-1B

1.

2.

JOURNAL PAGE

	DATE		DESCRIPTION	POST. REF.	DEBIT	CREDIT	
1							1
2							2
3							3
4							4
5							5
6							6
7							7
8							8
9							9

Exercise 9-2B

JOURNAL PAGE

	DATE	DESCRIPTION	POST. REF.	DEBIT	CREDIT	
1						1
2						2
3						3
4						4
5						5
6						6
7						7
8						8

Exercise 9-3B

Taxable Earnings

Name	Total Earnings	Unemploy. Comp.	Social Security
Carlson			
Delgado			
Lewis			
Nixon			
Shippe			
Watts			
Total			

Exercise 9-3B (Concluded)

JOURNAL PAGE

	DATE	DESCRIPTION	POST. REF.	DEBIT	CREDIT	
1						1
2						2
3						3
4						4
5						5
6						6
7						7
8						8
9						9

Exercise 9-4B: See page WP-264

Exercise 9-5B

JOURNAL PAGE

	DATE	DESCRIPTION	POST. REF.	DEBIT	CREDIT	
1						1
2						2
3						3
4						4
5						5
6						6
7						7
8						8
9						9
10						10
11						11
12						12

Exercise 9-4B

Exercise 9-6B

1.

	DATE	DESCRIPTION	POST. REF.	DEBIT	CREDIT	
1						1
2						2
3						3
4						4
5						5

JOURNAL PAGE

2.

JOURNAL PAGE

	DATE	DESCRIPTION	POST. REF.	DEBIT	CREDIT	
1						1
2						2
3						3
4						4
5						5

Problem 9-1B

		Taxable Earnings	
Name	**Total Earnings**	**Unemploy. Comp.**	**Social Security**
Ackers, Alice			
Conley, Dorothy			
Davis, James			
Lawrence, Kevin			
Rawlings, Judy			
Tanaka, Sumio			
Vadillo, Raynette			
Total			

2.

JOURNAL PAGE

	DATE	DESCRIPTION	POST. REF.	DEBIT	CREDIT	
1						1
2						2
3						3
4						4
5						5
6						6
7						7
8						8
9						9
10						10
11						11
12						12

Problem 9-2B

1.

<div align="center">JOURNAL</div>

PAGE

	DATE		DESCRIPTION	POST. REF.	DEBIT	CREDIT	
1							1
2							2
3							3
4							4
5							5
6							6
7							7
8							8
9							9
10							10
11							11
12							12
13							13
14							14
15							15
16							16
17							17
18							18
19							19
20							20
21							21
22							22
23							23
24							24
25							25
26							26
27							27
28							28
29							29
30							30
31							31
32							32
33							33
34							34

Problem 9-2B (Continued)

JOURNAL PAGE

	DATE		DESCRIPTION	POST. REF.	DEBIT	CREDIT	
1							1
2							2
3							3
4							4
5							5
6							6
7							7
8							8
9							9
10							10
11							11
12							12
13							13
14							14
15							15
16							16
17							17
18							18
19							19
20							20
21							21
22							22
23							23
24							24
25							25
26							26
27							27
28							28
29							29
30							30
31							31
32							32
33							33
34							34
35							35

Problem 9-2B(Concluded)

2.

Cash	101

Employ. Inc. Tax Pay.	211

Social Security Tax Payable	212

Medicare Tax Payable	213

Savings Bond Deductions Payable	218

FUTA Tax Payable	221

SUTA Tax Payable	222

Wages and Salaries Expense	511

Payroll Taxes Expense	530

Problem 9-3B

1.

JOURNAL PAGE

	DATE	DESCRIPTION	POST. REF.	DEBIT	CREDIT	
1						1
2						2
3						3
4						4
5						5
6						6

2.

JOURNAL PAGE

	DATE	DESCRIPTION	POST. REF.	DEBIT	CREDIT	
1						1
2						2
3						3
4						4
5						5
6						6

Problem 9-3B (Concluded)

3.

JOURNAL

PAGE

	DATE	DESCRIPTION	POST. REF.	DEBIT	CREDIT	
1						1
2						2
3						3
4						4

Challenge Problem

a.

b.

JOURNAL

PAGE

	DATE	DESCRIPTION	POST. REF.	DEBIT	CREDIT	
1						1
2						2
3						3
4						4
5						5
6						6
7						7

c.

Name _____

Mastery Problem

JOURNAL PAGE

	DATE	DESCRIPTION	POST. REF.	DEBIT	CREDIT	
1						1
2						2
3						3
4						4
5						5
6						6
7						7
8						8
9						9
10						10
11						11
12						12
13						13
14						14
15						15
16						16
17						17
18						18
19						19
20						20
21						21
22						22
23						23
24						24
25						25
26						26
27						27
28						28
29						29
30						30
31						31
32						32
33						33
34						34
35						35

Mastery Problem (Concluded)

JOURNAL PAGE

	DATE	DESCRIPTION	POST. REF.	DEBIT	CREDIT	
1						1
2						2
3						3
4						4
5						5
6						6
7						7
8						8
9						9
10						10
11						11
12						12
13						13
14						14
15						15
16						16
17						17
18						18
19						19
20						20
21						21
22						22
23						23
24						24
25						25
26						26
27						27
28						28
29						29
30						30
31						31
32						32
33						33
34						34
35						35

Exercise 10-1A

	Cash Basis	Modified Cash Basis	Accrual Basis
1. Purchase supplies on account.			
2. Make payment on asset previously purchased.			
3. Purchase supplies for cash.			
4. Purchase insurance for cash.			
5. Pay cash for wages.			
6. Pay cash for telephone expense.			
7. Pay cash for new equipment.			
8. Wages earned but not paid.			
9. Prepaid item purchased, partly used.			
10. Depreciation on long-term assets.			

Exercise 10-2A

COMBINATION JOURNAL

	DATE		CASH				DESCRIPTION	POST. REF.	
			DEBIT		CREDIT				
1									1
2									2
3									3
4									4
5									5
6									6
7									7
8									8
9									9
10									10
11									11
12									12
13									13
14									14
15									15
16									16
17									17
18									18
19									19
20									20
21									21
22									22
23									23
24									24
25									25
26									26
27									27
28									28
29									29
30									30
31									31
32									32
33									33
34									34

Exercise 10-2A (Concluded)

PAGE 1

	GENERAL					
	DEBIT	CREDIT				
1						1
2						2
3						3
4						4
5						5
6						6
7						7
8						8
9						9
10						10
11						11
12						12
13						13
14						14
15						15
16						16
17						17
18						18
19						19
20						20
21						21
22						22
23						23
24						24
25						25
26						26
27						27
28						28
29						29
30						30
31						31
32						32
33						33
34						34

Exercise 10-3A

COMBINATION JOURNAL

	DATE		CASH				DESCRIPTION	POST. REF.	
			DEBIT		CREDIT				
1									1
2									2
3									3
4									4
5									5
6									6
7									7
8									8
9									9
10									10
11									11
12									12
13									13
14									14
15									15
16									16
17									17
18									18
19									19
20									20
21									21
22									22
23									23
24									24
25									25
26									26
27									27
28									28

Proving the Combination Journal:

Exercise 10-3A (Concluded)

PAGE 1

	GENERAL		REPAIR FEES	WAGES EXPENSE	
	DEBIT	CREDIT	CREDIT	DEBIT	
1					1
2					2
3					3
4					4
5					5
6					6
7					7
8					8
9					9
10					10
11					11
12					12
13					13
14					14
15					15
16					16
17					17
18					18
19					19
20					20
21					21
22					22
23					23
24					24
25					25
26					26
27					27
28					28

Problem 10-1A

1. and 4.

COMBINATION JOURNAL

	DATE		CASH				DESCRIPTION	POST. REF.	
			DEBIT		CREDIT				
1									1
2									2
3									3
4									4
5									5
6									6
7									7
8									8
9									9
10									10
11									11
12									12
13									13
14									14
15									15
16									16
17									17
18									18
19									19
20									20
21									21
22									22
23									23
24									24
25									25
26									26
27									27
28									28
29									29
30									30
31									31
32									32
33									33
34									34

Problem 10-1A (Continued)

PAGE 1

	GENERAL					
	DEBIT	CREDIT				
1						
2						
3						
4						
5						
6						
7						
8						
9						
10						
11						
12						
13						
14						
15						
16						
17						
18						
19						
20						
21						
22						
23						
24						
25						
26						
27						
28						
29						
30						
31						
32						
33						
34						

Problem 10-1A (Continued)

2. **Cash Balance, January 12:**

3. **Proving the Combination Journal:**

5.

ACCOUNT	ACCT. NO.	DEBIT BALANCE	CREDIT BALANCE	

Problem 10-1A (Continued)

4.

PARTIAL GENERAL LEDGER

ACCOUNT Cash ACCOUNT NO. 101

DATE	ITEM	POST. REF.	DEBIT	CREDIT	BALANCE	
					DEBIT	CREDIT

ACCOUNT Office Supplies ACCOUNT NO. 142

DATE	ITEM	POST. REF.	DEBIT	CREDIT	BALANCE	
					DEBIT	CREDIT

ACCOUNT Office Equipment ACCOUNT NO. 181

DATE	ITEM	POST. REF.	DEBIT	CREDIT	BALANCE	
					DEBIT	CREDIT

ACCOUNT Accounts Payable ACCOUNT NO. 202

DATE	ITEM	POST. REF.	DEBIT	CREDIT	BALANCE	
					DEBIT	CREDIT

Problem 10-1A (Continued)

ACCOUNT Angela McWharton, Capital ACCOUNT NO. 311

DATE	ITEM	POST. REF.	DEBIT	CREDIT	BALANCE	
					DEBIT	CREDIT

ACCOUNT Angela McWharton, Drawing ACCOUNT NO. 312

DATE	ITEM	POST. REF.	DEBIT	CREDIT	BALANCE	
					DEBIT	CREDIT

ACCOUNT Nursing Care Fees ACCOUNT NO. 401

DATE	ITEM	POST. REF.	DEBIT	CREDIT	BALANCE	
					DEBIT	CREDIT

ACCOUNT Wages Expense ACCOUNT NO. 511

DATE	ITEM	POST. REF.	DEBIT	CREDIT	BALANCE	
					DEBIT	CREDIT

ACCOUNT Advertising Expense ACCOUNT NO. 512

DATE	ITEM	POST. REF.	DEBIT	CREDIT	BALANCE	
					DEBIT	CREDIT

Problem 10-1A (Concluded)

ACCOUNT Rent Expense ACCOUNT NO. 521

DATE	ITEM	POST. REF.	DEBIT	CREDIT	BALANCE	
					DEBIT	CREDIT

ACCOUNT Telephone Expense ACCOUNT NO. 525

DATE	ITEM	POST. REF.	DEBIT	CREDIT	BALANCE	
					DEBIT	CREDIT

ACCOUNT Transportation Expense ACCOUNT NO. 526

DATE	ITEM	POST. REF.	DEBIT	CREDIT	BALANCE	
					DEBIT	CREDIT

ACCOUNT Electricity Expense ACCOUNT NO. 533

DATE	ITEM	POST. REF.	DEBIT	CREDIT	BALANCE	
					DEBIT	CREDIT

ACCOUNT Miscellaneous Expense ACCOUNT NO. 549

DATE	ITEM	POST. REF.	DEBIT	CREDIT	BALANCE	
					DEBIT	CREDIT

Problem 10-2A

1. and 4.

COMBINATION JOURNAL

	DATE		CASH				DESCRIPTION	POST. REF.	
			DEBIT		CREDIT				
1									1
2									2
3									3
4									4
5									5
6									6
7									7
8									8
9									9
10									10
11									11
12									12
13									13
14									14
15									15
16									16
17									17
18									18
19									19
20									20
21									21
22									22
23									23
24									24
25									25
26									26
27									27
28									28
29									29
30									30
31									31
32									32
33									33
34									34

Problem 10-2A (Continued)

PAGE 5

	GENERAL		TAILORING FEES CREDIT	WAGES EXPENSE DEBIT	ADVERTISING EXPENSE DEBIT	
	DEBIT	CREDIT				
1						1
2						2
3						3
4						4
5						5
6						6
7						7
8						8
9						9
10						10
11						11
12						12
13						13
14						14
15						15
16						16
17						17
18						18
19						19
20						20
21						21
22						22
23						23
24						24
25						25
26						26
27						27
28						28
29						29
30						30
31						31
32						32
33						33
34						34

Problem 10-2A (Continued)

2. **Cash Balance, November 12:**

3. **Proving the Combination Journal:**

4.

GENERAL LEDGER

ACCOUNT Cash ACCOUNT NO. 101

DATE	ITEM	POST. REF.	DEBIT	CREDIT	BALANCE DEBIT	CREDIT

ACCOUNT Tailoring Supplies ACCOUNT NO. 141

DATE	ITEM	POST. REF.	DEBIT	CREDIT	BALANCE DEBIT	CREDIT

Problem 10-2A (Continued)

ACCOUNT Office Supplies ACCOUNT NO. 142

DATE	ITEM	POST. REF.	DEBIT	CREDIT	BALANCE	
					DEBIT	CREDIT

ACCOUNT Prepaid Insurance ACCOUNT NO. 145

DATE	ITEM	POST. REF.	DEBIT	CREDIT	BALANCE	
					DEBIT	CREDIT

ACCOUNT Tailoring Equipment ACCOUNT NO. 188

DATE	ITEM	POST. REF.	DEBIT	CREDIT	BALANCE	
					DEBIT	CREDIT

ACCOUNT Accumulated Depreciation—Tailoring Equipment ACCOUNT NO. 188.1

DATE	ITEM	POST. REF.	DEBIT	CREDIT	BALANCE	
					DEBIT	CREDIT

Problem 10-2A (Continued)

ACCOUNT Accounts Payable ACCOUNT NO. 202

DATE	ITEM	POST. REF.	DEBIT	CREDIT	BALANCE	
					DEBIT	CREDIT

ACCOUNT Sue Reyton Capital ACCOUNT NO. 311

DATE	ITEM	POST. REF.	DEBIT	CREDIT	BALANCE	
					DEBIT	CREDIT

ACCOUNT Sue Reyton, Drawing ACCOUNT NO. 312

DATE	ITEM	POST. REF.	DEBIT	CREDIT	BALANCE	
					DEBIT	CREDIT

ACCOUNT Income Summary ACCOUNT NO. 313

DATE	ITEM	POST. REF.	DEBIT	CREDIT	BALANCE	
					DEBIT	CREDIT

Problem 10-2A (Continued)

ACCOUNT Tailoring Fees ACCOUNT NO. 401

DATE	ITEM	POST. REF.	DEBIT	CREDIT	BALANCE	
					DEBIT	CREDIT

ACCOUNT Wages Expense ACCOUNT NO. 511

DATE	ITEM	POST. REF.	DEBIT	CREDIT	BALANCE	
					DEBIT	CREDIT

ACCOUNT Advertising Expense ACCOUNT NO. 512

DATE	ITEM	POST. REF.	DEBIT	CREDIT	BALANCE	
					DEBIT	CREDIT

ACCOUNT Rent Expense ACCOUNT NO. 521

DATE	ITEM	POST. REF.	DEBIT	CREDIT	BALANCE	
					DEBIT	CREDIT

Problem 10-2A (Continued)

ACCOUNT Office Supplies Expense ACCOUNT NO. 523

DATE	ITEM	POST. REF.	DEBIT	CREDIT	BALANCE DEBIT	BALANCE CREDIT

ACCOUNT Tailoring Supplies Expense ACCOUNT NO. 524

DATE	ITEM	POST. REF.	DEBIT	CREDIT	BALANCE DEBIT	BALANCE CREDIT

ACCOUNT Telephone Expense ACCOUNT NO. 525

DATE	ITEM	POST. REF.	DEBIT	CREDIT	BALANCE DEBIT	BALANCE CREDIT

ACCOUNT Electricity Expense ACCOUNT NO. 533

DATE	ITEM	POST. REF.	DEBIT	CREDIT	BALANCE DEBIT	BALANCE CREDIT

Problem 10-2A (Continued)

ACCOUNT Insurance Expense ACCOUNT NO. 535

DATE	ITEM	POST. REF.	DEBIT	CREDIT	BALANCE	
					DEBIT	CREDIT

ACCOUNT Depreciation Expense—Tailoring Equipment ACCOUNT NO. 542

DATE	ITEM	POST. REF.	DEBIT	CREDIT	BALANCE	
					DEBIT	CREDIT

ACCOUNT Miscellaneous Expense ACCOUNT NO. 549

DATE	ITEM	POST. REF.	DEBIT	CREDIT	BALANCE	
					DEBIT	CREDIT

Problem 10-2A (Continued)

5.

		TRIAL BALANCE		ADJUSTMENTS	
		DEBIT	CREDIT	DEBIT	CREDIT
1					
2					
3					
4					
5					
6					
7					
8					
9					
10					
11					
12					
13					
14					
15					
16					
17					
18					
19					
20					
21					
22					
23					
24					
25					
26					
27					
28					
29					
30					
31					
32					

Problem 10-2A (Continued)

ADJUSTED TRIAL BALANCE		INCOME STATEMENT		BALANCE SHEET		
DEBIT	CREDIT	DEBIT	CREDIT	DEBIT	CREDIT	
						1
						2
						3
						4
						5
						6
						7
						8
						9
						10
						11
						12
						13
						14
						15
						16
						17
						18
						19
						20
						21
						22
						23
						24
						25
						26
						27
						28
						29
						30
						31
						32

Problem 10-2A (Continued)

6.

Problem 10-2A (Continued)

Problem 10-2A (Continued)

7.

COMBINATION JOURNAL

	DATE		CASH				DESCRIPTION	POST. REF.	
			DEBIT		CREDIT				
1									1
2									2
3									3
4									4
5									5
6									6
7									7
8									8
9									9
10									10
11									11
12									12
13									13
14									14
15									15
16									16
17									17
18									18
19									19
20									20
21									21
22									22
23									23
24									24
25									25
26									26
27									27
28									28
29									29
30									30
31									31
32									32
33									33
34									34

Problem 10-2A (Concluded)

PAGE 6

	GENERAL		TAILORING FEES CREDIT	WAGES EXPENSE DEBIT	ADVERTISING EXPENSE DEBIT	
	DEBIT	CREDIT				
1						1
2						2
3						3
4						4
5						5
6						6
7						7
8						8
9						9
10						10
11						11
12						12
13						13
14						14
15						15
16						16
17						17
18						18
19						19
20						20
21						21
22						22
23						23
24						24
25						25
26						26
27						27
28						28
29						29
30						30
31						31
32						32
33						33
34						34

Exercise 10-1B

	Cash Basis	Modified Cash Basis	Accrual Basis
1. Office Equipment Cash Purchased equipment for cash.			
2. Office Equipment Accounts Payable Purchased equipment on account.			
3. Cash Revenue Cash receipts for week.			
4. Accounts Receivable Revenue Services performed on account.			
5. Prepaid Insurance Cash Purchased prepaid asset.			
6. Supplies Accounts Payable Purchased prepaid asset.			
7. Telephone Expense Cash Paid telephone bill.			
8. Wages Expense Cash Paid wages for month.			
9. Accounts Payable Cash Made payment on account.			
10. Supplies Expense Supplies			

	Cash Basis	Modified Cash Basis	Accrual Basis
11. Wages Expense Wages Payable			
12. Depreciation Expense—Office Equipment Accum. Depr. —Office Equipment			

Exercise 10-2B

	DATE	CASH			DESCRIPTION	POST. REF.	
		DEBIT		CREDIT			
1							1
2							2
3							3
4							4
5							5
6							6
7							7
8							8
9							9
10							10
11							11
12							12
13							13
14							14
15							15
16							16
17							17
18							18
19							19
20							20
21							21
22							22
23							23
24							24
25							25
26							26
27							27
28							28
29							29
30							30
31							31
32							32
33							33
34							34

Name _____

Exercise 10-2B (Concluded)

PAGE 1

	GENERAL			
	DEBIT	CREDIT		
1				
2				
3				
4				
5				
6				
7				
8				
9				
10				
11				
12				
13				
14				
15				
16				
17				
18				
19				
20				
21				
22				
23				
24				
25				
26				
27				
28				
29				
30				
31				
32				
33				
34				

Exercise 10-3B

COMBINATION JOURNAL

| | DATE | CASH | | DESCRIPTION | POST. REF. | |
		DEBIT	CREDIT			
1						1
2						2
3						3
4						4
5						5
6						6
7						7
8						8
9						9
10						10
11						11
12						12
13						13
14						14
15						15
16						16
17						17
18						18
19						19
20						20
21						21
22						22
23						23
24						24
25						25
26						26
27						27
28						28

Proving the Combination Journal:

Name _____

Exercise 10-3B (Concluded)

PAGE 1

	GENERAL		DELIVERY FEES CREDIT	WAGES EXPENSE DEBIT	
	DEBIT	CREDIT			
1					1
2					2
3					3
4					4
5					5
6					6
7					7
8					8
9					9
10					10
11					11
12					12
13					13
14					14
15					15
16					16
17					17
18					18
19					19
20					20
21					21
22					22
23					23
24					24
25					25
26					26
27					27
28					28

Problem 10-1B

1. and 4.

COMBINATION JOURNAL

	DATE		CASH				DESCRIPTION	POST. REF.	
			DEBIT		CREDIT				
1									1
2									2
3									3
4									4
5									5
6									6
7									7
8									8
9									9
10									10
11									11
12									12
13									13
14									14
15									15
16									16
17									17
18									18
19									19
20									20
21									21
22									22
23									23
24									24
25									25
26									26
27									27
28									28
29									29
30									30
31									31
32									32
33									33
34									34

Problem 10-1B (Continued)

PAGE 1

	GENERAL							
	DEBIT	CREDIT						
1								1
2								2
3								3
4								4
5								5
6								6
7								7
8								8
9								9
10								10
11								11
12								12
13								13
14								14
15								15
16								16
17								17
18								18
19								19
20								20
21								21
22								22
23								23
24								24
25								25
26								26
27								27
28								28
29								29
30								30
31								31
32								32
33								33
34								34

Problem 10-1B (Continued)

2. **Cash Balance, July 14:**

3. **Proving the Combination Journal:**

5.

ACCOUNT	ACCT. NO.	DEBIT BALANCE	CREDIT BALANCE

Problem 10-1B (Continued)

4.

GENERAL LEDGER

ACCOUNT Cash ACCOUNT NO. 101

DATE	ITEM	POST. REF.	DEBIT	CREDIT	BALANCE	
					DEBIT	CREDIT

ACCOUNT Office Supplies ACCOUNT NO. 142

DATE	ITEM	POST. REF.	DEBIT	CREDIT	BALANCE	
					DEBIT	CREDIT

ACCOUNT Skiing Equipment ACCOUNT NO. 183

DATE	ITEM	POST. REF.	DEBIT	CREDIT	BALANCE	
					DEBIT	CREDIT

ACCOUNT Accounts Payable ACCOUNT NO. 202

DATE	ITEM	POST. REF.	DEBIT	CREDIT	BALANCE	
					DEBIT	CREDIT

Problem 10-1B (Continued)

ACCOUNT J. B. Hoyt, Capital ACCOUNT NO. 311

DATE	ITEM	POST. REF.	DEBIT	CREDIT	BALANCE	
					DEBIT	CREDIT

ACCOUNT J. B. Hoyt, Drawing ACCOUNT NO. 312

DATE	ITEM	POST. REF.	DEBIT	CREDIT	BALANCE	
					DEBIT	CREDIT

ACCOUNT Training Fees ACCOUNT NO. 401

DATE	ITEM	POST. REF.	DEBIT	CREDIT	BALANCE	
					DEBIT	CREDIT

ACCOUNT Wages Expense ACCOUNT NO. 511

DATE	ITEM	POST. REF.	DEBIT	CREDIT	BALANCE	
					DEBIT	CREDIT

ACCOUNT Rent Expense ACCOUNT NO. 521

DATE	ITEM	POST. REF.	DEBIT	CREDIT	BALANCE	
					DEBIT	CREDIT

Problem 10-1B (Concluded)

ACCOUNT Telephone Expense ACCOUNT NO. 525

DATE	ITEM	POST. REF.	DEBIT	CREDIT	BALANCE	
					DEBIT	CREDIT

ACCOUNT Transportation Expense ACCOUNT NO. 526

DATE	ITEM	POST. REF.	DEBIT	CREDIT	BALANCE	
					DEBIT	CREDIT

ACCOUNT Electricity Expense ACCOUNT NO. 533

DATE	ITEM	POST. REF.	DEBIT	CREDIT	BALANCE	
					DEBIT	CREDIT

ACCOUNT Repair Expense ACCOUNT NO. 537

DATE	ITEM	POST. REF.	DEBIT	CREDIT	BALANCE	
					DEBIT	CREDIT

ACCOUNT Miscellaneous Expense ACCOUNT NO. 549

DATE	ITEM	POST. REF.	DEBIT	CREDIT	BALANCE	
					DEBIT	CREDIT

Problem 10-2B

1. and 4.

COMBINATION JOURNAL

	DATE		CASH				DESCRIPTION	POST. REF.	
			DEBIT		CREDIT				
1									1
2									2
3									3
4									4
5									5
6									6
7									7
8									8
9									9
10									10
11									11
12									12
13									13
14									14
15									15
16									16
17									17
18									18
19									19
20									20
21									21
22									22
23									23
24									24
25									25
26									26
27									27
28									28
29									29
30									30
31									31
32									32
33									33
34									34

Name _____

Problem 10-2B (Continued)

PAGE 5

	GENERAL		LAWN CARE FEES CREDIT	REPAIR EXPENSE DEBIT	WAGES EXPENSE DEBIT	
	DEBIT	CREDIT				
1						1
2						2
3						3
4						4
5						5
6						6
7						7
8						8
9						9
10						10
11						11
12						12
13						13
14						14
15						15
16						16
17						17
18						18
19						19
20						20
21						21
22						22
23						23
24						24
25						25
26						26
27						27
28						28
29						29
30						30
31						31
32						32
33						33
34						34

Problem 10-2B (Continued)

2. Cash Balance, June 12:

3. Proving the Combination Journal:

4.

GENERAL LEDGER

ACCOUNT Cash ACCOUNT NO. 101

DATE	ITEM	POST. REF.	DEBIT	CREDIT	BALANCE DEBIT	BALANCE CREDIT

ACCOUNT Lawn Care Supplies ACCOUNT NO. 141

DATE	ITEM	POST. REF.	DEBIT	CREDIT	BALANCE DEBIT	BALANCE CREDIT

Problem 10-2B (Continued)

ACCOUNT Office Supplies

ACCOUNT NO. 142

DATE	ITEM	POST. REF.	DEBIT	CREDIT	BALANCE DEBIT	BALANCE CREDIT

ACCOUNT Prepaid Insurance

ACCOUNT NO. 145

DATE	ITEM	POST. REF.	DEBIT	CREDIT	BALANCE DEBIT	BALANCE CREDIT

ACCOUNT Lawn Care Equipment

ACCOUNT NO. 189

DATE	ITEM	POST. REF.	DEBIT	CREDIT	BALANCE DEBIT	BALANCE CREDIT

ACCOUNT Accumulated Depreciation—Lawn Care Equipment

ACCOUNT NO. 189.1

DATE	ITEM	POST. REF.	DEBIT	CREDIT	BALANCE DEBIT	BALANCE CREDIT

Problem 10-2B (Continued)

ACCOUNT Accounts Payable ACCOUNT NO. 202

DATE	ITEM	POST. REF.	DEBIT	CREDIT	BALANCE DEBIT	BALANCE CREDIT

ACCOUNT Molly Claussen, Capital ACCOUNT NO. 311

DATE	ITEM	POST. REF.	DEBIT	CREDIT	BALANCE DEBIT	BALANCE CREDIT

ACCOUNT Molly Claussen, Drawing ACCOUNT NO. 312

DATE	ITEM	POST. REF.	DEBIT	CREDIT	BALANCE DEBIT	BALANCE CREDIT

ACCOUNT Income Summary ACCOUNT NO. 313

DATE	ITEM	POST. REF.	DEBIT	CREDIT	BALANCE DEBIT	BALANCE CREDIT

Problem 10-2B (Continued)

ACCOUNT Lawn Care Fees ACCOUNT NO. 401

DATE	ITEM	POST. REF.	DEBIT	CREDIT	BALANCE	
					DEBIT	CREDIT

ACCOUNT Wages Expense ACCOUNT NO. 511

DATE	ITEM	POST. REF.	DEBIT	CREDIT	BALANCE	
					DEBIT	CREDIT

ACCOUNT Rent Expense ACCOUNT NO. 521

DATE	ITEM	POST. REF.	DEBIT	CREDIT	BALANCE	
					DEBIT	CREDIT

ACCOUNT Office Supplies Expense ACCOUNT NO. 523

DATE	ITEM	POST. REF.	DEBIT	CREDIT	BALANCE	
					DEBIT	CREDIT

Problem 10-2B (Continued)

ACCOUNT Lawn Care Supplies Expense ACCOUNT NO. 524

DATE	ITEM	POST. REF.	DEBIT	CREDIT	BALANCE DEBIT	BALANCE CREDIT

ACCOUNT Telephone Expense ACCOUNT NO. 525

DATE	ITEM	POST. REF.	DEBIT	CREDIT	BALANCE DEBIT	BALANCE CREDIT

ACCOUNT Electricity Expense ACCOUNT NO. 533

DATE	ITEM	POST. REF.	DEBIT	CREDIT	BALANCE DEBIT	BALANCE CREDIT

ACCOUNT Insurance Expense ACCOUNT NO. 535

DATE	ITEM	POST. REF.	DEBIT	CREDIT	BALANCE DEBIT	BALANCE CREDIT

Problem 10-2B (Continued)

Problem 10-2B (Continued)

7.

COMBINATION JOURNAL

	DATE		CASH				DESCRIPTION	POST. REF.	
			DEBIT		CREDIT				
1									1
2									2
3									3
4									4
5									5
6									6
7									7
8									8
9									9
10									10
11									11
12									12
13									13
14									14
15									15
16									16
17									17
18									18
19									19
20									20
21									21
22									22
23									23
24									24
25									25
26									26
27									27
28									28
29									29
30									30
31									31
32									32
33									33
34									34

Problem 10-2B (Concluded)

PAGE 6

	GENERAL		LAWN CARE FEES CREDIT	REPAIR EXPENSE DEBIT	WAGES EXPENSE DEBIT	
	DEBIT	CREDIT				
1						1
2						2
3						3
4						4
5						5
6						6
7						7
8						8
9						9
10						10
11						11
12						12
13						13
14						14
15						15
16						16
17						17
18						18
19						19
20						20
21						21
22						22
23						23
24						24
25						25
26						26
27						27
28						28
29						29
30						30
31						31
32						32
33						33
34						34

Challenge Problem

Restler Financial Consulting

Income Statements

For Month Ended June 20--

	Cash Basis		Modified Cash Basis		Accrual Basis	

Mastery Problem

1. **The Combination Journal can be found on pages WP-330 and WP-331**

2. **Proving the Combination Journal:**

3.

GENERAL LEDGER

ACCOUNT Cash ACCOUNT NO. 101

DATE	ITEM	POST. REF.	DEBIT	CREDIT	BALANCE	
					DEBIT	CREDIT

Mastery Problem (Continued)

ACCOUNT Office Supplies ACCOUNT NO. 142

DATE	ITEM	POST. REF.	DEBIT	CREDIT	BALANCE	
					DEBIT	CREDIT

ACCOUNT Food Supplies ACCOUNT NO. 144

DATE	ITEM	POST. REF.	DEBIT	CREDIT	BALANCE	
					DEBIT	CREDIT

ACCOUNT Tennis Facilities ACCOUNT NO. 184

DATE	ITEM	POST. REF.	DEBIT	CREDIT	BALANCE	
					DEBIT	CREDIT

ACCOUNT Accumulated Depreciation—Tennis Facilities ACCOUNT NO. 184.1

DATE	ITEM	POST. REF.	DEBIT	CREDIT	BALANCE	
					DEBIT	CREDIT

ACCOUNT Exercise Equipment ACCOUNT NO. 186

DATE	ITEM	POST. REF.	DEBIT	CREDIT	BALANCE	
					DEBIT	CREDIT

Mastery Problem (Continued)

ACCOUNT Accumulated Depreciation—Exercise Equipment ACCOUNT NO. 186.1

DATE	ITEM	POST. REF.	DEBIT	CREDIT	BALANCE DEBIT	BALANCE CREDIT

ACCOUNT Accounts Payable ACCOUNT NO. 202

DATE	ITEM	POST. REF.	DEBIT	CREDIT	BALANCE DEBIT	BALANCE CREDIT

ACCOUNT John McRoe, Capital ACCOUNT NO. 311

DATE	ITEM	POST. REF.	DEBIT	CREDIT	BALANCE DEBIT	BALANCE CREDIT

ACCOUNT John McRoe, Drawing ACCOUNT NO. 312

DATE	ITEM	POST. REF.	DEBIT	CREDIT	BALANCE DEBIT	BALANCE CREDIT

Mastery Problem (Continued)

ACCOUNT Income Summary ACCOUNT NO. 313

DATE	ITEM	POST. REF.	DEBIT	CREDIT	BALANCE DEBIT	BALANCE CREDIT

ACCOUNT Registration Fees ACCOUNT NO. 401

DATE	ITEM	POST. REF.	DEBIT	CREDIT	BALANCE DEBIT	BALANCE CREDIT

ACCOUNT Wages Expense ACCOUNT NO. 511

DATE	ITEM	POST. REF.	DEBIT	CREDIT	BALANCE DEBIT	BALANCE CREDIT

ACCOUNT Rent Expense ACCOUNT NO. 521

DATE	ITEM	POST. REF.	DEBIT	CREDIT	BALANCE DEBIT	BALANCE CREDIT

ACCOUNT Office Supplies Expense ACCOUNT NO. 523

DATE	ITEM	POST. REF.	DEBIT	CREDIT	BALANCE DEBIT	BALANCE CREDIT

Mastery Problem (Continued)

ACCOUNT Food Supplies Expense ACCOUNT NO. 524

DATE	ITEM	POST. REF.	DEBIT	CREDIT	BALANCE DEBIT	BALANCE CREDIT

ACCOUNT Telephone Expense ACCOUNT NO. 525

DATE	ITEM	POST. REF.	DEBIT	CREDIT	BALANCE DEBIT	BALANCE CREDIT

ACCOUNT Utilities Expense ACCOUNT NO. 533

DATE	ITEM	POST. REF.	DEBIT	CREDIT	BALANCE DEBIT	BALANCE CREDIT

ACCOUNT Insurance Expense ACCOUNT NO. 535

DATE	ITEM	POST. REF.	DEBIT	CREDIT	BALANCE DEBIT	BALANCE CREDIT

ACCOUNT Postage Expense ACCOUNT NO. 536

DATE	ITEM	POST. REF.	DEBIT	CREDIT	BALANCE DEBIT	BALANCE CREDIT

Mastery Problem (Continued)

ACCOUNT Depreciation Expense—Tennis Facilities ACCOUNT NO. 541

DATE	ITEM	POST. REF.	DEBIT	CREDIT	BALANCE	
					DEBIT	CREDIT

ACCOUNT Depreciation Expense—Exercise Equipment ACCOUNT NO. 542

DATE	ITEM	POST. REF.	DEBIT	CREDIT	BALANCE	
					DEBIT	CREDIT

Mastery Problem (Continued)
1.

COMBINATION JOURNAL

	DATE		CASH				DESCRIPTION	POST. REF.	
			DEBIT		CREDIT				
1									1
2									2
3									3
4									4
5									5
6									6
7									7
8									8
9									9
10									10
11									11
12									12
13									13
14									14
15									15
16									16
17									17
18									18
19									19
20									20
21									21
22									22
23									23
24									24
25									25
26									26
27									27
28									28
29									29
30									30
31									31
32									32
33									33
34									34

Name _____

Mastery Problem (Continued)

PAGE 1

	GENERAL		REGISTRATION FEES CREDIT	WAGES EXPENSE DEBIT	FOOD SUPPLIES DEBIT	
	DEBIT	CREDIT				
1						1
2						2
3						3
4						4
5						5
6						6
7						7
8						8
9						9
10						10
11						11
12						12
13						13
14						14
15						15
16						16
17						17
18						18
19						19
20						20
21						21
22						22
23						23
24						24
25						25
26						26
27						27
28						28
29						29
30						30
31						31
32						32
33						33
34						34

Mastery Problem (Concluded)

4.

ACCOUNT	ACCT. NO.	DEBIT BALANCE	CREDIT BALANCE

Exercise 11-1A

1. _____ 4. _____

2. _____ 5. _____

3. _____ 6. _____

Exercise 11-2A

1.

Cash	Accounts Receivable

Sales Tax Payable	Sales

Sales Returns and Allowances	Sales Discounts

2.

Cash	Accounts Receivable

Sales Tax Payable	Sales

Sales Returns and Allowances	Sales Discounts

Exercise 11-2A (Concluded)

3.

Cash	Accounts Receivable

Sales Tax Payable	Sales

Sales Returns and Allowances	Sales Discounts

4.

Cash	Accounts Receivable

Sales Tax Payable	Sales

Sales Returns and Allowances	Sales Discounts

5.

Cash	Accounts Receivable

Sales Tax Payable	Sales

Sales Returns and Allowances	Sales Discounts

Exercise 11-3A

Exercise 11-4A

JOURNAL PAGE

	DATE	DESCRIPTION	POST. REF.	DEBIT	CREDIT	
1						1
2						2
3						3
4						4
5						5
6						6
7						7
8						8
9						9
10						10
11						11
12						12
13						13
14						14
15						15
16						16
17						17
18						18
19						19
20						20
21						21
22						22
23						23
24						24
25						25

Exercise 11-5A

JOURNAL

PAGE 60

	DATE		DESCRIPTION	POST. REF.	DEBIT	CREDIT	
1							1
2							2
3							3
4							4
5							5
6							6
7							7
8							8
9							9
10							10
11							11
12							12
13							13
14							14
15							15

GENERAL LEDGER

ACCOUNT Accounts Receivable ACCOUNT NO. 122

DATE		ITEM	POST. REF.	DEBIT	CREDIT	BALANCE	
						DEBIT	CREDIT
20-- June	1	Balance	✓			4 2 0 0 00	

ACCOUNT Sales Returns and Allowances ACCOUNT NO. 401.1

DATE		ITEM	POST. REF.	DEBIT	CREDIT	BALANCE	
						DEBIT	CREDIT

Exercise 11-5A (Concluded)

ACCOUNTS RECEIVABLE LEDGER

NAME John B. Abramovitz

ADDRESS 3201 West Judkins Road, Seattle, WA 98201-1079

DATE		ITEM	POST. REF.	DEBIT	CREDIT	BALANCE
20-- June	1	Balance	✓			8 5 0 00

NAME L. B. Gruder

ADDRESS 44 Western Blvd., Spokane, WA 98601-4092

DATE		ITEM	POST. REF.	DEBIT	CREDIT	BALANCE
20-- June	1	Balance	✓			4 2 8 00

NAME Marie L. Perez

ADDRESS 158 West Adams Point, Bellvue, WA 98401-0663

DATE		ITEM	POST. REF.	DEBIT	CREDIT	BALANCE
20-- June	1	Balance	✓			1 0 1 8 00

Exercise 11-6A

<div align="center">JOURNAL</div>

PAGE

	DATE		DESCRIPTION	POST. REF.	DEBIT	CREDIT	
1							1
2							2
3							3
4							4
5							5
6							6
7							7
8							8
9							9
10							10
11							11
12							12
13							13
14							14
15							15
16							16
17							17
18							18
19							19
20							20
21							21
22							22
23							23

Exercise 11-7A

Problem 11-1A

1.

<div align="center">

JOURNAL

</div>

	DATE	DESCRIPTION	POST. REF.	DEBIT	CREDIT	
1						1
2						2
3						3
4						4
5						5
6						6
7						7
8						8
9						9
10						10
11						11
12						12
13						13
14						14
15						15
16						16
17						17
18						18
19						19
20						20
21						21
22						22
23						23
24						24
25						25
26						26
27						27
28						28
29						29
30						30
31						31
32						32
33						33
34						34

Problem 11-1A (Continued)

2.

GENERAL LEDGER

ACCOUNT Accounts Receivable ACCOUNT NO. 122

DATE	ITEM	POST. REF.	DEBIT	CREDIT	BALANCE	
					DEBIT	CREDIT

ACCOUNT Sales Tax Payable ACCOUNT NO. 231

DATE	ITEM	POST. REF.	DEBIT	CREDIT	BALANCE	
					DEBIT	CREDIT

ACCOUNT Sales ACCOUNT NO. 401

DATE	ITEM	POST. REF.	DEBIT	CREDIT	BALANCE	
					DEBIT	CREDIT

Name _____

Problem 11-1A (Concluded)

ACCOUNTS RECEIVABLE LEDGER

NAME R. B. Hassad Co.

ADDRESS 1225 W. Temperance Street, Elletsville, IN 47429-9976

DATE	ITEM	POST. REF.	DEBIT	CREDIT	BALANCE

NAME Helsinki, Inc.

ADDRESS 125 Fishers Driver, Noblesville, IN 47870-8867

DATE	ITEM	POST. REF.	DEBIT	CREDIT	BALANCE

NAME Jung Manufacturing Co.

ADDRESS 8825 Old State Road, Bloomington, IN 47401-8823

DATE	ITEM	POST. REF.	DEBIT	CREDIT	BALANCE

NAME Ardis Myler

ADDRESS 2100 Greer Lane, Bedford, IN 47421-8876

DATE	ITEM	POST. REF.	DEBIT	CREDIT	BALANCE

Problem 11-2A

1.

<div align="center">JOURNAL</div>

	DATE		DESCRIPTION	POST. REF.	DEBIT	CREDIT	
1							1
2							2
3							3
4							4
5							5
6							6
7							7
8							8
9							9
10							10
11							11
12							12
13							13
14							14
15							15
16							16
17							17
18							18
19							19
20							20
21							21
22							22
23							23
24							24
25							25
26							26
27							27
28							28
29							29
30							30
31							31
32							32
33							33
34							34

Problem 11-2A (Continued)

JOURNAL

	DATE		DESCRIPTION	POST. REF.	DEBIT	CREDIT	
1							1
2							2
3							3
4							4
5							5
6							6
7							7
8							8
9							9
10							10
11							11
12							12
13							13
14							14
15							15
16							16
17							17
18							18
19							19
20							20
21							21
22							22
23							23
24							24
25							25
26							26
27							27
28							28
29							29
30							30
31							31
32							32
33							33
34							34

Problem 11-2A (Continued)

2.

GENERAL LEDGER

ACCOUNT Cash ACCOUNT NO. 101

DATE		ITEM	POST. REF.	DEBIT	CREDIT	BALANCE	
						DEBIT	CREDIT
20-- Dec.	1	Balance	✓			9 8 6 2 00	

ACCOUNT Accounts Receivable ACCOUNT NO. 122

DATE		ITEM	POST. REF.	DEBIT	CREDIT	BALANCE	
						DEBIT	CREDIT
20-- Dec.	1	Balance	✓			9 3 5 2 00	

Problem 11-2A (Continued)

ACCOUNT Sales Tax Payable ACCOUNT NO. 231

DATE	ITEM	POST. REF.	DEBIT	CREDIT	BALANCE	
					DEBIT	CREDIT

ACCOUNT Sales ACCOUNT NO. 401

DATE	ITEM	POST. REF.	DEBIT	CREDIT	BALANCE	
					DEBIT	CREDIT

ACCOUNT Sales Returns and Allowances ACCOUNT NO. 401.1

DATE	ITEM	POST. REF.	DEBIT	CREDIT	BALANCE	
					DEBIT	CREDIT

ACCOUNT Bank Credit Card Expense ACCOUNT NO. 513

DATE	ITEM	POST. REF.	DEBIT	CREDIT	BALANCE	
					DEBIT	CREDIT

Problem 11-2A (Continued)

ACCOUNTS RECEIVABLE LEDGER

NAME Michael Anderson

ADDRESS 233 West 11th Avenue, Detroit, MI 59500-1154

DATE		ITEM	POST. REF.	DEBIT	CREDIT	BALANCE
20-- Dec.	1	Balance	✓			2 4 8 0 00

NAME Ansel Manufacturing

ADDRESS 284 West 88 Street, Detroit, MI 59522-1168

DATE		ITEM	POST. REF.	DEBIT	CREDIT	BALANCE
20-- Dec.	1	Balance	✓			9 8 2 00

NAME J. Gorbea

ADDRESS P.O. BOX 864, Detroit, MI 59552-0864

DATE		ITEM	POST. REF.	DEBIT	CREDIT	BALANCE
20-- Dec.	1	Balance	✓			8 8 0 00

Problem 11-2A (Concluded)

NAME Rachel Carson

ADDRESS 11312 Fourteenth Avenue South, Detroit, MI 59221-1142

DATE		ITEM	POST. REF.	DEBIT	CREDIT	BALANCE
20-- Dec.	1	Balance	✓			3 2 0 0 00

NAME Tom Wilson

ADDRESS 100 NW Seward St., Detroit, MI 59210-1337

DATE		ITEM	POST. REF.	DEBIT	CREDIT	BALANCE
20-- Dec.	1	Balance	✓			1 8 1 0 00

Problem 11-3A

1.

<div align="center">

JOURNAL

</div>

	DATE		DESCRIPTION	POST. REF.	DEBIT	CREDIT	
1							1
2							2
3							3
4							4
5							5
6							6
7							7
8							8
9							9
10							10
11							11
12							12
13							13
14							14
15							15
16							16
17							17
18							18
19							19
20							20
21							21
22							22
23							23
24							24
25							25
26							26
27							27
28							28
29							29
30							30
31							31
32							32
33							33
34							34

Problem 11-3A (Continued)

JOURNAL PAGE 8

	DATE		DESCRIPTION	POST. REF.	DEBIT	CREDIT	
1							1
2							2
3							3
4							4
5							5
6							6
7							7
8							8
9							9
10							10
11							11
12							12
13							13
14							14
15							15
16							16
17							17
18							18
19							19
20							20
21							21
22							22
23							23
24							24
25							25
26							26
27							27
28							28
29							29
30							30
31							31
32							32
33							33
34							34

Problem 11-3A (Continued)

JOURNAL PAGE 9

	DATE	DESCRIPTION	POST. REF.	DEBIT	CREDIT	
1						1
2						2
3						3
4						4
5						5
6						6
7						7
8						8
9						9
10						10

2.

GENERAL LEDGER

ACCOUNT Cash ACCOUNT NO. 101

DATE		ITEM	POST. REF.	DEBIT	CREDIT	BALANCE DEBIT	BALANCE CREDIT
20-- Mar.	1	Balance	✓			9 7 4 1 00	

Problem 11-3A (Continued)

ACCOUNT Accounts Receivable ACCOUNT NO. 122

DATE		ITEM	POST. REF.	DEBIT	CREDIT	BALANCE	
						DEBIT	CREDIT
20-- Mar.	1	Balance	✓			1 0 5 8 25	

ACCOUNT Sales Tax Payable ACCOUNT NO. 231

DATE		ITEM	POST. REF.	DEBIT	CREDIT	BALANCE	
						DEBIT	CREDIT

Problem 11-3A (Continued)

ACCOUNT Sales ACCOUNT NO. 401

DATE	ITEM	POST. REF.	DEBIT	CREDIT	BALANCE	
					DEBIT	CREDIT

ACCOUNT Sales Returns and Allowances ACCOUNT NO. 401.1

DATE	ITEM	POST. REF.	DEBIT	CREDIT	BALANCE	
					DEBIT	CREDIT

ACCOUNTS RECEIVABLE LEDGER

NAME Able & Co.

ADDRESS 1424 Jackson Creek Road, Nashville, IN 47448-2245

DATE	ITEM	POST. REF.	DEBIT	CREDIT	BALANCE

Problem 11-3A (Concluded)

NAME Blevins Bakery

ADDRESS 6422 E. Bender Road, Bloomington, IN 47401-7756

DATE	ITEM	POST. REF.	DEBIT	CREDIT	BALANCE

NAME R. J. Kalas, Inc.

ADDRESS 3315 Longview Avenue, Bloomington, IN 47401-7223

DATE	ITEM	POST. REF.	DEBIT	CREDIT	BALANCE

NAME Thompson Group

ADDRESS 2300 E. National Road, Cumberland, IN 46229-4824

DATE	ITEM	POST. REF.	DEBIT	CREDIT	BALANCE
20-- Mar. 1	Balance	✓			1 0 5 8 25

Problem 11-4A

Exercise 11-1B

1.	_____	4.	_____
2.	_____	5.	_____
3.	_____	6.	_____

Exercise 11-2B

1.

Cash	Accounts Receivable

Sales Tax Payable	Sales

Sales Returns and Allowances	Sales Discounts

2.

Cash	Accounts Receivable

Sales Tax Payable	Sales

Sales Returns and Allowances	Sales Discounts

Name _____

Exercise 11-2B (Concluded)

3.

Cash		Accounts Receivable

Sales Tax Payable		Sales

Sales Returns and Allowances		Sales Discounts

4.

Cash		Accounts Receivable

Sales Tax Payable		Sales

Sales Returns and Allowances		Sales Discounts

5.

Cash		Accounts Receivable

Sales Tax Payable		Sales

Sales Returns and Allowances		Sales Discounts

Exercise 11-3B

Exercise 11-4B

JOURNAL PAGE

	DATE	DESCRIPTION	POST. REF.	DEBIT	CREDIT	
1						1
2						2
3						3
4						4
5						5
6						6
7						7
8						8
9						9
10						10
11						11
12						12
13						13
14						14
15						15
16						16
17						17
18						18
19						19
20						20
21						21
22						22
23						23
24						24

Exercise 11-5B

JOURNAL

	DATE		DESCRIPTION	POST. REF.	DEBIT	CREDIT	
1							1
2							2
3							3
4							4
5							5
6							6
7							7
8							8
9							9
10							10
11							11
12							12
13							13
14							14

GENERAL LEDGER

ACCOUNT Accounts Receivable ACCOUNT NO. 122

DATE		ITEM	POST. REF.	DEBIT	CREDIT	BALANCE DEBIT	BALANCE CREDIT
20-- June	1	Balance	✓			3 9 0 0 00	

ACCOUNT Sales Returns and Allowances ACCOUNT NO. 401.1

DATE	ITEM	POST. REF.	DEBIT	CREDIT	BALANCE DEBIT	BALANCE CREDIT

Exercise 11-5B (Concluded)

ACCOUNTS RECEIVABLE LEDGER

NAME John B. Adams

ADDRESS 127 Strawberry Lane, Manchester, CT 06040-0865

DATE		ITEM	POST. REF.	DEBIT	CREDIT	BALANCE
20— June	1	Balance	✓			8 5 0 00

NAME L. B. Green

ADDRESS 2254 Blackrock, Bronx, NY 10472-1974

DATE		ITEM	POST. REF.	DEBIT	CREDIT	BALANCE
20— June	1	Balance	✓			4 2 8 00

NAME Marie L. Phillips

ADDRESS 334 Fern St., W. Hartford, CT 06119-2314

DATE		ITEM	POST. REF.	DEBIT	CREDIT	BALANCE
20— June	1	Balance	✓			1 0 1 8 00

Exercise 11-6B

JOURNAL PAGE 1

	DATE		DESCRIPTION	POST. REF.	DEBIT	CREDIT	
1							1
2							2
3							3
4							4
5							5
6							6
7							7
8							8
9							9
10							10
11							11
12							12
13							13
14							14
15							15
16							16
17							17
18							18
19							19
20							20
21							21
22							22
23							23

Exercise 11-7B

Problem 11-1B

1.

	JOURNAL				PAGE 15

	DATE	DESCRIPTION	POST. REF.	DEBIT	CREDIT	
1						1
2						2
3						3
4						4
5						5
6						6
7						7
8						8
9						9
10						10
11						11
12						12
13						13
14						14
15						15
16						16
17						17
18						18
19						19
20						20
21						21
22						22
23						23
24						24
25						25
26						26
27						27
28						28
29						29
30						30
31						31
32						32
33						33
34						34

Problem 11-1B (Continued)

2.

GENERAL LEDGER

ACCOUNT Accounts Receivable ACCOUNT NO. 122

DATE	ITEM	POST. REF.	DEBIT	CREDIT	BALANCE	
					DEBIT	CREDIT

ACCOUNT Sales Tax Payable ACCOUNT NO. 231

DATE	ITEM	POST. REF.	DEBIT	CREDIT	BALANCE	
					DEBIT	CREDIT

ACCOUNT Sales ACCOUNT NO. 401

DATE	ITEM	POST. REF.	DEBIT	CREDIT	BALANCE	
					DEBIT	CREDIT

Problem 11-1B (Concluded)

ACCOUNTS RECEIVABLE LEDGER

NAME Dvorak Manufacturing Co.

ADDRESS 2105 Williams Drive, Muncie, IN 47304-2437

DATE	ITEM	POST. REF.	DEBIT	CREDIT	BALANCE

NAME Saga, Inc.

ADDRESS 1453 Parnell Avenue, Indianapolis, IN 46201-6870

DATE	ITEM	POST. REF.	DEBIT	CREDIT	BALANCE

NAME Vinnie Ward

ADDRESS 308 So. Muirhead Drive, Okemos, MI 48864-5356

DATE	ITEM	POST. REF.	DEBIT	CREDIT	BALANCE

NAME Zapata Co.

ADDRESS 789 Stafford Road, Bloomington, IN 47401-6201

DATE	ITEM	POST. REF.	DEBIT	CREDIT	BALANCE

Problem 11-2B

1.

	DATE		DESCRIPTION	POST. REF.	DEBIT	CREDIT	
1							1
2							2
3							3
4							4
5							5
6							6
7							7
8							8
9							9
10							10
11							11
12							12
13							13
14							14
15							15
16							16
17							17
18							18
19							19
20							20
21							21
22							22
23							23
24							24
25							25
26							26
27							27
28							28
29							29
30							30
31							31
32							32
33							33
34							34

JOURNAL PAGE 20

Problem 11-2B (Continued)

	DATE		DESCRIPTION	POST. REF.	DEBIT	CREDIT	
1							1
2							2
3							3
4							4
5							5
6							6
7							7
8							8
9							9
10							10
11							11
12							12
13							13
14							14
15							15
16							16
17							17
18							18
19							19
20							20
21							21
22							22
23							23
24							24
25							25
26							26
27							27
28							28
29							29
30							30
31							31
32							32
33							33
34							34

The table above is the JOURNAL, PAGE 21.

Problem 11-2B (Continued)

2.

GENERAL LEDGER

ACCOUNT Cash ACCOUNT NO. 101

DATE		ITEM	POST. REF.	DEBIT	CREDIT	BALANCE	
						DEBIT	CREDIT
20-- Jan.	1	Balance	✓			2 8 9 0 75	

ACCOUNT Accounts Receivable ACCOUNT NO. 122

DATE		ITEM	POST. REF.	DEBIT	CREDIT	BALANCE	
						DEBIT	CREDIT
20-- Jan.	1	Balance	✓			6 3 0 0 00	

Problem 11-2B (Continued)

ACCOUNT Sales Tax Payable ACCOUNT NO. 231

DATE	ITEM	POST. REF.	DEBIT	CREDIT	BALANCE	
					DEBIT	CREDIT

ACCOUNT Sales ACCOUNT NO. 401

DATE	ITEM	POST. REF.	DEBIT	CREDIT	BALANCE	
					DEBIT	CREDIT

ACCOUNT Sales Returns and Allowances ACCOUNT NO. 401.1

DATE	ITEM	POST. REF.	DEBIT	CREDIT	BALANCE	
					DEBIT	CREDIT

ACCOUNT Bank Credit Card Expense ACCOUNT NO. 513

DATE	ITEM	POST. REF.	DEBIT	CREDIT	BALANCE	
					DEBIT	CREDIT

Problem 11-2B (Continued)

ACCOUNTS RECEIVABLE LEDGER

NAME Ray Boyd

ADDRESS 229 SE 65th Avenue, Portland, OR 97215-1451

DATE		ITEM	POST. REF.	DEBIT	CREDIT	BALANCE
20-- Jan.	1	Balance	✓			1 4 0 0 00

NAME Dazai Manufacturing

ADDRESS 447 6th Avenue, Flagstaff, AZ 86004-6842

DATE		ITEM	POST. REF.	DEBIT	CREDIT	BALANCE
20-- Jan.	1	Balance	✓			3 1 8 00

NAME Clint Hassell

ADDRESS 1462 N. Steves Blvd., Los Cruces, NM 88012-7791

DATE		ITEM	POST. REF.	DEBIT	CREDIT	BALANCE
20-- Jan.	1	Balance	✓			8 1 5 00

Problem 11-2B (Concluded)

NAME Jan Sowada

ADDRESS 5997 Blackgold Lane, Grapevine, TX 76051-2366

DATE		ITEM	POST. REF.	DEBIT	CREDIT	BALANCE
20-- Jan.	1	Balance	✓			1 4 8 1 00

NAME Robert Zehnle

ADDRESS 6881 Seneca Drive, San Diego, CA 92127-8671

DATE		ITEM	POST. REF.	DEBIT	CREDIT	BALANCE
20-- Dec.	1	Balance	✓			2 2 8 6 00

Name _____

Problem 11-3B
1.

JOURNAL PAGE 7

	DATE	DESCRIPTION	POST. REF.	DEBIT	CREDIT	
1						1
2						2
3						3
4						4
5						5
6						6
7						7
8						8
9						9
10						10
11						11
12						12
13						13
14						14
15						15
16						16
17						17
18						18
19						19
20						20
21						21
22						22
23						23
24						24
25						25
26						26
27						27
28						28
29						29
30						30
31						31
32						32
33						33
34						34

Problem 11-3B (Continued)

<div align="center">JOURNAL</div>

	DATE		DESCRIPTION	POST. REF.	DEBIT	CREDIT	
1							1
2							2
3							3
4							4
5							5
6							6
7							7
8							8
9							9
10							10
11							11
12							12
13							13
14							14
15							15
16							16
17							17
18							18
19							19
20							20
21							21
22							22
23							23
24							24
25							25
26							26
27							27
28							28
29							29
30							30
31							31
32							32
33							33
34							34

Problem 11-3B (Continued)

2.

GENERAL LEDGER

ACCOUNT Cash ACCOUNT NO. 101

DATE		ITEM	POST. REF.	DEBIT	CREDIT	BALANCE	
						DEBIT	CREDIT
20-- Apr.	1	Balance	✓			2 8 6 4 54	

ACCOUNT Accounts Receivable ACCOUNT NO. 122

DATE		ITEM	POST. REF.	DEBIT	CREDIT	BALANCE	
						DEBIT	CREDIT
20-- Apr.	1	Balance	✓			2 7 2 6 25	

Problem 11-3B (Continued)

ACCOUNT Sales Tax Payable ACCOUNT NO. 231

DATE	ITEM	POST. REF.	DEBIT	CREDIT	BALANCE DEBIT	BALANCE CREDIT

ACCOUNT Sales ACCOUNT NO. 401

DATE	ITEM	POST. REF.	DEBIT	CREDIT	BALANCE DEBIT	BALANCE CREDIT

ACCOUNT Sales Returns and Allowances ACCOUNT NO. 401.1

DATE	ITEM	POST. REF.	DEBIT	CREDIT	BALANCE DEBIT	BALANCE CREDIT

Problem 11-3B (Concluded)

ACCOUNTS RECEIVABLE LEDGER

NAME O. L. Meyers

ADDRESS 119 Hartford Turnpike, Vernon, CT 06066-0113

DATE		ITEM	POST. REF.	DEBIT	CREDIT	BALANCE
20-- Apr.	1	Balance	✓			2 1 8 6 00

NAME Kelsay Munkres

ADDRESS 233 Cambridge Dr., Branford, CT 06405-9276

DATE		ITEM	POST. REF.	DEBIT	CREDIT	BALANCE
20-- Apr.	1	Balance	✓			4 8 2 00

NAME Andrew Plaa

ADDRESS 51 Bissell Ave., Old Saybrook, CT 06475-0212

DATE		ITEM	POST. REF.	DEBIT	CREDIT	BALANCE

NAME Melissa Richfield

ADDRESS 1107 Silver Lane, East Hartford, CT 06108-1907

DATE		ITEM	POST. REF.	DEBIT	CREDIT	BALANCE
20-- Apr.	1	Balance	✓			5 8 25

Problem 11-4B

Challenge Problem

JOURNAL

PAGE

	DATE		DESCRIPTION	POST. REF.	DEBIT	CREDIT	
1							1
2							2
3							3
4							4
5							5
6							6
7							7
8							8
9							9
10							10
11							11
12							12
13							13
14							14
15							15
16							16
17							17
18							18
19							19
20							20
21							21
22							22
23							23
24							24
25							25
26							26
27							27
28							28
29							29
30							30
31							31
32							32
33							33
34							34

Mastery Problem

1.

	DATE		DESCRIPTION	POST. REF.	DEBIT	CREDIT	
1							1
2							2
3							3
4							4
5							5
6							6
7							7
8							8
9							9
10							10
11							11
12							12
13							13
14							14
15							15
16							16
17							17
18							18
19							19
20							20
21							21
22							22
23							23
24							24
25							25
26							26
27							27
28							28
29							29
30							30
31							31
32							32
33							33
34							34

JOURNAL PAGE 7

Mastery Problem (Continued)

JOURNAL

	DATE		DESCRIPTION	POST. REF.	DEBIT	CREDIT	
1							1
2							2
3							3
4							4
5							5
6							6
7							7
8							8
9							9
10							10
11							11
12							12
13							13
14							14
15							15
16							16
17							17
18							18
19							19
20							20
21							21
22							22
23							23
24							24
25							25
26							26
27							27
28							28
29							29
30							30
31							31
32							32
33							33
34							34

Mastery Problem (Continued)

	DATE		DESCRIPTION	POST. REF.	DEBIT	CREDIT	
1							1
2							2
3							3
4							4
5							5
6							6
7							7
8							8
9							9
10							10
11							11
12							12
13							13
14							14
15							15
16							16
17							17
18							18
19							19
20							20
21							21
22							22
23							23
24							24
25							25
26							26
27							27
28							28
29							29
30							30
31							31
32							32
33							33
34							34

Mastery Problem (Continued)

JOURNAL

	DATE		DESCRIPTION	POST. REF.	DEBIT	CREDIT	
1							1
2							2
3							3
4							4
5							5
6							6
7							7
8							8
9							9
10							10

2.

GENERAL LEDGER

ACCOUNT Cash ACCOUNT NO. 101

DATE		ITEM	POST. REF.	DEBIT	CREDIT	BALANCE DEBIT	BALANCE CREDIT
20-- Sept.	1	Balance	✓			23 5 0 0 25	

Mastery Problem (Continued)

ACCOUNT Accounts Receivable ACCOUNT NO. 122

DATE		ITEM	POST. REF.	DEBIT	CREDIT	BALANCE	
						DEBIT	CREDIT
20-- Sept.	1	Balance	✓			8 5 0 75	

ACCOUNT Notes Payable ACCOUNT NO. 201

DATE		ITEM	POST. REF.	DEBIT	CREDIT	BALANCE	
						DEBIT	CREDIT
20-- Sept.	1	Balance	✓				2 5 0 0 00

Name _____

Mastery Problem (Continued)

ACCOUNT Sales Tax Payable ACCOUNT NO. 231

DATE	ITEM	POST. REF.	DEBIT	CREDIT	BALANCE DEBIT	BALANCE CREDIT
20-- Sept. 1	Balance	✓				9 0 9 90

ACCOUNT Sales ACCOUNT NO. 401

DATE	ITEM	POST. REF.	DEBIT	CREDIT	BALANCE DEBIT	BALANCE CREDIT
20-- Sept. 1	Balance	✓				13 0 5 0 48

Mastery Problem (Continued)

ACCOUNT Sales Returns and Allowances ACCOUNT NO. 401.1

DATE		ITEM	POST. REF.	DEBIT	CREDIT	BALANCE	
						DEBIT	CREDIT
20-- Sept.	1	Balance	✓			8 6 00	

ACCOUNT Boarding and Grooming Revenue ACCOUNT NO. 402

DATE		ITEM	POST. REF.	DEBIT	CREDIT	BALANCE	
						DEBIT	CREDIT
20-- Sept.	1	Balance	✓				2 1 1 5 00

ACCOUNTS RECEIVABLE LEDGER

NAME All American Day Camp

ADDRESS 3025 Old Mill Run, Bloomington, IN 47408-1080

DATE		ITEM	POST. REF.	DEBIT	CREDIT	BALANCE

Mastery Problem (Continued)

NAME Rosa Alanso

ADDRESS 2541 East 2nd Street, Bloomington, IN 47401-5356

DATE		ITEM	POST. REF.	DEBIT	CREDIT	BALANCE
20-- Sept.	1	Balance	✓			4 5 6 00

NAME Ed Cochran

ADDRESS 2669 Windcrest Dr., Bloomington, IN 47401-5446

DATE		ITEM	POST. REF.	DEBIT	CREDIT	BALANCE
20-- Sept.	1	Balance	✓			6 3 25

NAME Joe Gloy

ADDRESS 1458 Parnell Ave., Muncie, IN 47304-2682

DATE		ITEM	POST. REF.	DEBIT	CREDIT	BALANCE
20-- Sept.	1	Balance	✓			2 7 3 25

NAME Susan Hays

ADDRESS 1424 Jackson Creek Road, Nashville, IN 47448-2245

DATE		ITEM	POST. REF.	DEBIT	CREDIT	BALANCE

Mastery Problem (Continued)

NAME Ken Shank

ADDRESS 6422 E. Bender Road, Bloomington, IN 47401-7756

DATE		ITEM	POST. REF.	DEBIT	CREDIT	BALANCE

NAME Tully Shaw

ADDRESS 3315 Longview Ave., Bloomington, IN 47401-7223

DATE		ITEM	POST. REF.	DEBIT	CREDIT	BALANCE

NAME Nancy Truelove

ADDRESS 2300 E. National Road, Cumberland, IN 46229-4824

DATE		ITEM	POST. REF.	DEBIT	CREDIT	BALANCE
20-- Sept.	1	Balance	✓			5 8 25

NAME Jean Warkentin

ADDRESS 1813 Deepwell Court, Bloomington, IN 47401-5124

DATE		ITEM	POST. REF.	DEBIT	CREDIT	BALANCE

Mastery Problem (Concluded)

3.

4.

Exercise 12-1A

1. _____
2. Purchase order _____
3. _____
4. _____

Exercise 12-2A

1.

2.

3.

JOURNAL PAGE

	DATE		DESCRIPTION	POST. REF.	DEBIT	CREDIT	
1							1
2							2
3							3
4							4
5							5
6							6
7							7
8							8
9							9
10							10
11							11
12							12
13							13
14							14
15							15

Exercise 12-3A

1.

Cash		Accounts Payable

Purchases		Purchases Returns & Allowances

Purchases Discounts		Freight-In

2.

Cash		Accounts Payable

Purchases		Purchases Returns & Allowances

Purchases Discounts		Freight-In

Exercise 12-3A (Concluded)

3.

Cash		Accounts Payable

Purchases		Purchases Returns & Allowances

Purchases Discounts		Freight-In

4.

Cash		Accounts Payable

Purchases		Purchases Returns & Allowances

Purchases Discounts		Freight-In

Exercise 12-4A

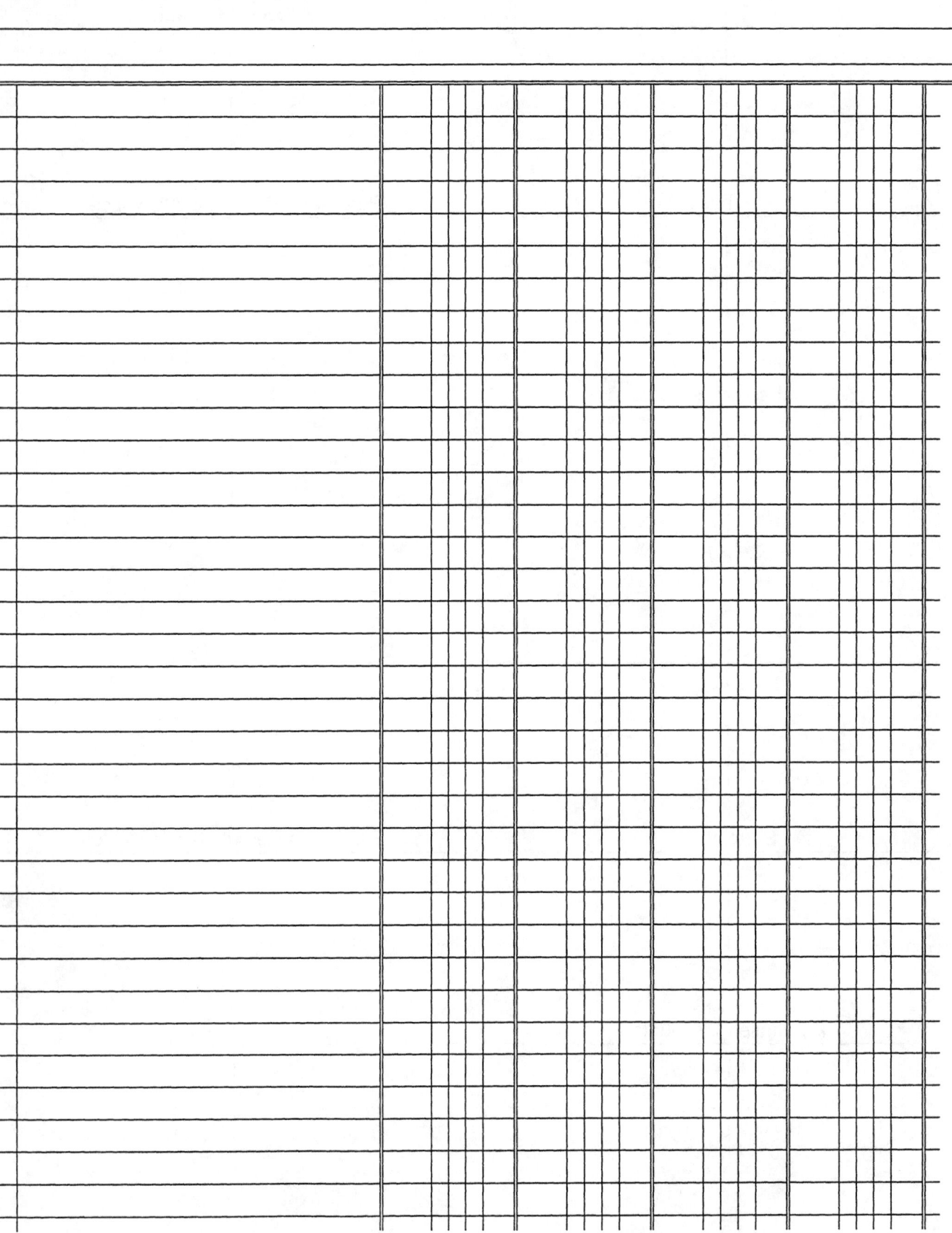

Name _____

Exercise 12-5A

JOURNAL PAGE

	DATE	DESCRIPTION	POST. REF.	DEBIT	CREDIT	
1						1
2						2
3						3
4						4
5						5
6						6
7						7
8						8
9						9
10						10
11						11
12						12
13						13
14						14
15						15
16						16
17						17
18						18
19						19
20						20
21						21
22						22
23						23
24						24
25						25
26						26
27						27
28						28
29						29
30						30
31						31
32						32
33						33
34						34

Exercise 12-6A

JOURNAL

PAGE

	DATE	DESCRIPTION	POST. REF.	DEBIT	CREDIT	
1						1
2						2
3						3
4						4
5						5
6						6
7						7
8						8
9						9
10						10
11						11
12						12

GENERAL LEDGER

ACCOUNT Accounts Payable ACCOUNT NO. 202

DATE		ITEM	POST. REF.	DEBIT	CREDIT	BALANCE DEBIT	BALANCE CREDIT
20-- July	1	Balance	✓				10 6 5 0 00

ACCOUNT Purchases Returns and Allowances ACCOUNT NO. 501.1

DATE	ITEM	POST. REF.	DEBIT	CREDIT	BALANCE DEBIT	BALANCE CREDIT

Exercise 12-6A (Concluded)

ACCOUNTS PAYABLE LEDGER

NAME Datamagic
ADDRESS

DATE	ITEM	POST. REF.	DEBIT	CREDIT	BALANCE
20-- July 1	Balance	✓			2 6 0 0 00

NAME Starcraft Industries
ADDRESS

DATE	ITEM	POST. REF.	DEBIT	CREDIT	BALANCE
20-- July 1	Balance	✓			4 3 0 0 00

NAME XYZ, Inc.
ADDRESS

DATE	ITEM	POST. REF.	DEBIT	CREDIT	BALANCE
20-- July 1	Balance	✓			3 7 5 0 00

Exercise 12-7A

	DATE		DESCRIPTION	POST. REF.	DEBIT	CREDIT	
1							1
2							2
3							3
4							4
5							5
6							6
7							7
8							8
9							9
10							10
11							11
12							12
13							13
14							14
15							15
16							16
17							17
18							18
19							19
20							20
21							21

Exercise 12-8A

Problem 12-1A

1.

| | JOURNAL | | | PAGE 16 |

	DATE		DESCRIPTION	POST. REF.	DEBIT	CREDIT	
1							1
2							2
3							3
4							4
5							5
6							6
7							7
8							8
9							9
10							10
11							11
12							12
13							13
14							14
15							15
16							16
17							17
18							18
19							19
20							20
21							21
22							22
23							23
24							24
25							25
26							26
27							27
28							28
29							29
30							30
31							31
32							32
33							33
34							34

Problem 12-1A (Continued)

2.

GENERAL LEDGER

ACCOUNT Accounts Payable ACCOUNT NO. 202

DATE	ITEM	POST. REF.	DEBIT	CREDIT	BALANCE	
					DEBIT	CREDIT

ACCOUNT Purchases ACCOUNT NO. 501

DATE	ITEM	POST. REF.	DEBIT	CREDIT	BALANCE	
					DEBIT	CREDIT

ACCOUNTS PAYABLE LEDGER

NAME

ADDRESS

DATE	ITEM	POST. REF.	DEBIT	CREDIT	BALANCE

Problem 12-1A (Concluded)

NAME

ADDRESS

DATE		ITEM	POST. REF.	DEBIT	CREDIT	BALANCE

NAME

ADDRESS

DATE		ITEM	POST. REF.	DEBIT	CREDIT	BALANCE

NAME

ADDRESS

DATE		ITEM	POST. REF.	DEBIT	CREDIT	BALANCE

NAME

ADDRESS

DATE		ITEM	POST. REF.	DEBIT	CREDIT	BALANCE

Problem 12-2A

1.

<div align="center">JOURNAL</div>

	DATE		DESCRIPTION	POST. REF.	DEBIT	CREDIT	
1							1
2							2
3							3
4							4
5							5
6							6
7							7
8							8
9							9
10							10
11							11
12							12
13							13
14							14
15							15
16							16
17							17
18							18
19							19
20							20
21							21
22							22
23							23
24							24
25							25
26							26
27							27
28							28
29							29
30							30
31							31
32							32
33							33
34							34

Problem 12-2A (Continued)

JOURNAL

PAGE 10

	DATE		DESCRIPTION	POST. REF.	DEBIT	CREDIT	
1							1
2							2
3							3
4							4
5							5

2.

GENERAL LEDGER

ACCOUNT Cash ACCOUNT NO. 101

DATE		ITEM	POST. REF.	DEBIT	CREDIT	BALANCE DEBIT	BALANCE CREDIT
20-- May	1	Balance	✓			40 0 0 0 00	

ACCOUNT Accounts Payable ACCOUNT NO. 202

DATE		ITEM	POST. REF.	DEBIT	CREDIT	BALANCE DEBIT	BALANCE CREDIT
20-- May	1	Balance	✓				20 0 0 0 00

Problem 12-2A (Continued)

ACCOUNT Purchases ACCOUNT NO. 501

DATE	ITEM	POST. REF.	DEBIT	CREDIT	BALANCE	
					DEBIT	CREDIT

ACCOUNT Purchases Discounts ACCOUNT NO. 501.2

DATE	ITEM	POST. REF.	DEBIT	CREDIT	BALANCE	
					DEBIT	CREDIT

ACCOUNT Freight-In ACCOUNT NO. 502

DATE	ITEM	POST. REF.	DEBIT	CREDIT	BALANCE	
					DEBIT	CREDIT

ACCOUNT Rent Expense ACCOUNT NO. 521

DATE	ITEM	POST. REF.	DEBIT	CREDIT	BALANCE	
					DEBIT	CREDIT

ACCOUNT Utilities Expense ACCOUNT NO. 533

DATE	ITEM	POST. REF.	DEBIT	CREDIT	BALANCE	
					DEBIT	CREDIT

Problem 12-2A (Concluded)

ACCOUNTS PAYABLE LEDGER

NAME Fantastic Toys
ADDRESS

DATE		ITEM	POST. REF.	DEBIT	CREDIT	BALANCE
20-- May	1	Balance	✓			5 2 0 0 00

NAME Goya Outlet
ADDRESS

DATE		ITEM	POST. REF.	DEBIT	CREDIT	BALANCE
20-- May	1	Balance	✓			3 8 0 0 00

NAME Mueller's Distributors
ADDRESS

DATE		ITEM	POST. REF.	DEBIT	CREDIT	BALANCE
20-- May	1	Balance	✓			3 6 0 0 00

NAME Van Kooning
ADDRESS

DATE		ITEM	POST. REF.	DEBIT	CREDIT	BALANCE
20-- May	1	Balance	✓			7 4 0 0 00

Problem 12-3A

1.

<div align="center">JOURNAL</div>

	DATE		DESCRIPTION	POST. REF.	DEBIT	CREDIT	
1							1
2							2
3							3
4							4
5							5
6							6
7							7
8							8
9							9
10							10
11							11
12							12
13							13
14							14
15							15
16							16
17							17
18							18
19							19
20							20
21							21
22							22
23							23
24							24
25							25
26							26
27							27
28							28
29							29
30							30
31							31
32							32
33							33
34							34

Problem 12-3A (Continued)

JOURNAL

	DATE	DESCRIPTION	POST. REF.	DEBIT	CREDIT	
1						1
2						2
3						3
4						4
5						5
6						6
7						7
8						8
9						9
10						10
11						11
12						12
13						13
14						14
15						15
16						16
17						17
18						18
19						19
20						20
21						21
22						22
23						23
24						24
25						25
26						26
27						27
28						28
29						29
30						30
31						31
32						32
33						33
34						34

Problem 12-3A (Continued)
2.

GENERAL LEDGER

ACCOUNT Cash ACCOUNT NO. 101

DATE		ITEM	POST. REF.	DEBIT	CREDIT	BALANCE	
						DEBIT	CREDIT
20-- July	1	Balance	✓			20 0 0 0 00	

ACCOUNT Accounts Payable ACCOUNT NO. 202

DATE	ITEM	POST. REF.	DEBIT	CREDIT	BALANCE	
					DEBIT	CREDIT

ACCOUNT Flint, Drawing ACCOUNT NO. 312

DATE	ITEM	POST. REF.	DEBIT	CREDIT	BALANCE	
					DEBIT	CREDIT

Problem 12-3A (Continued)

ACCOUNT Purchases ACCOUNT NO. 501

DATE	ITEM	POST. REF.	DEBIT	CREDIT	BALANCE DEBIT	BALANCE CREDIT

ACCOUNT Purchase Returns and Allowances ACCOUNT NO. 501.1

DATE	ITEM	POST. REF.	DEBIT	CREDIT	BALANCE DEBIT	BALANCE CREDIT

ACCOUNT Purchases Discounts ACCOUNT NO. 501.2

DATE	ITEM	POST. REF.	DEBIT	CREDIT	BALANCE DEBIT	BALANCE CREDIT

ACCOUNT Rent Expense ACCOUNT NO. 521

DATE	ITEM	POST. REF.	DEBIT	CREDIT	BALANCE DEBIT	BALANCE CREDIT

Problem 12-3A (Concluded)

ACCOUNTS PAYABLE LEDGER

NAME

ADDRESS

DATE	ITEM	POST. REF.	DEBIT	CREDIT	BALANCE

NAME

ADDRESS

DATE	ITEM	POST. REF.	DEBIT	CREDIT	BALANCE

NAME

ADDRESS

DATE	ITEM	POST. REF.	DEBIT	CREDIT	BALANCE

NAME

ADDRESS

DATE	ITEM	POST. REF.	DEBIT	CREDIT	BALANCE

Problem 12-4A

Exercise 12-1B

1. _____
2. _____
3. _____
4. _____

Exercise 12-2B

1.

2.

3.

JOURNAL PAGE

	DATE		DESCRIPTION	POST. REF.	DEBIT	CREDIT	
1							1
2							2
3							3
4							4
5							5
6							6
7							7
8							8
9							9
10							10
11							11
12							12
13							13
15							15

Exercise 12-3B

1.

Cash	Accounts Payable

Purchases	Purchases Returns & Allowances

Purchases Discounts	Freight-In

2.

Cash	Accounts Payable

Purchases	Purchases Returns & Allowances

Purchases Discounts	Freight-In

Exercise 12-3B (Concluded)

3.

Cash		Accounts Payable

Purchases		Purchases Returns & Allowances

Purchases Discounts		Freight-In

4.

Cash		Accounts Payable

Purchases		Purchases Returns & Allowances

Purchases Discounts		Freight-In

Exercise 12-4B

Exercise 12-5B

<div align="center">

JOURNAL
</div>

	DATE		DESCRIPTION	POST. REF.	DEBIT	CREDIT	
1							1
2							2
3							3
4							4
5							5
6							6
7							7
8							8
9							9
10							10
11							11
12							12
13							13
14							14
15							15
16							16
17							17
18							18
19							19
20							20
21							21
22							22
23							23
24							24
25							25
26							26
27							27
28							28
29							29
30							30
31							31
32							32
33							33
34							34

Exercise 12-6B

JOURNAL

	DATE	DESCRIPTION	POST. REF.	DEBIT	CREDIT	
1						1
2						2
3						3
4						4
5						5
6						6
7						7
8						8
9						9
10						10
11						11
12						12

GENERAL LEDGER

ACCOUNT Accounts Payable ACCOUNT NO. 202

DATE		ITEM	POST. REF.	DEBIT	CREDIT	BALANCE DEBIT	BALANCE CREDIT
20-- Mar.	1	Balance	✓				8 3 5 0 00

ACCOUNT Purchases Returns and Allowances ACCOUNT NO. 501.1

DATE	ITEM	POST. REF.	DEBIT	CREDIT	BALANCE DEBIT	BALANCE CREDIT

Exercise 12-6B (Concluded)

ACCOUNTS PAYABLE LEDGER

NAME A & D Arms

ADDRESS

DATE		ITEM	POST. REF.	DEBIT	CREDIT	BALANCE
20-- Mar.	1	Balance	✓			2 3 0 0 00

NAME Mighty Mansion

ADDRESS

DATE		ITEM	POST. REF.	DEBIT	CREDIT	BALANCE
20-- Mar.	1	Balance	✓			1 4 5 0 00

NAME Tower Industries

ADDRESS

DATE		ITEM	POST. REF.	DEBIT	CREDIT	BALANCE
20-- Mar.	1	Balance	✓			4 6 0 0 00

Exercise 12-7B

	DATE		DESCRIPTION	POST. REF.	DEBIT	CREDIT	
1							1
2							2
3							3
4							4
5							5
6							6
7							7
8							8
9							9
10							10
11							11
12							12
13							13
14							14
15							15
16							16
17							17
18							18
19							19
20							20
21							21

Exercise 12-8B

Problem 12-1B

1.

JOURNAL PAGE 16

	DATE		DESCRIPTION	POST. REF.	DEBIT	CREDIT	
1							1
2							2
3							3
4							4
5							5
6							6
7							7
8							8
9							9
10							10
11							11
12							12
13							13
14							14
15							15
16							16
17							17
18							18
19							19
20							20
21							21
22							22
23							23
24							24
25							25
26							26
27							27
28							28
29							29
30							30
31							31
32							32
33							33
34							34

Problem 12-1B (Continued)

2.

GENERAL LEDGER

ACCOUNT Accounts Payable ACCOUNT NO. 202

DATE	ITEM	POST. REF.	DEBIT	CREDIT	BALANCE	
					DEBIT	CREDIT

ACCOUNT Purchases ACCOUNT NO. 501

DATE	ITEM	POST. REF.	DEBIT	CREDIT	BALANCE	
					DEBIT	CREDIT

ACCOUNTS PAYABLE LEDGER

NAME

ADDRESS

DATE	ITEM	POST. REF.	DEBIT	CREDIT	BALANCE

Problem 12-1B (Concluded)

NAME

ADDRESS

DATE	ITEM	POST. REF.	DEBIT	CREDIT	BALANCE

NAME

ADDRESS

DATE	ITEM	POST. REF.	DEBIT	CREDIT	BALANCE

NAME

ADDRESS

DATE	ITEM	POST. REF.	DEBIT	CREDIT	BALANCE

NAME

ADDRESS

DATE	ITEM	POST. REF.	DEBIT	CREDIT	BALANCE

Problem 12-2B

1.

<div align="center">

JOURNAL
</div>

<div align="right">

PAGE 9
</div>

	DATE		DESCRIPTION	POST. REF.	DEBIT	CREDIT	
1							1
2							2
3							3
4							4
5							5
6							6
7							7
8							8
9							9
10							10
11							11
12							12
13							13
14							14
15							15
16							16
17							17
18							18
19							19
20							20
21							21
22							22
23							23
24							24
25							25
26							26
27							27
28							28
29							29
30							30
31							31
32							32
33							33
34							34

Problem 12-2B (Continued)

JOURNAL PAGE 10

	DATE		DESCRIPTION	POST. REF.	DEBIT	CREDIT	
1							1
2							2
3							3
4							4
5							5

2.

GENERAL LEDGER

ACCOUNT Cash ACCOUNT NO. 101

DATE		ITEM	POST. REF.	DEBIT	CREDIT	BALANCE DEBIT	BALANCE CREDIT
20-- May	1	Balance	✓			40 0 0 0 00	

ACCOUNT Accounts Payable ACCOUNT NO. 202

DATE		ITEM	POST. REF.	DEBIT	CREDIT	BALANCE DEBIT	BALANCE CREDIT
20-- May	1	Balance	✓				20 0 0 0 00

Problem 12-2B (Continued)

ACCOUNT Purchases ACCOUNT NO. 501

DATE	ITEM	POST. REF.	DEBIT	CREDIT	BALANCE	
					DEBIT	CREDIT

ACCOUNT Purchases Discounts ACCOUNT NO. 501.2

DATE	ITEM	POST. REF.	DEBIT	CREDIT	BALANCE	
					DEBIT	CREDIT

ACCOUNT Freight-In ACCOUNT NO. 502

DATE	ITEM	POST. REF.	DEBIT	CREDIT	BALANCE	
					DEBIT	CREDIT

ACCOUNT Rent Expense ACCOUNT NO. 521

DATE	ITEM	POST. REF.	DEBIT	CREDIT	BALANCE	
					DEBIT	CREDIT

ACCOUNT Utilities Expense ACCOUNT NO. 533

DATE	ITEM	POST. REF.	DEBIT	CREDIT	BALANCE	
					DEBIT	CREDIT

Problem 12-2B (Concluded)

ACCOUNTS PAYABLE LEDGER

NAME Cortez Distributors

ADDRESS

DATE		ITEM	POST. REF.	DEBIT	CREDIT	BALANCE
20-- May	1	Balance	✓			4 2 0 0 00

NAME Indra & Velga

ADDRESS

DATE		ITEM	POST. REF.	DEBIT	CREDIT	BALANCE
20-- May	1	Balance	✓			6 8 0 0 00

NAME Toy Corner

ADDRESS

DATE		ITEM	POST. REF.	DEBIT	CREDIT	BALANCE
20-- May	1	Balance	✓			4 6 0 0 00

NAME Troutman Outlet

ADDRESS

DATE		ITEM	POST. REF.	DEBIT	CREDIT	BALANCE
20-- May	1	Balance	✓			4 4 0 0 00

Problem 12-3B

1.

JOURNAL

	DATE		DESCRIPTION	POST. REF.	DEBIT	CREDIT	
1							1
2							2
3							3
4							4
5							5
6							6
7							7
8							8
9							9
10							10
11							11
12							12
13							13
14							14
15							15
16							16
17							17
18							18
19							19
20							20
21							21
22							22
23							23
24							24
25							25
26							26
27							27
28							28
29							29
30							30
31							31
32							32
33							33
34							34

Problem 12-3B (Continued)

	JOURNAL				PAGE 17

	DATE	DESCRIPTION	POST. REF.	DEBIT	CREDIT	
1						1
2						2
3						3
4						4
5						5
6						6
7						7
8						8
9						9
10						10
11						11
12						12
13						13
14						14
15						15
16						16
17						17
18						18
19						19
20						20
21						21
22						22
23						23
24						24
25						25
26						26
27						27
28						28
29						29
30						30
31						31
32						32
33						33
34						34

Problem 12-3B (Continued)

2.

GENERAL LEDGER

ACCOUNT Cash ACCOUNT NO. 101

DATE		ITEM	POST. REF.	DEBIT	CREDIT	BALANCE	
						DEBIT	CREDIT
20-- July	1	Balance	✓			20 0 0 0 00	

ACCOUNT Accounts Payable ACCOUNT NO. 202

DATE	ITEM	POST. REF.	DEBIT	CREDIT	BALANCE	
					DEBIT	CREDIT

ACCOUNT Mueller, Drawing ACCOUNT NO. 312

DATE	ITEM	POST. REF.	DEBIT	CREDIT	BALANCE	
					DEBIT	CREDIT

Problem 12-3B (Continued)

ACCOUNT Purchases ACCOUNT NO. 501

DATE	ITEM	POST. REF.	DEBIT	CREDIT	BALANCE	
					DEBIT	CREDIT

ACCOUNT Purchases Returns and Allowances ACCOUNT NO. 501.1

DATE	ITEM	POST. REF.	DEBIT	CREDIT	BALANCE	
					DEBIT	CREDIT

ACCOUNT Purchases Discounts ACCOUNT NO. 501.2

DATE	ITEM	POST. REF.	DEBIT	CREDIT	BALANCE	
					DEBIT	CREDIT

ACCOUNT Rent Expense ACCOUNT NO. 521

DATE	ITEM	POST. REF.	DEBIT	CREDIT	BALANCE	
					DEBIT	CREDIT

Problem 12-3B (Concluded)

ACCOUNTS PAYABLE LEDGER

NAME

ADDRESS

DATE	ITEM	POST. REF.	DEBIT	CREDIT	BALANCE

NAME

ADDRESS

DATE	ITEM	POST. REF.	DEBIT	CREDIT	BALANCE

NAME

ADDRESS

DATE	ITEM	POST. REF.	DEBIT	CREDIT	BALANCE

NAME

ADDRESS

DATE	ITEM	POST. REF.	DEBIT	CREDIT	BALANCE

Problem 12-4B

Exercise 12-3B

1.

Cash		
	(a)	*2,300*
	(b)	*3,600*

Accounts Payable

Purchases	
(a)	*2,300*
(b)	*3,600*

Purchases Returns & Allowances

Purchases Discounts

Freight In

2.

Cash		
	(c)	*3,920*
	(d)	*2,800*

Accounts Payable			
(c)	*4,000*	*(a)*	*4,000*
(d)	*2,800*	*(b)*	*2,800*

Purchases	
(a)	*4,000*
(b)	*2,800*

Purchases Returns & Allowances

Purchases Discounts		
	(c)	*80*

Freight-In

Mastery Problem

1.

	DATE		DESCRIPTION	POST. REF.	DEBIT	CREDIT	
1							1
2							2
3							3
4							4
5							5
6							6
7							7
8							8
9							9
10							10
11							11
12							12
13							13
14							14
15							15
16							16
17							17
18							18
19							19
20							20
21							21
22							22
23							23
24							24
25							25
26							26
27							27
28							28
29							29
30							30
31							31
32							32
33							33
34							34

JOURNAL PAGE 16

Mastery Problem (Continued)

JOURNAL PAGE 17

	DATE		DESCRIPTION	POST. REF.	DEBIT	CREDIT	
1							1
2							2
3							3
4							4
5							5
6							6
7							7
8							8
9							9
10							10
11							11
12							12
13							13
14							14
15							15
16							16
17							17
18							18
19							19
20							20
21							21
22							22
23							23
24							24
25							25
26							26
27							27
28							28
29							29
30							30
31							31
32							32
33							33
34							34

Mastery Problem (Continued)

2.

GENERAL LEDGER

ACCOUNT Cash ACCOUNT NO. 101

DATE		ITEM	POST. REF.	DEBIT	CREDIT	BALANCE	
						DEBIT	CREDIT
20-- June	1	Balance	✓			32 2 0 0 00	

ACCOUNT Accounts Payable ACCOUNT NO. 202

DATE		ITEM	POST. REF.	DEBIT	CREDIT	BALANCE	
						DEBIT	CREDIT
20-- June	1	Balance	✓				2 0 0 0 00

Mastery Problem (Continued)

ACCOUNT Michelle French, Drawing ACCOUNT NO. 312

DATE		ITEM	POST. REF.	DEBIT	CREDIT	BALANCE DEBIT	BALANCE CREDIT
20-- June	1	Balance	✓			18 0 0 0 00	

ACCOUNT Purchases ACCOUNT NO. 501

DATE		ITEM	POST. REF.	DEBIT	CREDIT	BALANCE DEBIT	BALANCE CREDIT
20-- June	1	Balance	✓			67 0 2 1 66	

ACCOUNT Purchases Returns and Allowances ACCOUNT NO. 501.1

DATE		ITEM	POST. REF.	DEBIT	CREDIT	BALANCE DEBIT	BALANCE CREDIT
20-- June	1	Balance	✓				2 3 1 5 23

ACCOUNT Purchases Discounts ACCOUNT NO. 501.2

DATE		ITEM	POST. REF.	DEBIT	CREDIT	BALANCE DEBIT	BALANCE CREDIT
20-- June	1	Balance	✓				9 0 5 00

Mastery Problem (Continued)

ACCOUNT Freight-In ACCOUNT NO. 502

DATE		ITEM	POST. REF.	DEBIT	CREDIT	BALANCE	
						DEBIT	CREDIT
20-- June	1	Balance	✓			5 2 2 60	

ACCOUNT Rent Expense ACCOUNT NO. 521

DATE		ITEM	POST. REF.	DEBIT	CREDIT	BALANCE	
						DEBIT	CREDIT
20-- June	1	Balance	✓			3 1 2 5 00	

ACCOUNT Utilities Expense ACCOUNT NO. 533

DATE		ITEM	POST. REF.	DEBIT	CREDIT	BALANCE	
						DEBIT	CREDIT
20-- June	1	Balance	✓			1 5 2 2 87	

ACCOUNTS PAYABLE LEDGER

NAME Broadway Publishing, Inc.

ADDRESS 2300 Goodman, Cincinnati, OH 45219-2901

DATE		ITEM	POST. REF.	DEBIT	CREDIT	BALANCE

Mastery Problem (Continued)

NAME Irving Publishing Company

ADDRESS 5200 N. Keystone Ave., Indianapolis, IN 46220-1986

DATE	ITEM	POST. REF.	DEBIT	CREDIT	BALANCE

NAME North-Eastern Publishing Company

ADDRESS 874 Crescent Drive, Flint, MI 48503-7564

DATE		ITEM	POST. REF.	DEBIT	CREDIT	BALANCE
20-- June	1	Balance	✓			2 0 0 0 00

NAME Riley Publishing Company

ADDRESS 5675 Pulaski Road, Chicago, IL 60629-6705

DATE	ITEM	POST. REF.	DEBIT	CREDIT	BALANCE

Mastery Problem (Concluded)

3.

4.

APPENDIX EXERCISES

Exercise 12Apx-1A

1.

<div align="center">JOURNAL</div>

PAGE

	DATE		DESCRIPTION	POST. REF.	DEBIT	CREDIT	
1							1
2							2
3							3
4							4
5							5
6							6
7							7
8							8
9							9
10							10
11							11
12							12
13							13
14							14
15							15
16							16

2.

1							1
2							2
3							3
4							4
5							5
6							6
7							7
8							8
9							9
10							10
11							11
12							12
13							13
14							14
15							15
16							16

Exercise 12Apx-1B

1.

	JOURNAL				PAGE

	DATE	DESCRIPTION	POST. REF.	DEBIT	CREDIT	
1						1
2						2
3						3
4						4
5						5
6						6
7						7
8						8
9						9
10						10
11						11
12						12
13						13
14						14
15						15
16						16

2.

1						1
2						2
3						3
4						4
5						5
6						6
7						7
8						8
9						9
10						10
11						11
12						12
13						13
14						14
15						15
16						16

Exercise 13-1A

SALES JOURNAL PAGE

DATE	SALE NO.	TO WHOM SOLD	POST. REF.	ACCOUNTS RECEIVABLE DR.	SALES CR.	SALES TAX PAYABLE CR.

Exercise 13-2A

CASH RECEIPTS JOURNAL PAGE

	DATE	ACCOUNT CREDITED	POST. REF.	GENERAL CR.	ACCTS. RECEIVABLE CR.	SALES CR.	SALES TAX PAY. CR.	CASH DR.	
1									1
2									2
3									3
4									4
5									5
6									6
7									7
8									8
9									9
10									10
11									11
12									12
13									13

Exercise 13-3A

PURCHASES JOURNAL PAGE

	DATE	INVOICE NO.	FROM WHOM PURCHASED	POST. REF.	PURCHASES DR. ACCTS. PAY. CR.	
1						1
2						2
3						3
4						4
5						5
6						6
7						7
8						8
9						9
10						10
11						11

Exercise 13-4A

CASH PAYMENTS JOURNAL PAGE

	DATE	CK. NO.	ACCOUNT DEBITED	POST. REF.	GENERAL DR.	ACCTS. PAYABLE DR.	PURCHASES DR.	PURCHASES DISCOUNTS CR.	CASH CR.	
1										1
2										2
3										3
4										4
5										5
6										6
7										7
8										8
9										9
10										10
11										11
12										12
13										13

Problem 13-1A

1.

SALES JOURNAL

PAGE 8

DATE	SALE NO.	TO WHOM SOLD	POST. REF.	ACCOUNTS RECEIVABLE DR.	SALES CR.	SALES TAX PAYABLE CR.

2.

GENERAL LEDGER

ACCOUNT Accounts Receivable ACCOUNT NO. 122

DATE	ITEM	POST. REF.	DEBIT	CREDIT	BALANCE DEBIT	BALANCE CREDIT

ACCOUNT Sales Tax Payable ACCOUNT NO. 231

DATE	ITEM	POST. REF.	DEBIT	CREDIT	BALANCE DEBIT	BALANCE CREDIT

Problem 13-1A (Concluded)

ACCOUNT Sales ACCOUNT NO. 401

DATE	ITEM	POST. REF.	DEBIT	CREDIT	BALANCE DEBIT	BALANCE CREDIT

ACCOUNTS RECEIVABLE LEDGER

NAME R. B. Hassad Co.

ADDRESS 1225 W. Temperance Street, Elletsville, IN 47429-9976

DATE	ITEM	POST. REF.	DEBIT	CREDIT	BALANCE

NAME Helsinki, Inc.

ADDRESS 125 Fishers Drive, Noblesville, IN 47870-8867

DATE	ITEM	POST. REF.	DEBIT	CREDIT	BALANCE

NAME Jung Manufacturing Co.

ADDRESS 8825 Old State Road, Bloomington, IN 47401-8823

DATE	ITEM	POST. REF.	DEBIT	CREDIT	BALANCE

NAME Ardis Myler

ADDRESS 2100 Greer Lane, Bedford, IN 47421-8876

DATE	ITEM	POST. REF.	DEBIT	CREDIT	BALANCE

Problem 13-2A

1.

<div align="center">

JOURNAL

</div>

PAGE 8

	DATE		DESCRIPTION	POST. REF.	DEBIT	CREDIT	
1							1
2							2
3							3
4							4
5							5
6							6
7							7
8							8
9							9
10							10
11							11
12							12
13							13
14							14
15							15
16							16
17							17
18							18
19							19
20							20
21							21
22							22
23							23
24							24
25							25
26							26
27							27
28							28
29							29
30							30
31							31
32							32
33							33
34							34

Problem 13-2A (Continued)

CASH RECEIPTS JOURNAL

	DATE	ACCOUNT CREDITED	POST. REF.	GENERAL CR.	ACCOUNTS RECEIVABLE CR.	
1						1
2						2
3						3
4						4
5						5
6						6
7						7
8						8
9						9
10						10
11						11
12						12
13						13
14						14
15						15
16						16
17						17
18						18
19						19
20						20
21						21
22						22
23						23
24						24
25						25
26						26
27						27
28						28

Problem 13-2A (Continued)

PAGE 10

	SALES CR.				SALES TAX PAYABLE CR.				BANK CREDIT CARD EXPENSE DR.				CASH DR.				
1																	1
2																	2
3																	3
4																	4
5																	5
6																	6
7																	7
8																	8
9																	9
10																	10
11																	11
12																	12
13																	13
14																	14
15																	15
16																	16
17																	17
18																	18
19																	19
20																	20
21																	21
22																	22
23																	23
24																	24
25																	25
26																	26
27																	27
28																	28

Problem 13-2A (Continued)

2.

GENERAL LEDGER

ACCOUNT Cash ACCOUNT NO. 101

DATE		ITEM	POST. REF.	DEBIT	CREDIT	BALANCE	
						DEBIT	CREDIT
20-- Dec.	1	Balance	✓			9 8 6 2 00	

ACCOUNT Accounts Receivable ACCOUNT NO. 122

DATE		ITEM	POST. REF.	DEBIT	CREDIT	BALANCE	
						DEBIT	CREDIT
20-- Dec.	1	Balance	✓			9 3 5 2 00	

ACCOUNT Sales Tax Payable ACCOUNT NO. 231

DATE		ITEM	POST. REF.	DEBIT	CREDIT	BALANCE	
						DEBIT	CREDIT

ACCOUNT Sales ACCOUNT NO. 401

DATE		ITEM	POST. REF.	DEBIT	CREDIT	BALANCE	
						DEBIT	CREDIT

Problem 13-2A (Continued)

ACCOUNT Sales Returns & Allowances ACCOUNT NO. 401.1

DATE	ITEM	POST. REF.	DEBIT	CREDIT	BALANCE	
					DEBIT	CREDIT

ACCOUNT Bank Credit Card Expense ACCOUNT NO. 513

DATE	ITEM	POST. REF.	DEBIT	CREDIT	BALANCE	
					DEBIT	CREDIT

ACCOUNTS RECEIVABLE LEDGER

NAME Michael Anderson

ADDRESS 233 West 11th Avenue, Detroit, MI 59500-1154

DATE		ITEM	POST. REF.	DEBIT	CREDIT	BALANCE
20-- Dec.	1	Balance	✓			2 4 8 0 00

NAME Ansel Manufacturing

ADDRESS 284 West 88 Street, Detroit, MI 59522-1168

DATE		ITEM	POST. REF.	DEBIT	CREDIT	BALANCE
20-- Dec.	1	Balance	✓			9 8 2 00

Problem 13-2A (Concluded)

NAME J. Gorbea

ADDRESS P.O. BOX 864, Detroit, MI 59552-0864

DATE		ITEM	POST. REF.	DEBIT	CREDIT	BALANCE
20-- Dec.	1	Balance	✓			8 8 0 00

NAME Rachel Carson

ADDRESS 11312 Fourteenth Avenue South, Detroit, MI 59221-1142

DATE		ITEM	POST. REF.	DEBIT	CREDIT	BALANCE
20-- Dec.	1	Balance	✓			3 2 0 0 00

NAME Tom Wilson

ADDRESS 100 NW Seward St., Detroit, MI 59210-1337

DATE		ITEM	POST. REF.	DEBIT	CREDIT	BALANCE
20-- Dec.	1	Balance	✓			1 8 1 0 00

Problem 13-3A

1.

SALES JOURNAL

PAGE 6

DATE	SALE NO.	TO WHOM SOLD	POST. REF.	ACCOUNTS RECEIVABLE DR.	SALES CR.	SALES TAX PAYABLE CR.

CASH RECEIPTS JOURNAL

PAGE 9

	DATE	ACCOUNT CREDITED	POST. REF.	GENERAL CR.	ACCTS. RECEIVABLE CR.	SALES CR.	SALES TAX PAY. CR.	CASH DR.	
1									1
2									2
3									3
4									4
5									5
6									6
7									7
8									8
9									9

Problem 13-3A (Continued)

JOURNAL PAGE 5

	DATE	DESCRIPTION	POST. REF.	DEBIT	CREDIT	
1						1
2						2
3						3
4						4
5						5
6						6
7						7
8						8
9						9
10						10
11						11
12						12
13						13
14						14

2.

GENERAL LEDGER

ACCOUNT Cash ACCOUNT NO. 101

DATE	ITEM	POST. REF.	DEBIT	CREDIT	BALANCE DEBIT	BALANCE CREDIT
20-- Mar. 1	Balance	✓			9 7 4 1 00	

ACCOUNT Accounts Receivable ACCOUNT NO. 122

DATE	ITEM	POST. REF.	DEBIT	CREDIT	BALANCE DEBIT	BALANCE CREDIT
20-- Mar. 1	Balance	✓			1 0 5 8 25	

Problem 13-3A (Continued)

ACCOUNT Sales Tax Payable ACCOUNT NO. 231

DATE		ITEM	POST. REF.	DEBIT	CREDIT	BALANCE	
						DEBIT	CREDIT

ACCOUNT Sales ACCOUNT NO. 401

DATE		ITEM	POST. REF.	DEBIT	CREDIT	BALANCE	
						DEBIT	CREDIT

ACCOUNT Sales Returns & Allowances ACCOUNT NO. 401.1

DATE		ITEM	POST. REF.	DEBIT	CREDIT	BALANCE	
						DEBIT	CREDIT

Problem 13-3A (Concluded)

ACCOUNTS RECEIVABLE LEDGER

NAME Able & Co.

ADDRESS 1424 Jackson Creek Road, Nashville, IN 47448-2245

DATE	ITEM	POST. REF.	DEBIT	CREDIT	BALANCE

NAME Blevins Bakery

ADDRESS 6422 E. Bender Road, Bloomington, IN 47401-7756

DATE	ITEM	POST. REF.	DEBIT	CREDIT	BALANCE

NAME R. J. Kalas, Inc.

ADDRESS 3315 Longview Avenue, Bloomington, IN 47401-7223

DATE	ITEM	POST. REF.	DEBIT	CREDIT	BALANCE

NAME Thompson Group

ADDRESS 2300 E. National Road, Cumberland, IN 46229-4824

DATE	ITEM	POST. REF.	DEBIT	CREDIT	BALANCE
20-- Mar. 1	Balance	✓			1 0 5 8 25

Name _____

Problem 13-4A

1.

PURCHASES JOURNAL PAGE 7

	DATE	INVOICE NO.	FROM WHOM PURCHASED	POST. REF.	PURCHASES DR. ACCTS. PAY. CR.	
1						1
2						2
3						3
4						4
5						5
6						6
7						7
8						8
9						9
10						10
11						11
12						12
13						13
14						14

2.

GENERAL LEDGER

ACCOUNT Accounts Payable ACCOUNT NO. 202

DATE	ITEM	POST. REF.	DEBIT	CREDIT	BALANCE DEBIT	BALANCE CREDIT

ACCOUNT Purchases ACCOUNT NO. 501

DATE	ITEM	POST. REF.	DEBIT	CREDIT	BALANCE DEBIT	BALANCE CREDIT

Problem 13-4A (Concluded)

ACCOUNTS PAYABLE LEDGER

NAME

ADDRESS

DATE		ITEM	POST. REF.	DEBIT	CREDIT	BALANCE

NAME

ADDRESS

DATE		ITEM	POST. REF.	DEBIT	CREDIT	BALANCE

NAME

ADDRESS

DATE		ITEM	POST. REF.	DEBIT	CREDIT	BALANCE

NAME

ADDRESS

DATE		ITEM	POST. REF.	DEBIT	CREDIT	BALANCE

NAME

ADDRESS

DATE		ITEM	POST. REF.	DEBIT	CREDIT	BALANCE

Problem 13-5A

1.

GENERAL LEDGER

ACCOUNT Accounts Payable ACCOUNT NO. 202

DATE	ITEM	POST. REF.	DEBIT	CREDIT	BALANCE	
					DEBIT	CREDIT

ACCOUNT Purchases ACCOUNT NO. 501

DATE	ITEM	POST. REF.	DEBIT	CREDIT	BALANCE	
					DEBIT	CREDIT

2.

ACCOUNTS PAYABLE LEDGER

NAME _____

ADDRESS _____

DATE	ITEM	POST. REF.	DEBIT	CREDIT	BALANCE

NAME _____

ADDRESS _____

DATE	ITEM	POST. REF.	DEBIT	CREDIT	BALANCE

Problem 13-5A (Concluded)

NAME

ADDRESS

DATE	ITEM	POST. REF.	DEBIT	CREDIT	BALANCE

NAME

ADDRESS

DATE	ITEM	POST. REF.	DEBIT	CREDIT	BALANCE

NAME

ADDRESS

DATE	ITEM	POST. REF.	DEBIT	CREDIT	BALANCE

Problem 13-6A

1.

<div align="center">CASH PAYMENTS JOURNAL</div>

PAGE 6

	DATE	CK. NO.	ACCOUNT DEBITED	POST. REF.	GENERAL DR.	ACCTS. PAYABLE DR.	PURCHASES DR.	PURCHASES DISCOUNTS CR.	CASH CR.	
1										1
2										2
3										3
4										4
5										5
6										6
7										7
8										8
9										9
10										10
11										11
12										12

2.

<div align="center">GENERAL LEDGER</div>

ACCOUNT Cash ACCOUNT NO. 101

DATE	ITEM	POST. REF.	DEBIT	CREDIT	BALANCE DEBIT	BALANCE CREDIT
20-- May 1	Balance	✓			40 0 0 0 00	

ACCOUNT Accounts Payable ACCOUNT NO. 202

DATE	ITEM	POST. REF.	DEBIT	CREDIT	BALANCE DEBIT	BALANCE CREDIT
20-- May 1	Balance	✓				20 0 0 0 00

Problem 13-6A (Continued)

ACCOUNT Purchases ACCOUNT NO. 501

DATE	ITEM	POST. REF.	DEBIT	CREDIT	BALANCE	
					DEBIT	CREDIT

ACCOUNT Purchases Discounts ACCOUNT NO. 501.2

DATE	ITEM	POST. REF.	DEBIT	CREDIT	BALANCE	
					DEBIT	CREDIT

ACCOUNT Freight-In ACCOUNT NO. 502

DATE	ITEM	POST. REF.	DEBIT	CREDIT	BALANCE	
					DEBIT	CREDIT

ACCOUNT Rent Expense ACCOUNT NO. 521

DATE	ITEM	POST. REF.	DEBIT	CREDIT	BALANCE	
					DEBIT	CREDIT

ACCOUNT Utilities Expense ACCOUNT NO. 533

DATE	ITEM	POST. REF.	DEBIT	CREDIT	BALANCE	
					DEBIT	CREDIT

Problem 13-6A (Concluded)

ACCOUNTS PAYABLE LEDGER

NAME Fantastic Toys

ADDRESS

DATE		ITEM	POST. REF.	DEBIT	CREDIT	BALANCE
20-- May	1	Balance	✓			5 2 0 0 00

NAME Goya Outlet

ADDRESS

DATE		ITEM	POST. REF.	DEBIT	CREDIT	BALANCE
20-- May	1	Balance	✓			3 8 0 0 00

NAME Mueller's Distributors

ADDRESS

DATE		ITEM	POST. REF.	DEBIT	CREDIT	BALANCE
20-- May	1	Balance	✓			3 6 0 0 00

NAME Van Kooning

ADDRESS

DATE		ITEM	POST. REF.	DEBIT	CREDIT	BALANCE
20-- May	1	Balance	✓			7 4 0 0 00

Problem 13-7A

1.

PURCHASES JOURNAL

	DATE	INVOICE NO.	FROM WHOM PURCHASED	POST. REF.	PURCHASES DR. ACCTS. PAY. CR.	
1						1
2						2
3						3
4						4
5						5
6						6
7						7
8						8
9						9
10						10

CASH PAYMENTS JOURNAL

	DATE	CK. NO.	ACCOUNT DEBITED	POST. REF.	GENERAL DR.	ACCTS. PAYABLE DR.	PURCHASES DR.	PURCHASES DISCOUNTS CR.	CASH CR.	
1										1
2										2
3										3
4										4
5										5
6										6
7										7
8										8
9										9
10										10
11										11
12										12

Problem 13-7A (Continued)

JOURNAL PAGE 3

	DATE	DESCRIPTION	POST. REF.	DEBIT	CREDIT	
1						1
2						2
3						3
4						4
5						5
6						6
7						7
8						8
9						9
10						10

2.

GENERAL LEDGER

ACCOUNT Cash ACCOUNT NO. 101

DATE	ITEM	POST. REF.	DEBIT	CREDIT	BALANCE DEBIT	BALANCE CREDIT
20-- July 1	Balance	✓			20 0 0 0 00	

ACCOUNT Accounts Payable ACCOUNT NO. 202

DATE	ITEM	POST. REF.	DEBIT	CREDIT	BALANCE DEBIT	BALANCE CREDIT

Problem 13-7A (Continued)

ACCOUNT Flint, Drawing ACCOUNT NO. 312

DATE	ITEM	POST. REF.	DEBIT	CREDIT	BALANCE	
					DEBIT	CREDIT

ACCOUNT Purchases ACCOUNT NO. 501

DATE	ITEM	POST. REF.	DEBIT	CREDIT	BALANCE	
					DEBIT	CREDIT

ACCOUNT Purchases Returns and Allowances ACCOUNT NO. 501.1

DATE	ITEM	POST. REF.	DEBIT	CREDIT	BALANCE	
					DEBIT	CREDIT

ACCOUNT Purchases Discounts ACCOUNT NO. 501.2

DATE	ITEM	POST. REF.	DEBIT	CREDIT	BALANCE	
					DEBIT	CREDIT

ACCOUNT Rent Expense ACCOUNT NO. 521

DATE	ITEM	POST. REF.	DEBIT	CREDIT	BALANCE	
					DEBIT	CREDIT

Problem 13-7A (Concluded)

ACCOUNTS PAYABLE LEDGER

NAME

ADDRESS

DATE	ITEM	POST. REF.	DEBIT	CREDIT	BALANCE

NAME

ADDRESS

DATE	ITEM	POST. REF.	DEBIT	CREDIT	BALANCE

NAME

ADDRESS

DATE	ITEM	POST. REF.	DEBIT	CREDIT	BALANCE

NAME

ADDRESS

DATE	ITEM	POST. REF.	DEBIT	CREDIT	BALANCE

Exercise 13-1B

SALES JOURNAL PAGE

DATE	SALE NO.	TO WHOM SOLD	POST. REF.	ACCOUNTS RECEIVABLE DR.	SALES CR.	SALES TAX PAYABLE CR.

Exercise 13-2B

CASH RECEIPTS JOURNAL PAGE

	DATE	ACCOUNT CREDITED	POST. REF.	GENERAL CR.	ACCTS. RECEIVABLE CR.	SALES CR.	SALES TAX PAY. CR.	CASH DR.	
1									1
2									2
3									3
4									4
5									5
6									6
7									7
8									8
9									9
10									10
11									11
12									12
13									13

Exercise 13-3B

PURCHASES JOURNAL

PAGE

	DATE	INVOICE NO.	FROM WHOM PURCHASED	POST. REF.	PURCHASES DR. ACCTS. PAY. CR.	
1						1
2						2
3						3
4						4
5						5
6						6
7						7
8						8
9						9
10						10
11						11

Exercise 13-4B

CASH PAYMENTS JOURNAL

PAGE

	DATE	CK. NO.	ACCOUNT DEBITED	POST. REF.	GENERAL DR.	ACCTS. PAYABLE DR.	PURCHASES DR.	PURCHASES DISCOUNTS CR.	CASH CR.	
1										1
2										2
3										3
4										4
5										5
6										6
7										7
8										8
9										9
10										10
11										11
12										12
13										13

Problem 13-1B

1.

| | | | SALES JOURNAL | | | | | | PAGE 8 |

DATE	SALE NO.	TO WHOM SOLD	POST. REF.	ACCOUNTS RECEIVABLE DR.	SALES CR.	SALES TAX PAYABLE CR.

2.

GENERAL LEDGER

ACCOUNT Accounts Receivable ACCOUNT NO. 122

DATE	ITEM	POST. REF.	DEBIT	CREDIT	BALANCE DEBIT	CREDIT

ACCOUNT Sales Tax Payable ACCOUNT NO. 231

DATE	ITEM	POST. REF.	DEBIT	CREDIT	BALANCE DEBIT	CREDIT

Problem 13-1B (Concluded)

ACCOUNT Sales ACCOUNT NO. 401

DATE	ITEM	POST. REF.	DEBIT	CREDIT	BALANCE	
					DEBIT	CREDIT

ACCOUNTS RECEIVABLE LEDGER

NAME Dvorak Manufacturing Co.

ADDRESS 2105 Williams Drive, Muncie, IN 47304-2437

DATE	ITEM	POST. REF.	DEBIT	CREDIT	BALANCE

NAME Saga, Inc.

ADDRESS 1453 Parnell Avenue, Indianapolis, IN 46201-6870

DATE	ITEM	POST. REF.	DEBIT	CREDIT	BALANCE

NAME Vinnie Ward

ADDRESS 308 So. Muirhead Drive, Okemos, MI 48864-5356

DATE	ITEM	POST. REF.	DEBIT	CREDIT	BALANCE

NAME Zapata Co.

ADDRESS 789 N. Stafford Road, Bloomington, IN 47401-6201

DATE	ITEM	POST. REF.	DEBIT	CREDIT	BALANCE

Problem 13-2B

1.

CASH RECEIPTS JOURNAL

	DATE		ACCOUNT CREDITED	POST. REF.	GENERAL CR.					ACCOUNTS RECEIVABLE CR.					
1															1
2															2
3															3
4															4
5															5
6															6
7															7
8															8
9															9
10															10
11															11
12															12
13															13
14															14
15															15
16															16
17															17
18															18
19															19
20															20
21															21
22															22
23															23
24															24
25															25
26															26
27															27
28															28

Problem 13-2B (Continued)

PAGE 10

	SALES CR.	SALES TAX PAYABLE CR.	BANK CREDIT CARD EXPENSE DR.	CASH DR.	
1					1
2					2
3					3
4					4
5					5
6					6
7					7
8					8
9					9
10					10
11					11
12					12
13					13
14					14
15					15
16					16
17					17
18					18
19					19
20					20
21					21
22					22
23					23
24					24
25					25
26					26
27					27
28					28

Problem 13-2B (Continued)

	JOURNAL					PAGE 8	

	DATE		DESCRIPTION	POST. REF.	DEBIT	CREDIT	
1							1
2							2
3							3
4							4
5							5
6							6
7							7
8							8
9							9
10							10
11							11
12							12
13							13
14							14
15							15
16							16
17							17
18							18
19							19
20							20
21							21
22							22
23							23
24							24
25							25
26							26
27							27
28							28
29							29
30							30
31							31
32							32
33							33
34							34

Problem 13-2B (Continued)

2.

GENERAL LEDGER

ACCOUNT Cash ACCOUNT NO. 101

DATE		ITEM	POST. REF.	DEBIT	CREDIT	BALANCE	
						DEBIT	CREDIT
20-- Jan.	1	Balance	✓			2 8 9 0 75	

ACCOUNT Accounts Receivable ACCOUNT NO. 122

DATE		ITEM	POST. REF.	DEBIT	CREDIT	BALANCE	
						DEBIT	CREDIT
20-- Jan.	1	Balance	✓			6 3 0 0 00	

ACCOUNT Sales Tax Payable ACCOUNT NO. 231

DATE	ITEM	POST. REF.	DEBIT	CREDIT	BALANCE	
					DEBIT	CREDIT

ACCOUNT Sales ACCOUNT NO. 401

DATE	ITEM	POST. REF.	DEBIT	CREDIT	BALANCE	
					DEBIT	CREDIT

Problem 13-2B (Continued)

ACCOUNT Sales Returns & Allowances ACCOUNT NO. 401.1

DATE	ITEM	POST. REF.	DEBIT	CREDIT	BALANCE DEBIT	BALANCE CREDIT

ACCOUNT Bank Credit Card Expense ACCOUNT NO. 513

DATE	ITEM	POST. REF.	DEBIT	CREDIT	BALANCE DEBIT	BALANCE CREDIT

ACCOUNTS RECEIVABLE LEDGER

NAME Ray Boyd

ADDRESS 229 SE 65th Avenue, Portland, OR 97215-1451

DATE		ITEM	POST. REF.	DEBIT	CREDIT	BALANCE
20-- Jan.	1	Balance	✓			1 4 0 0 00

NAME Dazai Manufacturing

ADDRESS 447 6th Avenue, Flagstaff, AZ 86004-6842

DATE		ITEM	POST. REF.	DEBIT	CREDIT	BALANCE
20-- Jan.	1	Balance	✓			3 1 8 00

Problem 13-2B (Concluded)

NAME Clint Hassell

ADDRESS 1462 N. Steves Blvd., Los Cruces, NM 88012-7791

DATE		ITEM	POST. REF.	DEBIT	CREDIT	BALANCE
20-- Jan.	1	Balance	✓			8 1 5 00

NAME Jan Sowada

ADDRESS 5997 Blackgold Lane, Grapevine, TX 76051-2366

DATE		ITEM	POST. REF.	DEBIT	CREDIT	BALANCE
20-- Jan.	1	Balance	✓			1 4 8 1 00

NAME Robert Zehnle

ADDRESS 6881 Seneca Drive, San Diego, CA 92127-8671

DATE		ITEM	POST. REF.	DEBIT	CREDIT	BALANCE
20-- Jan.	1	Balance	✓			2 2 8 6 00

Problem 13-3B

1.

		SALES JOURNAL					PAGE 6

DATE	SALE NO.	TO WHOM SOLD	POST. REF.	ACCOUNTS RECEIVABLE DR.	SALES CR.	SALES TAX PAYABLE CR.

		CASH RECEIPTS JOURNAL						PAGE 9

	DATE	ACCOUNT CREDITED	POST. REF.	GENERAL CR.	ACCTS. RECEIVABLE CR.	SALES CR.	SALES TAX PAY. CR.	CASH DR.	
1									1
2									2
3									3
4									4
5									5
6									6
7									7
8									8
9									9

Problem 13-3B (Continued)

JOURNAL PAGE 5

	DATE		DESCRIPTION	POST. REF.	DEBIT	CREDIT	
1							1
2							2
3							3
4							4
5							5
6							6
7							7
8							8
9							9
10							10
11							11
12							12
13							13
14							14

2.

GENERAL LEDGER

ACCOUNT Cash ACCOUNT NO. 101

DATE		ITEM	POST. REF.	DEBIT	CREDIT	BALANCE DEBIT	BALANCE CREDIT
20-- Apr.	1	Balance	✓			2 8 6 4 54	

ACCOUNT Accounts Receivable ACCOUNT NO. 122

DATE		ITEM	POST. REF.	DEBIT	CREDIT	BALANCE DEBIT	BALANCE CREDIT
20-- Apr.	1	Balance	✓			2 7 2 6 25	

Problem 13-3B (Continued)

ACCOUNT Sales Tax Payable ACCOUNT NO. 231

DATE	ITEM	POST. REF.	DEBIT	CREDIT	BALANCE	
					DEBIT	CREDIT

ACCOUNT Sales ACCOUNT NO. 401

DATE	ITEM	POST. REF.	DEBIT	CREDIT	BALANCE	
					DEBIT	CREDIT

ACCOUNT Sales Returns & Allowances ACCOUNT NO. 401.1

DATE	ITEM	POST. REF.	DEBIT	CREDIT	BALANCE	
					DEBIT	CREDIT

Problem 13-3B (Concluded)

ACCOUNTS PAYABLE LEDGER

NAME O. L. Meyers

ADDRESS 119 Hartford Turnpike, Vernon, CT 06066-0113

DATE		ITEM	POST. REF.	DEBIT	CREDIT	BALANCE
20-- Apr.	1	Balance	✓			2 1 8 6 00

NAME Kelsay Munkres

ADDRESS 233 Cambridge Dr., Branford, CT 06405-9276

DATE		ITEM	POST. REF.	DEBIT	CREDIT	BALANCE
20-- Apr.	1	Balance	✓			4 8 2 00

NAME Andrew Plaa

ADDRESS 51 Bissell Ave., Old Saybrook, CT 06475-0212

DATE		ITEM	POST. REF.	DEBIT	CREDIT	BALANCE

NAME Melissa Richfield

ADDRESS 1107 Silver Lane, East Hartford, CT 06108-1907

DATE		ITEM	POST. REF.	DEBIT	CREDIT	BALANCE
20-- Apr.	1	Balance	✓			5 8 25

Problem 13-4B

1.

<div align="center">

PURCHASES JOURNAL PAGE 7

</div>

	DATE	INVOICE NO.	FROM WHOM PURCHASED	POST. REF.	PURCHASES DR. ACCTS. PAY. CR.	
1						1
2						2
3						3
4						4
5						5
6						6
7						7
8						8
9						9
10						10
11						11
12						12
13						13
14						14

2.

<div align="center">

GENERAL LEDGER

</div>

ACCOUNT Accounts Payable ACCOUNT NO. 202

DATE	ITEM	POST. REF.	DEBIT	CREDIT	BALANCE DEBIT	BALANCE CREDIT

ACCOUNT Purchases ACCOUNT NO. 501

DATE	ITEM	POST. REF.	DEBIT	CREDIT	BALANCE DEBIT	BALANCE CREDIT

Problem 13-4B (Concluded)

ACCOUNTS PAYABLE LEDGER

NAME _____
ADDRESS _____

DATE	ITEM	POST. REF.	DEBIT	CREDIT	BALANCE

NAME _____
ADDRESS _____

DATE	ITEM	POST. REF.	DEBIT	CREDIT	BALANCE

NAME _____
ADDRESS _____

DATE	ITEM	POST. REF.	DEBIT	CREDIT	BALANCE

NAME _____
ADDRESS _____

DATE	ITEM	POST. REF.	DEBIT	CREDIT	BALANCE

NAME _____
ADDRESS _____

DATE	ITEM	POST. REF.	DEBIT	CREDIT	BALANCE

Problem 13-5B

1.

GENERAL LEDGER

ACCOUNT Accounts Payable ACCOUNT NO. 202

DATE	ITEM	POST. REF.	DEBIT	CREDIT	BALANCE	
					DEBIT	CREDIT

ACCOUNT Purchases ACCOUNT NO. 501

DATE	ITEM	POST. REF.	DEBIT	CREDIT	BALANCE	
					DEBIT	CREDIT

2.

ACCOUNTS PAYABLE LEDGER

NAME

ADDRESS

DATE	ITEM	POST. REF.	DEBIT	CREDIT	BALANCE

NAME

ADDRESS

DATE	ITEM	POST. REF.	DEBIT	CREDIT	BALANCE

Problem 13-5B (Concluded)

NAME

ADDRESS

DATE	ITEM	POST. REF.	DEBIT	CREDIT	BALANCE

NAME

ADDRESS

DATE	ITEM	POST. REF.	DEBIT	CREDIT	BALANCE

NAME

ADDRESS

DATE	ITEM	POST. REF.	DEBIT	CREDIT	BALANCE

Problem 13-6B

1.

<div align="center">

CASH PAYMENTS JOURNAL PAGE 6

</div>

	DATE	CK. NO.	ACCOUNT DEBITED	POST. REF.	GENERAL DR.	ACCTS. PAYABLE DR.	PURCHASES DR.	PURCHASES DISCOUNTS CR.	CASH CR.	
1										1
2										2
3										3
4										4
5										5
6										6
7										7
8										8
9										9
10										10
11										11
12										12

2.

<div align="center">

GENERAL LEDGER

</div>

ACCOUNT Cash ACCOUNT NO. 101

DATE		ITEM	POST. REF.	DEBIT	CREDIT	BALANCE DEBIT	BALANCE CREDIT
20-- May	1	Balance	✓			40 0 0 0 00	

ACCOUNT Accounts Payable ACCOUNT NO. 202

DATE		ITEM	POST. REF.	DEBIT	CREDIT	BALANCE DEBIT	BALANCE CREDIT
20-- May	1	Balance	✓				20 0 0 0 00

Name _____

Problem 13-6B (Continued)

ACCOUNT Purchases ACCOUNT NO. 501

DATE	ITEM	POST. REF.	DEBIT	CREDIT	BALANCE DEBIT	BALANCE CREDIT

ACCOUNT Purchases Discounts ACCOUNT NO. 501.2

DATE	ITEM	POST. REF.	DEBIT	CREDIT	BALANCE DEBIT	BALANCE CREDIT

ACCOUNT Freight-In ACCOUNT NO. 502

DATE	ITEM	POST. REF.	DEBIT	CREDIT	BALANCE DEBIT	BALANCE CREDIT

ACCOUNT Rent Expense ACCOUNT NO. 521

DATE	ITEM	POST. REF.	DEBIT	CREDIT	BALANCE DEBIT	BALANCE CREDIT

ACCOUNT Utilities Expense ACCOUNT NO. 533

DATE	ITEM	POST. REF.	DEBIT	CREDIT	BALANCE DEBIT	BALANCE CREDIT

Problem 13-6B (Concluded)

ACCOUNTS PAYABLE LEDGER

NAME Cortez Distributors

ADDRESS

DATE		ITEM	POST. REF.	DEBIT	CREDIT	BALANCE
20-- May	1	Balance	✓			4 2 0 0 00

NAME Indra & Velga

ADDRESS

DATE		ITEM	POST. REF.	DEBIT	CREDIT	BALANCE
20-- May	1	Balance	✓			6 8 0 0 00

NAME Toy Corner

ADDRESS

DATE		ITEM	POST. REF.	DEBIT	CREDIT	BALANCE
20-- May	1	Balance	✓			4 6 0 0 00

NAME Troutman Outlet

ADDRESS

DATE		ITEM	POST. REF.	DEBIT	CREDIT	BALANCE
20-- May	1	Balance	✓			4 4 0 0 00

Problem 13-7B

1.

PURCHASES JOURNAL PAGE 7

	DATE	INVOICE NO.	FROM WHOM PURCHASED	POST. REF.	PURCHASES DR. ACCTS. PAY. CR.	
1						1
2						2
3						3
4						4
5						5
6						6
7						7
8						8
9						9
10						10

CASH PAYMENTS JOURNAL PAGE 9

	DATE	CK. NO.	ACCOUNT DEBITED	POST. REF.	GENERAL DR.	ACCTS. PAYABLE DR.	PURCHASES DR.	PURCHASES DISCOUNTS CR.	CASH CR.	
1										1
2										2
3										3
4										4
5										5
6										6
7										7
8										8
9										9
10										10
11										11
12										12

Problem 13-7B (Continued)

JOURNAL

PAGE

	DATE		DESCRIPTION	POST. REF.	DEBIT	CREDIT	
1							1
2							2
3							3
4							4
5							5
6							6
7							7
8							8
9							9
10							10

2.

GENERAL LEDGER

ACCOUNT Cash ACCOUNT NO. 101

DATE		ITEM	POST. REF.	DEBIT	CREDIT	BALANCE DEBIT	BALANCE CREDIT
20-- July	1	Balance	✓			20 0 0 0 00	

ACCOUNT Accounts Payable ACCOUNT NO. 202

DATE	ITEM	POST. REF.	DEBIT	CREDIT	BALANCE DEBIT	BALANCE CREDIT

Problem 13-7B (Continued)

ACCOUNT Mueller, Drawing ACCOUNT NO. 312

DATE	ITEM	POST. REF.	DEBIT	CREDIT	BALANCE DEBIT	CREDIT

ACCOUNT Purchases ACCOUNT NO. 501

DATE	ITEM	POST. REF.	DEBIT	CREDIT	BALANCE DEBIT	CREDIT

ACCOUNT Purchases Returns and Allowances ACCOUNT NO. 501.1

DATE	ITEM	POST. REF.	DEBIT	CREDIT	BALANCE DEBIT	CREDIT

ACCOUNT Purchases Discounts ACCOUNT NO. 501.2

DATE	ITEM	POST. REF.	DEBIT	CREDIT	BALANCE DEBIT	CREDIT

ACCOUNT Rent Expense ACCOUNT NO. 521

DATE	ITEM	POST. REF.	DEBIT	CREDIT	BALANCE DEBIT	CREDIT

Problem 13-7B (Concluded)

ACCOUNTS PAYABLE LEDGER

NAME

ADDRESS

DATE		ITEM	POST. REF.	DEBIT	CREDIT	BALANCE

NAME

ADDRESS

DATE		ITEM	POST. REF.	DEBIT	CREDIT	BALANCE

NAME

ADDRESS

DATE		ITEM	POST. REF.	DEBIT	CREDIT	BALANCE

NAME

ADDRESS

DATE		ITEM	POST. REF.	DEBIT	CREDIT	BALANCE

Challenge Problem

1.

<div align="center">

JOURNAL

</div>

PAGE

	DATE		DESCRIPTION	POST. REF.	DEBIT	CREDIT	
1							1
2							2
3							3
4							4
5							5
6							6
7							7
8							8
9							9
10							10
11							11
12							12
13							13
14							14
15							15
16							16
17							17
18							18
19							19
20							20
21							21
22							22
23							23
24							24
25							25
26							26
27							27
28							28
29							29
30							30
31							31
32							32
33							33
34							34

Challenge Problem (Continued)

	DATE		DESCRIPTION	POST. REF.	DEBIT	CREDIT	
1							1
2							2
3							3
4							4
5							5
6							6
7							7
8							8
9							9
10							10
11							11
12							12
13							13
14							14
15							15
16							16
17							17
18							18
19							19
20							20
21							21
22							22
23							23
24							24
25							25
26							26
27							27
28							28
29							29
30							30
31							31
32							32
33							33
34							34

JOURNAL PAGE

Challenge Problem (Continued)

JOURNAL PAGE

	DATE		DESCRIPTION	POST. REF.	DEBIT	CREDIT	
1							1
2							2
3							3
4							4
5							5
6							6
7							7
8							8
9							9
10							10
11							11
12							12
13							13
14							14
15							15
16							16
17							17
18							18
19							19
20							20
21							21
22							22
23							23
24							24
25							25
26							26
27							27
28							28
29							29
30							30
31							31
32							32
33							33
34							34

Challenge Problem (Concluded)

Mastery Problem

1.

SALES JOURNAL

PAGE 7

DATE	SALE NO.	TO WHOM SOLD	POST. REF.	ACCOUNTS RECEIVABLE DR.	SALES CR.	SALES TAX PAYABLE CR.

CASH RECEIPTS JOURNAL

PAGE 10

	DATE	ACCOUNT CREDITED	POST. REF.	GENERAL CR.	ACCTS. RECEIVABLE CR.	SALES CR.	SALES TAX PAY. CR.	CASH DR.	
1									1
2									2
3									3
4									4
5									5
6									6
7									7
8									8
9									9
10									10
11									11
12									12
13									13

Mastery Problem (Continued)

PURCHASES JOURNAL

	DATE	INVOICE NO.	FROM WHOM PURCHASED	POST. REF.	PURCHASES DR. ACCTS. PAY. CR.	
1						1
2						2
3						3
4						4
5						5
6						6
7						7
8						8
9						9
10						10
11						11

CASH PAYMENTS JOURNAL

	DATE	CK. NO.	ACCOUNT DEBITED	POST. REF.	GENERAL DR.	ACCTS. PAYABLE DR.	PURCHASES DR.	PURCHASES DISCOUNTS CR.	CASH CR.	
1										1
2										2
3										3
4										4
5										5
6										6
7										7
8										8
9										9
10										10
11										11
12										12
13										13

Mastery Problem (Continued)

JOURNAL

PAGE 5

	DATE	DESCRIPTION	POST. REF.	DEBIT	CREDIT	
1						1
2						2
3						3
4						4
5						5
6						6
7						7
8						8
9						9
10						10
11						11
12						12

2.

GENERAL LEDGER

ACCOUNT Cash ACCOUNT NO. 101

DATE	ITEM	POST. REF.	DEBIT	CREDIT	BALANCE DEBIT	BALANCE CREDIT
20-- Oct. 1	Balance	✓			18 2 2 5 00	

ACCOUNT Accounts Receivable ACCOUNT NO. 122

DATE	ITEM	POST. REF.	DEBIT	CREDIT	BALANCE DEBIT	BALANCE CREDIT
20-- Oct. 1	Balance	✓			9 6 1 9 00	

Mastery Problem (Continued)

ACCOUNT Accounts Payable ACCOUNT NO. 202

DATE		ITEM	POST. REF.	DEBIT	CREDIT	BALANCE	
						DEBIT	CREDIT
20-- Oct.	1	Balance	✓				5 1 2 0 00

ACCOUNT Sales Tax Payable ACCOUNT NO. 231

DATE		ITEM	POST. REF.	DEBIT	CREDIT	BALANCE	
						DEBIT	CREDIT

ACCOUNT Sales ACCOUNT NO. 401

DATE		ITEM	POST. REF.	DEBIT	CREDIT	BALANCE	
						DEBIT	CREDIT

ACCOUNT Sales Returns and Allowances ACCOUNT NO. 401.1

DATE		ITEM	POST. REF.	DEBIT	CREDIT	BALANCE	
						DEBIT	CREDIT

Name _____

Mastery Problem (Continued)

ACCOUNT Purchases ACCOUNT NO. 501

DATE	ITEM	POST. REF.	DEBIT	CREDIT	BALANCE DEBIT	CREDIT

ACCOUNT Purchases Returns and Allowances ACCOUNT NO. 501.1

DATE	ITEM	POST. REF.	DEBIT	CREDIT	BALANCE DEBIT	CREDIT

ACCOUNT Purchases Discounts ACCOUNT NO. 501.2

DATE	ITEM	POST. REF.	DEBIT	CREDIT	BALANCE DEBIT	CREDIT

ACCOUNT Wages Expense ACCOUNT NO. 511

DATE	ITEM	POST. REF.	DEBIT	CREDIT	BALANCE DEBIT	CREDIT

ACCOUNT Telephone Expense ACCOUNT NO. 525

DATE	ITEM	POST. REF.	DEBIT	CREDIT	BALANCE DEBIT	CREDIT

Mastery Problem (Continued)

ACCOUNTS RECEIVABLE LEDGER

NAME David's Decorating

ADDRESS 12 Jude Lane, Hartford, CT 06117

DATE		ITEM	POST. REF.	DEBIT	CREDIT	BALANCE
20-- Oct.	1	Balance	✓			3 3 4 0 00

NAME Meg Johnson

ADDRESS 700 Hobbes Dr., Avon, CT 06108

DATE		ITEM	POST. REF.	DEBIT	CREDIT	BALANCE
20-- Oct.	1	Balance	✓			4 0 0 0 00

NAME Elizabeth Shoemaker

ADDRESS 52 Juniper Road, Hartford, CT 06118

DATE		ITEM	POST. REF.	DEBIT	CREDIT	BALANCE
20-- Oct.	1	Balance	✓			2 7 9 00

NAME Leigh Summers

ADDRESS 5200 Hamilton Ave., Hartford, CT 06111

DATE		ITEM	POST. REF.	DEBIT	CREDIT	BALANCE
20-- Oct.	1	Balance	✓			2 0 0 0 00

Mastery Problem (Concluded)

ACCOUNTS PAYABLE LEDGER

NAME Flower Wholesalers

ADDRESS 43 Lucky Lane, Bristol, CT 06007

DATE		ITEM	POST. REF.	DEBIT	CREDIT	BALANCE
20-- Oct.	1	Balance	✓			1 5 0 0 00

NAME Jill Hand

ADDRESS 1009 Drake Rd., Farmington, CT 06082

DATE		ITEM	POST. REF.	DEBIT	CREDIT	BALANCE
20-- Oct.	1	Balance	✓			5 0 0 00

NAME Seidl Enterprises

ADDRESS 888 Anders Street, Newington, CT 06789

DATE		ITEM	POST. REF.	DEBIT	CREDIT	BALANCE

NAME Vases Etc.

ADDRESS 34 Harry Ave., East Hartford, CT 05234

DATE		ITEM	POST. REF.	DEBIT	CREDIT	BALANCE
20-- Oct.	1	Balance	✓			3 1 2 0 00

Exercise 14-1A

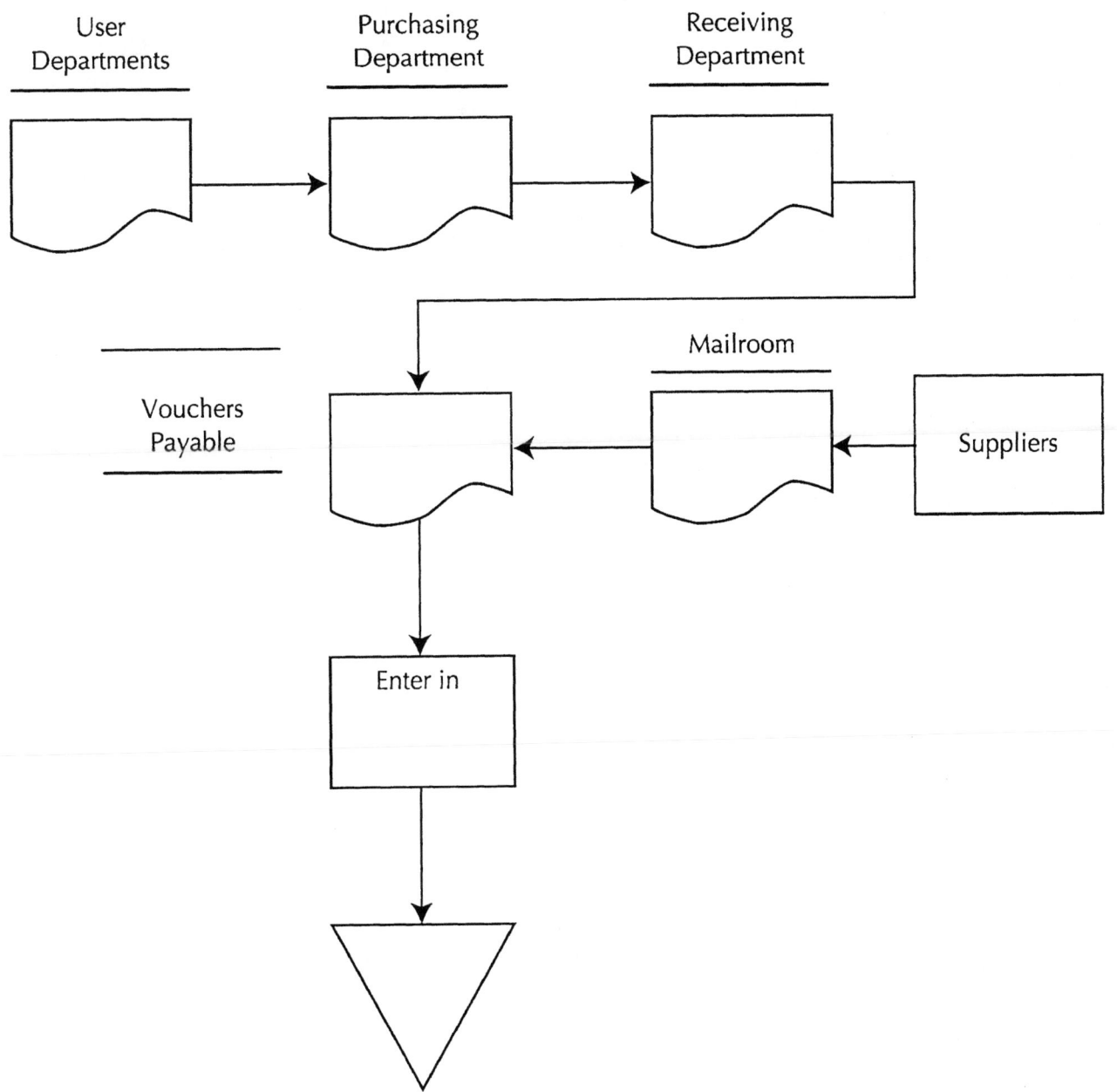

Exercise 14-2A
Voucher (front)

Mitchell & Jenkins Sporting Goods

2200 E. Washington St.
Indianapolis, IN 46201-3216

Date
To:

Terms:

Due:

Voucher No. **164**

Invoice Date	Invoice No.	Description	Amount

Authorization _____ Prepared By _____

Voucher No. **164**

Account Debited	Account No.	Amount	Summary
			Invoice
			Discount
			Net

Payment	Date	Check No.	Amount

Approved Distribution _____ Payment _____

Voucher (back)

Exercise 14-3A

See pages 504 and 505.

Exercise 14-4A

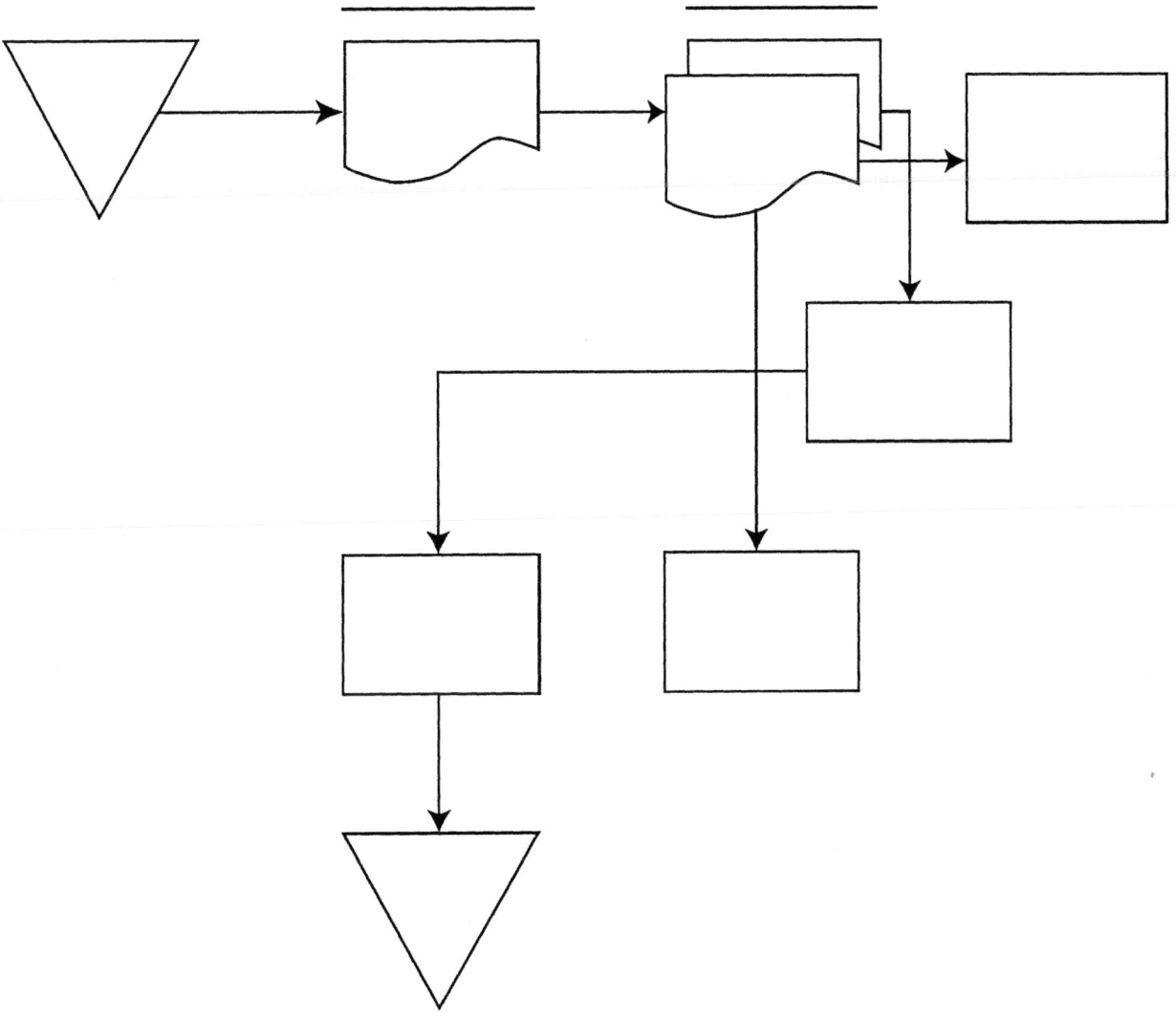

Voucher System—Payment Process

Exercise 14-3A

VOUCHER REGISTER

	DATE	VOUCHER NO.	ISSUED TO	PURCHASES DR.				
1								
2								
3								
4								
5								
6								
7								
8								
9								
10								
11								
12								
13								
14								

Exercise 14-3A (Concluded)

PAGE

SUPPLIES DR.	WAGES AND SALARIES EXP. DR.	GENERAL DR.			VOUCHERS PAYABLE CR.	PAYMENT		
		ACCOUNT	POST. REF.	AMOUNT		DATE	CK. NO.	
								1
								2
								3
								4
								5
								6
								7
								8
								9
								10
								11
								12
								13
								14

Exercise 14-5A

CHECK REGISTER

PAGE

	DATE	CHECK NO.	PAYEE	VOUCHERS PAY. DR.		PURCHASES DISCOUNTS CR.	CASH CR.	
				VOU. NO.	AMOUNT			
1								1
2								2
3								3
4								4
5								5
6								6
7								7
8								8
9								9
10								10
11								11
12								12
13								13

Exercise 14-6A

Exercise 14-7A

VOUCHER REGISTER

	DATE	VOUCHER NO.	ISSUED TO	PURCHASES DR.			
1	9/6/--	202	Briggs Store	6	0	0	00
2	9/8/--	203	XYZ Co.	8	0	0	00
3	9/10/--	204	Arbiters, Inc.	7	0	0	00
4	9/11/--	205	Paper Traders				
5	9/15/--	206	Trizon Suppliers	3	5	0	00
6	9/16/--	207	Payroll				
7	9/18/--	208	F. B. Jones Co.	6	0	0	00
8							
9							
10							
11							
12							

Exercise 14-7A (Concluded)

JOURNAL

PAGE _____

	DATE		DESCRIPTION	POST. REF.	DEBIT	CREDIT	
1							1
2							2
3							3
4							4
5							5
6							6
7							7
8							8
9							9
10							10
11							11
12							12
13							13
14							14
15							15
16							16

PAGE _____

SUPPLIES DR.	WAGES AND SALARIES EXP. DR.	GENERAL DR. ACCOUNT	POST. REF.	AMOUNT	VOUCHERS PAYABLE CR.	PAYMENT DATE	CK. NO.	
					6 0 0 00	9/8	681	1
					8 0 0 00			2
					7 0 0 00			3
1 8 6 00					1 8 6 00			4
					3 5 0 00			5
	1 2 0 0 00				1 2 0 0 00			6
					6 0 0 00			7
								8
								9
								10
								11
								12

Problem 14-1A

1.

VOUCHER REGISTER

	DATE	VOUCHER NO.	ISSUED TO	PURCHASES DR.				
1								
2								
3								
4								
5								
6								
7								
8								
9								
10								
11								
12								
13								
14								
15								
16								
17								
18								
19								
20								

Proof

Problem 14-1A (Continued)

SUPPLIES DR.	WAGES AND SALARIES EXP. DR.	GENERAL DR. ACCOUNT	POST. REF.	AMOUNT	VOUCHERS PAYABLE CR.	PAYMENT DATE	CK. NO.	
								1
								2
								3
								4
								5
								6
								7
								8
								9
								10
								11
								12
								13
								14
								15
								16
								17
								18
								19
								20

Problem 14-1A (Continued)

2.

GENERAL LEDGER

ACCOUNT Supplies ACCOUNT NO. 141

DATE	ITEM	POST. REF.	DEBIT	CREDIT	BALANCE	
					DEBIT	CREDIT

ACCOUNT Vouchers Payable ACCOUNT NO. 202

DATE	ITEM	POST. REF.	DEBIT	CREDIT	BALANCE	
					DEBIT	CREDIT

ACCOUNT Purchases ACCOUNT NO. 501

DATE	ITEM	POST. REF.	DEBIT	CREDIT	BALANCE	
					DEBIT	CREDIT

ACCOUNT Wages and Salaries Expense ACCOUNT NO. 511

DATE	ITEM	POST. REF.	DEBIT	CREDIT	BALANCE	
					DEBIT	CREDIT

ACCOUNT Rent Expense ACCOUNT NO. 521

DATE	ITEM	POST. REF.	DEBIT	CREDIT	BALANCE	
					DEBIT	CREDIT

Problem 14-1A (Concluded)

3.

Problem 14-2A

1.

CHECK REGISTER

PAGE 8

	DATE	CHECK NO.	PAYEE	VOUCHERS PAY. DR.		PURCHASES DISCOUNTS CR.	CASH CR.	
				VOU. NO.	AMOUNT			
1								1
2								2
3								3
4								4
5								5
6								6
7								7
8								8
9								9
10								10
11								11
12								12

Problem 14-2A (Concluded)

2.

GENERAL LEDGER

ACCOUNT Cash ACCOUNT NO. 101

DATE		ITEM	POST. REF.	DEBIT	CREDIT	BALANCE DEBIT	BALANCE CREDIT
20-- Aug.	1	Balance	✓			9 8 6 2 00	

ACCOUNT Vouchers Payable ACCOUNT NO. 202

DATE		ITEM	POST. REF.	DEBIT	CREDIT	BALANCE DEBIT	BALANCE CREDIT
20-- Aug.	1	Balance	✓				8 4 8 2 00

ACCOUNT Purchases Discounts ACCOUNT NO. 501.2

DATE		ITEM	POST. REF.	DEBIT	CREDIT	BALANCE DEBIT	BALANCE CREDIT

Problem 14-3A

1. See pages 514 and 515.

2.

CHECK REGISTER PAGE 4

	DATE	CHECK NO.	PAYEE	VOUCHERS PAY. DR.		PURCHASES DISCOUNTS CR.	CASH CR.	
				VOU. NO.	AMOUNT			
1								1
2								2
3								3
4								4
5								5
6								6
7								7
8								8
9								9
10								10
11								11
12								12
13								13
14								14
15								15
16								16
17								17
18								18
19								19
20								20
21								21
22								22
23								23
24								24
25								25
26								26

Problem 14-3A (Continued)

1.

VOUCHER REGISTER

	DATE	VOUCHER NO.	ISSUED TO	PURCHASES DR.
1				
2				
3				
4				
5				
6				
7				
8				
9				
10				
11				
12				
13				
14				
15				
16				
17				
18				
19				
20				

Proof

Problem 14-3A (Continued)

SUPPLIES DR.	WAGES AND SALARIES EXP. DR.	GENERAL DR. ACCOUNT	POST. REF.	AMOUNT	VOUCHERS PAYABLE CR.	PAYMENT DATE	CK. NO.	
								1
								2
								3
								4
								5
								6
								7
								8
								9
								10
								11
								12
								13
								14
								15
								16
								17
								18
								19
								20

Problem 14-3A (Continued)

3.

GENERAL LEDGER

ACCOUNT Cash ACCOUNT NO. 101

DATE		ITEM	POST. REF.	DEBIT	CREDIT	BALANCE DEBIT	BALANCE CREDIT
20-- Apr.	1	Balance	✓			5 1 8 9 00	

ACCOUNT Supplies ACCOUNT NO. 141

DATE		ITEM	POST. REF.	DEBIT	CREDIT	BALANCE DEBIT	BALANCE CREDIT
20-- Apr.	1	Balance	✓			4 0 8 00	

ACCOUNT Vouchers Payable ACCOUNT NO. 202

DATE	ITEM	POST. REF.	DEBIT	CREDIT	BALANCE DEBIT	BALANCE CREDIT

ACCOUNT Purchases ACCOUNT NO. 501

DATE	ITEM	POST. REF.	DEBIT	CREDIT	BALANCE DEBIT	BALANCE CREDIT

ACCOUNT Purchases Discounts ACCOUNT NO. 501.2

DATE	ITEM	POST. REF.	DEBIT	CREDIT	BALANCE DEBIT	BALANCE CREDIT

Problem 14-3A (Concluded)

ACCOUNT Wages and Salaries Expense ACCOUNT NO. 511

DATE	ITEM	POST. REF.	DEBIT	CREDIT	BALANCE DEBIT	BALANCE CREDIT

ACCOUNT Rent Expense ACCOUNT NO. 521

DATE	ITEM	POST. REF.	DEBIT	CREDIT	BALANCE DEBIT	BALANCE CREDIT

4.

Problem 14-4A

1.

VOUCHER REGISTER

	DATE	VOUCHER NO.	ISSUED TO	PURCHASES DR.
1				
2				
3				
4				
5				
6				
7				
8				
9				
10				
11				
12				
13				
14				
15				
16				
17				
18				
19				
20				

Proof

Problem 14-4A (Continued)

SUPPLIES DR.	WAGES AND SALARIES EXP. DR.	GENERAL DR.			VOUCHERS PAYABLE CR.	PAYMENT		
		ACCOUNT	POST. REF.	AMOUNT		DATE	CK. NO.	
								1
								2
								3
								4
								5
								6
								7
								8
								9
								10
								11
								12
								13
								14
								15
								16
								17
								18
								19
								20

Problem 14-4A (Concluded)

2.

<div align="center">

CHECK REGISTER PAGE 5

</div>

	DATE	CHECK NO.	PAYEE	VOUCHERS PAY. DR.		PURCHASES DISCOUNTS CR.	CASH CR.	
				VOU. NO.	AMOUNT			
1								1
2								2
3								3
4								4
5								5
6								6
7								7
8								8
9								9
10								10
11								11

3.

<div align="center">

JOURNAL PAGE 5

</div>

	DATE	DESCRIPTION	POST. REF.	DEBIT	CREDIT	
1						1
2						2
3						3
4						4
5						5
6						6
7						7
8						8
9						9
10						10
11						11
12						12

Exercise 14-1B

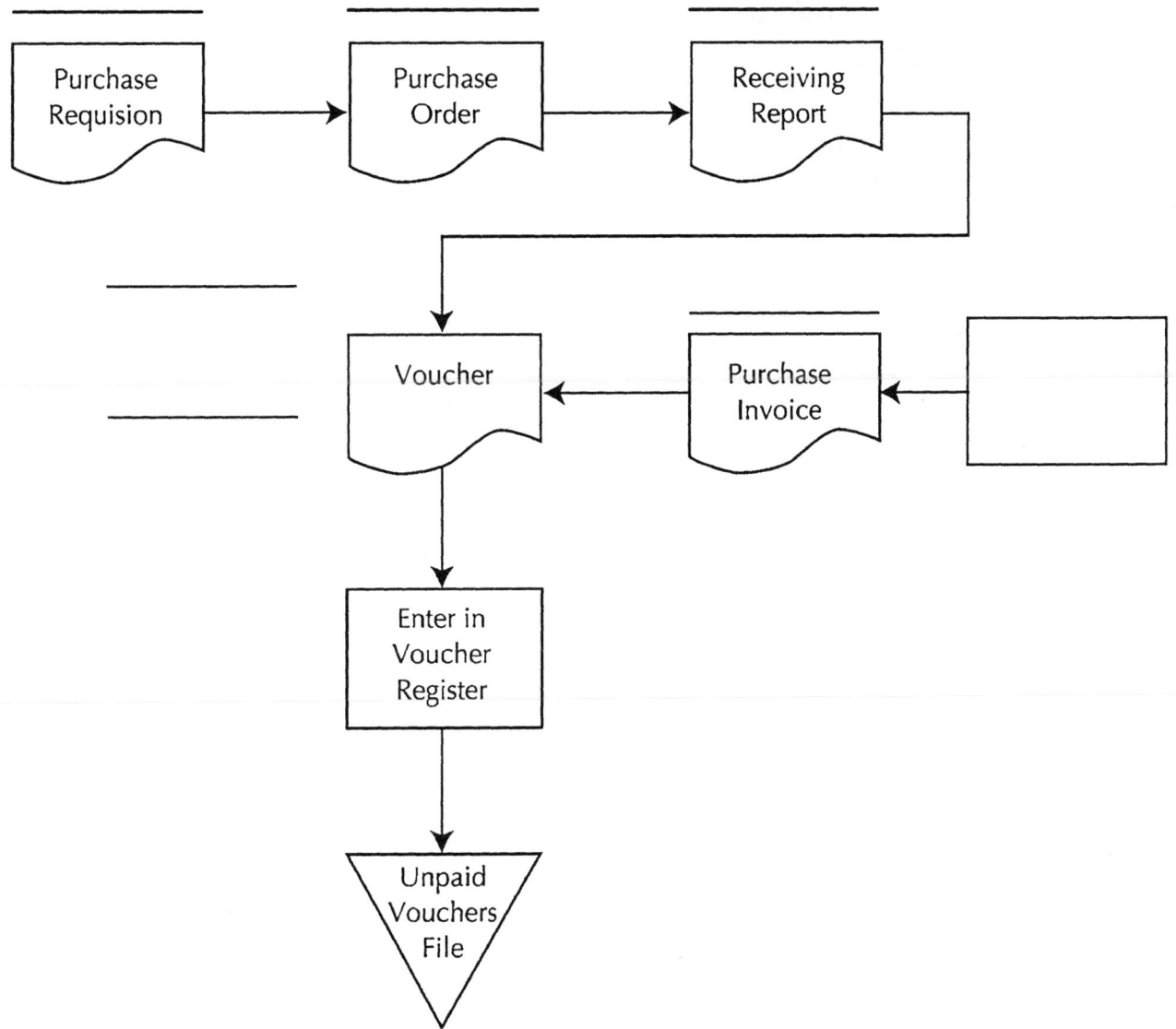

Exercise 14-2B

Voucher (front)

				Voucher No. **193**

Mitchell & Jenkins Sporting Goods

Date
To:

Terms:

Due:

2200 E. Washington St.
Indianapolis, IN 46201-3216

Invoice Date	Invoice No.	Description	Amount

Authorization _____

Prepared By _____

			Voucher No. **193**

Account Debited	Account No.	Amount	Summary
			Invoice
			Discount
			Net

Payment	Date	Check No.	Amount

Approved Distribution _____ Payment _____

Voucher (back)

Exercise 14-3B

See pages 524 and 525.

Exercise 14-4B

Exercise 14-5B

CHECK REGISTER PAGE

	DATE	CHECK NO.	PAYEE	VOUCHERS PAY. DR.		PURCHASES DISCOUNTS CR.	CASH CR.	
				VOU. NO.	AMOUNT			
1								1
2								2
3								3
4								4
5								5
6								6
7								7
8								8
9								9
10								10
11								11
12								12
13								13

Exercise 14-3B

VOUCHER REGISTER

	DATE	VOUCHER NO.	ISSUED TO	PURCHASES DR.				
1								
2								
3								
4								
5								
6								
7								
8								
9								
10								
11								
12								
13								
14								

Exercise 14-3B (Concluded)

PAGE _____

| SUPPLIES DR. | | | | WAGES AND SALARIES EXP. DR. | | | | GENERAL DR. | | | | | | VOUCHERS PAYABLE CR. | | | | PAYMENT | | |
|---|
| | | | | | | | | ACCOUNT | POST. REF. | AMOUNT | | | | | | | | DATE | CK. NO. |
| 1 |
| 2 |
| 3 |
| 4 |
| 5 |
| 6 |
| 7 |
| 8 |
| 9 |
| 10 |
| 11 |
| 12 |
| 13 |
| 14 |

Exercise 14-6B

Exercise 14-7B

VOUCHER REGISTER

	DATE	VOUCHER NO.	ISSUED TO	PURCHASES DR.			
1	9/6/--	202	Briggs Store	6	0	0	00
2	9/8/--	203	XYZ Co.	8	0	0	00
3	9/10/--	204	Arbiters, Inc.	7	0	0	00
4	9/11/--	205	Paper Traders				
5	9/15/--	206	Trizon Suppliers	3	5	0	00
6	9/16/--	207	Payroll				
7	9/18/--	208	F. B. Jones Co.	6	0	0	00
8							
9							
10							
11							
12							

Exercise 14-7B (Concluded)

PAGE

SUPPLIES DR.	WAGES AND SALARIES EXP. DR.	GENERAL DR. ACCOUNT	POST. REF.	AMOUNT	VOUCHERS PAYABLE CR.	PAYMENT DATE	CK. NO.	
					6 0 0 00	9/8	681	1
					8 0 0 00			2
					7 0 0 00			3
1 8 6 00					1 8 6 00			4
					3 5 0 00			5
	1 2 0 0 00				1 2 0 0 00			6
					6 0 0 00			7
								8
								9
								10
								11
								12

JOURNAL

PAGE

	DATE	DESCRIPTION	POST. REF.	DEBIT	CREDIT	
1						1
2						2
3						3
4						4
5						5
6						6
7						7
8						8
9						9
10						10
11						11
12						12
13						13
14						14
15						15
16						16

Problem 14-1B

1.

VOUCHER REGISTER

	DATE	VOUCHER NO.	ISSUED TO	PURCHASES DR.				
1								
2								
3								
4								
5								
6								
7								
8								
9								
10								
11								
12								
13								
14								
15								
16								
17								
18								
19								
20								

Proof

Problem 14-1B (Continued)

SUPPLIES DR.	WAGES AND SALARIES EXP. DR.	GENERAL DR.			VOUCHERS PAYABLE CR.	PAYMENT		
		ACCOUNT	POST. REF.	AMOUNT		DATE	CK. NO.	
								1
								2
								3
								4
								5
								6
								7
								8
								9
								10
								11
								12
								13
								14
								15
								16
								17
								18
								19
								20

Problem 14-1B (Continued)

2.

GENERAL LEDGER

ACCOUNT Supplies ACCOUNT NO. 141

DATE	ITEM	POST. REF.	DEBIT	CREDIT	BALANCE	
					DEBIT	CREDIT

ACCOUNT Vouchers Payable ACCOUNT NO. 202

DATE	ITEM	POST. REF.	DEBIT	CREDIT	BALANCE	
					DEBIT	CREDIT

ACCOUNT Purchases ACCOUNT NO. 501

DATE	ITEM	POST. REF.	DEBIT	CREDIT	BALANCE	
					DEBIT	CREDIT

ACCOUNT Wages and Salaries Expense ACCOUNT NO. 511

DATE	ITEM	POST. REF.	DEBIT	CREDIT	BALANCE	
					DEBIT	CREDIT

ACCOUNT Rent Expense ACCOUNT NO. 521

DATE	ITEM	POST. REF.	DEBIT	CREDIT	BALANCE	
					DEBIT	CREDIT

Problem 14-1B (Concluded)

3.

Problem 14-2B

1.

CHECK REGISTER PAGE 8

	DATE	CHECK NO.	PAYEE	VOUCHERS PAY. DR.		PURCHASES DISCOUNTS CR.	CASH CR.	
				VOU. NO.	AMOUNT			
1								1
2								2
3								3
4								4
5								5
6								6
7								7
8								8
9								9
10								10
11								11
12								12
13								13

Problem 14-2B (Concluded)

2.

GENERAL LEDGER

ACCOUNT Cash ACCOUNT NO. 101

DATE		ITEM	POST. REF.	DEBIT	CREDIT	BALANCE	
						DEBIT	CREDIT
20-- Aug.	1	Balance	✓			9 8 6 2 00	

ACCOUNT Vouchers Payable ACCOUNT NO. 202

DATE		ITEM	POST. REF.	DEBIT	CREDIT	BALANCE	
						DEBIT	CREDIT
20-- Aug.	1	Balance	✓				8 4 8 2 00

ACCOUNT Purchases Discounts ACCOUNT NO. 501.2

DATE		ITEM	POST. REF.	DEBIT	CREDIT	BALANCE	
						DEBIT	CREDIT

Problem 14-3B

1. See pages 534 and 535.

2.

CHECK REGISTER PAGE 4

	DATE	CHECK NO.	PAYEE	VOUCHERS PAY. DR.		PURCHASES DISCOUNTS CR.	CASH CR.	
				VOU. NO.	AMOUNT			
1								1
2								2
3								3
4								4
5								5
6								6
7								7
8								8
9								9
10								10
11								11
12								12
13								13
14								14
15								15
16								16
17								17
18								18
19								19
20								20
21								21
22								22
23								23
24								24
25								25
26								26

Problem 14-3B (Continued)

1.

VOUCHER REGISTER

	DATE	VOUCHER NO.	ISSUED TO	PURCHASES DR.				
1								
2								
3								
4								
5								
6								
7								
8								
9								
10								
11								
12								
13								
14								

Proof

Problem 14-3B (Continued)

PAGE 4

SUPPLIES DR.	WAGES AND SALARIES EXP. DR.	GENERAL DR.			VOUCHERS PAYABLE CR.	PAYMENT		
		ACCOUNT	POST. REF.	AMOUNT		DATE	CK. NO.	
								1
								2
								3
								4
								5
								6
								7
								8
								9
								10
								11
								12
								13
								14

3.

GENERAL LEDGER

ACCOUNT Cash ACCOUNT NO. 101

DATE		ITEM	POST. REF.	DEBIT	CREDIT	BALANCE	
						DEBIT	CREDIT
20-- Apr.	1	Balance	✓			5 1 8 9 00	

ACCOUNT Supplies ACCOUNT NO. 141

DATE		ITEM	POST. REF.	DEBIT	CREDIT	BALANCE	
						DEBIT	CREDIT
20-- Apr.	1	Balance	✓			4 0 8 00	

Problem 14-3B (Continued)

ACCOUNT Vouchers Payable ACCOUNT NO. 202

DATE	ITEM	POST. REF.	DEBIT	CREDIT	BALANCE DEBIT	BALANCE CREDIT

ACCOUNT Purchases ACCOUNT NO. 501

DATE	ITEM	POST. REF.	DEBIT	CREDIT	BALANCE DEBIT	BALANCE CREDIT

ACCOUNT Purchases Discounts ACCOUNT NO. 501.2

DATE	ITEM	POST. REF.	DEBIT	CREDIT	BALANCE DEBIT	BALANCE CREDIT

ACCOUNT Wages and Salaries Expense ACCOUNT NO. 511

DATE	ITEM	POST. REF.	DEBIT	CREDIT	BALANCE DEBIT	BALANCE CREDIT

ACCOUNT Rent Expense ACCOUNT NO. 521

DATE	ITEM	POST. REF.	DEBIT	CREDIT	BALANCE DEBIT	BALANCE CREDIT

Problem 14-3B (Concluded)

4.

Problem 14-4B

1.

VOUCHER REGISTER

	DATE	VOUCHER NO.	ISSUED TO	PURCHASES DR.
1				
2				
3				
4				
5				
6				
7				
8				
9				
10				
11				
12				
13				
14				
15				
16				
17				
18				
19				
20				

Proof

Name _____

Problem 14-4B (Continued)

SUPPLIES DR.	WAGES AND SALARIES EXP. DR.	GENERAL DR.			VOUCHERS PAYABLE CR.	PAYMENT	
		ACCOUNT	POST. REF.	AMOUNT		DATE	CK. NO.
							1
							2
							3
							4
							5
							6
							7
							8
							9
							10
							11
							12
							13
							14
							15
							16
							17
							18
							19
							20

Problem 14-4B (Concluded)

2.

<div align="center">

CHECK REGISTER PAGE 5

</div>

	DATE	CHECK NO.	PAYEE	VOUCHERS PAY. DR.		PURCHASES DISCOUNTS CR.	CASH CR.	
				VOU. NO.	AMOUNT			
1								1
2								2
3								3
4								4
5								5
6								6
7								7
8								8
9								9
10								10
11								11

3.

<div align="center">

JOURNAL PAGE 5

</div>

	DATE	DESCRIPTION	POST. REF.	DEBIT	CREDIT	
1						1
2						2
3						3
4						4
5						5
6						6
7						7
8						8
9						9
10						10
11						11
12						12

Challenge Problem

<div align="center">

JOURNAL

</div>

PAGE

	DATE		DESCRIPTION	POST. REF.	DEBIT	CREDIT	
1							1
2							2
3							3
4							4
5							5
6							6
7							7
8							8
9							9
10							10
11							11
12							12
13							13
14							14
15							15
16							16
17							17
18							18
19							19
20							20
21							21
22							22
23							23
24							24
25							25
26							26
27							27
28							28
29							29
30							30
31							31
32							32
33							33
34							34

Challenge Problem (Continued)

VOUCHER REGISTER

	DATE	VOUCHER NO.	ISSUED TO	PURCHASES DR.	SUPPLIES DR.
1					
2					
3					
4					
5					
6					
7					
8					
9					
10					
11					
12					
13					
14					
15					
16					
17					
18					
19					
20					

Challenge Problem (Concluded)

PAGE _____

WAGES AND SALARIES EXP. DR.	GENERAL				VOUCHERS PAYABLE CR.	PAYMENT		
	ACCOUNT	POST. REF.	DEBIT	CREDIT		DATE	CK. NO.	
								1
								2
								3
								4
								5
								6
								7
								8
								9
								10
								11
								12
								13
								14
								15
								16
								17
								18
								19
								20

Mastery Problem

1.

VOUCHER REGISTER

	DATE	VOUCHER NO.	ISSUED TO	PURCHASES DR.
1				
2				
3				
4				
5				
6				
7				
8				
9				
10				
11				
12				
13				
14				
15				
16				
17				
18				
19				
20				

Mastery Problem (Continued)

SUPPLIES DR.	WAGES AND SALARIES EXP. DR.	GENERAL DR.			VOUCHERS PAYABLE CR.	PAYMENT		
		ACCOUNT	POST. REF.	AMOUNT		DATE	CK. NO.	
								1
								2
								3
								4
								5
								6
								7
								8
								9
								10
								11
								12
								13
								14
								15
								16
								17
								18
								19
								20

Mastery Problem (Continued)

1.

<div align="center">CHECK REGISTER</div>

PAGE 1

	DATE	CHECK NO.	PAYEE	VOUCHERS PAY. DR.		PURCHASES DISCOUNTS CR.	CASH CR.	
				VOU. NO.	AMOUNT			
1								1
2								2
3								3
4								4
5								5
6								6
7								7
8								8
9								9
10								10
11								11
12								12

<div align="center">JOURNAL</div>

PAGE 1

	DATE	DESCRIPTION	POST. REF.	DEBIT	CREDIT	
1						1
2						2
3						3
4						4
5						5
6						6
7						7
8						8
9						9
10						10
11						11
12						12

Mastery Problem (Continued)

2.

GENERAL LEDGER

ACCOUNT Cash ACCOUNT NO. 101

DATE		ITEM	POST. REF.	DEBIT	CREDIT	BALANCE	
						DEBIT	CREDIT
20-- July	1	Balance	✓			6 0 0 0 00	

ACCOUNT Supplies ACCOUNT NO. 141

DATE	ITEM	POST. REF.	DEBIT	CREDIT	BALANCE	
					DEBIT	CREDIT

ACCOUNT Vouchers Payable ACCOUNT NO. 202

DATE	ITEM	POST. REF.	DEBIT	CREDIT	BALANCE	
					DEBIT	CREDIT

ACCOUNT Purchases ACCOUNT NO. 501

DATE	ITEM	POST. REF.	DEBIT	CREDIT	BALANCE	
					DEBIT	CREDIT

Mastery Problem (Continued)

ACCOUNT Purchases Returns and Allowances ACCOUNT NO. 501.1

DATE		ITEM	POST. REF.	DEBIT	CREDIT	BALANCE	
						DEBIT	CREDIT

ACCOUNT Purchases Discounts ACCOUNT NO. 501.2

DATE		ITEM	POST. REF.	DEBIT	CREDIT	BALANCE	
						DEBIT	CREDIT

ACCOUNT Freight-In ACCOUNT NO. 502

DATE		ITEM	POST. REF.	DEBIT	CREDIT	BALANCE	
						DEBIT	CREDIT

ACCOUNT Wages and Salaries Expense ACCOUNT NO. 511

DATE		ITEM	POST. REF.	DEBIT	CREDIT	BALANCE	
						DEBIT	CREDIT

ACCOUNT Rent Expense ACCOUNT NO. 521

DATE		ITEM	POST. REF.	DEBIT	CREDIT	BALANCE	
						DEBIT	CREDIT

Mastery Problem (Concluded)

3.

Exercise 15-1A

Merchandise Inventory	Income Summary

Exercise 15-2A

Cost of Goods Sold								
Beg. Inv. Mech.						26000		
Purchases				71000				
Less: Purch. Ret.+Allw	3500							
Purch. Disc.	5500			9000				
Net Purchases				62000				
Add Freight-In				500				
Cost of Gds. Prchs						62500		
Goods Available						88500		
Less: Merchandise Inv. Ending						23000		
Cost of Goods Sold							65500	

Exercise 15-3A

Cash		Unearned Ticket Revenue	
$45,000		adj. 35,000	45,000

Ticket Revenue	
	35,000 adj.

Exercise 15-4A

1., 2., & 3.

Kevin's

Work

For Year Ended

		TRIAL BALANCE												ADJUSTMENTS										
		DEBIT					CREDIT					DEBIT					CREDIT							
1	Merchandise Inventory	40	0	0	0	00						50	0	0	0	—	40	0	0	0	—			
12	Income Summary											40	0	0	0	—	50	0	0	0	—			
13	Purchases	90	0	0	0	00																		
14	Purchases Returns and Allow.						2	0	0	0	00													
15	Purchases Discounts						3	0	0	0	00													
16	Freight-In		5	0	0	00																		
17																								
18																								
19																								
20																								
21																								
22																								
23																								
24																								
25																								

Exercise 15-4A (Concluded)

Gift Shop

Sheet (Partial)

December 31, 20--

ADJUSTED TRIAL BALANCE		INCOME STATEMENT		BALANCE SHEET		
DEBIT	CREDIT	DEBIT	CREDIT	DEBIT	CREDIT	
50 000 —						1
40 000 —	50 000 —	40 000 —	50 000 —			12
90 000 —		90 000 —				13
	2 000 —		2 000 —			14
	3 000 —		3 000 —			15
500 —		500 —				16
						17
						18
						19
						20
						21
						22
						23
						24
						25

4.

Exercise 15-5A

Exercise 15-6A

JOURNAL PAGE

	DATE		DESCRIPTION	POST. REF.	DEBIT	CREDIT	
1							1
2							2
3							3
4							4
5							5
6							6
7							7
8							8
9							9
10							10
11							11
12							12
13							13
14							14
15							15
16							16
17							17
18							18
19							19
20							20
21							21
22							22
23							23
24							24
25							25
26							26
27							27

Problem 15-2A (Continued)

Shop _____

Sheet _____

December 31, 20-- _____

	ADJUSTED TRIAL BALANCE		INCOME STATEMENT		BALANCE SHEET		
	DEBIT	CREDIT	DEBIT	CREDIT	DEBIT	CREDIT	
							1
							2
							3
							4
							5
							6
							7
							8
							9
							10
							11
							12
							13
							14
							15
							16
							17
							18
							19
							20
							21
							22
							23
							24
							25
							26
							27
							28
							29
							30
							31
							32
							33
							34
							35
							36
							37
							38

Problem 15-2A (Concluded)

3.

<div align="center">

JOURNAL PAGE

</div>

	DATE		DESCRIPTION	POST. REF.	DEBIT	CREDIT	
1							1
2							2
3							3
4							4
5							5
6							6
7							7
8							8
9							9
10							10
11							11
12							12
13							13
14							14
15							15
16							16
17							17
18							18
19							19
20							20
21							21
22							22
23							23
24							24
25							25
26							26
27							27
28							28
29							29
30							30
31							31
32							32
33							33
34							34
35							35

Problem 15-3A

1.

Stark Street Computers

Work Sheet (Partial)

For Year Ended December 31, 20--

	Account Title	Trial Balance		Adjustments		Adjusted Trial Balance		
		Debit	Credit	Debit	Credit	Debit	Credit	
1	Cash	18 0 0 0 00				18 0 0 0 00		1
2	Accounts Receivable	11 0 0 0 00				11 0 0 0 00		2
3	Merchandise Inventory	25 0 0 0 00				35 0 0 0 00		3
4	Supplies	8 0 0 0 00				2 8 2 0 00		4
5	Prepaid Insurance	5 4 0 0 00				1 2 2 5 00		5
6	Land	27 0 0 0 00				27 0 0 0 00		6
7	Building	48 0 0 0 00				48 0 0 0 00		7
8	Accum. Depr.—Building		20 0 0 0 00				27 0 0 0 00	8
9	Store Equipment	33 0 0 0 00				33 0 0 0 00		9
10	Accu. Depr.—Store Equip.		8 7 0 0 00				12 8 0 0 00	10
11	Accounts Payable		6 4 0 0 00				6 4 0 0 00	11
12	Wages Payable						1 3 0 0 00	12
13	Sales Tax Payable		5 7 0 0 00				5 7 0 0 00	13
14	Unearned Repair Rev.		8 2 0 0 00				1 8 0 0 00	14
15	Mortgage Payable		44 0 0 0 00				44 0 0 0 00	15
16	Logan Cowart, Capital		80 0 2 5 00				80 0 2 5 00	16
17	Logan Cowart, Drawing	35 0 0 0 00				35 0 0 0 00		17
18	Income Summary					25 0 0 0 00	35 0 0 0 00	18
19	Sales		122 0 0 0 00				122 0 0 0 00	19
20	Sales Returns and Allow.	2 2 5 0 00				2 2 5 0 00		20
21	Repair Revenue						6 4 0 0 00	21
22	Purchases	29 7 5 0 00				29 7 5 0 00		22
23	Purchases Ret. and Allow.		1 8 5 0 00				1 8 5 0 00	23
24	Purchases Discounts		1 4 2 5 00				1 4 2 5 00	24
25	Freight-In	3 2 0 0 00				3 2 0 0 00		25
26	Wages Expense	37 0 0 0 00				38 3 0 0 00		26
27	Advertising Expense	4 1 2 5 00				4 1 2 5 00		27
28	Supplies Expense					5 1 8 0 00		28
29	Telephone Expense	1 6 5 0 00				1 6 5 0 00		29
30	Utilities Expense	9 1 5 0 00				9 1 5 0 00		30
31	Insurance Expense					4 1 7 5 00		31
32	Depr. Exp.—Building					7 0 0 0 00		32
33	Depr. Exp.—Store Equip.					4 1 0 0 00		33
34	Miscellaneous Expense	7 7 5 00				7 7 5 00		34
35		298 3 0 0 00	298 3 0 0 00			345 7 0 0 00	345 7 0 0 00	35
36								36
37								37
38								38

Problem 15-3A (Concluded)

2.

JOURNAL PAGE

	DATE		DESCRIPTION	POST. REF.	DEBIT	CREDIT	
1							1
2							2
3							3
4							4
5							5
6							6
7							7
8							8
9							9
10							10
11							11
12							12
13							13
14							14
15							15
16							16
17							17
18							18
19							19
20							20
21							21
22							22
23							23
24							24
25							25
26							26
27							27
28							28
29							29
30							30
31							31
32							32
33							33
34							34
35							35

Problem 15-4A

1. See pages 564-565.

2.

<div align="center">

JOURNAL PAGE

</div>

	DATE		DESCRIPTION	POST. REF.	DEBIT	CREDIT	
1							1
2							2
3							3
4							4
5							5
6							6
7							7
8							8
9							9
10							10
11							11
12							12
13							13
14							14
15							15
16							16
17							17
18							18
19							19
20							20
21							21
22							22
23							23
24							24
25							25
26							26
27							27
28							28
29							29
30							30
31							31
32							32
33							33
34							34

Problem 15-4A (Continued)

1.

Lewis Music

Work

For Year Ended

		TRIAL BALANCE											ADJUSTMENTS										
		DEBIT						CREDIT						DEBIT					CREDIT				
1	Cash	27	0	0	0	00																	
2	Accounts Receivable	13	3	0	0	00																	
3	Merchandise Inventory	34	0	0	0	00																	
4	Supplies	5	3	0	0	00																	
5	Prepaid Insurance	6	1	0	0	00																	
6	Land	31	0	0	0	00																	
7	Building	52	0	0	0	00																	
8	Accumulated Depr.—Building						17	0	0	0	00												
9	Store Equipment	39	0	0	0	00																	
10	Accumulated Depr.—Store Equip.						11	9	0	0	00												
11	Accounts Payable						6	2	5	0	00												
12	Wages Payable																						
13	Sales Tax Payable						6	2	0	0	00												
14	Unearned Rent Revenue						7	4	0	0	00												
15	Mortgage Payable						46	0	0	0	00												
16	Hugo Lewis, Capital						111	6	2	0	00												
17	Hugo Lewis, Drawing	37	0	0	0	00																	
18	Income Summary																						
19	Sales						136	0	0	0	00												
20	Sales Returns and Allowances	3	5	0	0	00																	
21	Rent Revenue																						
22	Purchases	39	0	0	0	00																	
23	Purchases Returns and Allow.						2	5	3	0	00												
24	Purchases Discounts						1	9	7	5	00												
25	Freight-In	2	6	5	0	00																	
26	Wages Expense	42	0	0	0	00																	
27	Advertising Expense	4	1	7	5	00																	
28	Supplies Expense																						
29	Telephone Expense	1	9	8	0	00																	
30	Utilities Expense	7	9	4	5	00																	
31	Insurance Expense																						
32	Depreciation Expense—Building																						
33	Depreciation Exp.—Store Equip.																						
34	Miscellaneous Expense		9	2	5	00																	
35		346	8	7	5	00	346	8	7	5	00												
36	Net Income																						
37																							
38																							

Problem 15-4A (Continued)

Store _____

Sheet _____

December 31, 20--

	ADJUSTED TRIAL BALANCE		INCOME STATEMENT		BALANCE SHEET		
	DEBIT	CREDIT	DEBIT	CREDIT	DEBIT	CREDIT	
1					27 0 0 0 00		
2					13 3 0 0 00		
3					38 0 0 0 00		
4					1 5 0 0 00		
5					1 7 8 5 00		
6					31 0 0 0 00		
7					52 0 0 0 00		
8						21 1 4 5 00	
9					39 0 0 0 00		
10						14 8 7 5 00	
11						6 2 5 0 00	
12						8 7 5 00	
13						6 2 0 0 00	
14						3 1 7 5 00	
15						46 0 0 0 00	
16						111 6 2 0 00	
17					37 0 0 0 00		
18			34 0 0 0 00	38 0 0 0 00			
19				136 0 0 0 00			
20			3 5 0 0 00				
21				4 2 2 5 00			
22			39 0 0 0 00				
23				2 5 3 0 00			
24				1 9 7 5 00			
25			2 6 5 0 00				
26			42 8 7 5 00				
27			4 1 7 5 00				
28			3 8 0 0 00				
29			1 9 8 0 00				
30			7 9 4 5 00				
31			4 3 1 5 00				
32			4 1 4 5 00				
33			2 9 7 5 00				
34			9 2 5 00				
35			152 2 8 5 00	182 7 3 0 00	240 5 8 5 00	210 1 4 0 00	
36			30 4 4 5 00			30 4 4 5 00	
37			182 7 3 0 00	182 7 3 0 00	240 5 8 5 00	240 5 8 5 00	
38							

Problem 15-4A (Concluded)

3.

Exercise 15-1B

Merchandise Inventory	Income Summary

Exercise 15-2B

Exercise 15-3B

Cash	Unearned Ticket Revenue

Ticket Revenue

Exercise 15-4B

1., 2., & 3.

Nicole's

Work

For Year Ended

| | | TRIAL BALANCE | | | ADJUSTMENTS | |
		DEBIT	CREDIT		DEBIT	CREDIT
1	Merchandise Inventory	30 0 0 0 00				
12	Income Summary					
13	Purchases	85 0 0 0 00				
14	Purchases Returns and Allow.		2 2 0 0 00			
15	Purchases Discounts		2 5 0 0 00			
16	Freight-In	1 0 0 00				
17						
18						
19						
20						
21						
22						
23						
24						
25						

Exercise 15-4B (Concluded)

Gift Shop

Sheet (Partial)

December 31, 20--

	ADJUSTED TRIAL BALANCE		INCOME STATEMENT		BALANCE SHEET		
	DEBIT	CREDIT	DEBIT	CREDIT	DEBIT	CREDIT	
							1
							12
							13
							14
							15
							16
							17
							18
							19
							20
							21
							22
							23
							24
							25

4.

Exercise 15-5B

Exercise 15-6B

JOURNAL

PAGE

	DATE		DESCRIPTION	POST REF.	DEBIT	CREDIT	
1							1
2							2
3							3
4							4
5							5
6							6
7							7
8							8
9							9
10							10
11							11
12							12
13							13
14							14
15							15
16							16
17							17
18							18
19							19
20							20
21							21
22							22
23							23
24							24
25							25
26							26
27							27

Problem 15-4B (Continued)

Store _____

Sheet _____

December 31, 20--

#	ADJUSTED TRIAL BALANCE DEBIT	ADJUSTED TRIAL BALANCE CREDIT	INCOME STATEMENT DEBIT	INCOME STATEMENT CREDIT	BALANCE SHEET DEBIT	BALANCE SHEET CREDIT
1					31 0 0 0 00	
2					11 9 8 0 00	
3					39 1 0 0 00	
4					1 9 6 5 00	
5					1 2 3 5 00	
6					36 2 0 0 00	
7					51 8 5 0 00	
8						18 8 7 5 00
9					32 6 7 5 00	
10						14 7 5 5 00
11						5 8 9 5 00
12						1 2 5 0 00
13						6 3 7 5 00
14						2 9 3 0 00
15						42 4 0 0 00
16						116 3 5 0 00
17					39 5 0 0 00	
18			33 6 0 0 00	39 1 0 0 00		
19				148 0 0 0 00		
20			2 8 0 0 00			
21				5 9 2 0 00		
22			40 7 0 0 00			
23				2 7 7 5 00		
24				2 3 2 5 00		
25			1 8 7 5 00			
26			48 2 5 0 00			
27			4 6 9 5 00			
28			5 1 7 5 00			
29			2 2 5 0 00			
30			6 8 2 5 00			
31			4 7 5 0 00			
32			5 2 8 5 00			
33			4 4 6 5 00			
34			7 7 5 00			
35			161 4 4 5 00	198 1 2 0 00	245 5 0 5 00	208 8 3 0 00
36			36 6 7 5 00			36 6 7 5 00
37			198 1 2 0 00	198 1 2 0 00	245 5 0 5 00	245 5 0 5 00

Problem 15-4B (Concluded)

3.

Name _____

Challenge Problem

Mastery Problem

1.

		TRIAL BALANCE		ADJUSTMENTS	
		DEBIT	CREDIT	DEBIT	CREDIT
1	Cash	30 0 0 0 00			
2	Accounts Receivable	22 5 0 0 00			
3	Merchandise Inventory	57 0 0 0 00			
4	Supplies	2 7 0 0 00			
5	Prepaid Insurance	3 6 0 0 00			
6	Land	15 0 0 0 00			
7	Building	135 0 0 0 00			
8	Accumulated Depr.—Building		24 0 0 0 00		
9	Store Equipment	75 0 0 0 00			
10	Accumulated Depr.—Store Equip.		22 5 0 0 00		
11	Notes Payable		7 5 0 0 00		
12	Accounts Payable		15 0 0 0 00		
13	Wages Payable				
14	Unearned Boat Rental Revenue		33 0 0 0 00		
15	John Neff, Capital		233 7 0 0 00		
16	John Neff, Drawing	30 0 0 0 00			
17	Income Summary				
18	Sales		300 7 5 0 00		
19	Sales Returns and Allowances	1 8 0 0 00			
20	Boat Rental Revenue				
21	Purchases	157 5 0 0 00			
22	Purchases Returns and Allow.		1 2 0 0 00		
23	Purchases Discounts		1 5 0 0 00		
24	Freight-In	4 5 0 0 00			
25	Wages Expense	63 0 0 0 00			
26	Advertising Expense	11 2 5 0 00			
27	Supplies Expense				
28	Telephone Expense	5 2 5 0 00			
29	Utilities Expense	18 0 0 0 00			
30	Insurance Expense				
31	Depreciation Expense—Building				
32	Depreciation Exp.—Store Equip.				
33	Miscellaneous Expense	10 8 7 5 00			
34	Interest Expense	2 2 5 00			
35		639 1 5 0 00	639 1 5 0 00		
36					
37					
38					

Mastery Problem (Continued)

Shop _____

Sheet _____

December 31, 20--

ADJUSTED TRIAL BALANCE		INCOME STATEMENT		BALANCE SHEET		
DEBIT	CREDIT	DEBIT	CREDIT	DEBIT	CREDIT	
						1
						2
						3
						4
						5
						6
						7
						8
						9
						10
						11
						12
						13
						14
						15
						16
						17
						18
						19
						20
						21
						22
						23
						24
						25
						26
						27
						28
						29
						30
						31
						32
						33
						34
						35
						36
						37
						38

Mastery Problem (Concluded)

2.

JOURNAL PAGE 3

	DATE		DESCRIPTION	POST REF.	DEBIT	CREDIT	
1							1
2							2
3							3
4							4
5							5
6							6
7							7
8							8
9							9
10							10
11							11
12							12
13							13
14							14
15							15
16							16
17							17
18							18
19							19
20							20
21							21
22							22
23							23
24							24
25							25
26							26
27							27
28							28
29							29
30							30
31							31
32							32
33							33
34							34

Exercise 15Apx-1A

JOURNAL PAGE

	DATE		DESCRIPTION	POST REF.	DEBIT	CREDIT	
1							1
2							2
3							3
4							4
5							5
6							6
7							7
8							8
9							9
10							10
11							11
12							12

Exercise 15Apx-1B

JOURNAL PAGE

	DATE		DESCRIPTION	POST REF.	DEBIT	CREDIT	
1							1
2							2
3							3
4							4
5							5
6							6
7							7
8							8
9							9
10							10
11							11
12							12
13							13
14							14
15							15
16							16

Exercise 16-1A

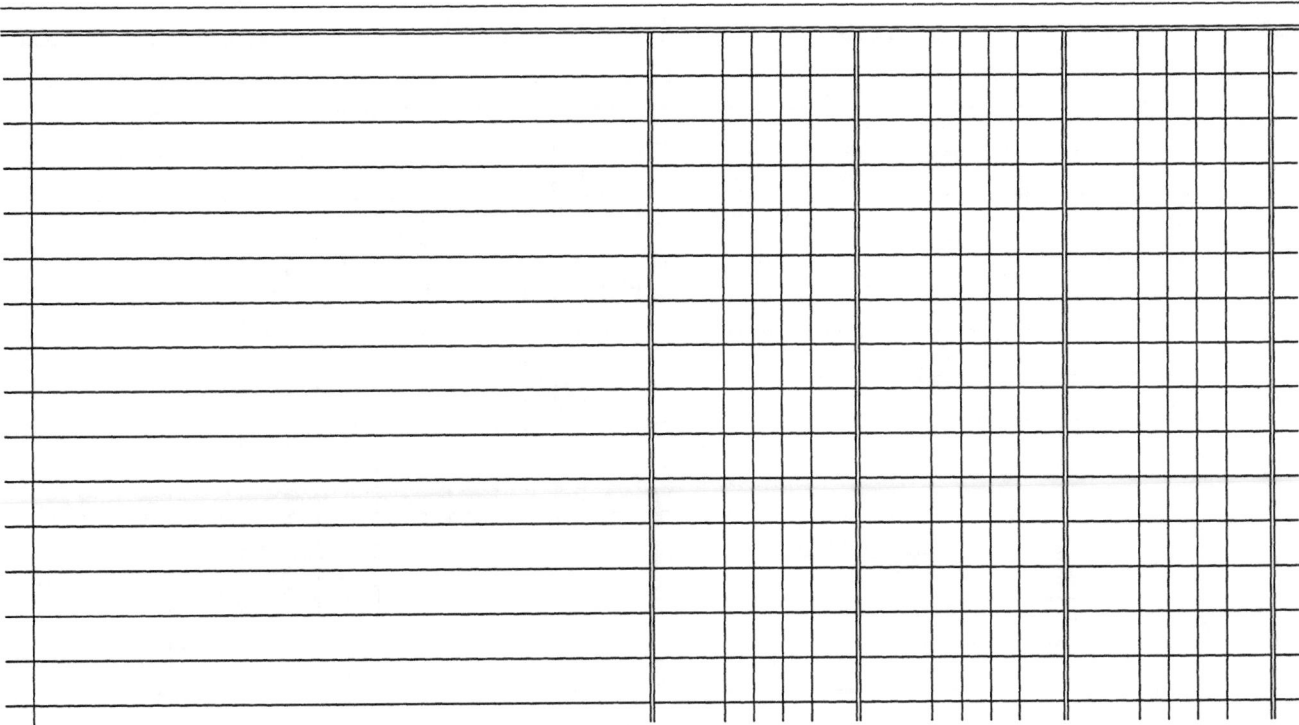

Exercise 16-2A

Exercise 16-3A

Exercise 16-4A

JOURNAL

PAGE

	DATE		DESCRIPTION	POST. REF.	DEBIT	CREDIT	
1							1
2							2
3							3
4							4
5							5
6							6
7							7
8							8
9							9
10							10
11							11
12							12
13							13
14							14
15							15
16							16
17							17
18							18
19							19
20							20
21							21
22							22
23							23
24							24
25							25
26							26
27							27
28							28
29							29
30							30
31							31
32							32
33							33
34							34

Exercise 16-5A

JOURNAL PAGE

	DATE	DESCRIPTION	POST. REF.	DEBIT	CREDIT	
1						1
2						2
3						3
4						4
5						5

Exercise 16-6A

DATE	WITHOUT REVERSING ENTRY	WITH REVERSING ENTRY
Adjusting Entry:		
Closing Entry:		
Reversing Entry:		
Payment of Payroll:		

Wages Expense Wages Expense

Wages Payable Wages Payable

Exercise 16-4B

JOURNAL

PAGE

	DATE		DESCRIPTION	POST. REF.	DEBIT	CREDIT	
1							1
2							2
3							3
4							4
5							5
6							6
7							7
8							8
9							9
10							10
11							11
12							12
13							13
14							14
15							15
16							16
17							17
18							18
19							19
20							20
21							21
22							22
23							23
24							24
25							25
26							26
27							27
28							28
29							29
30							30
31							31
32							32
33							33
34							34

Exercise 16-5B

JOURNAL PAGE

	DATE		DESCRIPTION	POST. REF.	DEBIT	CREDIT	
1							1
2							2
3							3
4							4
5							5

Exercise 16-6B

DATE	WITHOUT REVERSING ENTRY	WITH REVERSING ENTRY
Adjusting Entry:		
Closing Entry:		
Reversing Entry:		
Payment of Payroll:		

Wages Expense

Wages Expense

Wages Payable

Wages Payable

Exercise 16-7B

Problem 16-1B

1.

Darby Kite

Work

For Year Ended

		TRIAL BALANCE				ADJUSTMENTS		
		DEBIT	CREDIT			DEBIT	CREDIT	
1	Cash	11 7 0 0 00						
2	Accounts Receivable	11 2 0 0 00						
3	Merchandise Inventory	25 0 0 0 00						
4	Supplies	1 2 0 0 00						
5	Prepaid Insurance	8 0 0 00						
6	Equipment	5 4 0 0 00						
7	Accumulated Depr.—Equipment		8 0 0 00					
8	Accounts Payable		7 6 0 0 00					
9	Wages Payable							
10	Sales Tax Payable		2 5 0 00					
11	M. D. Akins, Capital		50 0 0 0 00					
12	M. D. Akins, Drawing	10 5 0 0 00						
13	Income Summary							
14	Sales		57 9 9 0 00					
15	Sales Returns and Allowances	1 4 5 0 00						
16	Purchases	34 5 0 0 00						
17	Purchases Returns and Allow.		1 1 0 0 00					
18	Purchases Discounts		6 3 0 00					
19	Freight-In	3 6 0 00						
20	Wages Expense	10 8 8 0 00						
21	Advertising Expense	7 4 0 00						
22	Supplies Expense							
23	Telephone Expense	1 1 0 0 00						
24	Utilities Expense	2 3 0 0 00						
25	Insurance Expense							
26	Depreciation Expense—Equip.							
27	Miscellaneous Expense	3 2 0 00						
28	Interest Expense	9 2 0 00						
29		118 3 7 0 00	118 3 7 0 00					
30								
31								
32								
33								

Problem 16-2B

1.

Problem 16-2B (Continued)

2.

Exercise 16-2B (Concluded)

3.

Problem 16-3B

Name _____

Challenge Problem

Mastery Problem

1.

Mastery Problem (Continued)

2.

Mastery Problem (Continued)

3.

Mastery Problem (Continued)

4.

Mastery Problem (Continued)

5.

		JOURNAL				PAGE

	DATE		DESCRIPTION	POST REF.	DEBIT	CREDIT	
1							1
2							2
3							3
4							4
5							5
6							6
7							7
8							8
9							9
10							10
11							11
12							12
13							13
14							14
15							15
16							16
17							17
18							18
19							19
20							20
21							21
22							22

Should the adjustment be reversed?

Mastery Problem (Concluded)

6. & 7.

JOURNAL PAGE 4

	DATE		DESCRIPTION	POST REF.	DEBIT	CREDIT	
1							1
2							2
3							3
4							4
5							5
6							6
7							7
8							8
9							9
10							10
11							11
12							12
13							13
14							14
15							15
16							16
17							17
18							18
19							19
20							20
21							21
22							22
23							23
24							24
25							25
26							26
27							27
28							28
29							29
30							30
31							31
32							32
33							33
34							34
35							35

Comprehensive Problem 2: Accounting Cycle With Subsidiary Ledgers, Part 1

2. and 3.

SALES JOURNAL PAGE 6

DATE	SALE NO.	TO WHOM SOLD	POST. REF.	ACCOUNTS RECEIVABLE DR.	SALES CR.	SALES TAX PAYABLE CR.

CASH RECEIPTS JOURNAL PAGE 9

	DATE	ACCOUNT CREDITED	POST. REF.	GENERAL CR.	ACCTS. RECEIVABLE CR.	SALES CR.	SALES TAX PAY. CR.	CASH DR.	
1									1
2									2
3									3
4									4
5									5
6									6
7									7
8									8
9									9

Comprehensive Problem 2, Part 1 (Continued)

PURCHASES JOURNAL

PAGE 5

	DATE	INVOICE NO.	FROM WHOM PURCHASED	POST. REF.	PURCHASES DR. ACCTS. PAY. CR.	
1						1
2						2
3						3
4						4
5						5
6						6
7						7
						10

CASH PAYMENTS JOURNAL

PAGE 10

	DATE	CK. NO.	ACCOUNT DEBITED	POST. REF.	GENERAL DR.	ACCTS. PAYABLE DR.	PURCHASES DR.	PURCHASES DISCOUNTS CR.	CASH CR.	
1										1
2										2
3										3
4										4
5										5
6										6
7										7
8										8
9										9
10										10
11										11
12										12
13										13
14										14
15										15

Comprehensive Problem 2, Part 1 (Continued)

JOURNAL PAGE 4

	DATE	DESCRIPTION	POST. REF.	DEBIT	CREDIT	
1						1
2						2
3						3
4						4
5						5
6						6
7						7
8						8
9						9
10						10
11						11

3., 6., & 7.

GENERAL LEDGER

ACCOUNT Cash ACCOUNT NO. 101

DATE		ITEM	POST. REF.	DEBIT	CREDIT	BALANCE DEBIT	BALANCE CREDIT
20-1 Dec.	1	Balance	✓			11 5 0 0 00	

ACCOUNT Accounts Receivable ACCOUNT NO. 122

DATE		ITEM	POST. REF.	DEBIT	CREDIT	BALANCE DEBIT	BALANCE CREDIT
20-1 Dec.	1	Balance	✓			8 6 0 0 00	

Comprehensive Problem 2, Part 1 (Continued)

ACCOUNT Merchandise Inventory ACCOUNT NO. 131

DATE	ITEM	POST. REF.	DEBIT	CREDIT	BALANCE DEBIT	BALANCE CREDIT
20-1 Dec. 1	Balance	✓			21 8 0 0 00	

ACCOUNT Supplies ACCOUNT NO. 141

DATE	ITEM	POST. REF.	DEBIT	CREDIT	BALANCE DEBIT	BALANCE CREDIT
20-1 Dec. 1	Balance	✓			1 0 3 5 00	

ACCOUNT Prepaid Insurance ACCOUNT NO. 145

DATE	ITEM	POST. REF.	DEBIT	CREDIT	BALANCE DEBIT	BALANCE CREDIT
20-1 Dec. 1	Balance	✓			1 3 8 0 00	

ACCOUNT Land ACCOUNT NO. 161

DATE	ITEM	POST. REF.	DEBIT	CREDIT	BALANCE DEBIT	BALANCE CREDIT
20-1 Dec. 1	Balance	✓			8 7 0 0 00	

Comprehensive Problem 2, Part 1 (Continued)

ACCOUNT Building ACCOUNT NO. 171

DATE		ITEM	POST. REF.	DEBIT	CREDIT	BALANCE DEBIT	BALANCE CREDIT
20-1 Dec.	1	Balance	✓			52 0 0 0 00	

ACCOUNT Accumulated Depreciation—Building ACCOUNT NO. 171.1

DATE		ITEM	POST. REF.	DEBIT	CREDIT	BALANCE DEBIT	BALANCE CREDIT
20-1 Dec.	1	Balance	✓				9 2 0 0 00

ACCOUNT Store Equipment ACCOUNT NO. 181

DATE		ITEM	POST. REF.	DEBIT	CREDIT	BALANCE DEBIT	BALANCE CREDIT
20-1 Dec.	1	Balance	✓			28 7 5 0 00	

ACCOUNT Accumulated Depreciation—Store Equipment ACCOUNT NO. 181.1

DATE		ITEM	POST. REF.	DEBIT	CREDIT	BALANCE DEBIT	BALANCE CREDIT
20-1 Dec.	1	Balance	✓				9 3 0 0 00

Comprehensive Problem 2, Part 1 (Continued)

ACCOUNT Accounts Payable ACCOUNT NO. 202

DATE		ITEM	POST. REF.	DEBIT	CREDIT	BALANCE	
						DEBIT	CREDIT
20-1 Dec.	1	Balance	✓				6 8 5 0 00

ACCOUNT Wages Payable ACCOUNT NO. 219

DATE		ITEM	POST. REF.	DEBIT	CREDIT	BALANCE	
						DEBIT	CREDIT

ACCOUNT Sales Tax Payable ACCOUNT NO. 231

DATE		ITEM	POST. REF.	DEBIT	CREDIT	BALANCE	
						DEBIT	CREDIT
20-1 Dec.	1	Balance	✓				9 7 0 00

ACCOUNT Mortgage Payable ACCOUNT NO. 251

DATE		ITEM	POST. REF.	DEBIT	CREDIT	BALANCE	
						DEBIT	CREDIT
20-1 Dec.	1	Balance	✓				12 5 2 5 00

Comprehensive Problem 2, Part 1 (Continued)

ACCOUNT Tom Jones, Capital ACCOUNT NO. 311

DATE		ITEM	POST. REF.	DEBIT	CREDIT	BALANCE	
						DEBIT	CREDIT
20-1 Dec.	1	Balance	✓				90 0 0 0 00

ACCOUNT Tom Jones, Drawing ACCOUNT NO. 312

DATE		ITEM	POST. REF.	DEBIT	CREDIT	BALANCE	
						DEBIT	CREDIT
20-1 Dec.	1	Balance	✓			8 5 0 0 00	

ACCOUNT Income Summary ACCOUNT NO. 313

DATE		ITEM	POST. REF.	DEBIT	CREDIT	BALANCE	
						DEBIT	CREDIT

ACCOUNT Sales ACCOUNT NO. 401

DATE		ITEM	POST. REF.	DEBIT	CREDIT	BALANCE	
						DEBIT	CREDIT
20-1 Dec.	1	Balance	✓				116 0 0 0 00

Comprehensive Problem 2, Part 1 (Continued)

ACCOUNT Sales Returns and Allowances ACCOUNT NO. 401.1

DATE		ITEM	POST. REF.	DEBIT	CREDIT	BALANCE DEBIT	BALANCE CREDIT
20-1 Dec.	1	Balance	✓			6 9 0 00	

ACCOUNT Purchases ACCOUNT NO. 501

DATE		ITEM	POST. REF.	DEBIT	CREDIT	BALANCE DEBIT	BALANCE CREDIT
20-1 Dec.	1	Balance	✓			60 5 0 0 00	

ACCOUNT Purchases Returns and Allowances ACCOUNT NO. 501.1

DATE		ITEM	POST. REF.	DEBIT	CREDIT	BALANCE DEBIT	BALANCE CREDIT
20-1 Dec.	1	Balance	✓				4 6 0 00

ACCOUNT Purchases Discounts ACCOUNT NO. 501.2

DATE		ITEM	POST. REF.	DEBIT	CREDIT	BALANCE DEBIT	BALANCE CREDIT
20-1 Dec.	1	Balance	✓				5 7 5 00

Comprehensive Problem 2, Part 1 (Continued)

ACCOUNT Freight-In ACCOUNT NO. 502

DATE		ITEM	POST. REF.	DEBIT	CREDIT	BALANCE	
						DEBIT	CREDIT
20-1 Dec.	1	Balance	✓			1 7 5 00	

ACCOUNT Wages Expense ACCOUNT NO. 511

DATE		ITEM	POST. REF.	DEBIT	CREDIT	BALANCE	
						DEBIT	CREDIT
20-1 Dec.	1	Balance	✓			25 0 0 0 00	

ACCOUNT Advertising Expense ACCOUNT NO. 512

DATE		ITEM	POST. REF.	DEBIT	CREDIT	BALANCE	
						DEBIT	CREDIT
20-1 Dec.	1	Balance	✓			4 3 0 0 00	

ACCOUNT Supplies Expense ACCOUNT NO. 524

DATE		ITEM	POST. REF.	DEBIT	CREDIT	BALANCE	
						DEBIT	CREDIT

Comprehensive Problem 2, Part 1 (Continued)

ACCOUNT Telephone Expense

ACCOUNT NO. 525

DATE		ITEM	POST. REF.	DEBIT	CREDIT	BALANCE	
						DEBIT	CREDIT
20-1 Dec.	1	Balance	✓			2 0 0 0 00	

ACCOUNT Utilities Expense

ACCOUNT NO. 533

DATE		ITEM	POST. REF.	DEBIT	CREDIT	BALANCE	
						DEBIT	CREDIT
20-1 Dec.	1	Balance	✓			6 9 0 0 00	

ACCOUNT Insurance Expense

ACCOUNT NO. 535

DATE		ITEM	POST. REF.	DEBIT	CREDIT	BALANCE	
						DEBIT	CREDIT

ACCOUNT Depreciation Expense—Building

ACCOUNT NO. 540

DATE		ITEM	POST. REF.	DEBIT	CREDIT	BALANCE	
						DEBIT	CREDIT

Comprehensive Problem 2, Part 1 (Continued)

ACCOUNT Depreciation Expense—Store Equipment ACCOUNT NO. 541

DATE		ITEM	POST. REF.	DEBIT	CREDIT	BALANCE DEBIT	BALANCE CREDIT

ACCOUNT Miscellaneous Expense ACCOUNT NO. 549

DATE		ITEM	POST. REF.	DEBIT	CREDIT	BALANCE DEBIT	BALANCE CREDIT
20-1 Dec.	1	Balance	✓			2 7 0 0 00	

ACCOUNT Interest Expense ACCOUNT NO. 551

DATE		ITEM	POST. REF.	DEBIT	CREDIT	BALANCE DEBIT	BALANCE CREDIT
20-1 Dec.	1	Balance	✓			1 3 5 0 00	

ACCOUNTS RECEIVABLE LEDGER

NAME Martha Boyle

ADDRESS 12 Jude Lane, Hartford, CT 06117

DATE		ITEM	POST. REF.	DEBIT	CREDIT	BALANCE
20-1 Dec.	1	Balance	✓			3 2 5 0 00

Comprehensive Problem 2, Part 1 (Continued)

NAME Anne Clark

ADDRESS 52 Juniper Road, Hartford, CT 06118

DATE		ITEM	POST. REF.	DEBIT	CREDIT	BALANCE
20-1 Dec.	1	Balance	✓			1 3 4 0 00

NAME John Dempsey

ADDRESS 700 Hobbes Dr., Avon, CT 06108

DATE		ITEM	POST. REF.	DEBIT	CREDIT	BALANCE
20-1 Dec.	1	Balance	✓			1 5 6 0 00

NAME Kim Fields

ADDRESS 5200 Hamilton Ave., Hartford, CT 06117

DATE		ITEM	POST. REF.	DEBIT	CREDIT	BALANCE

NAME Lucy Greene

ADDRESS 236 Bally Lane, Simsbury, CT 06123

DATE		ITEM	POST. REF.	DEBIT	CREDIT	BALANCE
20-1 Dec.	1	Balance	✓			1 9 6 0 00

Comprehensive Problem 2, Part 1 (Continued)

NAME Heather Waters

ADDRESS 447 Drury Lane, West Hartford, CT 06107

DATE		ITEM	POST. REF.	DEBIT	CREDIT	BALANCE
20-1 Dec.	1	Balance	✓			4 9 0 00

ACCOUNTS PAYABLE LEDGER

NAME Evans Essentials

ADDRESS 34 Harry Ave., East Hartford, CT 05234

DATE		ITEM	POST. REF.	DEBIT	CREDIT	BALANCE
20-1 Dec.	1	Balance	✓			1 2 5 0 00

NAME Nathen Co.

ADDRESS 1009 Drake Rd., Farmington, CT, 06082

DATE		ITEM	POST. REF.	DEBIT	CREDIT	BALANCE
20-1 Dec.	1	Balance	✓			3 0 0 0 00

Comprehensive Problem 2, Part 1 (Continued)

NAME Owen Enterprises

ADDRESS 43 Lucky Lane, Bristol, CT 06007

DATE		ITEM	POST. REF.	DEBIT	CREDIT	BALANCE
20-1 Dec.	1	Balance	✓			1 6 0 0 00

NAME West Wholesalers

ADDRESS 888 Anders Street, Newington, CT 06789

DATE		ITEM	POST. REF.	DEBIT	CREDIT	BALANCE
20-1 Dec.	1	Balance	✓			1 0 0 0 00

Comprehensive Problem 2, Part 1 (Continued)

4.

Comprehensive Problem 2, Part 1 (Continued)
5.

	TRIAL BALANCE		ADJUSTMENTS	
	DEBIT	CREDIT	DEBIT	CREDIT
1				
2				
3				
4				
5				
6				
7				
8				
9				
10				
11				
12				
13				
14				
15				
16				
17				
18				
19				
20				
21				
22				
23				
24				
25				
26				
27				
28				
29				
30				
31				
32				
33				
34				
35				
36				

Comprehensive Problem 2, Part 1 (Continued)

ADJUSTED TRIAL BALANCE		INCOME STATEMENT		BALANCE SHEET		
DEBIT	CREDIT	DEBIT	CREDIT	DEBIT	CREDIT	
						1
						2
						3
						4
						5
						6
						7
						8
						9
						10
						11
						12
						13
						14
						15
						16
						17
						18
						19
						20
						21
						22
						23
						24
						25
						26
						27
						28
						29
						30
						31
						32
						33
						34
						35
						36

Comprehensive Problem 2, Part 1 (Continued)

Comprehensive Problem 2, Part 1 (Continued)

Comprehensive Problem 2, Part 1 (Continued)

Comprehensive Problem 2, Part 1 (Continued)

6.

JOURNAL

PAGE 5

	DATE		DESCRIPTION	POST. REF.	DEBIT	CREDIT	
1							1
2							2
3							3
4							4
5							5
6							6
7							7
8							8
9							9
10							10
11							11
12							12
13							13
14							14
15							15
16							16
17							17
18							18
19							19
20							20
21							21
22							22
23							23
24							24
25							25
26							26
27							27
28							28
29							29
30							30
31							31
32							32
33							33
34							34

Comprehensive Problem 2, Part 1 (Continued)

7. & 9.

JOURNAL

	DATE		DESCRIPTION	POST. REF.	DEBIT	CREDIT	
1							1
2							2
3							3
4							4
5							5
6							6
7							7
8							8
9							9
10							10
11							11
12							12
13							13
14							14
15							15
16							16
17							17
18							18
19							19
20							20
21							21
22							22
23							23
24							24
25							25
26							26
27							27
28							28
29							29
30							30
31							31
32							32
33							33
34							34

Name _____

Comprehensive Problem 2, Part 1 (Concluded)
8.

ACCOUNT	DEBIT BALANCE	CREDIT BALANCE

Comprehensive Problem 2: Accounting Cycle With Subsidiary Ledgers, Part 2
2. and 3.

SALES JOURNAL

PAGE 7

DATE	SALE NO.	TO WHOM SOLD	POST. REF.	ACCOUNTS RECEIVABLE DR.	SALES CR.	SALES TAX PAYABLE CR.

CASH RECEIPTS JOURNAL

PAGE 10

	DATE	ACCOUNT CREDITED	POST. REF.	GENERAL CR.	ACCTS. RECEIVABLE CR.	SALES CR.	SALES TAX PAY. CR.	CASH DR.	
1									1
2									2
3									3
4									4
5									5
6									6
7									7
8									8

Comprehensive Problem 2, Part 2 (Continued)

PURCHASES JOURNAL

	DATE	INVOICE NO.	FROM WHOM PURCHASED	POST. REF.	PURCHASES DR. ACCTS. PAY. CR.	
1						1
2						2
3						3
4						4
5						5
6						6
7						7
8						8

CASH PAYMENTS JOURNAL

	DATE	CK. NO.	ACCOUNT DEBITED	POST. REF.	GENERAL DR.	ACCTS. PAYABLE DR.	PURCHASES DR.	PURCHASES DISCOUNTS CR.	CASH CR.	
1										1
2										2
3										3
4										4
5										5
6										6
7										7
8										8
9										9
10										10

Comprehensive Problem 2, Part 2 (Continued)

JOURNAL

PAGE 5

	DATE	DESCRIPTION	POST. REF.	DEBIT	CREDIT	
1						1
2						2
3						3
4						4
5						5
6						6
7						7
8						8
9						9
10						10
11						11

3., 6., & 7.

GENERAL LEDGER

ACCOUNT Cash ACCOUNT NO. 101

DATE		ITEM	POST. REF.	DEBIT	CREDIT	BALANCE DEBIT	BALANCE CREDIT
20-2 Jan.	1	Balance	✓			12 5 4 8 00	

ACCOUNT Accounts Receivable ACCOUNT NO. 122

DATE		ITEM	POST. REF.	DEBIT	CREDIT	BALANCE DEBIT	BALANCE CREDIT
20-2 Jan.	1	Balance	✓			7 2 0 3 00	

Comprehensive Problem 2, Part 2 (Continued)

ACCOUNT Merchandise Inventory ACCOUNT NO. 131

DATE		ITEM	POST. REF.	DEBIT	CREDIT	BALANCE	
						DEBIT	CREDIT
20-2 Jan.	1	Balance	✓			19 7 0 0 00	

ACCOUNT Supplies ACCOUNT NO. 141

DATE		ITEM	POST. REF.	DEBIT	CREDIT	BALANCE	
						DEBIT	CREDIT
20-2 Jan.	1	Balance	✓			5 2 5 00	

ACCOUNT Prepaid Insurance ACCOUNT NO. 145

DATE		ITEM	POST. REF.	DEBIT	CREDIT	BALANCE	
						DEBIT	CREDIT
20-2 Jan.	1	Balance	✓			1 0 0 0 00	

ACCOUNT Land ACCOUNT NO. 161

DATE		ITEM	POST. REF.	DEBIT	CREDIT	BALANCE	
						DEBIT	CREDIT
20-2 Jan.	1	Balance	✓			8 7 0 0 00	

Comprehensive Problem 2, Part 2 (Continued)

ACCOUNT **Building** ACCOUNT NO. **171**

DATE		ITEM	POST. REF.	DEBIT	CREDIT	BALANCE DEBIT	BALANCE CREDIT
20-2 Jan.	1	Balance	✓			52 0 0 0 00	

ACCOUNT **Accumulated Depreciation—Building** ACCOUNT NO. **171.1**

DATE		ITEM	POST. REF.	DEBIT	CREDIT	BALANCE DEBIT	BALANCE CREDIT
20-2 Jan.	1	Balance	✓				10 0 0 0 00

ACCOUNT **Store Equipment** ACCOUNT NO. **181**

DATE		ITEM	POST. REF.	DEBIT	CREDIT	BALANCE DEBIT	BALANCE CREDIT
20-2 Jan.	1	Balance	✓			28 7 5 0 00	

ACCOUNT **Accumulated Depreciation—Store Equipment** ACCOUNT NO. **181.1**

DATE		ITEM	POST. REF.	DEBIT	CREDIT	BALANCE DEBIT	BALANCE CREDIT
20-2 Jan.	1	Balance	✓				9 7 5 0 00

Comprehensive Problem 2, Part 2 (Continued)

ACCOUNT Accounts Payable ACCOUNT NO. 202

DATE		ITEM	POST. REF.	DEBIT	CREDIT	BALANCE DEBIT	BALANCE CREDIT
20-2 Jan.	1	Balance	✓				4 3 5 0 00

ACCOUNT Wages Payable ACCOUNT NO. 219

DATE		ITEM	POST. REF.	DEBIT	CREDIT	BALANCE DEBIT	BALANCE CREDIT

ACCOUNT Sales Tax Payable ACCOUNT NO. 231

DATE		ITEM	POST. REF.	DEBIT	CREDIT	BALANCE DEBIT	BALANCE CREDIT
20-2 Jan.	1	Balance	✓				1 5 1 8 00

ACCOUNT Mortgage Payable ACCOUNT NO. 251

DATE		ITEM	POST. REF.	DEBIT	CREDIT	BALANCE DEBIT	BALANCE CREDIT
20-2 Jan.	1	Balance	✓				12 5 2 5 00

Comprehensive Problem 2, Part 2 (Continued)

ACCOUNT Tom Jones, Capital ACCOUNT NO. 311

DATE		ITEM	POST. REF.	DEBIT	CREDIT	BALANCE	
						DEBIT	CREDIT
20-2 Jan.	1	Balance	✓				91 9 5 3 00

ACCOUNT Tom Jones, Drawing ACCOUNT NO. 312

DATE		ITEM	POST. REF.	DEBIT	CREDIT	BALANCE	
						DEBIT	CREDIT

ACCOUNT Income Summary ACCOUNT NO. 313

DATE		ITEM	POST. REF.	DEBIT	CREDIT	BALANCE	
						DEBIT	CREDIT

ACCOUNT Sales ACCOUNT NO. 401

DATE		ITEM	POST. REF.	DEBIT	CREDIT	BALANCE	
						DEBIT	CREDIT

Comprehensive Problem 2, Part 2 (Continued)

ACCOUNT Sales Returns and Allowances ACCOUNT NO. 401.1

DATE	ITEM	POST. REF.	DEBIT	CREDIT	BALANCE	
					DEBIT	CREDIT

ACCOUNT Purchases ACCOUNT NO. 501

DATE	ITEM	POST. REF.	DEBIT	CREDIT	BALANCE	
					DEBIT	CREDIT

ACCOUNT Purchases Returns and Allowances ACCOUNT NO. 501.1

DATE	ITEM	POST. REF.	DEBIT	CREDIT	BALANCE	
					DEBIT	CREDIT

ACCOUNT Purchases Discounts ACCOUNT NO. 501.2

DATE	ITEM	POST. REF.	DEBIT	CREDIT	BALANCE	
					DEBIT	CREDIT

Comprehensive Problem 2, Part 2 (Continued)

ACCOUNT Freight-In ACCOUNT NO. 502

DATE	ITEM	POST. REF.	DEBIT	CREDIT	BALANCE DEBIT	BALANCE CREDIT

ACCOUNT Wages Expense ACCOUNT NO. 511

DATE	ITEM	POST. REF.	DEBIT	CREDIT	BALANCE DEBIT	BALANCE CREDIT
20-2 Jan. 1	Balance	✓				3 3 0 00

ACCOUNT Advertising Expense ACCOUNT NO. 512

DATE	ITEM	POST. REF.	DEBIT	CREDIT	BALANCE DEBIT	BALANCE CREDIT

ACCOUNT Supplies Expense ACCOUNT NO. 524

DATE	ITEM	POST. REF.	DEBIT	CREDIT	BALANCE DEBIT	BALANCE CREDIT

Comprehensive Problem 2, Part 2 (Continued)

ACCOUNT Telephone Expense ACCOUNT NO. 525

DATE	ITEM	POST. REF.	DEBIT	CREDIT	BALANCE DEBIT	BALANCE CREDIT

ACCOUNT Utilities Expense ACCOUNT NO. 533

DATE	ITEM	POST. REF.	DEBIT	CREDIT	BALANCE DEBIT	BALANCE CREDIT

ACCOUNT Insurance Expense ACCOUNT NO. 535

DATE	ITEM	POST. REF.	DEBIT	CREDIT	BALANCE DEBIT	BALANCE CREDIT

ACCOUNT Depreciation Expense—Building ACCOUNT NO. 540

DATE	ITEM	POST. REF.	DEBIT	CREDIT	BALANCE DEBIT	BALANCE CREDIT

Comprehensive Problem 2, Part 2 (Continued)

ACCOUNT Depreciation Expense—Store Equipment ACCOUNT NO. 541

DATE	ITEM	POST. REF.	DEBIT	CREDIT	BALANCE	
					DEBIT	CREDIT

ACCOUNT Miscellaneous Expense ACCOUNT NO. 549

DATE	ITEM	POST. REF.	DEBIT	CREDIT	BALANCE	
					DEBIT	CREDIT

ACCOUNT Interest Expense ACCOUNT NO. 551

DATE	ITEM	POST. REF.	DEBIT	CREDIT	BALANCE	
					DEBIT	CREDIT

ACCOUNTS RECEIVABLE LEDGER

NAME Martha Boyle

ADDRESS 12 Jude Lane, Hartford, CT 06117

DATE		ITEM	POST. REF.	DEBIT	CREDIT	BALANCE
20-2 Jan.	1	Balance	✓			1 3 2 3 00

Comprehensive Problem 2, Part 2 (Continued)

NAME Anne Clark

ADDRESS 52 Juniper Road, Hartford, CT 06118

DATE		ITEM	POST. REF.	DEBIT	CREDIT	BALANCE
20-2 Jan.	1	Balance	✓			2 1 0 0 00

NAME John Dempsey

ADDRESS 700 Hobbes Dr., Avon, CT 06108

DATE		ITEM	POST. REF.	DEBIT	CREDIT	BALANCE
20-2 Jan.	1	Balance	✓			2 1 2 1 00

NAME Kim Fields

ADDRESS 5200 Hamilton Ave., Hartford, CT 06117

DATE		ITEM	POST. REF.	DEBIT	CREDIT	BALANCE
20-2 Jan.	1	Balance	✓			1 6 8 00

NAME Lucy Greene

ADDRESS 236 Bally Lane, Simsbury, CT 06123

DATE		ITEM	POST. REF.	DEBIT	CREDIT	BALANCE
20-2 Jan.	1	Balance	✓			1 4 9 1 00

Comprehensive Problem 2, Part 2 (Continued)

NAME Heather Waters

ADDRESS 447 Drury Lane, West Hartford, CT 06107

DATE	ITEM	POST. REF.	DEBIT	CREDIT	BALANCE

ACCOUNTS PAYABLE LEDGER

NAME Evans Essentials

ADDRESS 34 Harry Ave., East Hartford, CT 05234

DATE		ITEM	POST. REF.	DEBIT	CREDIT	BALANCE
20-2 Jan.	1	Balance	✓			2 3 5 0 00

NAME Nathen Co.

ADDRESS 1009 Drake Rd., Farmington, CT, 06082

DATE		ITEM	POST. REF.	DEBIT	CREDIT	BALANCE
20-2 Jan.	1	Balance	✓			8 0 0 00

NAME Owen Enterprises

ADDRESS 43 Lucky Lane, Bristol, CT 06007

DATE	ITEM	POST. REF.	DEBIT	CREDIT	BALANCE

Name _____

COMPREHENSIVE PROBLEM WP-661

Comprehensive Problem 2, Part 2 (Continued)

NAME West Wholesalers

ADDRESS 888 Anders Street, Newington, CT 06789

DATE		ITEM	POST. REF.	DEBIT	CREDIT	BALANCE
20-2 Jan.	1	Balance	✓			1 2 0 0 00

4.

Comprehensive Problem 2, Part 2 (Continued)

5.

	TRIAL BALANCE		ADJUSTMENTS	
	DEBIT	CREDIT	DEBIT	CREDIT
1				
2				
3				
4				
5				
6				
7				
8				
9				
10				
11				
12				
13				
14				
15				
16				
17				
18				
19				
20				
21				
22				
23				
24				
25				
26				
27				
28				
29				
30				
31				
32				
33				
34				
35				
36				

Comprehensive Problem 2, Part 2 (Continued)

ADJUSTED TRIAL BALANCE		INCOME STATEMENT		BALANCE SHEET		
DEBIT	CREDIT	DEBIT	CREDIT	DEBIT	CREDIT	
						1
						2
						3
						4
						5
						6
						7
						8
						9
						10
						11
						12
						13
						14
						15
						16
						17
						18
						19
						20
						21
						22
						23
						24
						25
						26
						27
						28
						29
						30
						31
						32
						33
						34
						35
						36

Comprehensive Problem 2, Part 2 (Continued)

Comprehensive Problem 2, Part 2 (Continued)

Comprehensive Problem 2, Part 2 (Continued)

Comprehensive Problem 2, Part 2 (Continued)

6.

<div align="center">

JOURNAL PAGE 6

</div>

	DATE	DESCRIPTION	POST. REF.	DEBIT	CREDIT	
1						1
2						2
3						3
4						4
5						5
6						6
7						7
8						8
9						9
10						10
11						11
12						12
13						13
14						14
15						15
16						16
17						17
18						18
19						19
20						20
21						21
22						22
23						23
24						24
25						25
26						26
27						27
28						28
29						29
30						30
31						31
32						32
33						33
34						34

Comprehensive Problem 2, Part 2 (Continued)
7.

	JOURNAL			PAGE 7

	DATE	DESCRIPTION	POST. REF.	DEBIT	CREDIT	
1						1
2						2
3						3
4						4
5						5
6						6
7						7
8						8
9						9
10						10
11						11
12						12
13						13
14						14
15						15
16						16
17						17
18						18
19						19
20						20
21						21
22						22
23						23
24						24
25						25
26						26
27						27
28						28
29						29
30						30
31						31
32						32
33						33
34						34

Comprehensive Problem 2, Part 2 (Concluded)
8.

ACCOUNT	DEBIT BALANCE	CREDIT BALANCE